Selected Writings

KARL MARX

Selected Writings

Edited, with Introduction, by
Lawrence H. Simon

Hackett Publishing Company, Inc.
Indianapolis/Cambridge

Karl Marx: 1818–1883
Copyright © 1994 by Hackett Publishing Company, Inc.
All rights reserved
Printed in the United States of America

13 12 11 10 09   7 8 9 10 11 12

Text design by Dan Kirklin
Cover by Listenberger Design & Associates

For further information, please address
    Hackett Publishing Company, Inc.
    P.O. Box 44937
    Indianapolis, Indiana 46244-0937

    www.hackettpublishing.com

Library of Congress Cataloging-in-Publication Data

Marx, Karl, 1818–1883.
    [Selections. English 1994]
    Selected writings/Karl Marx; edited, with introduction, by
Lawrence H. Simon.
        p.   cm.
    Includes bibliographical references.
    ISBN 0-87220-219-4 (cloth).   ISBN 0-87220-218-6 (pbk.)
    1. Communism.   2. Socialism.   I. Simon, Lawrence Hugh, 1947–
II. Title.
HX39.5.A2   1994
335.4—dc20
                                                    94-362
                                                    CIP

ISBN-13: 978-0-87220-219-1 (cloth)
ISBN-13: 978-0-87220-218-4 (pbk.)

Contents

IV. Late Political Writings

Acknowledgments

"On the Jewish Question," "Toward a Critique of Hegel's *Philosophy of Right:* Introduction," "Excerpt-Notes of 1844," "Economic and Philosophic Manuscripts," "Theses on Feuerbach," and *The German Ideology*, translated by Loyd D. Easton and Kurt H. Guddat, copyright © 1967, are reprinted here with the generous permission of Loyd D. Easton.

The Eighteenth Brumaire of Louis Bonaparte, "Preface to *A Contribution to the Critique of Political Economy*," "Critique of the Gotha Program," and "Marginal Notes on Bakunin's *Statism and Anarchy*" are reprinted here with the kind permission of International Publishers, Inc., New York.

I would like to thank David Ruccio, Paul Franco, Susan Bell, and Philip Spencer for their advice on choosing the selections for this volume. Gerlinde Rickel deserves special thanks for her many contributions to the preparation of the book. Lastly, I would like to thank my wife, Lynne Miller, for her support and forbearance.

Introduction

I

Karl Marx is the most influential thinker of the modern period. Indeed, one could go further and claim that, in terms of sheer numbers, Marx's ideas have had a greater impact on more people than those of anyone else in history, with Jesus, Buddha, and Muhammad his closest rivals. Yet most people today would probably say that Marxism's day is over, that Marx's ideas have been proven empirically false and morally bankrupt, and that it is time to sweep away the remnants of Marx's influence into the "dustbin of history." If these claims are true, then one would study Marx's philosophical writings today only as a matter of historical curiosity, viewing them as part of a dead end in western thought.

Such a conclusion would, of course, be overly hasty and premature to say the least. Marx's legacy to the world of thought, to how we understand ourselves and our society, to major perspectives and issues in a wide variety of disciplines, cannot be dismissed that easily. Understanding the modern world is inevitably caught up with understanding Marx. For as Robert Heilbroner has observed:

> We turn to Marx, therefore, not because he is infallible, but because he is inescapable. Everyone who wishes to pursue the kind of investigation that Marx opened up, finds Marx there ahead of him, and must thereafter agree with or confute, expand or discard, explain or explain away the ideas that are his legacy.[1]

No one who wants a full account of philosophy in the nineteenth and twentieth centuries, or who is interested in politics and political theory, or sociology and social theory, or aesthetics, and literary and cultural theory, can avoid a serious encounter with Marx's work. There is much still to be learned from Marx's theoretical system, a complex mixture of philosophical analysis, normative and critical argument, and empirical investigation, despite the many ways in which it is open to criticism. And Marx's blend of revolutionary theory and practice will remain a beacon

---

1. Robert L. Heilbroner, *Marxism: For and Against* (New York and London: W. W. Norton and Company, 1980) p. 15.

for those engaged in radical politics, despite the events of recent years which seem to signal its failure.

But what kind of investigation did Marx open up? On the one hand, Marx was the culmination of a major line of development in modern social and political philosophy that started at least as far back as Hobbes and Locke and continued through Rousseau, Kant, and Hegel and on to Marx. From this point of view, Marx's project is to philosophically explain and criticize the nature of power in modern society, and to reveal the relations between the state, the political order, on the one hand, and the market and the economic order, on the other. This philosophical task has at least two elements. Like his predecessors but perhaps more deeply than any but Hegel, Marx was concerned to develop a philosophical anthropology, an understanding of human beings as historical and social creatures. And like all of the great political philosophers going back to the Greeks, Marx was concerned with the normative task of criticizing certain forms of political life and outlining a view of how the political community should properly be organized. Thus, the dimension of moral critique is never far from the surface in Marx's writings. He is often compared to an Old Testament prophet attempting to awaken his society to the ways in which their misunderstandings support unjust and corrupt practices and to help lead them on the road to salvation.

But Marx was more than just a political philosopher, for the political was only one aspect of modern social existence and for Marx, not the determining one. Perhaps more important is Marx's contribution as one of the towering figures at the beginning of modern social science. As such, he attempted to provide an empirical analysis of the deep structure of capitalism, the social formation that in the nineteenth century was emerging as the dominant form of social existence in the west. Although capitalism was the particular object of his inquiry, his larger empirical project was the understanding of all of human history and in particular, why and how one social formation evolved into the next. To this end he formulated his theory of historical materialism, which is in the first instance an empirical theory, but inseparable from Marx's philosophical and methodological views.

Marx was not, of course, just interested in theory, in understanding the historical and social reality of human beings. Beyond philosophical analysis, normative argument, and empirical investigation, Marx's focus was on changing the world. His ultimate task was to hasten the time when capitalism would prove no longer viable and a new social formation, socialism (and finally communism) would emerge.

The central theme in all of Marx's work is liberation. Human beings are in and of nature and have always lived under the yoke of natural forces. Their major weapon against the domination by nature is the technology they create. Throughout all of history thus far, however, humans have not been able to overcome a constant condition of scarcity. Given their natural circumstances and the often precarious level of material well-being that is all they have been able to produce with the available technology, people have had to resort to living in social structures which have required various forms of social and political oppression and domination. That is, our inability to fend off natural forces threatening human well-being and our inability to produce enough to satisfy all existing needs have required that we live in circumstances where some exploit and dominate others. But according to Marx's understanding of history and the development of capitalism, a time was approaching when our technology would be able to, if not master nature totally, then use it largely to our purposes and buffer our lives against its harsher aspects and forces. At that point in history, it would no longer be necessary for humans to live in ways that allowed social and political domination of others. True human liberation would then and only then be possible. Central to the fight for liberation, according to Marx, was the understanding of the forces that oppress us; and to this end and the furtherance of human freedom he dedicated his life.

Marx's theoretical work, then—understanding the nature of human beings and how they have constructed their historical world, discovering the deeper nature of capitalism and why it is unstable, morally unjustifiable, and open to change, and unmasking the nature of political power—was put to the service of moving the social world towards what Marx saw as its ultimate form and structure. For Marx, theory and practice are intertwined in complicated ways on a number of levels and one cannot appreciate what is special about his "kind of investigation" unless that point is kept constantly in mind. His theory, that is, is informed by both a critical and an emancipatory element beyond that of "mere" understanding. If, for convenience sake, we say that the modern age of revolution began in 1789 (and according to some, ended in 1989), then Marx is not only the most important thinker of that age but its greatest revolutionary and guiding light.

II

Marx's life spanned the greater part of the nineteenth century, a time of rapid and profound social, economic, and political change in western Europe and America. His life must be understood against the backdrop of the forces propelling Europe into the modern age of capitalism, industrial development, and technology. Marx was born in 1818 in the small Rhineland town of Trier in what is now the western part of Germany. His family was Jewish and had deep rabbinical roots on both the paternal and maternal sides. Marx's father, Heinrich, broke early with his family and his Jewish upbringing and became a lawyer. In order to pursue his career, given Prussian legal restrictions on posts that could be held by Jews, Heinrich converted to Christianity (Lutheranism, even though the Rhineland was predominately Catholic) just before the birth of Karl, his eldest son. Marx himself was baptized in 1824.

Trier had been incorporated into Prussia in 1814, but in the preceding years it had been occupied by French troops under Napoleon and the ideas of the Enlightenment, and the French Revolution had more currency there than in the eastern parts of Prussia. Notions of human progress, reason, skepticism towards religion and tradition, and the promotion of social change and even utopian socialism were very much in the air during Marx's early years. Marx's father subscribed in general to the ideas of the Enlightenment and undoubtedly gave Marx his first exposure to themes that were to loom large in his work. This rationalistic impulse was balanced to some degree by an enthusiasm for romanticism on the part of Baron von Westphalen, a neighbor who greatly influenced Marx during his youth and whose daughter Jenny Marx would later marry.

In 1835, Marx entered the university at Bonn to study law as his father wished. His first year of university was not a success, however. He got caught up in fraternity drinking, dueling, and writing romantic poetry and after a year, at his father's insistence, he transferred to the university in Berlin. In Berlin, Marx became a more serious student and his reading in law led him to the Faculty of Philosophy. Philosophy in the University of Berlin at that time was still very much under the influence of Hegel, who had been a professor there from 1818 until his death in 1831. Hegel's philosophy offered a grand historical and metaphysical theory in which Reason, embodied in the human mind, both caused and explained the domains of nature, history, and spirit (the latter including art, religion, and philosophy). History was seen as the development of human consciousness through various stages of contradiction and alienation until a point of self-understanding was attained. At this point, freedom could be fully realized and alienation overcome. What Hegel's philosophy seemed to promise was a rational world of progress towards human fulfillment. The modern age, just coming into existence in the form of emerging political and economics institutions, was taken as the historical achievement of this philosophical promise.

By the late 1830's Hegel's followers had split into contending camps, principally the conservative Right Hegelians and the more liberal Young,

or Left, Hegelians. At issue was whether Hegel's philosophy as interpreted through his writings lent support to the increasingly conservative
Prussian state, or whether the correct understanding of Hegel provided a
philosophical basis from which to criticize that state. Part of the controversy concerned the status and nature of religion, which the Young
Hegelians tended to see as providing a conservative bulwark for the state
and thus open to criticism. Marx soon sided with the Young Hegelians
and in particular was attracted to the political and philosophical ideas of
Bruno Bauer, one of the leading members of that circle of radical young
philosophers. In 1841, Marx completed a dissertation on Greek philosophy after Aristotle and received his doctorate from the University of
Jena, Berlin being too politically charged to welcome a dissertation from
another Young Hegelian.

Unable to secure an academic appointment because of his political
and religious views, Marx, following Bauer, went into journalism. He
soon became editor of the *Rheinische Zeitung,* an opposition newspaper
in Cologne, but resigned in 1843 in protest of the state censorship.
Meanwhile, he continued his writings, working in the summer of 1843
on, among other pieces, "On the Jewish Question," a critical review of a
new book by Bruno Bauer, and on Hegel's political philosophy, drafting
an essay, intended as an introduction to a book on Hegel that was never
completed. The essay became known as "Toward a Critique of Hegel's
Philosophy of Law: Introduction" and contains some of Marx's most
famous remarks about religion. At this point, he was already moving away
from his Young Hegelian philosophical roots, clearly distancing himself
from Bauer, and increasingly attracted by the more radical ideas of
Moses Hess and Ludwig Feuerbach, among others.

In the fall of 1843, after marrying Jenny von Westphalen, he moved to
Paris to continue his political work as a journalist. Paris was at that point
the political capital of Europe, and Marx found himself in the midst of
the most radical circles. It was also in Paris that Marx first came into
contact with workers and gained a first hand sense of the emerging
industrial working class, the proletariat. Working for the *Deutsch-
Französische Jahrbücher,* a journal which brought together many of his
old associates from Germany, he threw himself into a study of politics
and political economy. The fruit of this intense work was a manuscript, a
complete edition of which was not published until 1932, that became
known as the *Economic and Philosophic Manuscripts,* also referred to as
the "Paris Manuscripts" or the "1844 Manuscripts." This early work
has, in the last half century, become a major focus of discussion and
interpretation. For many, it is the crucial text defining Marx's position as
a radical humanist. During this period, he also set down his reactions

after reading the work of various political economists, including James Mill, the father of John Stuart Mill. These reflections, which include some interesting early thoughts on communism, have come to be known as the "Excerpt-Notes of 1844."

During 1843–44, Marx was greatly influenced by the work of Ludwig Feuerbach. Feuerbach had made a name for himself as a critic of Christianity, having published *The Essence of Christianity* in 1841. There he argued that religion was the alienated projection of the human essence. He then moved on to a critique of Hegel's idealism from a materialist point of view in *Preliminary Theses for the Reform of Philosophy* (1842). Feuerbach's argument that philosophy should start with real people as they actually existed as sensory beings in the material world, and not with the Hegelian abstractions of Reason, Idea, or Geist (Mind, Spirit), inspired Marx to shake off whatever vestiges of Hegelian idealism remained in his thought.

He did not remain a Feuerbachian materialist for long, however. By the spring of 1845, Marx realized, perhaps influenced by the historicist dimension in Hegel, that Feuerbach's position was insufficiently social and historical. These insights were aphoristically summarized in a short manuscript published only posthumously, known as the "Theses on Feuerbach."

It was in this period as well that Marx first met the person who would become his closest friend, chief support, political companion, and collaborator, Friedrich Engels. Engels, too, was a young German radical, but from a well-to-do family that had industrial holdings in Manchester, England, as well as in Germany. The two first met in 1842, but it was not until Engels visited Marx in Paris in 1844 that their friendship and collaboration really began. Engels had been living from 1842 to 1844 in Manchester, which was one of the most advanced industrialized cities in Europe. There he experienced the new industrial age and what it was doing to the lives of factory workers. The dismal and impoverished conditions of their lives, which he described in his classic *The Condition of the Working Class in England in 1844*, greatly impressed him and Marx. From the time of their second encounter in 1844 until the end of Marx's life, Engels was so much a part of Marx's work and life that experts still argue over how much of Marx's thought should be credited to Engels.

Paris was filled with political exiles in the 1840's, and the French government, perhaps as a legacy of the 1789 Revolution, had been generally sympathetic to providing a haven for them. By the early 1840's, however, the political climate there was becoming more conservative. The Prussian government, increasingly irritated by the work of Marx and his colleagues, pressured the French to silence them. At the beginning of 1845, the French succumbed to the pressure and expelled Marx and several others, and the Marx family moved to Brussels. There Marx continued his work, writing (but not publishing) in collaboration with Engels in 1845–46 *The German Ideology,* his first and in some ways most influential statement of the materialist theory of history and the text in which his theory of class clearly emerges for the first time.

Marx had identified himself as a communist for a number of years, but the term carried very little explicit meaning other than some general sense of opposition to private property. Marx began to sharpen up his views on communism first in a polemic against the anarchist Proudhon in *The Poverty of Philosophy* (1847) and most famously in what is perhaps the best known of all of Marx's works, *The Communist Manifesto. The Manifesto* was written by Marx (it is a matter of some dispute as to how much Engels contributed to the manuscript) in 1847–48 at the invitation of The Communist League, an association of revolutionary German workers then headquartered in London. It was intended to serve both as the public statement of the political views and goals of the "party" and to provide a statement, albeit compressed, of the theoretical foundations of communism as understood by Marx and those who were beginning to emerge as his followers.

Almost immediately after the publication of *The Manifesto* in 1848, revolutionary activity burst out across Europe. Marx was forced out of Belgium and he returned to Paris where revolutionary events were underway. He soon left France for Germany, however, when word reached him of political turmoil there. He settled in Cologne and started up once again a radical newspaper, *Neue Rheinische Zeitung,* to encourage the revolution along. By 1849, however, it was clear that the revolution in Germany would not succeed. Marx was once again forced to flee and this time he settled in London, where he would remain but for a few trips abroad for the remainder of his life.

After the failure of the 1848 Revolution, the political order was reinstated in the various European countries, and radical activity was put very much on the defensive. Marx remained active in the revolutionary workers' activities in London, but the politics had largely to do with the intrigues of refugees. While the 1850's were a period of relative political quietism, the decade proved enormously important for Marx in terms of his theoretical work. He went back to his studies, and using the library of the British Museum, immersed himself in economic theory and history. To earn some money to support his family, he took a post as a part-time foreign correspondent for the New York Daily Tribune, and he relied on support from Engels, who had gone to Manchester to help run the family firm there.

In late 1851, early 1852, Marx wrote *The Eighteenth Brumaire of Louis*

Bonaparte, analyzing Bonaparte's coup d'état of 1851 in France. Over the next ten years, he worked on what would be his magnum opus, the three volumes of *Capital.* In line with his usual procedures, he wrote draft manuscripts both criticizing the theories of others and working out his own views in opposition. These manuscripts include the *Grundrisse* (notebooks from 1857–58, first published in 1939–40) and *A Contribution to the Critique of Political Economy,* published by Marx in 1859. In the preface to the latter, Marx provided a thumbnail sketch of the development of his ideas and gave what has become a famous and controversially concise statement of his theory of history. In the early 1860's he wrote the three volumes of *Theories of Surplus Value,* which contain his closest and most extensive critique of the classical political economists, especially Smith and Ricardo.

By the mid-1860's, working class activism was reviving in England and elsewhere. This activity increasingly took the form of trade union organizing, with links being forged among union groups across national boundaries. This activity led in 1864 to the formation of the International Working Men's Association, otherwise known as the First International. The International proved a watershed in the history of the working class movement and was very influential for the first eight years or so of its existence; during this period, Marx was one of its most powerful leaders. Internal fights and struggles between, for example, Marx and the anarchist Bakunin, tore the International apart, and it died finally in 1876 in Philadelphia. During this period of intense political involvement, Marx brought out the first volume of *Capital* in 1867. Although Volumes Two and Three were largely done by this point, Marx delayed publication and continued to work on them. They were finally published after Marx's death by Engels, Volume Two in 1885 and Volume Three in 1894.

In 1870, war broke out between Prussia and France. In the aftermath of the quick rout of the French and the unification of Germany under the Prussians, a republic was declared in Paris. The republic grew increasingly radical and by March of 1871, it declared itself the *Commune de Paris;* but within two months it had been defeated by the conservative French government. Marx was ambivalent about the Commune while it existed, but after its demise he wrote *The Civil War in France* as both a eulogy and analysis of the events that transpired. What has become famous from this essay, which was first given as an address to the General Council of the International, are remarks Marx makes about the organization of communism and the dictatorship of the proletariat.

By the 1870's Marx had become the leading theoretician for much of the European, and especially the German, working-class movement, and in that role, he became quite notorious across Europe as the "Red Doctor" Marx. In 1875, two of the major factions of the German movement prepared to meet in Gotha to unify their efforts, and they sent a draft of their common platform to Marx and Engels in London for comment. Marx, in a lengthy commentary, criticized the document for various deviations from his views. This commentary, which has become known as the "Critique of the Gotha Program," also contains important comments about Marx's views on communism and the organization of the state. About the same time, Marx prepared notes for a reply to an important book by Bakunin, *Statism and Anarchy*. These notes, not published until 1926, also give insight into Marx's thinking about the state and political matters towards the end of his life.

Marx died in London in 1883. His wife, Jenny, had died two years earlier. They had lived a hard life, struggling especially in the 1850's against poverty, and living in extremely difficult circumstances. Only three of their six children survived to adulthood. Marx himself was quite ill during the last years of his life. Yet Marx lived to see the dramatic growth of a working-class movement alongside the development of an ever more powerful capitalism. While he did not live to see a successful revolution inspired by his work, he had reason to believe that his ideas gave him some insight into the future and that his efforts had not been futile. Those who read Marx today, just over one hundred years after his death, must ask whether he was correct to believe this. What would he have made of the events of the twentieth century carried on in his name, and what analysis would he have given of the present juncture of history? In order to better think about these questions, we must examine some of the central ideas and concepts in Marx's work.

III

As a way of organizing the immense body of material that Marx developed, I will discuss three central dimensions of his work: his theory of history, historical materialism; his analysis and critique of capitalism; and his vision of a fully human society at the end of history, communism.

Historical Materialism

While Marx early on rejected Hegel's philosophical idealism and the account of history that it supported, he put in its place a theory of history that is as wide in scope and explanatory ambitions as was Hegel's. In a certain broad measure, Marx's theory is the inversion of Hegel's, as Marx noted in the "Postface to the Second Edition" of Volume One of *Capital*,

My dialectical method is, in its foundations, not only different from the Hegelian, but exactly opposite to it. For Hegel, the process of thinking, which he even transforms into an independent subject, under the name of 'the Idea', is the creator of the real world, and the real world is only the external appearance of the idea. With me the reverse is true: the ideal is nothing but the material world reflected in the mind of man, and translated into forms of thought.[2]

Marx, that is, inverted Hegel "in order to discover the rational kernel within the mystical shell."[3] Hegel was wrong to claim that ideas, whether in some cosmic Mind or in the mind of humans, could causally explain the historical and social world. Rather, the cause was to be found in the human productive encounter with the material conditions of nature, the subject matter ultimately of economics. The rational kernel in Hegel was the idea that humans have created their own history through their labor, but thus far only under conditions of ignorance, alienation, and exploitation. Thus they are dominated both by the forces of nature they encounter and by social forces they confront, social forces they have constructed but do not control. "Men," Marx wrote in *The Eighteenth Brumaire of Louis Bonaparte*, "make their own history, but they do not make it just as they please; they do not make it under circumstances chosen by themselves, but under circumstances directly encountered, given and transmitted from the past."[4] The key to understanding history was to understand these circumstances. The key to liberation from domination was to use that understanding to control the circumstances and thus be able to make history knowingly and intentionally.

The aim of Marx's historical project is to explain the overall course of human history, how "men make their own history." As such, it is largely an empirical task. But as with any such theory, what is crucial are the categories chosen to carry the explanatory weight.

Marx's starting point, he tells us in *The German Ideology*, is "real individuals, their actions, and their material conditions of life, those which they find existing as well as those which they produce through

2. Karl Marx, "Postface to the Second Edition," *Capital*, vol. 1, trans. Ben Fowkes, The Marx Library (New York: Random House/Vintage Books, 1977), p. 102.

3. Ibid., p. 103.

4. Karl Marx, *The Eighteenth Brumaire of Louis Bonaparte, Karl Marx/Friedrich Engels, Collected Works*, vol. 11 (New York: International Publishers, 1979), p. 103 [p. 188 below].

their actions."[5] What is of central importance about real historical human beings and their material conditions is how they produce their means of existence in and from nature. Humans express themselves in the first instance through their labor. "As individuals express their life, so they are. What they are, therefore, coincides with what they produce, with *what* they produce and *how* they produce."[6] The core insight of Marx's philosophical anthropology then, is that humans are laboring beings, *Homo faber*, and that their development, their creativity, their freedom, and their flourishing all arise out of and are dependent on the conditions of their labor.

How humans produce their existence, of course, changes through time, and the key to history, for Marx, was the ever expanding power of humans to produce and reproduce themselves. This power, productive power, is contained in the tools and technology, developed by humans in their efforts to improve their material conditions, plus the human labor that goes into employing these tools. Marx uses the term, means of production, for the physical tools, technology, and natural resources that enter into the process of production. The forces of production are the means of production plus the human labor that ultimately powers them. The basic logic of history, then, is the logic behind the development of the forces of production.

The forces of production, however, are always utilized within some system of social relations that govern their use. These social relations, which Marx called the relations of production, are in effect relations of power that determine who has access to and control over the means of production. For example, if the means of production consist of certain tools and raw materials, then the relations of production stipulate who owns or otherwise controls those forces, either through legal ownership or social convention. With control over the means of production comes control, formally and informally, over labor, which without access to the means can do little, as well as, generally, control over the product. So for instance, in a society based on slave labor, the dominant relation of production is that between the slavemaster and the slave, and this relation as defined in social tradition and perhaps in the law governs the nature of the major economic roles in that society. The class of masters

5. Karl Marx and Friedrich Engels, *The German Ideology*, trans. Loyd D. Easton and Kurt H. Guddat, in *Writings of the Young Marx on Philosophy and Society*, eds. Loyd D. Easton and Kurt H. Guddat (Garden City, N.Y.: Anchor Books/ Doubleday and Company, Inc., 1967), p. 409 [p. 107 below].

6. Ibid., [pp. 107–108 below].

has all the power, economically and politically, controlling the means of production and the labor of their slaves. They also, of course, own the product of their slaves' labor.

According to Marx, it is not arbitrary what relations of production obtain at different points in history. As a general rule, the forces of production tend to increase over time. Simplifying a great deal, Marx's claim is that at different levels in the development of the forces of production, different kinds of relations of production are best suited to allow further development of the existing forces. It is these relations that tend to develop at any given point.[7] As the forces of production continue to grow within the constraints of the existing relations, a point is reached when those relations are no longer the ones best suited to allow the continued development of the forces. At this point, the old relations tend to break down and new relations emerge which are better suited to further the development of the forces. These points of transition are periods of revolution, although they might not involve revolutionary activity in the modern sense of rapid and often violent change of political regime. The transition in fact might take place over a long period of time and be hardly noticed by the participants.

The combination of the forces of production as utilized at any given historical moment within determinant relations of production forms an economic system called by Marx the mode of production. According to Marx, there have been three modes of production prior to capitalism. The ancient mode of production as found, for instance, in Greece and Rome, was the first large scale form of social organization. It was succeeded by the feudal mode of production. The feudal mode was then followed by the emergence of capitalism. The third precapitalist mode was what Marx calls the Asiatic mode of production, which he locates in several major Asian societies and which he holds to be static in the sense

---

7. These remarks have, of course, simplified the theory considerably. The best and most careful exposition of Marx's theory of history is G. A. Cohen, *Karl Marx's Theory of History: A Defence* (Princeton, N.J.: Princeton University Press, 1978). For replies to and refinements of Cohen's reading of Marx, see Jon Elster, *Making Sense of Marx* (Cambridge: Cambridge University Press, 1985), Philippe Van Parijs, "Marxism's Central Puzzle," and Richard Miller, "Producing Change: Work, Technology, and Power in Marx's Theory of History," both in *After Marx*, eds. Terence Ball and James Farr (Cambridge: Cambridge University Press, 1984), and Erik Olin Wright, Andrew Levine, and Elliott Sober, *Reconstructing Marxism: Essays on Explanation and the Theory of History* (London and New York: Verso, 1992).

that it does not develop into a successor mode as, for instance, feudalism developed into capitalism.

As mentioned above, the relations of production are relations of economic power in that they determine which people have power over, access to, and use of the means of production while leaving others dependent on those who control the forces. Typically, those who control the means of production do not contribute their labor to the production process but live off the labor of others, while those who contribute their labor do not have independent access, for the most part, to the means of production. This insight is the core of Marx's theory of class. In any given mode of production, those who control the means of production are the ruling class and those who contribute the labor are the workers.

While the actual form of the relation between the ruling class and the workers differs in each mode of production and must be specified carefully (the master-serf relation in feudalism is, for instance, very different from the capitalist-proletarian relation in capitalism), still in general, each class contributes something to the production process. The ruling class contributes the technology and raw materials it typically controls, and the workers their labor. But the situation is not one of equality; the relation is not symmetrical. The ruling class, which contributes little or no labor, controls most or all of the product produced and lives off the economic surplus (that part of the product over and above what is necessary to keep people alive at subsistence). The working class, meanwhile, since it has no, or at best, limited, access to the means of production is forced to contribute its labor (if necessary, this force is exerted as political coercion). In contributing its labor to the production process, the workers do the work, make the product, and yet typically they retain only a small part of it.

It is not surprising that under these sorts of conditions antagonisms tend to exist between the dominant ruling class and the subservient working class. The story of these antagonisms is what Marx calls the history of class struggle. As Marx and Engels announce near the opening of *The Communist Manifesto,* "The history of all hitherto existing society is the history of class struggles."[8] Ruling classes rise and fall with each mode of production, and the composition and nature of the working class changes. But within a given mode of production there is always class struggle. How exactly history as the story of the development of the

8. Karl Marx and Friedrich Engels, *The Manifesto of the Communist Party, Karl Marx/Friedrich Engels, Collected Works,* vol. 6 (New York: International Publishers, 1976), p. 482 [p. 158 below].

forces of production and history as the story of class struggle can be unified in a single explanatory account was never made clear by Marx. It remains one of the major questions for historical materialism, one which I can do no more than mention here.

The relations of production are, of course, not the only important social relations in society. Insofar as historical materialism was to be an adequate historical sociology, it had to give an account of, at the very least, political, legal, cultural, and religious institutions and relations. "[T]he economic structure of society," Marx writes in the 1859 Preface, is "the real foundation [of society], on which arises a legal and political superstructure and to which correspond definite forms of social consciousness."[9] Marx is suggesting here a model of how social institutions are related. The economic structure, principally the relations of production, comprise what Marx calls the base, and the other institutions in society, principally the political and legal ones, and the various relations that comprise them are referred to as the superstructure. The non-economic relations and institutions in a given mode of production, then, in this model correspond to and are to be explained by the nature of the relations of production. Just as Marx holds that the level of development of the forces of production determines the nature of the existing relations of production, so the relations of production (taken as the base) determine the nature of the existing superstructural institutions and relations.

From this point of view, what is especially important is that the state and legal and political institutions in general are of secondary importance with regard to the relations of production and are to be understood in terms of how they contribute to the stability of these relations of the base. Traditional history, which focuses on matters of state and political, diplomatic and military affairs, misses, according to Marx, the crucial level of historical explanation. Developments at the level of the relations of production explain political events rather than the other way around.

Insofar as culture, the realm of ideas, is part of the superstructure as well, it too is to be explained in terms of its relation to the base. "It is not the consciousness of men that determines their existence, but their so-

9. Karl Marx, "Preface" to *A Contribution to the Critique of Political Economy, Karl Marx/Friedrich Engels, Collected Works,* vol. 29 (New York: International Publishers, 1987), p. 263. For a careful discussion of the base/superstructure model, see Cohen, *Karl Marx's Theory of History: A Defence,* Chapter VIII, and a reply by Steven Lukes, "Can the Base Be Distinguished from the Superstructure?" in *The Nature of Political Theory,* eds. David Miller and Larry Siedentop (Oxford: Clarendon Press, 1983) [p. 211 below].

cial existence that determines their consciousness."[10] That is, the consciousness of an age, the beliefs and values that prevail, are to be explained in terms of the nature of the relations of production and how the ideas function to help stabilize those relations.

The realm of consciousness is sometimes referred to by Marx as the ideology of an age. In all class societies, the relations of production favor the situation of the dominant class. The ideology of a society, the beliefs and values that pervade the society, in effect functions to help stabilize the relations of production to the degree that widespread acceptance of the ideology helps make domination of the ruling class appear legitimate if not inevitable. We would expect, then, as Marx puts it, that "In every epoch the ideas of the ruling class are the ruling ideas, that is, the class that is the ruling *material* power of society is at the same time its ruling *intellectual* power."[11] Put crudely, if the workers can be made to believe that their masters and rulers have legitimate power, they will be more resigned to their lot and less likely to revolt. Thus, among others things, according to Marx, one would expect that the ideologies of class societies involve false ideas and understanding on the part of both the rulers and the ruled, for a true understanding of class relations of domination would reveal that they are neither fair nor necessary. It follows that one of the first tasks of a revolutionary is to break through the dominant ideology and help others to do the same. The critique of ideology, then, the unmasking of false beliefs at both the popular and theoretical levels, was one of the central aims of Marx's theoretical work.

The Analysis and Critique of Capitalism

Historical materialism is the grand social theory that Marx developed to explain his world. The point of the explanation always remained to change that world, and so the particular world that needed to be explained in order to be changed was capitalism. Capitalism, then, was the specific object on which the general theory of historical materialism was brought to bear in the most detail.

To this end, Marx developed an economic theory that at the same time attempted to reveal the nature of the capitalist market and production processes and relations and to show the deficiencies in all prior economic theories. For the purposes of this introduction, the more technical aspects of Marx's economic theory are not important. What are important are the two philosophical concepts that are central to Marx's critique of

10. Ibid.
11. Karl Marx and Friedrich Engels, *The German Ideology,* p. 438 [p. 129 below].

capitalism, alienation, and exploitation. While both alienation and exploitation can be said to occur in other modes of production, I will focus on the form they take in capitalism.

The more general concept, alienation, must be understood against the backdrop of Marx's philosophical anthropology. As mentioned above, Marx saw labor as the essential human activity, and human potential at any point in history was determined by the forms that labor took. This idea of the fundamental role of labor is expressed in historical materialism in the claim that the development of the forces and relations of production determines and explains the course of history. Implicit in this idea is the further claim that human beings can only be free and flourish when they freely labor under conditions they control.

In capitalism, the dominant relation of production is that between the capitalist and the proletarian. The dominant form that labor takes is wage labor. The proletarian in effect has no access to the means of production except as allowed by the capitalist; the capitalist controls the means, that is, owns the factories and can purchase the raw materials. The worker does, however, initially control her labor. In order to gain what is minimally needed to stay alive, the proletarian must work; but because the proletarian does not have access to tools and raw materials on which to labor, the conditions of labor are determined by the capitalist. The worker must give the capitalist the only thing in her possession, labor (or more correctly, as we will see, labor-power). In return, the capitalist gives the worker, not the product produced, but a wage with which to buy the goods necessary for subsistence. It is this exchange of labor (power) for a wage, what is experienced in capitalism as the buying and selling of labor, that is the crucial relation in capitalism. Unlocking the nature of this relation was, for Marx, the key to understanding that mode of production.

Once having sold her labor to the capitalist, the worker has no choice but to labor to the specifications of the capitalist. This situation condemns the worker to a condition of alienated labor. Alienation means, in one sense, to be separated or estranged from one's essential properties or attributes, from one's real self. The wage laborer, in giving command over her labor to the capitalist, has in effect separated herself from her essential human capacity. What the worker has sold is that which is the core of human existence, the ability to labor. She is no longer her own person, and bereft of control over her own labor, she cannot be fully human. For Marx, this situation is tragic and condemns the worker to a life without the possibility of meaningful purpose and fulfillment.

In the *Economic and Philosophic Manuscripts*, Marx describes the alienation of labor as having four aspects or moments. The worker is separated from her product, that which is in theory the concrete expression of the worker's will and powers. Second, the worker is separated from the process of labor; without control over the place, rhythm, and duration of labor, a worker is not free to express her nature and develop her person in her labor. Third, the worker is separated from her species-being. "Species-being" is a Feuerbachian term that Marx used in his early writings but dropped later for the most part. To be separated from one's species-being is to be separated from one's essential capacities and potential as a human and as part of a human community where, at least potentially, each contributes to the welfare the whole. Last, Marx describes the worker in capitalism as alienated from her fellow worker. In capitalism, where market relations separate and divide individuals and set each against the others, the relation of a person to her fellows cannot but be one of competition rather than genuine community. The result of this fourfold structure of alienation is that the worker in capitalism experiences life as meaningless and empty, filled with frustration, and devoid of real satisfactions.

The exchange between the wage laborer and the capitalist boss appears to be one of freedom and equality. As Marx describes it in *Capital*, the two freely meet in the marketplace and enter into a normal market transaction. The exchange is commodity for commodity, like the buying and selling of any object in the capitalist market, but in this case the exchange is money for the ability to labor, what Marx calls labor-power. Each can refuse to enter into the exchange, although each has obvious needs that can only be satisfied by consummating the exchange. What is important to note, Marx emphasizes, is that the wage is an offer of an amount of money per period of time, $5.00 per hour, for instance. What the capitalist buys from the worker is the ability to labor for that period of time covered by the wage agreement, for instance, eight hours a day for $40. The capitalist takes what he has purchased, the labor-power, which of course as it turns out cannot be detached from the body of the worker, back to his factory to use as he, the capitalist, sees fit.

The key to what happens in the factory is that the capitalist has purchased the worker's ability to labor for a specified period of time, but how much labor that entails is not specified in advance. That is, two capitalists might purchase equivalent labor-power from two workers in the form of the ability to labor for eight hours in exchange for $40. However, if one capitalist can squeeze more effort out of his worker than the other, which will mean that his worker will produce more goods in the same amount of time compared to the other worker, then that capitalist will clearly be in an advantageous position. How much labor a capitalist can squeeze out of the amount of labor-power purchased depends on a number of factors, according to Marx. Chief among these factors are the discipline imposed on the workers in the factory and the level of technology available on which to work.

Whatever the conditions of the labor, the entire product produced in the factory belongs to the capitalist. He, after all, owns all the factors of production: the factory and the machines and other technology in it, the raw materials he bought to be used in the manufacturing process, and the labor-power also purchased in the market that is used to combine these other ingredients into the final product. The worker can claim only the wage, which, after all, was stipulated in the marketplace exchange that she agreed to.

Surplus product (or as Marx would put it, surplus value) is whatever is produced over and above what is required to support life. The part of the product that is required to sustain life is called the necessary product (or necessary value). If we need to consume one loaf of bread a day to stay alive, and yet we have the resources to produce 400 per year, the necessary value is 365 loaves per year, and we are capable of producing a surplus value of some 35 loaves per year. Probably ever since they created the first real tools, humans have had the capacity to produce a surplus. This surplus generally went to support the nonlaboring ruling class, the warrior chiefs or the priests, for instance. But most obviously and dramatically with the advent of the Industrial Revolution in the middle of the eighteenth century, humans have had the ability to produce a surplus far beyond what is necessary to sustain life. How is this surplus distributed in capitalism?

This question, one might think, is not difficult to answer. Clearly, the capitalist gets the surplus product, for as we have seen, he owns the entire product, the necessary part and the surplus. But, one might object, he doesn't really own the entire product, for he has had, in effect, to surrender part of it to the worker in the form of the wage. Where does the wage come from if not from part of the product that the capitalist converts into money by selling it in order to be able to pay his workers? The question for Marx thus becomes, what does the wage represent in terms of the concepts of necessary and surplus value? Is part of the surplus given to the worker in the form of the wage, or is the entire surplus retained by the capitalist?

Marx's answer to this question is complicated, and I cannot provide a full explanation here. In outline, however, Marx's answer is as follows. According to the labor theory of value, the basic economic theory that Marx took from Adam Smith and David Ricardo and developed in his own way, the value (or price) of a commodity (an object produced specifically to be sold) is determined by the amount of labor necessary to produce it. Since the labor-power of the worker is treated in capitalism like any other market commodity, its price, too, can be determined by the same method. But the amount of labor necessary to produce labor-power is the amount necessary to keep the worker healthy and able to appear each morning at the factory gates ready and willing to sell the capitalist another day's worth of labor-power.[12] This amount, however, is just what Marx calls the necessary product (or more strictly, necessary value), for it is the amount necessary to sustain the worker. If the worker is given a wage that is less than necessary value, the worker will not be able to buy those things required to keep her alive and thus able to replenish the supply of labor-power consumed in each day's laboring. If the worker is paid a wage greater than necessary value, the worker is, according to the labor theory of value, being overpaid. If a competitor can manage to pay his workers a lower wage, one just equal to necessary value, he will have a competitive edge. Thus market forces and the nature of the process of producing labor-power keep the wages at the value of the necessary product as an equilibrium price.[13]

But if the wage is equivalent to the value of the necessary product, and that is all the worker gets and can rightfully claim, that means that the entire surplus is kept by the capitalist. There is a seeming imbalance here. The worker has done all the work, produced the entire product.[14] But at the end of the day, she has no more than what she began with. (Remember, the wage is that value necessary to bring you back to parity with the condition you were in at the beginning of the laboring day.) The capitalist, meanwhile, has done nothing, but has all of the surplus value. That is, the capitalist claims part of the product in virtue of nothing

---

12. Technically, the amount has to include enough to support the worker's family, for in the long run, the labor necessary to produce labor-power must include the cost of producing and raising children who are the future suppliers of labor-power. If this were not taken into account by the system, capitalists would soon run out of a steady supply of their most important commodity.

13. Of course, the story Marx tells is much more complicated than this. He tries to show that there are real market forces that keep the wage at the level of necessary value. Importantly among these forces is unemployment which means that the supply of labor is greater than the demand for it and thus that there is downward pressure on the price. Whether he has a convincing account of this matter is open to dispute.

14. If the capitalist has actually worked, actually added labor to the production process, then he deserves a part of the product in return—think of this as the capitalist's wage. But a capitalist need not actually contribute labor in order to be able to claim the surplus product.

except the function of ownership of the means of production (capital, roughly). Because of this ownership, the capitalist is in a position to buy and be able to use labor-power; and conversely, because they lack access to the means of production, the workers have no choice but to sell their labor-power to the capitalist. It is this structured relation of imbalance whereby the worker contributes all of the labor that becomes the necessary and surplus value but gets only the necessary portion in return that Marx calls exploitation. Thus, the initial appearance of freedom and equality in the marketplace belies the true nature of the relationship between capitalist and worker, which now seems to be one of coercion and unfair exchange.[15] The explanation of alienated labor in capitalism, its nature and conditions of reproduction, then, is given by the theory of exploitation.[16]

Communism

Capitalism, Marx was sure, would be followed by a new and different mode of production, communism. Communism as a mode of production would be unique in that it would be a society of true freedom and equality, a society without alienation, exploitation, or class domination. But what, in detail, would communist society look like? And how would it come about?

To take the second question first, Marx thought that communism would be created as a result of a revolution by the proletariat which would overthrow the capitalist class and institute socialist relations of production. This revolution would occur because capitalism would find it increasingly hard to reproduce the conditions under which surplus could be generated and accumulated in the form of capital. Further development of the forces of production would be stymied. Depressions, unem-

15. Whether the exchange is indeed coerced, as Marx seems to think, and whether it is indeed unfair have both been subjects of some controversy. The exchange is not coerced if the worker has some other reasonable avenue open that would avoid wage labor. And it is not unfair if the standards of fairness are determined by the rules of the capitalist market, where, after all, the worker is getting just what the value of her labor-power is and ought to be.

16. Another important aspect of Marx's theory of capitalism is, of course, his account of why and how capitalism will cease to function properly and become vulnerable to revolution. Part of that account involves economic matters too technical for this introduction, and part involves questions about the possibility of communism which will be discussed in the next section.

ployment, and other disruptions and ill-effects of capitalism would become more frequent and worsen the conditions of the proletariat. At the same time, the working class, led by its more militant and radical elements, would come to see the nature of its alienation and exploitation in capitalism and the possibilities of changing the system. Capitalism would be experienced increasingly as a lack of freedom. The irrationalities of the capitalist market, an institution that has immense influence over the lives of the workers but over which they can exert no control, would become increasingly obvious. At some point, these two interrelated vectors, the difficulties of capitalist reproduction and the growing revolutionary nature of the working class, would collide and a revolution would occur.

Especially in his younger days, Marx seems to have thought that this revolution would happen in the near future and would be violent and sudden. But there are remarks in his latter writings that indicate that he came to see that the revolution might not happen for a while, that capitalism might be resilient enough to continue for some time, and also that it was possible that the revolution might be engineered nonviolently through the election of a working class party.[17] Marx did not, I believe, think that a socialist revolution was inevitable, certainly not in a strong sense of nomic necessity. But he certainly thought that there were good reasons to believe that one would happen at some point in history; that capitalism was not a stable and viable mode of production in the long run; that it did not best serve human needs; and that this would be understood and appreciated by the majority of the people in capitalist society, the proletariat. All of Marx's energy was spent trying to bring this realization closer.

As is well known, Marx did not discuss in any detail what society after the revolution would be like. His focus was primarily on capitalism, and he felt that the construction of communism would be the concern of those for whom it was an immediate task. His concern had to be with the problems at hand. Nonetheless, remarks about communism are scattered across several of his works.

In "The Critique of the Gotha Program," Marx talks of postrevolutionary society as going through two stages of development. The two stages can be differentiated largely in terms of their principles of distribution and the nature of the political state. The first stage (which is

17. These two issues, the point in the development of capitalism at which a revolution might and should occur, and the possibility of a nonviolent revolution, are still very much matters of debate among Marxists.

sometimes referred to as socialism, although Marx does not use the term in this context) is seen as one of transition. The remnants of capitalism still exist. Changes need to be made and safeguarded against the still possible threat of counter-revolution. The means of production have to be further developed to the point where the surplus product begins to make possible basic changes in the relation of humans to their work. During this stage, then, there is still a need for some authority operating on behalf of the interests of the working class. It will be, Marx calls it, a period of the dictatorship of the proletariat.

Also, during the first stage, the means of production will be socialized, that is, private ownership of the means of production will be eliminated, and with it, the capitalist class. With no way of gaining access to the means of life except through one's labor, all individuals will in effect become workers. With the means of production owned and organized by society as a whole, all will be in the same class, that is, all will have the same relation to the means of production. In effect, then, class will be eliminated in general. Socialist society thus is classless.

With the elimination of capitalist ownership, exploitation will be ended. Everyone will have access to the social product in virtue of the labor performed. Society will still function in terms of market exchange relations, but the surplus product will be distributed according to the principle of "from each according to his ability, to each according to his contribution." With no need to support relations of production that involve the domination of one class by another, political institutions can be open and democratic. Decisions about the allocation of resources will be made rationally through centrally coordinated social planning and not left to the vagaries of the market, which, as in capitalism, was under the control of no one. Social relations, in general, will no longer need, as they did in capitalism, to mask the nature of alienated and exploitative exchanges. Ideology, then, in the form of false or distorted beliefs that serve the function of stabilizing relations of domination, will disappear.

But, Marx notes, the first postrevolutionary stage will still have its defects. There will still be a need for state authority, albeit of a lesser and more benign sort. And distributing the social product according to contribution still involves treating people unequally for reasons that seem morally irrelevant. Some people, because of natural abilities, will be able to contribute more and thus will receive more of the product and be able to better satisfy their needs; others will, because of their family and personal responsibilities, have to spread their share of the product more thinly.

Eventually, however, the means of production will increase until a point is reached where scarcity is overcome and true abundance is achieved.[18] At this point, questions of authority and distribution will effectively disappear. If abundance means that we can satisfy our needs without depriving others of the satisfaction of their needs and without having to spend most of our time engaged in undesirable activities that are not experienced as ends in themselves, then conflicts concerning the just allocation of time and social product will be less likely to arise and more amenable to social consensus. In this case, state authority that ultimately functions to enforce class relations and settle matters of dispute about property will no longer be necessary. The state will, as Engels put it, wither away.

With true abundance, we will no longer have to worry about having enough, about accumulating wealth beyond the point required to satisfy our immediate needs, for there will be a socially shared confidence that our future needs will be satisfied through the normal course of development. The motivation to acquire goods and wealth will no longer make sense as a basis for organizing our lives. In effect, the conditions in which greed and selfishness seem natural, even rational, reactions will no longer obtain. Under the new conditions of abundance, the social product can be distributed according to the principle, "from each according to his ability, to each according to his needs."

In this second and higher stage of communism, necessary labor that has to be done but that is undesirable will be minimized through the use of technology. This will leave people able to spend their time creatively and freely. Productive activity will be engaged in for its own sake, not merely in order to produce a product needed for some other need satisfaction. The process as well as the product of our creative activity will be valued as an essential part of life. The line between art and labor will be blurred if not eliminated. With the end of alienated labor and exploitation, the forces that distort human relations will be lessened. Truly human social relations will develop in which people relate to each

18. Defining scarcity is a rather tricky business. G. A. Cohen usefully defines it as "given men's wants and the character of external nature, they cannot satisfy their wants unless they spend the better part of their time and energy doing what they would rather not do, engaged in labour which is not experienced as an end in itself." *Karl Marx's Theory of History: A Defence*, p. 152. Abundance, then, would involve being able to satisfy most of one's needs while still being able to spend most of one's time engaged in activity that is experienced as an end in itself and not merely as a means to gain an object to satisfy some need not otherwise related to the activity.

other as part of a genuinely human community. Exchange relations, from which we can never entirely eliminate an alienating aspect, will disappear. The distinction between my product and your product, between your need and my need, will no longer be important. As Marx put it in the "Excerpt-Notes of 1844," "In my individual life I would have directly created your life; in my individual activity I would have immediately *confirmed* and *realized* my true *human* and *social* nature."[19]

Communism, then, represents for Marx the conditions of the realization of human potential and fulfillment. The basic sources of human conflict would be eliminated. There would no longer be a need to overcome existing social and economic relations, thus, no further human evolution in terms of new modes of production would be necessary. Communism in this sense would be the end of history; it is "the riddle of history solved and knows itself as this solution."[20]

Whether Marx thought that this obviously utopian vision could ever really be realized is not, I think, of much importance. Even if he did think that communism was an unobtainable end, he certainly thought that we could come closer to it than we were in capitalism. In that sense, it represents a sort of moral vision and standard by which to judge our progress, and it stands as the philosophical completion of Marx's project.

IV

Virtually all of Marx's substantive and theoretical views have been challenged, and in some cases, all but refuted. Few, if any, thinkers have been subject to the level and intensity of criticism that Marx has, and from so many different points of view. Yet as I indicated in the opening section, many would say, nonetheless, that Marx remains inescapable as a figure with whom we must come to terms if we are to understand ourselves, our world, and our history. Marxist scholarship, especially in the English speaking world, has experienced an impressive rebirth in the last twenty-five years, and more and better philosophy about Marx and from a Marxist point of view is being written in English now than ever before. Yet the influence of Marx on political events beyond the towers of academia seems on the wane, for now at least. What are we to make of this confusing situation?

This is not the place to go into a discussion of the ways in which Marx's views have been criticized. The issues are complicated and sometimes technical, and the debates are often long and fierce. One can easily

19. *Writings of the Young Marx on Philosophy and Society*, p. 281 [p. 53 below].
20. Ibid., p. 304 [p. 71 below].

find any number of incompatible answers to the question, what is living and what is dead in Marx?[21] But whatever scorecard one eventually draws up, one must first encounter Marx directly and attempt to understand the texts. Only then can one hope to navigate successfully through the tricky currents of commentaries and criticism.

I will end this introduction, then, not with a survey of criticisms or defenses of Marx but with a brief discussion of several of the central ideas of Marx that I believe are of continuing interest. These ideas are all controversial, and they may ultimately prove to be unsound. But they are ideas with which we must in various ways still struggle.

The first is the idea at the core of Marx's philosophical anthropology. Humans, according to Marx, are essentially active, creative beings, and labor is the paradigm of human creative activity. In our labor, we express the nature of our selves and find self-realization. If this claim is true, then the conditions of our labor go a long way towards explaining the nature of our lives, whether they are happy and fulfilling or stunted and deformed. It would also follow from this claim that human freedom cannot be understood except in terms of the conditions of free labor. On the other hand, if the claim is false, then it is still important to ask about the role of labor in a full human life. What else, in addition to or instead of the conditions of labor, must we attend to in order to have a proper picture of human flourishing, growth, and expression?

Marx not only held that labor was the essential human activity, but also that human labor thus far in history has, for the most part, been alienated. Certainly, his philosophical critique of capitalism centers on the related concepts of alienated labor and exploitation. Few of Marx's critics, even those who believe that Marx's vision of communism is both unattainable and undesirable, would claim that present day capitalism is devoid of alienation. People may disagree about the nature, causes, and pervasiveness of alienation, and in particular, about how much the alienation experienced by various marginalized groups has to do with the nature of their labor (or in the case of the unemployed, the lack of labor). But most would admit alienation in some form is among the ills of capitalism. Marx's analysis, then, remains relevant.

Also of continuing relevance are two of the central ideas of historical materialism: that history is to be explained in terms of economic developments rather than the development of ideas (or as Marx would put it, social being determines social consciousness); and that class remains a central explanatory variable in social theory. In a way, these two ideas have

21. For an example, see the last chapter of Jon Elster, *An Introduction to Karl Marx* (Cambridge: Cambridge University Press, 1986).

so deeply infiltrated our common sense understanding of the world that we tend to take them for granted. But not always. For there are still many attempts to explain major historical developments in terms of moral values, religious commitments, or political ideologies. Among the most significant events going on in the world today is surely the transformation of Eastern Europe. An analysis from a self-consciously Marxist perspective would tend to explain these events in terms of underlying economic and class factors, as complicated as they might be. Is this the correct way to understand the religious, ethnic, and nationalist currents now so powerful in that part of the world?

Class remains one of the categories most associated with Marx. His class analysis, which basically saw capitalism in terms of two major classes, the capitalist and the proletariat, was too simplistic to do justice to nineteenth-century Europe, and it is surely inadequate to make sense of our society. But is there a concept of class and class struggle that has some explanatory power? Or is class simply the wrong concept to use in trying to understand our complex social reality? If one wants to hold on to something like a Marxist class analysis, is there today a class (or even more generally, a social group) that can play the role of the revolutionary agent that Marx assigned to the proletariat?

Three important features of communist society, as Marx sketched it, also remain relevant: the rejection of the market as an organizing principle of social relations, the abolishment of private ownership of the means of production, and the nature and meaning of egalitarianism. Although at the moment socialism appears to be receding from the political agenda in most places, the question of the market persists. Is there a viable alternative to the use of the market as an organizing principle of our economy and more generally, of society? To what extent do we want to continue to rely on the market to allocate resources and distribute wealth, and to what extent should we assign these tasks to a centralized authority? Which institutional approach, or some combination of the two, offers the best way to maximize efficiency, freedom, and rationality? In Marx himself one can detect two tendencies or moments in this regard. On the one hand, he was clearly critical of the capitalist market as ultimately inefficient, irrational, and alienating, and was drawn towards a model of centralized social planning as the rational, and in a certain sense, liberating alternative. On the other hand, there is an anarchist tendency in Marx in places. When he talks about decentralization and direct participatory control of the production process and of the product, it is not clear how this is consistent with centralized planning. While the capitalist market of the late twentieth century is a far cry from that of Marx's day, we are still wrestling with where we should be along both the state/market and the centralized/decentralized continuums.

We are also still struggling with the issue of private ownership of the means of production, with, that is, the nature of capital. There have, of course, been various attempts to address this question, social experiments ranging on a continuum from the Soviet Union to Sweden to the United States. The issue, however, is still not resolved, as the present debate over the role of the government in the health care industry clearly indicates.

Lastly, the idea of an egalitarian society remains relevant. Marx is often taken to be an enemy of individualism and individual freedom. This is far from the truth. His vision was of a society in which individuals could for the first time be free to develop their talents and abilities. But importantly, it was a society in which all individuals would be equally free to do this. Communism is again often misrepresented as a leveling society where all would be reduced to a common level. This is the sense of egalitarianism associated with Marx. But what Marx saw as the true value was not equality of result but equality of potential, not equality in tension with freedom but equality that could only be realized along side of true freedom for all. Communism would not be a society of equal result or equal achievement. But it would be a society in which differences in achievement would not be the cause of jealousy, envy, or greed. It would be egalitarian in the sense that all would be equally free of unnecessary and harmful barriers to individual achievement. This is, for sure, a heady and utopian vision. But properly understanding the sense in which Marx was an egalitarian does give us some purchase on the ways in which we are not.

Selected Bibliography

The literature on Marx is, needless to say, enormous. The following list includes, for the most part, works that have been published in English in the recent past. They are predominantly philosophical studies that focus on Marx rather than the Marxist tradition.

I. Writings of Marx

Capital, Volume 1, trans. Ben Fowkes. Pelican Marx Library. New York: Random House, 1977.

Capital, Volume 2, trans. David Fernbach. Pelican Marx Library. New York: Random House, 1981.

Capital, Volume 3, trans. David Fernbach. Pelican Marx Library. New York: Random House, 1981.

Grundrisse: Foundations of the Critique of Political Economy, trans. Martin Nicolaus. Harmondsworth: Penguin Books, 1974.

Marx Engels Collected Works. New York: International Publishers, 1975–.

Marx Engels Gesamtausgabe. Berlin: Dietz Verlag, 1972–.

Theories of Surplus Value. London: Lawrence & Wishart, 1969–72. 3 volumes.

Writings of the Young Marx on Philosophy and Society. Loyd D. Easton and Kurt H. Guddat, eds. and trans. Garden City: Doubleday Anchor Books, 1967.

II. Biographies

Berlin, Sir Isaiah. *Karl Marx: His Life and Environment.* 4th edition. Oxford: Oxford University Press, 1978.

McLellan, David. *Karl Marx: His Life and Thought.* New York: Harper & Row, 1973.

III. Secondary Literature

Avineri, Shlomo. *The Social and Political Thought of Karl Marx.* Cambridge: Cambridge University Press, 1968.

Ball, T. and J. Farr, eds. *After Marx.* Cambridge: Cambridge University Press, 1984.

Buchanan, Allen. *Marx and Justice.* Totowa: Rowman and Littlefield, 1982.

Callinicos, Alex, ed. *Marxist Theory.* Oxford: Oxford University Press, 1989.

Carver, Terrell, ed. *The Cambridge Companion to Marx.* Cambridge: Cambridge University Press, 1991.

Cohen, G. A. *History, Labour and Freedom: Themes from Marx.* Oxford: Clarendon Press, 1988.

Cohen, G. A. *Karl Marx's Theory of History: A Defence.* Princeton: Princeton University Press, 1978.

Cohen, M., T. Nagel, and T. Scanlon, eds. *Marx, Justice and History.* Princeton: Princeton University Press, 1981.

Draper, Hal. *Karl Marx's Theory of Revolution.* 2 volumes. New York: Monthly Review Press, 1977–78.

Elster, Jon. *An Introduction to Karl Marx.* Cambridge: Cambridge University Press, 1986.

Elster, Jon. *Making Sense of Marx.* Cambridge: Cambridge University Press, 1985.

Geras, Norman. *Marx and Human Nature.* London: New Left Books, 1983.

Heilbronner, Richard. *Marxism: For and Against.* New York: Norton. 1980.

Kolakowski, Leszek. *Main Currents of Marxism.* 3 volumes. Oxford: Oxford University Press, 1978.

Little, Daniel. *The Scientific Marx.* Minneapolis: University of Minnesota Press, 1986.

Lukes, Steven. *Marxism and Morality.* Oxford: Clarendon Press, 1984.

Miller, Richard. *Analyzing Marx: Morality, Power and History.* Princeton: Princeton University Press, 1984.

Peffer, R. G. *Marxism, Morality, and Social Justice.* Princeton: Princeton University Press, 1990.

Plamenatz, John. *Karl Marx's Philosophy of Man.* Oxford: Oxford University Press, 1975.

Roemer, John, ed. *Analytical Marxism.* Cambridge: Cambridge University Press, 1986.

Schmidt, Alfred. *The Concept of Nature in Marx.* London: New Left Books, 1971.

Schmitt, Richard. *Introduction to Marx and Engels: A Critical Reconstruction.* Boulder: Westview Press, 1987.

Shaw, William H. *Marx's Theory of History.* Stanford: Stanford University Press, 1978.

Singer, Peter. *Marx.* Oxford: Oxford University Press, 1980.

Wolff, Robert Paul. *Understanding Marx.* Princeton: Princeton University Press, 1984.

Wood, Allen W. *Karl Marx.* London: Routledge and Kegan Paul, 1981.

Wright, Erik Olin, Andrew Levine, and Elliott Sober. *Reconstructing Marxism: Essays on Explanation and the Theory of History.* New York: Verso, 1992.

I.

EARLY

PHILOSOPHICAL

WRITINGS

On the Jewish Question

Karl Marx

In 1842, Bruno Bauer published a series of articles in the Deutsche Jahrbücher *on the subject of Jewish emancipation in Germany. Marx wrote a review of and response to Bauer's articles (and subsequent book) in the fall of 1843 in Kreuznach, where he had gone on return from his honeymoon, and just before he moved to Paris in October. Marx's review was published in the* Deutsch-Französische Jahrbücher *in February, 1844. The essay is in the first instance about civil rights: whether Jews should be granted the same rights as Christians. Laws in Prussia restricted Jews with regard to commercial activities and occupational opportunities. Marx's father had been a victim of this policy.*

In the early 1840's, the question of Jewish emancipation was of some interest to German radicals. Bauer had argued that for Jews to be granted the same rights as Christians, both had to renounce their religions. Religion was too great a divide; a state dominated by Christians could not grant Jews equal rights. This position made some sense in the context of the general Young Hegelian critique of religion. In fact, however, it served the interests of those opposed to Jewish emancipation.

Marx takes exception to Bauer's argument. A liberal state could grant equality to Jews qua citizens of the state. America, he notes, is an example of this. Likewise, a state could, from a constitutional point of view, free citizens from property by doing away with a property qualification for the franchise without liberating people from the effects of private property in civil society. The real question of Jewish emancipation, Marx goes on to argue, should be seen as a question of real emancipation in general. Being free to practice religion in civil society is possible without being free of the alienation that is religion. Likewise, granting everyone the rights of citizenship in relation to the state does not ensure that we live a species-life as a communal being outside of our role of citizen. Indeed, granting everyone the rights of "man" and "citizen" means ultimately that all are free to be egotistical and unfree in civil society. Overcoming the alienation and separation of human from human in the sphere of the state does not end the alienation of civil society from the state. Political emancipation should not be confused with real, human emancipation to be achieved in a community of species-beings. The essay, then, can be seen as an attempt to expose the limitations of liberalism in the context of an unreformed sphere of private property.

1

In the second part of the essay, Marx goes on to criticize the economic rela-
tions and attitudes characteristic of civil society. These he identifies, in a
manner typical of his time, with stereotypes of Jews. Some have seen these re-
marks as evidence of Marx's own anti-Semitism. While he does exploit anti-
Semitic imagery and rhetoric, his real target is civil society (and ultimately
capitalism) and not Jews per se.

Bruno Bauer, The Jewish Question, *Braunschweig, 1843*

The German Jews want emancipation. What kind of emancipation? *Civil, political* emancipation.

Bruno Bauer answers them: No one in Germany is politically emancipated. We are not free ourselves. How shall we liberate you? You Jews are *egoists* when you claim a special emancipation for yourselves as Jews. As Germans, you should work for the political emancipation of Germany, as men, for the emancipation of mankind; and you should feel the particular form of your oppression and shame not as an exception to the rule but rather as its confirmation.

Or do Jews desire to be put on an equal footing with *Christian subjects?* If so, they recognize the *Christian state* as legitimate, as the regime of general subjugation. Why should they be displeased at their particular yoke if the general yoke pleases them? Why should Germans be interested in the liberation of Jews if Jews are not interested in the liberation of Germans?

The *Christian* state takes cognizance only of *privileges.* In it the Jew has the privilege of being a Jew. As a Jew he has rights that Christians do not have. Why does he want rights he does not have and that Christians enjoy?

If the Jew wants to be emancipated from the Christian state, he is demanding that the Christian state abandon its *religious* prejudice. But does the Jew abandon *his* religious prejudice? Has he, then, the right to demand of another this abdication of religion?

By *its very nature* the Christian state cannot emancipate the Jew; but, Bauer adds, the Jew by his very nature cannot be emancipated. So long as the state remains Christian and the Jew remains Jewish, both are equally incapable of giving as well as receiving emancipation.

The Christian state can only behave toward the Jew in the manner of the Christian state—that is, permitting the separation of the Jew from

Translated from the German by Loyd D. Easton and Kurt H. Guddat.

other subjects as a privilege but making him feel the pressure of the other separate spheres of society, and feel them all the more heavily, since he stands in *religious* opposition to the predominant religion. But the Jew in turn can behave toward the state only in a Jewish manner, that is as a foreigner, since he opposes his chimerical nationality to actual nationality, his illusory law to actual law. He imagines that his separation from humanity is justified, abstains on principle from participation in the historical movement, looks to a future that has nothing in common with the future of mankind as a whole, and regards himself as a part of the Jewish people, the chosen people.

On what basis, then, do you Jews want emancipation? On the basis of your religion? It is the mortal enemy of the religion of the state. As citizens? There are no citizens in Germany. As men? You are not men, just as those to whom you appeal are not men.

After criticizing previous positions and solutions, Bauer formulates the question of Jewish emancipation in a new way. What is the *nature*, he asks, of the Jew who is to be emancipated and the Christian state that is to emancipate him? He answers with a critique of the Jewish religion, analyzes the *religious* antagonism between Judaism and Christianity, and explains the essence of the Christian state—all this with dash, acuteness, wit, and thoroughness in a style as precise as it is pregnant and energetic.

How then does Bauer settle the Jewish question? What is the result? The formulation of a question is its solution. Criticism of the Jewish question provides the answer to the Jewish question. The résumé thus follows:

We must emancipate ourselves before we can emancipate others.

The most persistent form of the antagonism between the Jew and the Christian is the *religious* antagonism. How is an antagonism to be resolved? By making it impossible. And how is a *religious* antagonism made impossible? By *abolishing religion.* Once Jew and Christian recognize their respective religions as nothing more than *different stages in the evolution of the human spirit,* as different snake skins shed by *history,* and recognize *man* as the snake that wore them, they will no longer find themselves in religious antagonism but only in a critical, *scientific,* and human relationship. *Science,* then, constitutes their unity. Contradictions in science, however, are resolved by science itself.

The *German* Jew is particularly affected by the general lack of political emancipation and the pronounced Christianity of the state. With Bauer, however, the Jewish question has a universal significance independent of specific German conditions. It is the question of the relation of religion to the state, of the *contradiction between religious prejudice and political emancipation.* Emancipation from religion is presented as a condition both for the Jew who seeks political emancipation and for the state which is to emancipate him and is to be emancipated itself as well.

"Very well, you say—and the Jew himself says it—the Jew should not be emancipated because he is Jew or because he has such excellent and universal ethical principles but rather because he takes second place to the *citizen* and becomes one in spite of being and wanting to remain a Jew. That is, he is and remains a Jew in spite of the fact that he is a *citizen* living in universally human relationships; his Jewish and restricted nature always triumphs in the end over his human and political obligations. The *prejudice* remains even though it has been overtaken by *universal* principles. But if it remains, it rather overtakes everything else." "The Jew could remain a Jew in political life only in a sophistical sense, only in appearance; thus if he wanted to remain a Jew, this mere appearance would become the essential thing and would triumph. In other words, his *life in the state* would be only a semblance or a momentary exception to the real nature of things, an exception to the rule." ("The Capacity of Present-day Jews and Christians to Become Free," *Twenty-one Sheets from Switzerland* [*Einundzwanzig Bogen aus der Schweiz*], p. 57.)

Let us see, on the other hand, how Bauer describes the role of the state:

"France," he says, "recently (Proceedings of the Chamber of Deputies, 26 December 1840) gave us, in connection with the Jewish question and all other *political* questions (since the July Revolution), a glimpse of a life which is free but which revokes its freedom by law, thus revealing it to be a sham, and on the other hand, denies its free law by its acts." (*The Jewish Question*, p. 64.)
   "Universal freedom is not yet established as law in France, and the *Jewish question is not yet settled* because legal freedom—that all citizens are equal—is limited in actual life which is still dominated and fragmented by religious privileges, and because the lack of freedom in actual life reacts on the law, compelling it to sanction the division of inherently free citizens into the oppressed and the oppressors" (p. 65).

When, therefore, would the Jewish question be settled in France?

"The Jew, for instance, would really have ceased being a Jew if he did not let himself be hindered by his code from fulfilling his duties toward the state and his fellow citizens—if he went, for example, to the Chamber of Deputies and took part in public affairs on the Sabbath. Every *religious privilege,* including the monopoly of a privileged church, would have to be abolished, and if a few or many or *even the overwhelming majority still felt obliged to fulfill their religious duties,* such a practice should be left to *them* as a *purely private matter"* (p. 65). "There is no longer any religion if there is no privileged religion. Take from religion its power of excommunication and it ceases to exist" (p. 66). "Just as M. Martin du Nord saw the proposal to omit any mention of Sunday in the law as a declaration that Christianity had ceased to exist, with equal right (and one well-founded) a declaration that the Sabbath-law is no longer binding for the Jew would proclaim the end of Judaism" (p. 71).

Bauer thus demands, on the one hand, that the Jew give up Judaism and man give up religion in order to be emancipated *as a citizen.* On the other hand, he holds that from the *political* abolition of religion there logically follows the abolition of religion altogether. The state which presupposes religion is as yet no true, no actual state. "To be sure, the religious view reinforces the state. But what state? *What kind of state?*" (p. 97).

At this point Bauer's *one-sided* approach to the Jewish question becomes apparent.

It is by no means sufficient to ask: Who should emancipate and who should be emancipated? Criticism has to be concerned with a third question. It must ask: *What kind of emancipation is involved and what are its underlying conditions?* Criticism of *political emancipation* itself is primarily the final critique of the Jewish question and its true resolution into the *"universal question of the age."*

Since Bauer does not raise the question to this level, he falls into contradictions. He presents conditions that are not based on the essence of *political* emancipation. He raises questions that are irrelevant to his problem and solves problems that leave his question untouched. Bauer says of the opponents of Jewish emancipation, "Their mistake simply lay in assuming the Christian state to be the only true state without subjecting it to the same criticism they applied to Judaism" (p. 3). Here we find Bauer's mistake in subjecting *only* the "Christian state," not the "state as such," to criticism, in failing to examine the *relation between political emancipation and human emancipation,* and hence presenting conditions that are only explicable from his uncritical confusion of political emancipation with universal human emancipation. Bauer asks the Jews: Have you the right to demand *political emancipation* from your standpoint? We ask, on the contrary: Has the standpoint of *political* emancipation the right to demand from the Jews the abolition of Judaism and from man the abolition of religion?

The Jewish question has a different aspect according to the state in which the Jew finds himself. In Germany, where there is no political state and no state as such exists, the Jewish question is purely *theological.* The Jew finds himself in *religious* opposition to a state acknowledging Christianity as its foundation. This state is a theologian *ex professo.* Criticism is here criticism of theology, double-edged criticism of Christian and of Jewish theology. But however *critical* we might be, we are still moving in theology.

In France, a *constitutional* state, the Jewish question is a question of constitutionalism, a question of the *incompleteness of political emancipation*. As the *semblance* of a state religion is preserved there, if only by the meaningless and self-contradictory formula of a *religion of the majority*, the relation of the Jew to the state also retains the *semblance* of a religious or theological opposition.

Only in the free states of North America—or at least in some of them—does the Jewish question lose its *theological* significance and become a truly *secular* question. Only where the political state exists in its complete development can the relation of the Jew, and generally speaking the religious man, to the political state, that is, the relation of religion to state, appear in its characteristic and pure form. Criticism of this relation ceases to be theological once the state abandons a *theological* posture toward religion, once it relates itself to religion as a state, that is, *politically*. Criticism then becomes *criticism of the political state*. Where the question here ceases to be *theological*, Bauer's criticism ceases to be critical. *"In the United States there is neither a state religion, nor a religion declared to be that of the majority, nor a pre-eminence of one faith over another. The state is foreign to all faiths."* (Gustave de Beaumont, *Marie ou l'esclave aux Etats-Unis* . . . [Brussels, 1835], p. 214.) There are even some states in North America where *"the constitution imposes no religious beliefs or sectarian practice as the condition of political rights"* (*loc. cit.*, p. 225). Yet *"no one in the United States believes that a man without religion can be an honest man"* (*loc. cit.*, p. 224). And North America is pre-eminently the land of religiosity as Beaumont, Tocqueville, and the Englishman Hamilton assure us unanimously. The North American states, however, serve only as an example. The question is: What is the relation of *complete* political emancipation to religion? If we find even in a country with full political emancipation that religion not only *exists* but is *fresh* and *vital*, we have proof that the existence of religion is not incompatible with the full development of the state. But since the existence of religion implies a defect, the source of this defect must be sought in the *nature* of the state itself. We no longer take religion to be the *basis* but only the *manifestation* of secular narrowness. Hence we explain religious restriction of free citizens on the basis of their secular restriction. We do not claim that they must transcend their religious restriction in order to transcend their secular limitations. We do claim that they will transcend their religious restriction once they have transcended their secular limitations. We do not convert secular questions into theological ones. We convert theological questions into secular ques-

tions. History has long enough been resolved into superstition, but now
we can resolve superstition into history. The question of the *relation of
political emancipation to religion* becomes for us a question of the *relation
of political emancipation to human emancipation*. We criticize the religious
weaknesses of the political state by criticizing the political state in its
secular constitution *apart from* the religious defects. In human terms we
resolve the contradiction between the state and a *particular religion* such
as *Judaism* into the contradiction between the state and *particular secular*
elements, the contradiction between the state and *religion generally* into
the contradiction between the state and its *presuppositions*.

The *political* emancipation of the Jew, the Christian, or the *religious*
man generally is the *emancipation of the state* from Judaism, from Christianity, from *religion* in general. In a form and manner corresponding to
its nature, the *state* as such emancipates itself from religion by emancipating itself from the *state religion*, that is, by recognizing no religion
and recognizing itself simply as the state. *Political* emancipation from
religion is not complete and consistent emancipation from religion because political emancipation is not the complete and consistent form of
human emancipation.

The limits of political emancipation are seen at once in the fact that
the *state* can free itself from a limitation without man *actually* being free
from it, in the fact that a state can be a *free state* without men becoming
free men. Bauer himself tacitly admits this in setting the following condition of political emancipation: "Every religious privilege, including the
monopoly of a privileged church, would have to be abolished. If a few or
many or even the *overwhelming majority still felt obliged to fulfill their
religious duties*, such a practice should be left to them as a *purely private
matter*." The *state* can thus emancipate itself from religion even though
the *overwhelming majority* is still religious. And the overwhelming majority does not cease being religious by being religious *in private*.

But the attitude of the state, particularly the *free state*, toward religion
is still only the attitude of the *men* who make up the state. Hence it
follows that man frees himself from a limitation *politically*, *through the
state*, by overcoming the limitation in an *abstract*, *limited*, and partial
manner, in contradiction with himself. Further, when man frees himself
politically, he does so *indirectly*, through an *intermediary*, even if the
intermediary is *necessary*. Finally, even when man proclaims himself an
atheist through the medium of the state—that is, when he declares the
state to be atheistic—he is still captive to religion since he only recognizes his atheism indirectly through an intermediary. Religion is merely
the indirect recognition of man through a *mediator*. The state is the
mediator between man and the freedom of man. As Christ is the mediator on whom man unburdens all his own divinity and all his *religious ties*,

so is the state the mediator to which man transfers all his unholiness and
all his *human freedom.*

   The *political* elevation of man above religion shares all the defects and
all the advantages of any political elevation. If the state as state, for
example, abolishes *private property,* man proclaims private property is
overcome politically once he abolishes the *property qualification* for active
and passive voting as has been done in many North American states.
Hamilton interprets this fact quite correctly in political terms: *"The great
majority of the people have gained a victory over property owners and financial wealth."*[*] Is not private property ideally abolished when the have-
nots come to legislate for the haves? The *property qualification* is the last
political form for recognizing private property.

   Yet the political annulment of private property not only does not
abolish it but even presupposes it. The state abolishes distinctions of
birth, rank, education, and *occupation* in its fashion when it declares them
to be *non-political* distinctions, when it proclaims that every member of
the community *equally* participates in popular sovereignty without regard
to these distinctions, and when it deals with all elements of the actual life
of the nation from the standpoint of the state. Nevertheless the state
permits private property, education, and occupation to *act* and manifest
their *particular* nature as private property, education, and occupation in
their *own* ways. Far from overcoming these *factual* distinctions, the state
exists only by presupposing them; it is aware of itself as a *political state*
and makes its *universality* effective only in opposition to these elements.
Hegel, therefore, defines the relation of the *political state* to religion quite
correctly in saying: "If the state is to have specific existence as the *self-
knowing ethical actuality* of Spirit, it must be *distinct* from the form of
authority and faith; this distinction emerges only as the ecclesiastical
sphere is *divided* within itself; *only* thus has the state attained *universality*
of thought, the principle of its form, *above particular* churches and only
thus does it bring that universality into existence." (Hegel's *Philosophy of
Law,* 1st ed., p. 346 [§ 270].) Exactly! Only thus *above* the *particular*
elements is the state a universality.

   By its nature the perfected political state is man's *species-life* in opposition to his material life. All the presuppositions of this egoistic life
remain in *civil society outside* the state, but as qualities of civil society.
Where the political state has achieved its full development, man leads a
double life, a heavenly and an earthly life, not only in thought or con-

[*Thomas Hamilton, *Men and Manners in America* (2 vols.; Edinburgh: William
Blackwood, 1833). Marx quotes from the German translation, *Die Menschen und
die Sitten in den Vereinigten Staaten von Nordamerika* (Mannheim: Hoff, 1834),
Vol. I, p. 146.]

sciousness but in *actuality*. In the *political community* he regards himself as a *communal being*; but in *civil society* he is active as a *private individual*, treats other men as means, reduces himself to a means, and becomes the plaything of alien powers. The political state is as spiritual in relation to civil society as heaven is in relation to earth. It stands in the same opposition to civil society and goes beyond it in the same way as religion goes beyond the limitation of the profane world, that is, by recognizing, reestablishing, and necessarily allowing itself to be dominated by it. In his *innermost* actuality, in civil society, man is a profane being. Here, where he counts as an actual individual to himself and others, he is an *illusory* phenomenon. In the state where he counts as a species-being, on the other hand, he is an imaginary member of an imagined sovereignty, divested of his actual individual life and endowed with an unactual universality.

The conflict in which man as believer in a *particular* religion finds himself—a conflict with his own citizenship and other men as members of the community—is reduced to the *secular* split between the *political* state and *civil society*. For man as *bourgeois* [or part of civil society], "life in the state is only a semblance or a momentary exception to the real nature of things, an exception to the rule." Certainly the *bourgeois*, like the Jew, participates in the life of the state only in a sophistical way just as the *citoyen* is only sophistically a Jew or *bourgeois;* but this sophistry is not personal. It is the *sophistry of the political state* itself. The difference between the religious man and the citizen is the difference between the shopkeeper and the citizen, between the day laborer and the citizen, between the landowner and the citizen, between the *living individual* and the *citizen*. The contradiction between the religious and political man is the same as that between *bourgeois* and *citoyen*, between the member of civil society and his *political lion skin*.

This secular conflict to which the Jewish question ultimately is reduced—the relation between the political state and its presuppositions, whether the presuppositions be material elements such as private property or spiritual elements such as education and religion, the conflict between *general* and *private interest*, the split betwen the *political state* and *civil society*—these secular contradictions Bauer leaves untouched while attacking their *religious* expression. "It is precisely its foundation, need, which assures the maintenance of *civil society* and *guarantees its necessity* but exposes its maintenance to constant danger, sustains an element of uncertainty in civil society, and produces that constantly alternating mixture of poverty and wealth, of adversity and prosperity, and change in general" (p. 8).

Consider his entire section, "Civil Society" (pp. 8–9), which closely follows the main features of Hegel's philosophy of law. Civil society in opposition to the political state is recognized as necessary since the political state is recognized as necessary.

Political emancipation is indeed a great step forward. It is not, to be sure, the final form of universal human emancipation, but it is the final form *within* the prevailing order of things. It is obvious that we are here talking about actual, practical emancipation.

Man emancipates himself *politically* from religion by banishing it from the sphere of public law into private right. It is no longer the spirit of the *state* where man—although in a limited way, under a particular form, and in a particular sphere—associates in community with other men as a species-being. It has become the spirit of *civil society*, of the sphere of egoism, of the *bellum omnium contra omnes.* It is no longer the essence of *community* but the essence of *division.* It has become what it was *originally*, an expression of the *separation* of man from his *community*, from himself and from other men. It is now only the abstract confession of particular peculiarity, of *private whim*, of caprice. The infinite splits of religion in North America, for example, already give it the *external* form of a purely individual matter. It has been tossed among numerous private interests and exiled from the community as a community. But one must not be deceived about the scope of political emancipation. The splitting of man into *public* and *private*, the *displacement* of religion from the state to civil society, is not just a step in political emancipation but its *completion.* It as little abolishes man's *actual* religiosity as it seeks to abolish it.

The *disintegration* of man into Jew and citizen, Protestent and citizen, religious man and citizen does not belie citizenship or circumvent political emancipation. It is *political emancipation itself,* the *political* mode of emancipation from religion. To be sure, in periods when the political state as such is forcibly born from civil society, when men strive to liberate themselves under the form of political self-liberation, the state can and must go as far as to *abolish* and *destroy religion*, but only in the way it abolishes private property by setting a maximum, confiscation, and progressive taxation or only in the way it abolishes life by the *guillotine.* In moments of special concern for itself political life seeks to repress its presupposition, civil society and its elements, and to constitute itself the actual, harmonious species-life of man. But it can do this only in *violent* contradiction with its own conditions of existence by declaring the revolution to be *permanent*, and thus the political drama is bound to end with the restoration of religion, private property, and all the elements of civil society just as war ends with peace.

Indeed, the perfected Christian state is not the so-called *Christian* state acknowledging Christianity as its foundation in the state religion and excluding all others. It is, rather, the *atheistic* state, the *democratic* state, the state that relegates religion to the level of other elements of civil society. The state that is still theological and still officially prescribes belief in Christianity has not yet dared to declare itself to be *a state* and has not yet succeeded in expressing in *secular* and *human* form, in its *actuality* as a state, those *human* foundations of which Christianity is the sublime expression. The so-called Christian state is simply a *non-state*, for it is only the *human foundation* of Christianity, not Christianity as a religion, which can realize itself in actual human creations.

The so-called Christian state is a Christian denial of the state, not in any way the political actualization of Christianity. The state that still professes Christianity in the form of religion does not profess it in political form because it still behaves religiously toward religion—that is, it is not the *actual expression* of the human basis of religion since it still deals with the *unreality* and *imaginary* form of this human core. The so-called Christian state is an *imperfect* one, which treats Christianity as the *supplement* and *sanctification* of its imperfection. Hence religion necessarily becomes a *means* to an end, and the state is a *hypocrite*. There is a great difference between a *perfected* state that counts religion as one of its *prerequisites* because of a lack in the general *nature* of the state and an *imperfect* state that proclaims religion as its *foundation* because of a lack in its *particular existence* as an imperfect state. In the latter, religion becomes *imperfect politics*. In the former, the inadequacy of even perfected *politics* is apparent in religion. The so-called Christian state needs the Christian religion to complete itself *as a state*. The democratic state, the real state, needs no religion for its political fulfillment. It can, rather, do without religion because it fulfills the human basis of religion in a secular way. The so-called Christian state, on the other hand, behaves toward religion in a political way and toward politics in a religious way. As it reduces political forms to mere appearance, it equally reduces religion to a mere appearance.

To express this contradiction clearly let us consider Bauer's construct of the Christian state, a construct derived from his perception of the Christian-Germanic state.

"To prove the *impossibility* or *non-existence* of a Christian state," says Bauer, "we have recently and more frequently been referred to those passages in the Gospel which the [present] state *not only* does *not* follow but *also cannot unless it wants to dissolve itself completely.*" "But the matter is not so easily settled. What do those Gospel passages demand? Supernatural self-renunciation and submission to the authority of revelation, turning away from the state, the abolition of secular relationships. But the Christian state demands and achieves all these things. It has made the *spirit of the Gospel* its own, and if it does not reproduce it in exactly the same words as the Gospel, that is because it expresses that spirit in political forms borrowed from the political system of this world but reduced to mere appearance by the religious rebirth they must undergo. This withdrawal from the state is realized through the forms of the state" (p. 55).

Bauer goes on to show how the people of a Christian state do not constitute a nation with a will of its own but have their true existence in the ruler to whom they are subject but who is alien to them by origin and nature since he was given to them by God without their consent. Further, the laws of this nation are not its own doing but are positive revelations. The supreme ruler requires privileged intermediaries in his relations with his own people, the masses, themselves split into a multitude of distinct spheres formed and determined by chance and differentiated from each other by their interests and particular passions and prejudices but permitted as a privilege to isolate themselves from each other, etc. (p. 56).

But Bauer himself says: "If politics is to be nothing more than religion, it cannot be politics any more than cleaning cooking pans can be regarded as an economic matter if it is to be treated religiously" (p. 108). But in the Christian-Germanic state, religion is an "economic matter" just as "economic matters" are religion. In the Christian-Germanic state, the dominance of religion is the religion of domination.

The separation of the "spirit of the Gospel" from the "letter of the Gospel" is an *irreligious act*. The state that permits the Gospel to speak in the letter of politics or in any other letter than that of the Holy Spirit commits a sacrilege if not in the eyes of men at least in the eyes of its own religion. The state that acknowledges Christianity as its highest rule and the *Bible* as its *charter* must be confronted with the *words* of Holy Writ, for the Writ is holy in every word. This state as well as the *human rubbish* on which it is based finds itself involved in a painful contradiction, a contradiction insoluble from the standpoint of religious consciousness based on the teaching of the Gospel, which it "not only does not follow but *also cannot unless it wants to dissolve itself completely as a state.*" And why does it not want to dissolve itself completely? It cannot answer this question either for itself or others. In its *own consciousness* the official Christian state is an *ought* whose realization is impossible. It knows it can affirm the *actuality* of its own existence only by lying to itself and hence remains dubious, unreliable, and problematic. Criticism is thus completely right in forcing the state that appeals to the Bible into a mental derangement in which it no longer knows whether it is an *illusion* or a *reality*, in which the infamy of its *secular* purposes cloaked by religion irreconcilably conflicts with the integrity of its *religious* consciousness viewing religion as the world's purpose. Such a state can only free itself of inner torment by becoming the *constable* of the Catholic

Church. In relation to that church, which claims secular power as its servant, the state, the *secular* power claiming to dominate the religious spirit, is impotent.

In the so-called Christian state what counts is indeed *alienation* but not *man*. The only man who does count, the *king*, is still religious, specifically distinguished from others and directly connected with heaven, with God. The relations prevailing here are still relations of *faith*. The religious spirit is still not actually secularized.

But the religious spirit cannot *actually* be secularized, for what is it, in fact, but the *unsecular* form of a stage in the development of the human spirit? The religious spirit can only be actualized if the stage of development of the human spirit it expresses religiously emerges into and assumes its *secular* form. This is what happens in the *democratic* state. The basis of the democratic state is not Christianity but the *human ground* of Christianity. Religion remains the ideal, unsecular consciousness of its members because it is the ideal form of the *stage of human development* attained in the democratic state.

The members of the political state are religious by virtue of the dualism between individual life and species-life, between the life of civil society and political life. They are religious inasmuch as man regards as his true life the political life remote from his actual individuality, inasmuch as religion is here the spirit of civil society expressing the generation and withdrawal of man from man. Political democracy is Christian in that it regards man—not merely one but every man—as *sovereign* and supreme. But this means man in his uncivilized and unsocial aspect, in his fortuitous existence and just as he is, corrupted by the entire organization of our society, lost and alienated from himself, oppressed by inhuman relations and elements—in a word, man who is not yet an *actual* species-being. The sovereignty of man—though as alien and distinct from actual men—which is the chimera, dream, and postulate of Christianity, is a tangible and present actuality, a secular maxim, in democracy.

In the perfected democracy the religious and theological consciousness appears to itself all the more religious and theological for being apparently without political significance or mundane purposes—for being a spiritual affair eschewing the world, an expression of reason's limitation, a product of whim and fantasy, an actual life in the beyond. Christianity here achieves the *practical* expression of its universal religious meaning in that the most varied views are grouped together in the form of Christianity and, what is more, others are not asked to profess Christianity but only religion in general, any kind of religion (cf. Beaumont, *op. cit.*). The religious consciousness revels in the wealth of religious contradictions and multiplicity.

We have thus shown: Political emancipation from religion permits

religion, though not privileged religion, to continue. The contradiction
in which the adherent of a specific religion finds himself in relation to
his citizenship is only *one aspect* of the universal *secular contradiction
between the political state and civil society.* The fulfillment of the Christian
state is a state that acknowledges itself as a state and ignores the religion
of its members. The emancipation of the state from religion is not the
emancipation of actual man from religion.

We thus do not say with Bauer to the Jews: You cannot be politically
emancipated without radically emancipating yourselves from Judaism.
Rather we tell them: Because you can be emancipated politically without
completely and fully renouncing Judaism, *political emancipation* by itself
is not *human* emancipation. If you Jews want to be politically emancipated without emancipating yourselves humanly, the incompleteness and
contradiction lies not only in you but in the *essence* and *category* of
political emancipation. If you are engrossed in this category, you share a
general bias. Just as the state *evangelizes* when, in spite of being a state, it
behaves toward the Jew in a Christian way, the Jew *acts politically* when,
in spite of being a Jew, he demands civil rights.

But if man can be emancipated politically and acquire civil rights even
though he is a Jew, can he claim and acquire the so-called *rights of man?*
Bauer *denies* it.

"The question is whether the Jew as such—i.e. the Jew who avows that his
true nature compels him to live in eternal separation from others—is able to
acquire the *universal rights of man* and grant them to others."

"The idea of the rights of man was discovered in the Christian world only
in the last century. It is not an innate idea but rather is acquired in struggle
against historical traditions in which man has hitherto been educated. Thus
the rights of man are neither a gift of nature nor a legacy from past history but
the reward of struggle against the accident of birth and privileges transmitted
by history from generation to generation up to the present. They are the result
of culture, and only he can possess them who has earned and deserved them."

"But can the Jew actually take possession of them? As long as he remains a
Jew the limited nature which makes him a Jew must triumph over the human
nature which should link him as a man with others and must separate him
from non-Jews. By this separation he proclaims that the special nature which
makes him a Jew is his true and highest nature to which his human nature
must yield."

"In the same way, the Christian as Christian cannot grant the rights of
man." (Pp. 19, 20.)

According to Bauer man must sacrifice the *"privilege of faith"* to be
able to acquire the universal rights of man. Let us consider for a moment

these so-called rights and indeed in their most authentic form, the form they have among their *discoverers*, the North Americans and the French. In part these rights are *political* rights that can be exercised only in community with others. *Participation* in the *community*, indeed the *political* community or *state*, constitutes their substance. They belong in the category of *political freedom*, of *civil rights*, which by no means presupposes the consistent and positive transcendence of religion and thus of Judaism, as we have seen. There is left for consideration the other part, the *rights of man* as distinct from the *rights of the citizen*.

Among these is freedom of conscience, the right to practice one's chosen religion. The *privilege of faith* is expressly recognized either as a *right of man* or as a consequence of a right of man, freedom.

> *Declaration of the Rights of Man and of the Citizen*, 1791, Art. 10: "No one is to be disturbed on account of his beliefs, even religious beliefs." In Title I of the Constitution of 1791 there is guaranteed as a human right: "The liberty of every man to practice the *religious worship* to which he is attached."
>
> The *Declaration of the Rights of Man*, etc., 1793, includes among human rights, Art. 7: "Freedom of worship." Moreover, it even maintains in regard to the right to express views and opinions, to assemble, and to worship: "The need to proclaim these *rights* assumes either the presence or recent memory of despotism." Compare the Constitution of 1795, Title XIV, Art. 354.
>
> *Constitution of Pennsylvania*, Art. 9, § 3: "All men have a natural and indefeasible *right* to worship Almighty God according to the dictates of their own consciences; no man can of right be compelled to attend, erect, or support any place of worship, or to maintain any ministry against his consent; no human authority can, in any case whatever, interfere with the rights of conscience and control the prerogatives of the soul."
>
> *Constitution of New Hampshire*, Arts. 5 and 6: "Among the natural rights, some are in their very nature unalienable, because no equivalent can be conceived for them. Of this kind are the *rights* of conscience." (Beaumont, *loc. cit.*, pp. 213, 214.)

The incompatibility between religion and the rights of man is so little implied in the concept of the rights of man that the *right to be religious* according to one's liking and to practice a particular religion is explicitly included among the rights of man. The *privilege of faith* is a *universal human right.*

The *rights of man* as *such* are distinguished from the *rights of the citizen*. Who is this *man* distinguished from the *citizen?* None other than the *member of civil society*. Why is the member of the civil society called "man," man without qualification, and why are his rights called the *rights of man?* How can we explain this? By the relation of the political state to civil society and by the nature of political emancipation.

Let us note first of all that the so-called *rights of man* as distinguished from the *rights of the citizen* are only the rights of the *member of civil society*, that is, of egoistic man, man separated from other men and from the community. The most radical constitution, the Constitution of 1793, may be quoted:

Declaration of the Rights of Man and of the Citizen.
   Art. 2. "These rights (the natural and imprescriptible rights) are: *equality, liberty, security, property.*"

What is this *liberty?*

Art. 6. "Liberty is the power belonging to each man to do anything which does not impair the rights of others," or according to the Declaration of the Rights of Man of 1791: "Liberty is the power to do anything which does not harm others."

Liberty is thus the right to do and perform anything that does not harm others. The limits within which each can act *without harming* others is determined by law just as the boundary between two fields is marked by a stake. This is the liberty of man viewed as an isolated monad, withdrawn into himself. Why, according to Bauer, is the Jew not capable of acquiring human rights? "As long as he remains a Jew the limited nature which makes him a Jew must triumph over the human nature which should link him as a man with others and must separate him from non-Jews." But liberty as a right of man is not based on the association of man with man but rather on the separation of man from man. It is the *right* of this separation, the right of the *limited* individual limited to himself.

The practical application of the right of liberty is the right of *private property.*

What is property as one of the rights of man?

Art. 16 (Constitution of 1793): "The right of *property* is that belonging to every citizen to enjoy and dispose of his goods, his revenues, the fruits of his labor and of his industry *as he wills.*"

The right of property is thus the right to enjoy and dispose of one's possessions as one wills, without regard for other men and independently of society. It is the right of self-interest. This individual freedom and its application as well constitutes the basis of civil society. It lets every man find in other men not the *realization* but rather the *limitation* of his own freedom. It proclaims above all the right of man "to enjoy and dispose of his goods, his revenues, the fruits of his labor and of his industry *as he wills.*"

There still remain the other rights of man, equality and security.

"Equality"—here used in its non-political sense—is only the equal right to *liberty* as described above, viz., that every man is equally viewed as a self-sufficient monad. The Constitution of 1705 defines the concept of equality with this significance:

> *Art. 3* (Constitution of 1795): "Equality consists in the fact that the law is the same for all, whether it protects or whether it punishes."

And security?

> *Art. 8* (Constitution of 1793): "Security consists in the protection accorded by society to each of its members for the preservation of his person, his rights and his property."

Security is the supreme social concept of civil society, the concept of the *police*, the concept that the whole society exists only to guarantee to each of its members the preservation of his person, his rights, and his property. In this sense Hegel calls civil society "the state as necessity and rationality."

Civil society does not raise itself above its egoism through the concept of security. Rather, security is the *guarantee* of the egoism.

Thus none of the so-called rights of men goes beyond the egoistic man, the man withdrawn into himself, his private interest and his private choice, and separated from the community as a member of civil society. Far from viewing man here in his species-being, his species-life itself—society—rather appears to be an external framework for the individual, limiting his original independence. The only bond between men is natural necessity, need and private interest, the maintenance of their property and egoistic persons.

It is somewhat curious that a nation just beginning to free itself, tearing down all the barriers between different sections of the people and founding a political community, should solemnly proclaim (Declaration of 1791) the justification of the egoistic man, man separated from his fellow men and from the community, and should even repeat this proclamation at a moment when only the most heroic sacrifice can save the nation and hence is urgently required, when the sacrifice of all the interests of civil society is highly imperative and egoism must be punished as crime (Declaration of the Rights of Man of 1793). This becomes even more curious when we observe that the political liberators reduce citizenship, the *political community*, to a mere *means* for preserving these so-called rights of man and that the citizen thus is proclaimed to be the servant of the egoistic man, the sphere in which man acts as a member of the community is degraded below that in which he acts as a fractional being, and finally man as bourgeois rather than man as citizen is considered to be the *proper* and *authentic* man.

"The *goal* of all *political association* is the *preservation* of the natural and imprescriptible rights of man." (Declaration of the Rights of Man, etc., of 1791, Art. 2.) "*Government* is instituted to guarantee man's enjoyment of his natural and imprescriptible rights." (Declaration, etc., of 1793, Art. 1.) Thus even at the time of its youthful enthusiasm fired by the urgency of circumstances political life is proclaimed to be a mere *means* whose end is life in civil society. To be sure, revolutionary practice flagrantly contradicts its theory. While security, for example, is proclaimed to be one of the rights of man, the violation of the privacy of correspondence is publicly established as the order of the day. While the "*unlimited* freedom of the press" (Constitution of 1793, Art. 122) as a consequence of the rights of man and individual freedom is guaranteed, freedom of the press is completely abolished because "freedom of the press should not be permitted to compromise public liberty." ("Robespierre jeune," *Parliamentary History of the French Revolution*, by Buchez and Roux, Vol. 28, p. 159.) This means that the human right of liberty ceases to be a right when it comes into conflict with *political* life while theoretically political life is only the guarantee of the rights of man, the rights of individual man, and should be abandoned once it contradicts its *end*, these rights of man. But the practice is only the exception, the theory is the rule. Even if we choose to regard revolutionary practice as the correct expression of this relationship, the problem still remains unsettled as to why the relationship is inverted in the consciousness of the political liberators so that the end appears as means and the means as the end. This optical illusion of their consciousness would always be the same problem, though a psychological, a theoretical problem.

The problem is easily settled.

Political emancipation is also the *dissolution* of the old society on which rests the sovereign power, the character of the state as alienated from the people. The political revolution is the revolution of civil society. What was the character of the old society? It can be described in one word *Feudalism*. The old civil society had a *directly political* character, that is, the elements of civil life such as property, the family, the mode and manner of work, for example, were raised into elements of political life in the form of landlordism, estates, and corporations. In this form they determined the relation of the particular individual to the *state as a whole*, that is, his *political* relation, his separation and exclusion from other parts of society. For the feudal organization of national life did not elevate property or labor to the level of social elements but rather completed their *separation* from the state as a whole and established them as *separate* societies within society. Thus the vital functions and conditions of civil society always remained political, but political in the feudal sense. That is, they excluded the individual from the state as a whole and transformed the *special* relation between his corporation and the state into his own general relation to national life, just as they transformed his specific civil activity and situation into a general activity and situation. As a consequence of this organization, there necessarily appears the unity of the state as well as its consciousness, will, and activity—the general political power—likewise the *special* business of the ruler and his servants, separated from the people.

The political revolution, which overthrew this domination, turned the business of the state into the people's business, and made the political state the business of *all*, that is, an actual state—this revolution inevitably destroyed all estates, corporations, guilds, and privileges variously expressing the separation of the people from their community. The political revolution thereby *abolished* the *political character of civil society*. It shattered civil society into its constituent elements—on the one hand *individuals* and on the other the *material* and *spiritual elements* constituting the vital content and civil situation of these individuals. It released the political spirit, which had been broken, fragmented, and lost, as it were, in the various cul-de-sacs of feudal society. It gathered up this scattered spirit, liberated it from its entanglement with civil life, and turned it into the sphere of the community, the *general* concern of the people ideally independent of these *particular* elements of civil life. A *particular* activity and situation in life sank into a merely individual significance, no longer forming the general relation of the individual to the state as a whole. Public business as such rather became the general business of every individual and the political function became his general function.

But the fulfillment of the idealism of the state was at the same time the fulfillment of the materialism of civil society. The throwing off of the political yoke was at the same time the throwing off of the bond that had fettered the egoistic spirit of civil society. Political emancipation was at the same time the emancipation of civil society from politics, from the *appearance* of a general content.

Feudal society was dissolved into its foundation, into *man*. But into man as he actually was the foundation of that society, into *egoistical* man.

This *man*, the member of civil society, is now the basis and presupposition of the *political* state. He is recognized as such by the state in the rights of man.

But the freedom of egoistic man and the recognition of this freedom is rather the recognition of the *unbridled* movement of the spiritual and material elements forming the content of his life.

Thus man was not freed from religion; he received religious freedom. He was not freed from property. He received freedom of property. He was not freed from the egoism of trade but received freedom to trade.

The *constitution* of the *political state* and the dissolution of civil society into independent *individuals*—whose relation is *law* just as the relation of estates and guilds was *privilege*—is accomplished in *one and the same act*. As a member of civil society man is the *non-political* man but necessarily appears to be *natural* man. The *rights of man* appear to be *natural rights* because *self-conscious activity* is concentrated on the *political act*. The *egoistic* man is the *passive* and *given* result of the dissolved society, an object of *immediate certainty* and thus a *natural* object. The *political revolution* dissolves civil life into its constituent elements without *revolutionizing* these elements themselves and subjecting them to criticism. It regards civil society—the realm of needs, labor, private interests, and private right—as the *basis of its existence*, as a *presupposition* needing no ground, and thus as its *natural basis*. Finally, man as a member of civil society is regarded as *authentic* man, *man* as distinct from *citizen*, since he is man in his sensuous, individual, and *most intimate* existence while *political* man is only the abstract and artificial man, man as an *allegorical*, *moral* person. Actual man is recognized only in the form of an *egoistic* individual, *authentic* man, only in the form of *abstract citizen*.

The abstraction of the political man was correctly depicted by Rousseau:

"Whoever dares to undertake the founding of a nation must feel himself capable of **changing**,[*] so to speak, **human nature** and **transforming** each individual who is in himself a complete but isolated whole, into a **part** of something greater than himself from which he somehow derives his life and existence, substituting a **limited** and **moral existence** for physical and independent existence. **Man** must be deprived of **his own powers** and given alien powers which he cannot use without the aid of others." (*Social Contract*, Bk. II, London, 1782, p. 67.)

All emancipation is *restoration* of the human world and the relationships of *men themselves*.

[* Boldface type identifies Marx's emphasis in the quotation.]

Political emancipation is a reduction of man to a member of civil society, to an *egoistic independent* individual on the one hand and to a *citizen,* a moral person, on the other.

Only when the actual, individual man has taken back into himself the abstract citizen and in his everyday life, his individual work, and his individual relationships has become a *species-being,* only when he has recognized and organized his own powers as *social* powers so that social force is no longer separated from him as *political* power, only then is human emancipation complete.

Bruno Bauer, *"The Capacity of Present-day Jews and Christians to Become Free,"* Twenty-one Sheets [from Switzerland *(ed. Georg Herwegh), Zurich and Winterthur, 1843]*, pp. 56–71.

Here Bauer deals with the relation between the *Jewish and Christian religion* and their relation to criticism. Their relation to criticism is their bearing "on the capacity to become free."

Accordingly: "The Christian has only one stage to surpass—namely, his religion—in order to abandon religion in general" and thus become free. "The Jew, on the other hand, has to break not only with his Jewish nature but also with the development, the completion, of his religion, a development which has remained alien to him" (p. 71).

Thus Bauer here transforms the question of Jewish emancipation into a purely religious one. The theological difficulty as to whether the Jew or the Christian has the better prospect of salvation is here reproduced in the enlightened form: Which of the two is *more capable of emancipation?* It is thus no longer the question: Does Judaism or Christianity emancipate? but rather, on the contrary: Which emancipates more, the negation of Judaism or the negation of Christianity?

"If they want to be free, the Jews should not embrace Christianity but Christianity in dissolution, religion generally in dissolution— enlightenment, criticism and its results, free humanity" (p. 70).

For the Jew it is still a matter of *professing faith,* not Christianity but rather Christianity in dissolution.

Bauer requires the Jew to break with the essence of the Christian religion, a requirement which does not follow, as he says himself, from the development of the Jewish nature.

When Bauer, at the end of his *Jewish Question,* interpreted Judaism merely as a crude religious criticism of Christianity and hence gave it "only" a religious significance, it was to be expected that he would also transform the emancipation of the Jews into a philosophico-theological act.

Bauer views the *ideal* and abstract essence of the Jew, his *religion,* as his *whole* nature. Hence he correctly infers: "The Jew contributes nothing to mankind if he disregards his narrow law," if he cancels all his Judaism (p. 65).

The relation of Jews to Christian thus becomes the following: the sole interest of the Christian in the emancipation of the Jew is a general human interest, a *theoretical* interest. Judaism is an offensive fact to the religious eye of the Christian. As soon as the Christian's eye ceases to be religious, this fact ceases to offend it. In and for itself the emancipation of the Jew is not a task for the Christian.

The Jew, on the other hand, not only has to finish his own task but also the task of the Christian—[Bruno Bauer's] *Critique of the* [*Gospel History of the*] *Synoptics* and [Strauss'] *Life of Jesus,* etc.—if he wants to emancipate himself.

"They can look after themselves: they will determine their own destiny; but history does not allow itself to be mocked" (p. 71).

We will try to break with the theological formulation of the issue. The question concerning the Jew's capacity for emancipation becomes for us the question: What specific *social element is to be overcome in order to* abolish Judaism? For the modern Jew's capacity for emancipation is the relation of Judaism to the emancipation of the modern world. This relation follows necessarily from the particular position of Judaism in the modern, subjugated world.

Let us consider the actual, secular Jew—not the *sabbath Jew,* as Bauer does, but the *everyday Jew.*

Let us look for the secret of the Jew not in his religion but rather for the secret of the religion in the actual Jew.

What is the secular basis of Judaism? *Practical* need, *self-interest.*

What is the worldly cult of the Jew? *Bargaining.* What is his worldly god? *Money.*

Very well! Emancipation from *bargaining* and *money,* and thus from practical and real Judaism would be the self-emancipation of our era.

An organization of society that would abolish the pre-conditions of bargaining and thus its possibility would render the Jew impossible. His religious consciousness would dissolve like a dull mist in the actual life-giving air of society. On the other hand, when the Jew recognizes this *practical* nature of his as futile and strives to eliminate it, he works away from his previous development toward general *human emancipation* and opposes the *supreme practical* expression of human self-alienation.

Thus we perceive in Judaism a general and *contemporary anti-social* element, which has been carried to its present high point by a historical development in which the Jews have contributed to this element, a point at which it must necessarily dissolve itself.

The *emancipation of the Jews*, in the final analysis, is the emancipation of mankind from *Judaism*.

The Jew has already emancipated himself in a Jewish way, "The Jew who is only tolerated in Vienna, for example, determines the fate of the whole empire through his financial power. The Jew who may be without rights in the smallest German state decides the destiny of Europe. While corporations and guilds exclude the Jew or are unfavorable to him, audacity in industry mocks the obstinacy of these medieval institutions." (B. Bauer, *The Jewish Question*, p. 114.)

This is no isolated fact. The Jew has emancipated himself in a Jewish way not only by acquiring financial power but also because, with and without him, *money* has become a world power, and the practical Jewish spirit has become the practical spirit of Christian nations. The Jews have emancipated themselves insofar as the Christian have become Jews.

For example, the pious and politically free inhabitant of New England, Captain Hamilton reports, is a kind of *Laocoön* who does not make the slightest effort to free himself from the serpents strangling him. *Mammon* is his idol to whom he prays not only with his lips but with all the power of his body and soul. In his eyes the world is nothing but a stock exchange, and he is convinced that here below he has no other destiny than to become richer than his neighbor. Bargaining dominates his every thought, exchange in things constitutes his only recreation. When he travels, he carries his shop or office on his back, as it were, and talks of nothing but interest and profit. If he loses sight of his own business for a moment, it is only in order to poke his nose into that of others.

Indeed, the practical domination of Judaism over the Christian world in North America has achieved such clear and common expression that the *very preaching of the Gospel*, the Christian ministry, has become an article of commerce and the bankrupt merchant takes to the Gospel while the minister who has become rich goes into business. *"That man whom you see at the head of a respectable congregation began as a merchant; his business having failed, he became a minister; the other started with the ministry, but as soon as he had acquired a sum of money, he left the pulpit for business. In the eyes of many, the religious ministry is a veritable commercial career."* (Beaumont, *loc. cit.*, pp. 185, 186.)

According to Bauer it is a hypocritical situation when the Jew is deprived of political rights in theory while he wields enormous power in practice, when he exercises the political influence *wholesale* denied to him in retail (*The Jewish Question*, p. 114).

The contradiction existing between the practical political power of the Jew and his political rights is the contradiction between politics and financial power in general. While politics ideally is superior to financial power, in actual fact it has become its serf.

Judaism has persisted *alongside* Christianity not only as the religious critique of Christianity, not only as the concrete doubt concerning the religious descent of Christianity, but equally because the practical Jewish spirit, Judaism, has perpetuated itself in Christian society and there even attained its highest development. The Jew, who exists as a special member of civil society, is only the special manifestation of civil society's Judaism.

Judaism has survived not in spite of but by means of history.

Out of its own entrails, civil society ceaselessly produces the Jew.

What actually was the foundation of the Jewish religion? Practical need, egoism.

Hence, the Jew's monotheism is actually the polytheism of many needs, a polytheism that makes even the toilet an object of divine law. *Practical need, egoism* is the principle of *civil society* and appears purely as such as soon as civil society has fully delivered itself of the political state. The god of *practical need and self-interest* is *money.*

Money is the jealous god of Israel before whom no other god may exist. Money degrades all the gods of mankind—and converts them into commodities. Money is the general, self-sufficient *value* of everything. Hence it has robbed the whole world, the human world as well as nature, of its proper worth. Money is the alienated essence of man's labor and life, and this alien essence dominates him as he worships it.

The god of the Jews has been secularized and has become the god of the world. The bill of exchange is the Jew's actual god. His god is only an illusory bill of exchange.

The view of nature achieved under the rule of private property and money is an actual contempt for and practical degradation of nature which does, to be sure, exist in the Jewish religion, but only in imagination.

In this sense Thomas Münzer declared it to be intolerable "that every creature should be turned into property, the fish in the water, the birds in the air, the plants of the earth—the creature must also become free."

That which is contained abstractly in the Jewish religion—contempt for theory, for art, for history, for man as an end in himself—is the *actual conscious* standpoint and virtue of the monied man. The species-relation itself, the relation between man and woman, etc., becomes an object of commerce. The woman is bought and sold.

The *chimerical* nationality of the Jew is the nationality of the merchant, particularly of the monied man.

The Jew's unfounded, superficial law is only the religious caricature of unfounded, superficial morality and law in general, the caricature of merely *formal* ceremonies encompassing the world of self-interest.

Here also the highest relation of man is the *legal* relation, the relation to laws which apply to him not because they are laws of his own will and nature but because they *dominate* him and because defection from them will be *avenged.*

Jewish Jesuitism, the same practical Jesuitism Bauer finds in the Talmud, is the relationship of the world of self-interest to the laws governing it, and the cunning circumvention of these laws is that world's main art.

Indeed, the movement of that world within its law is necessarily a continuous abrogation of the law.

Judaism could not develop further as *religion,* could not develop further theoretically, because the perspective of practical need is limited by its very nature and soon exhausted.

By its very nature, the religion of practical need could not find fulfillment in theory but only in *practice* [*Praxis*], simply because practice is its truth.

Judaism could create no new world; it could only draw the new creations and conditions of the world into the compass of its own activity because practical need, whose rationale is self-interest, remains passive, never willfully extending itself but only *finding* itself extended with the continuous development of social conditions.

Judaism reaches its height with the perfection of civil society, but civil society achieves perfection only in the *Christian* world. Only under the reign of Christianity, which makes *all* national, natural, moral, and theoretical relationships *external* to man, was civil society able to separate itself completely from political life, sever all man's species-ties, substitute egoism and selfish need for those ties, and dissolve the human world into a world of atomistic, mutually hostile individuals.

Christianity arose out of Judaism. It has again dissolved itself into Judaism.

From the outset the Christian was the theorizing Jew. Hence, the Jew is the practical Christian, and the practical Christian has again become a Jew.

Christianity overcame real Judaism only in appearance. It was too *noble,* too spiritual, to eliminate the crudeness of practical need except by elevating it into the blue.

Christianity is the sublime thought of Judaism, and Judaism is the common practical application of Christianity. But this application could only become universal after Christianity as religion par excellence had *theoretically* completed the alienation of man from himself and from nature.

Only then could Judaism attain universal dominion and convert externalized man and nature into *alienable* and saleable objects subservient to egoistic need, dependent on bargaining.

Selling is the practice of externalization. As long as man is captivated in religion, knows his nature only as objectified, and thereby converts his nature into an *alien* illusory being, so under the dominion of egoistic need he can only act practically, only practically produce objects, by subordinating both his products and his activity to the domination of an alien being, bestowing upon them the significance of an alien entity—of money.

The Christian egoism of eternal bliss in its practical fulfillment necessarily becomes the material egoism of the Jew, heavenly need is converted into earthly need, and subjectivism becomes selfishness. We do not explain the Jew's tenacity from his religion but rather from the human basis of his religion, from practical need, from egoism.

Since the Jew's real nature has been generally actualized and secularized in civil society, civil society could not convince the Jew of the *unreality* of his *religious* nature which is precisely the ideal representation of practical need. Thus not only in the Pentateuch or Talmud but also in present society we find the nature of the contemporary Jew, not as an abstract nature but a supremely empirical nature, not only as the Jew's narrowness but as the Jewish narrowness of society.

When society succeeds in transcending the *empirical* essence of Judaism—bargaining and all its conditions—the Jew becomes *impossible* because his consciousness no longer has an object, the subjective basis of Judaism—practical need—is humanized, and the conflict between the individual sensuous existence of man and his species-existence is transcended.

The *social* emancipation of the Jew is the *emancipation of society from Judaism.*

Toward A Critique of Hegel's
Philosophy of Right: Introduction

Karl Marx

One of Marx's chief projects in 1843 was to study and critique Hegel's political philosophy, especially as presented in The Philosophy of Right. *Marx's work took the form of notebooks in which he wrote detailed commentary on specific sections of Hegel's volume that he copied out. After moving to Paris in the fall of 1843, Marx wrote an essay that was intended to be the introduction to his planned book on Hegel's political philosophy. Although the book was never completed (the manuscript in draft form was published first in 1927), the introduction was published in the* Deutsch-Französische Jahrbücher *in 1844.*

The essay is less an introduction to Hegel than an introduction to the general political context in Germany at that time. It is of particular interest for two reasons. The opening contains Marx's best-known remarks about religion, including the famous comment that religion "is the opium of the people." Continuing his analysis beyond that of "On the Jewish Question," Marx sees religion as a symptom of the alienation rooted in civil society. Religion, then, is not the problem, and the criticism and even abolition of religion is not the solution. As he puts it, "The criticism of heaven turns into the criticism of the earth, . . . the criticism of theology into the criticism of politics." In this way he clearly goes beyond the Young Hegelian analysis.

The second important point in the essay has to do with his analysis of criticism. Mere philosophical criticism will be insufficient to change the world. "The weapon of criticism," he observes, "obviously cannot replace the criticism of weapons. Material force must be overthrown by material force." And where will this material force come from? Here Marx turns to a Hegelian concept but uses it for his own purposes. What is needed is a universal class that has nothing at stake in the status quo and therefore nothing to lose in overthrowing it. Such a class exists in Germany, Marx asserts, in the proletariat. The proletariat will take the theory of philosophical criticism and turn it into the practice of revolution. Thus Marx announces his "discovery" of the proletariat and its role in the uniting of theory and practice.

The following essay is translated from the German by Loyd D. Easton and Kurt H. Guddat.

For Germany the *criticism of religion* has been essentially completed, and criticism of religion is the premise of all criticism.

The *profane* existence of error is compromised when its *heavenly oratio pro aris et focis* [defense of altar and hearth] has been refuted. Man, who has found only the *reflection* of himself in the fantastic reality of heaven where he sought a supernatural being, will no longer be inclined to find the *semblance* of himself, only the non-human being, where he seeks and must seek his true reality.

The basis of irreligious criticism is: *Man makes religion,* religion does not make man. And indeed religion is the self-consciousness and self-regard of man who has either not yet found or has already lost himself. But *man* is not an abstract being squatting outside the world. Man is *the world of men,* the state, society. This state and this society produce religion, which is an *inverted consciousness of the world* because they are an *inverted world.* Religion is the generalized theory of this world, its encyclopaedic compendium, its logic in popular form, its spiritualistic point d'honneur, its enthusiasm, its moral sanction, its solemn complement, its general ground of consolation and justification. It is the *fantastic realization* of the human essence inasmuch as the *human essence* possesses no true reality. The struggle against religion is therefore indirectly the struggle against *that world* whose spiritual *aroma* is religion.

Religious suffering is the *expression* of real suffering and at the same time the *protest* against real suffering. Religion is the sigh of the oppressed creature, the heart of a heartless world, as it is the spirit of spiritless conditions. It is the *opium* of the people.

The abolition of religion as people's *illusory* happiness is the demand for their *real* happiness. The demand to abandon illusions about their condition is a *demand to abandon a condition which requires illusions.* The criticism of religion is thus in *embryo* a *criticism of the vale of tears* whose *halo* is religion.

Criticism has plucked imaginary flowers from the chain, not so that man will wear the chain that is without fantasy or consolation but so that he will throw it off and pluck the living flower. The criticism of religion disillusions man so that he thinks, acts, and shapes his reality like a disillusioned man who has come to his senses, so that he revolves around himself and thus around his true sun. Religion is only the illusory sun that revolves around man so long as he does not revolve about himself.

Thus it is the *task of history,* once the *otherworldly truth* has disappeared, to establish the *truth of this world.* The immediate *task of philosophy* which is in the service of history is to unmask human self-alienation in its *unholy forms* now that it has been unmasked in its *holy form.* Thus the criticism of heaven turns into the criticism of the earth, the *criticism*

[left margin, handwritten:] change material conditions

of religion into the *criticism of law,* and the *criticism of theology* into the *criticism of politics.*

The following exposition—a contribution to this undertaking [developed from the unpublished "Critique of Hegel's Philosophy of the State" written in Kreuznach]—does not directly pertain to the original but to a copy, the German *philosophy* of the state and law, for the simple reason that it deals with *Germany.*

If one were to proceed from the *status quo* itself in Germany, even in the only appropriate way, *that is,* negatively, the result would still be an *anachronism.* Even the negation of our political present is already a dusty fact in the historical lumber room of modern nations. If I negate powdered wigs, I am still left with unpowdered wigs. If I negate German conditions of 1843, I am hardly, according to French chronology, in the year 1789 and still less in the focus of the present.

Indeed, German history plumes itself on a development no nation in the historical firmament previously exhibited or will ever copy. We have in point of fact shared in the restorations of the modern nations without sharing in their revolutions. We have been restored, first because other nations dared to make revolutions, and secondly because other nations suffered counter-revolutions—on the one hand because our masters were afraid, and on the other because they were not afraid. Led by our shepherds, we found ourselves in the company of freedom only once, on the *day of its burial.*

A school of thought that legitimizes today's infamy by yesterday's, a school of thought that explains every cry of the serf against the knout as rebellion once the knout is time-honored, ancestral, and historical, a school to which history shows only its *a posteriori,* as the God of Israel did to his servant Moses—the *Historical School of Law*—might have invented German history if it were not an invention of German history. A Shylock, but a servile Shylock, that school swears on its bond, on its historical bond, its Christian-Germanic bond, for every pound of flesh cut from the heart of the people.

Good-natured enthusiasts, German chauvinists by extraction and liberals by reflection, on the other hand, seek our history of freedom beyond our history in the primeval Teutonic forests. But how does the history of our freedom differ from the history of the wild boar's freedom if it is only to be found in the forests? As the proverb says, what is shouted into the forest, the forest echoes back. So peace to the primeval Teutonic forests!

War on German conditions! By all means! They are *below the level of history, beneath all criticism,* but they are still an object of criticism just as the criminal below the level of humanity is still an object of the *executioner.* In its struggle against these conditions criticism is not a passion of the head but the head of passion. It is not a lancet, it is a weapon. Its object is an *enemy* it wants not to refute but to *destroy.* For the spirit of these conditions has already been refuted. In and for themselves they are objects not *worthy of thought* but *existences* as despicable as they are despised. Criticism itself does not even need to be concerned with this matter, for it is already clear about it. Criticism is no longer an *end in itself* but simply a *means.* Its essential pathos is *indignation,* its essential task, *denunciation.*

It is a matter of describing the pervasive, suffocating pressure of all social spheres on one another, the general but passive dejection, the narrowness that recognizes but misunderstands itself—this framed in a system of government that lives on the conservation of all meanness and is nothing but *meanness* in government.

What a sight! Society is forever splitting into the most varied races opposing one another with petty antipathies, bad consciences, and brutal mediocrity, and precisely because of their mutually ambiguous and distrustful situation they are all treated by their *rulers* as merely *tolerated existences,* without exception, though with varying formalities. And they are forced to recognize and acknowledge their being *dominated, ruled,* and *possessed* as a *concession from heaven!* On the other side are the rulers themselves whose greatness is inversely proportional to their number!

The criticism dealing with this matter is criticism in *hand-to-hand* combat, and in such a combat the point is not whether the opponent is noble, equal, or *interesting,* the point is to *strike* him. The point is to permit the Germans not even a moment of self-deception and resignation. We must make the actual pressure more pressing by adding to it the consciousness of pressure and make the shame more shameful by publicizing it. Every sphere of German society must be shown as the *partie honteuse* of German society, and we have to make these petrified social relations dance by singing their own tune! The people must be taught to be *terrified* of themselves to give them *courage.* This will fulfill an imperative need of the German nation, and the needs of nations are themselves the ultimate grounds of their satisfaction.

And even for *modern* nations this struggle against the restricted content of the German *status quo* cannot be without interest, for the German *status quo* is the *open fulfillment of the Ancien Régime,* and the *Ancien Régime* is the *hidden deficiency of the modern state.* The struggle against the German political present is the struggle against the past of modern nations, and they are still burdened with reminders of that past. It is instructive for them to see the *Ancien Régime,* which lived through its *tragedy* with them, play its *comedy* as a German ghost. The history of the

Ancien Régime was *tragic* so long as it was the established power in the world, while freedom on the other hand was a personal notion—in short, as long as it believed and had to believe in its own validity. As long as the *Ancien Régime* as an existing world order struggled against a world that was just coming into being, there was on its side a historical but not a personal error. Its downfall was therefore tragic.

On the other hand, the present German regime—an anachronism, a flagrant contradiction of generally accepted axioms, the nullity of the *Ancien Régime* exhibited to the whole world—only imagines that it believes in itself and demands that the world imagine the same thing. If it is believed in its own *nature*, would it try to hide that nature under the *semblance* of an alien nature and seek its salvation in hypocrisy and sophism? The modern *Ancien Régime* is merely the *comedian* in a world whose *real heroes* are dead. History is thorough and goes through many phases as it conducts an old form to the grave. The final phase of a world-historical form is *comedy*. The Greek gods, already tragically and mortally wounded in Aeschylus' *Prometheus Bound*, had to die again comically in Lucian's dialogues. Why this course of history? So that mankind may part from its past *happily*. This *happy* historical destiny we vindicate for the political authorities of Germany.

But once *modern* political and social reality itself is subjected to criticism, once criticism arrives at truly human problems, it either finds itself outside the German *status quo* or it would deal with its object at *a level below* its objects. For example! The relation of industry and the world of wealth in general to the political world is a major problem of modern times. In what form is this problem beginning to preoccupy the Germans? In the form of <u>*protective tariffs,*</u> the <u>*system of prohibition,*</u> and <u>*political economy.*</u> German chauvinism has gone from man to matter and thus one fine day our barons of cotton and heroes of iron saw themselves transformed into patriots. Thus in Germany we are beginning to recognize the sovereignty of monopoly at home by investing it with *sovereignty abroad*. We are about to begin in Germany where France and England are about to end. <u>The old rotten condition against which these countries are revolting in theory and which they bear as chains is greeted in Germany as the dawn of a glorious future which as yet hardly dares to pass from *crafty*</u> [*listigen:* Friedrich List] <u>theory to the most ruthless practice.</u> Whereas the problem in France and England reads: *political economy* or the *rule of society over wealth*, in Germany it reads: *political economy* or the *rule of private property over nationality*. Thus in France and England it is a question of abolishing monopoly that has developed to its final consequences; in Germany it is a question of proceeding to the final consequences of monopoly. There it is a question of solution;

here, still a question of collision. This is an adequate example of the *German* form of modern problems, an example of how our history, like a raw recruit, still has had to do extra drill on matters threshed over in history.

If the *total* German development were not in advance of its *political* development, a German could at the most have a share in the problems of the present like that of a *Russian*. But if the single individual is not bound by the limitations of his nation, still less is the nation as a whole liberated by the liberation of one individual. The Scythians made no progress toward Greek culture even though Greece had a Scythian among her philosophers.

Fortunately we are Germans and not Scythians.

As the ancient countries lived their pre-history in imagination, in *mythology,* so we Germans have lived our post-history in thought, in *philosophy.* We are *philosophical* contemporaries of the present without being its *historical* contemporaries. German philosophy is the *ideal extension* of German history. If, therefore, we criticize the *œuvres posthumes* of our ideal history—philosophy—instead of the *œuvres incomplètes* of our real history, our criticism is in the center of questions of which the present says: *That is the question.* That which in progressive nations is a *practical* break with modern political conditions is in Germany, where these conditions do not yet exist, just a *critical* break with the philosophical reflection of those conditions.

The *German philosophy of law and of the state* is the only *German history* which stands *al pari* with the *official* modern present. The German nation must therefore join its dream-history to its present conditions and criticize not only these present conditions but also their abstract continuation. Its future can be *limited* neither to the direct negation of its real political and legal conditions nor to their direct fulfillment, for it has the direct negation of its real conditions in its ideal conditions and has almost *outlived* the direct fulfillment of its ideal conditions in the view of neighboring countries. Hence, the *practical* political party in Germany rightly demands the *negation of philosophy.* It is wrong not in its demand but in stopping at the demand it neither seriously fulfills nor can fulfill. It supposes that it accomplishes that negation by turning its back on philosophy, looking aside, and muttering a few petulant and trite phrases about it. Because its outlook is so limited it does not even count philosophy as part of *German* actuality or even imagines it is *beneath* German practice and its theories. You demand starting from *actual germs of life* but forget that the actual life-germ of the German nation has so far sprouted only inside its *cranium*. In short: *you cannot transcend [aufheben] philosophy without actualizing it.*

The same error, but with the factors *reversed*, was committed by the *theoretical* party which originated in philosophy.

In the present struggle the theoretical party saw *only* the *critical struggle of philosophy against the German world.* It did not consider that *previous philosophy* itself belongs to this world and is its *complement*, although an ideal one. Critical toward its counterpart, it was not critical of itself. Starting from the *presuppositions* of philosophy, it either stopped at philosophy's given results or passed off demands and results from somewhere else as direct demands and results from philosophy. But these latter—their legitimacy assumed—can only be obtained by the *negation of previous philosophy*, by the negation of philosophy as philosophy. We shall later give a closer account of this party. Its main defect may be summarized as follows: *It believed that it could actualize philosophy without transcending it.*

The criticism of the *German philosophy of the state and law*, which attained its most consistent, profound, and final formulation with *Hegel*, is at once a critical analysis of the modern state and the actuality connected with it and also the decisive negation of all previous *forms* of *German political and legal consciousness* whose most prominent and general expression at the level of *science* is precisely the *speculative philosophy of law.* If the speculative philosophy of law—that abstract and extravagant *thinking* about the modern state whose reality remains in the beyond, if only beyond the Rhine—was possible only in Germany, conversely the *German* conception of the modern state in abstraction from *actual man* was possible only because and insofar as the modern state abstracts itself from *actual man* or satisfies the *whole* man only in an illusory way. In politics the Germans have *thought* what other nations have *done.* Germany has been their *theoretical conscience.* The abstraction and presumption of its thought always kept pace with the one-sided and stunted character of their actuality. If the *status quo* of the *German political system* [*Staatswesen*] expresses *the completion of the Ancien Régime,* the thorn in the flesh of the modern state, the *status quo* of *German political science* [*Staatswissen*] expresses the *incompletion of the modern state,* the damage to the flesh itself.

As the resolute opponent of the previous mode of *German* political consciousness, the criticism of speculative philosophy of law does not proceed in its own sphere but proceeds to *tasks* that can be solved by only one means—*practice* [*Praxis*].

The question arises: Can Germany reach a practice *à la hauteur des principes, that is,* a *revolution,* which will raise it not only to the *official level* of modern nations but to the *human level* which will be their immediate future?

The weapon of criticism obviously cannot replace the criticism of weapons. Material force must be overthrown by material force. But theory also becomes a material force once it has gripped the masses. Theory is capable of gripping the masses when it demonstrates *ad hominem,* and it demonstrates *ad hominem* when it becomes radical. To be radical is to grasp things by the root. But for man the root is man himself. The clear proof of the radicalism of German theory and hence of its political energy is that it proceeds from the decisive *positive* transcendence of religion. The criticism of religion ends with the doctrine that *man is the highest being for man,* hence with the *categorical imperative to overthrow all conditions* in which man is a degraded, enslaved, neglected, contemptible being—conditions that cannot better be described than by the exclamation of a Frenchman on the occasion of a proposed dog tax: Poor dogs! They want to treat you like human beings!

Even historically, theoretical emancipation has a specific practical significance for Germany. For Germany's *revolutionary* past is theoretical—it is the *Reformation.* As the revolution then began in the brain of the *monk,* now it begins in the brain of the *philosopher.*

Luther, to be sure, overcame bondage based on *devotion* by replacing it with bondage based on *conviction.* He shattered faith in authority by restoring the authority of faith. He turned priests into laymen by turning laymen into priests. He freed man from outward religiosity by making religiosity the inwardness of man. He emancipated the body from its chains by putting chains on the heart.

But if Protestantism was not the true solution, it was the true formulation of the problem. The question was no longer the struggle of the layman against the *priest external to him* but of his struggle against *his own inner priest,* his *priestly nature.* And if the Protestant transformation of German laymen into priests emancipated the lay popes—the *princes* with their clerical set, the privileged, and the Philistines—the philosophical transformation of priestly Germans into men will emancipate the *people.* But little as emancipation stops with princes, just as little will *secularization* of property stop with the *confiscation of church property* set in motion chiefly by hypocritical Prussia. At that time the Peasants' War, the most radical fact of German history, came to grief because of theology. Today, when theology itself has come to grief, the most unfree fact of German history—our *status quo*—will be shattered by philosophy. On the eve of the Reformation official Germany was the most abject vassal of Rome. On the eve of its revolution Germany is the abject vassal of something less than Rome—of Prussia and Austria, of ignorant country squires and Philistines.

But a major difficulty seems to stand in the way of a *radical* German revolution.

Revolutions require a *passive* element, a *material* basis. Theory is actualized in a people only insofar as it actualizes their needs. But will the enormous discrepancy between the demands of German thought and the answers of German actuality correspond to a similar discrepancy between civil society and the state, and within civil society itself? Will theoretical needs be immediate practical needs? It is not enough that thought should seek its actualization; actuality must itself strive toward thought.

But Germany has not risen to the intermediate stages of political emancipation at the same time as the modern nations. It has not yet reached in practice even the stages it has surpassed in theory. How can it clear with a *salto mortale* not only its own limitations but also those of modern nations—limitations which in actuality it must experience and strive for as an emancipation from its actual limitations? A radical revolution can only be a revolution of radical needs whose preconditions and birthplaces appear to be lacking.

But if Germany has attended the development of modern nations only through the abstract activity of thought without taking an active part in the real struggles of this development, it has also shared the *sufferings* of this development without sharing its enjoyments or partial satisfaction. Abstract activity on one side corresponds to abstract suffering on the other. One fine day Germany will find itself at the level of European decadence before ever having reached the level of European emancipation. It will be comparable to a *fetishist* wasting away from the diseases of Christianity.

Considering *German governments*, we find that owing to the circumstances of the time, the situation of Germany, the outlook of German culture, and finally their own fortunate instinct they are driven to combine the *civilized deficiencies* of the *modern political order* (whose advantages we do not enjoy) with the *barbarous deficiencies* of the *Ancien Régime* (which we enjoy in full). Hence Germany must participate more and more if not in the sense [*Verstand*] at least in the nonsense [*Unverstand*] of those political forms transcending its *status quo*. Is there, for example, another country in the whole world which as naïvely as so-called constitutional Germany shares all the illusions of constitutional statehood without sharing its realities? And was it not, necessarily, a German government's bright idea to combine the tortures of censorship with the tortures of the French September laws [of 1835] presupposing freedom of the press? As the *gods* of all nations were found in the Roman Pantheon, the *sins* of all forms of the state will be found in the Holy German Empire. That this eclecticism will reach an unprecedented height is particularly guaranteed by the *politico-aesthetic gourmanderie* of a German king [Friedrich Wilhelm IV] who plans to play all the roles of monarchy—feudal or bureaucratic, absolute or constitutional, autocratic or democratic—if not in the person of the people at least in his *own,* and if not for the people at least for *himself. As the deficiency of the political present erected into a system,* Germany will not be able to shed the specifically German limitations without shedding the general limitations of the political present.

. *Radical* revolution, *universal human* emancipation, is not a utopian dream for Germany. What is utopian is the partial, the *merely* political revolution, the revolution which would leave the pillars of the house standing. What is the basis of a partial and merely political revolution? It is *part of civil society* emancipating itself and attaining *universal* supremacy, a particular class by virtue of its *special situation* undertaking the general emancipation of society. This class emancipates the whole of society but only on the condition that the whole of society is in the same position as this class, *for example,* that it has or can easily acquire money and education.

No class in civil society can take this role without arousing an impulse of enthusiasm in itself and in the masses, an impulse in which it fraternizes and merges with society at large, identifies itself with it, and is experienced and recognized as its *general representative*—an impulse in which its claims and rights are truly the rights and claims of society itself and in which it is actually the social head and the social heart. Only in the name of the general rights of society can a particular class claim general supremacy. Revolutionary energy and intellectual self-confidence are not by themselves sufficient to seize this emancipatory position and hence the political control of all spheres of society in the interest of its own. If a *popular revolution* is to coincide with the *emancipation of a particular* class of civil society, if *one* class is to stand for the whole society, all the defects of society must conversely be concentrated in another class. A particular class must be the class of general offense and the incorporation of general limitation. A particular social sphere must stand for the *notorious crime* of society as a whole so that emancipation from this sphere appears as general self-emancipation. For *one* class to be the class of emancipation *par excellence,* conversely another must be the obvious class of oppression. The negative, general significance of the French nobility and clergy determined the positive, general significance of the *bourgeoisie* standing next to and opposing them.

But in Germany every class lacks not only the consistency, penetration, courage, and ruthlessness which could stamp it as the negative representative of society. There is equally lacking in every class that breadth of soul which identifies itself, if only momentarily, with the soul of the people—that genius for inspiring material force toward political power, that revolutionary boldness which flings at its adversary the defiant words, *I am nothing and I should be everything*. The main feature of German morality and honor in classes as well as individuals is rather a *modest egoism* displaying its narrowness and allowing it to be displayed against itself. The relationship of the different spheres of German society is therefore not dramatic but epic. Each of them begins to be aware of itself and place itself beside the others, not as soon as it is oppressed but as soon as circumstances, without its initiative, create a social layer on which it can exert pressure in turn. Even the *moral self-esteem of the German middle class* rests only on its awareness of being the general representative of the philistine mediocrity of all the other classes. Hence, not only do German kings ascend their thrones *mal à propos*, but every section of civil society goes through a defeat before it celebrates victory, develops its own obstacles before it overcomes those facing it, asserts its narrow-minded nature before it can assert its generosity so that even the opportunity of playing a great role has always passed before it actually existed and each class is involved in a struggle against the class beneath as soon as it begins to struggle with the class above it. Hence princes struggle against kings, the bureaucrat against the nobility, and the bourgeoisie against them all, while the proletariat is already beginning to struggle against the bourgeoisie. The middle class hardly dares to conceive the idea of emancipation from its own perspective. The development of social conditions and the progress of political theory show that perspective to be already antiquated or at least problematic.

In France it is enough to be something for one to want to be everything. In Germany no one can be anything unless he is prepared to renounce everything. In France partial emancipation is the basis of universal emancipation. In Germany universal emancipation is the *conditio sine qua non* of any partial emancipation. In France it is the actuality, in Germany the impossibility, of gradual emancipation which must give birth to complete freedom. In France every class of the nation is *politically idealistic* and experiences itself first of all not as a particular class but as representing the general needs of society. The role of *emancipator* thus passes successively and dramatically to different classes of people until it finally reaches the class which actualizes social freedom, no longer assuming certain conditions external to man and yet created by human society but rather organizing all the conditions of human existence on the basis of social freedom. In Germany, by contrast, where practical life is as mindless as mental life is impractical, no class in civil society has any need or capacity for general emancipation until it is forced to it by its *immediate* condition, by material necessity, by its *very* chains.

Where then, is the *positive* possibility of German emancipation?

Answer: In the formation of a class with *radical chains*, a class in civil society that is not of civil society, a class that is the dissolution of all classes, a sphere of society having a universal character because of its universal suffering and claiming no *particular* right because no *particular wrong* but *unqualified wrong* is perpetrated on it; a sphere that can invoke no *traditional* title but only a *human* title, which does not partially oppose the consequences but totally opposes the premises of the German political system; a sphere, finally, that cannot emancipate itself without emancipating itself from all the other spheres of society, thereby emancipating them; a sphere, in short, that is the *complete loss* of humanity and can only redeem itself through the *total redemption of humanity.* This dissolution of society as a particular class is the *proletariat.*

The proletariat is only beginning to appear in Germany as a result of the rising *industrial* movement. For it is not poverty from *natural circumstances* but *artificially produced* poverty, not the human masses mechanically oppressed by the weight of society but the masses resulting from the *acute disintegration* of society, and particularly of the middle class, which gives rise to the proletariat—though also, needless to say, poverty from natural circumstances and Christian-Germanic serfdom gradually join the proletariat.

Heralding the *dissolution of the existing order of things*, the proletariat merely announces the *secret of its own existence* because it *is the real* dissolution of this order. Demanding the *negation of private property*, the proletariat merely raises to the *principle of society* what society has raised to the principle *of the proletariat*, what the proletariat already embodies as the negative result of society without its action. The proletarian thus has the same right in the emerging order of things as the *German king* has in the existing order when he calls the people *his* people or a horse *his* horse. Declaring the people to be his private property, the king merely proclaims that the private owner is king.

As philosophy finds its *material* weapons in the proletariat, the proletariat finds its *intellectual* weapons in philosophy. And once the lightning of thought has deeply struck this unsophisticated soil of the people, the *Germans* will emancipate themselves to become *men*.

Let us summarize the result:

The only emancipation of Germany possible *in practice* is emancipation based on *the* theory proclaiming that man is the highest essence of man. In Germany emancipation from the *Middle Ages* is possible only as emancipation at the same time from *partial* victories over the Middle Ages. In Germany *no* brand of bondage can be broken without *every* brand of bondage being broken. Always seeking *fundamentals*, Germany can only make a *fundamental* revolution. The *emancipation of the German* is the *emancipation of mankind.* The *head* of this emancipation is *philosophy,* its *heart* is the *proletariat.* Philosophy cannot be actualized without the transcendence [*Aufhebung*] of the proletariat, the proletariat cannot be transcended without the actualization of philosophy.

When all the inner conditions are fulfilled, the *day of German resurrection* will be announced by the *crowing of the French rooster.*

Excerpt-Notes of 1844
(selections)

Karl Marx

*In the spring of 1844, Marx began a serious study of political economy.
He worked through the writings of a number of theorists, including Adam
Smith, David Ricardo, Jean Baptiste Say, and James Mill (the father of
John Stuart), among others. In his typical fashion, he copied out passages
from the their works into a notebook and commented on them. What follows is
some of his commentary on Mill's* Elements of Political Economy *(1821).*

*Marx's main theme in these passages is the dehumanizing effects of market
exchange relations. This discussion, then, parallels the discussions of alienated
labor and money in the* Economic and Philosophic Manuscripts *on which
Marx was working at the same time. The emphasis here is less on the process
of production and more on the nature of exchange in the market, especially as
it is a function of the credit system. Credit and the banking system in general,
Marx argues, alienate people and distort the true nature of our species-life.
Our true communal life, or species-being, is expressed in how we organize our
mutual activity to better satisfy our needs. "The* exchange of human activity
within production itself as well as the exchange of *human products with one
another is equivalent to the* generic activity *and generic spirit whose actual,
conscious, and authentic existence is* social activity *and* social satisfaction."
*You have a human relation to my product insofar as it is universal and can
satisfy a human need that you have. Our relations qua human are mediated
by needs and not by possession.*

*But within a system of private property and market relations, we relate to
each other only through our property and only from the point of view of how
each of us can best satisfy his or her own individual needs. Thus, your need
for my product, "far from being the* means of giving you power over my
production . . . is the *means of giving me power over you." Our relation
becomes one of mutual exploitation, expressed first and foremost in the relation of our objects. I am only interested in you insofar as you possess an object
that I desire to have, and vice versa. "Our objects in their relation to one
another constitute the only intelligible language we use with one another.
We would not understand a human language, and it would remain without
effect."*

What would a truly human relation look like, then? Marx tells us at the end of this excerpt in a famous passage that some have taken as an indication of how nonalienated people would relate to each other in a communist society.

Money and Alienated Man

In comparing money with precious metals, as well as in the discussion of the costs of production as the only factor in determining value, Mill makes the mistake—generally like Ricardo's school—of giving the *abstract law* without the variation and continuous suspension by which it comes into being. If it is an *independent* law, for example, that the costs of production ultimately—or rather with the periodic and accidental coincidence of supply and demand—determine price (value), it is equally an *independent* law that this relationship does not hold and that value and production costs have no necessary relationship. Indeed, supply and demand coincide only momentarily because of previous fluctuations of supply and demand, because of the discrepancy of costs and exchange value, just as this fluctuation and discrepancy in turn succeed the momentary coincidence of supply and demand. This *actual* process, in which this law is only an abstract, accidental, and one-sided factor, becomes something accidental, something unessential with the modern economists. Why? Since they reduce the economic order to precise and exact formulas, the basic formula, abstractly expressed, would have to be: In the economic order lawfulness is determined by its opposite, lawlessness. The real law of the economic order is *contingency* from which we scientists arbitrarily stabilize some aspects in the form of laws.

In designating *money* as the *medium* of exchange, Mill puts the matter very well and succinctly in a single concept. The essence of money is not primarily that it externalizes property, but that the *mediating activity* or process—the *human* and social act in which man's products reciprocally complement one another—becomes *alienated* and takes on the quality of a *material thing, money, external to man*. By externalizing this mediating activity, man is active only as he is lost and dehumanized. The very *relationship* of things and the human dealings with them become an operation beyond and above man. Through this *alien mediation* man regards his will, his activity, and his relationships to others as a power independent of himself and of them—instead of man himself being the mediator for man. His slavery thus reaches a climax. It is clear that this

Translated from the German by Loyd D. Easton and Kurt H. Guddat.

mediator becomes an *actual god,* for the mediator is the *actual power* over that which he mediates to me. His worship becomes an end in itself. Apart from this mediation, objects lose their value. They have value only insofar as they *represent* it while originally it appeared that the mediation would have value only insofar as *it* represents *objects.* This inversion of the original relationship is necessary. The *mediation,* therefore, is the lost, alienated *essence* of private property, exteriorated and *externalized* private property, just as it is the *externalized exchange* of human production with human production, the *externalized* species-activity of man. All qualities involved in this activity are transmitted to the mediator. Man as separated from this mediator thus becomes so much the poorer as the mediator becomes *richer.*

Christ originally *represents:* (1) man before God; (2) God for man; (3) man for man.

Likewise, *money* originally represents by its very concept: (1) private property for private property; (2) society for private property; (3) private property for society.

But Christ is God *externalized,* externalized *man.* God has value only insofar as he represents Christ; man has value only insofar as he represents Christ. It is the same with money.

Why must private property end up in *money?* Because man as a social being must resort to *exchange* and because exchange—under the presupposition of private property—must end up in value. The mediating process of man making exchanges is no social, no *human process,* no human relationship; rather, it is the *abstract relationship* of private property to private property, and this *abstract* relationship is the *value* whose actual existence as value is primarily *money.* Because men making exchanges do not relate to one another as men, *things* lose the significance of being human and personal property. The social relationship of private property to private property is a relationship in which private property has alienated itself. The reflexive existence of this relationship, money, is thus the externalization of private property, an abstraction from its *specific* and personal nature.

Despite all its cleverness, the modern economic order in opposition to the monetary system cannot achieve a decisive victory. The crude economic superstitions of people and their governments hold on to the *perceptible, palpable,* and *observable* moneybag and believe in the absolute value of precious metals and their possession as the only real form of wealth. The enlightened and knowledgeable economist comes along and proves to them that money is a commodity like any other and that its value, like that of any other commodity, depends on the relationship of the costs of production to demand (competition) and supply, and to the quantity or competition of other commodities. The correct reply to this economist is that the *actual* value of things, after all, is their *exchange value*, and the exchange value resides in money, just as money exists in precious metals. Money, therefore, is the *true* value of things and hence the most desirable thing. The economist's doctrines yield the same wisdom, except that he can abstractly recognize the existence of money in all forms of commodities and not believe in the exchange value of its official metallic existence. The metallic existence of money is only the official sensuous expression of the very soul of money existing in all branches of production and in all operations of civil society.

The modern economists, in opposition to the monetary system, have grasped *money* in its abstraction and generality and are enlightened about the *sensuous* superstition which believes that money exists only in precious metals. They substitute refined superstition for this crude one. But since both have a single root, the enlightened form of the superstition does not entirely replace the crude sensuous form because it does not deal with its essence but only with the particular form of its essence.—The *personal* existence of money as money—and not only as the inner, implicitly existing, and hidden relationship of commodities to one another in respect to their conversion and status—this existence more corresponds to the essence of money, the more abstract it is and the less *natural* relationship it has to other commodities. The more it appears as a product and yet again as something not produced by man, the less is its element of existence something *produced by nature*. The more it is produced by man or produced in economics, the greater is the *inverted* relationship of its *value as money* to the exchange value or to the monetary value of the material in which it exists. Hence *paper money* and *paper substitutes for money* such as bills of exchange, checks, promissory notes, etc., constitute the more *complete* existence of *money as money* and a necessary phase in the progressive development in the monetary system. In the *credit system*, fully expressed in *banking*, it appears as if the power of an alien, material force is broken, the relationships of self-alienation overcome, and man again is humanly related to man. The *followers of Saint-Simon*, misled by this *appearance*, consider the development of money, bills of exchange, paper money, paper substitutes for money, *credit*, and *banking* as a gradual transcendence of the separation of man from things, capital from labor, private property from money, and of money from man—a gradual transcendence of the separation of man from man. Hence the organized *bank system* is their ideal. But this transcendence of alienation, this *return* of man to himself and thus to other men is only *apparent*. Its self-alienation, its dehumanization is all the more *odious* and *extreme*, insofar as its element is no longer the commodity, metal, or paper, but the *moral* and *social* existence, the very *inwardness* of the human heart; insofar as it is the highest *distrust* of man for man and complete alienation, under the appearance of trust of man for man.

What is the nature of *credit?* We are here completely disregarding the *content* of credit which is again money. We thus disregard the *content* of this trust, wherein a man *recognizes* another by lending him values—let us assume that he does not take interest and is no profiteer—and by trusting that his fellow man is a "good" man and not a rascal. By a "good" man the trusting man here understands, like Shylock, the man who can pay.—Credit is possible under two relationships and under two distinct conditions. Take the case where a wealthy man gives credit to a poor man whom he considers diligent and reliable. This kind of credit belongs in the romantic and sentimental part of economics, belongs to its departures, excesses, *exceptions,* not to its *rule.* Even if this exception and this romantic possibility are assumed, the life, talent, and activity of the poor man *guarantee* for the rich man the repayment for the money loaned. All social virtues of the poor man, then, the substance of his living and his very existence represent for the rich man the reimbursement of his capital with the usual interest. The death of the poor man is the worst possibility for the creditor. It is the death of his capital and the interest as well. Consider the ignominy in the *evaluation* of a man in terms of *money* as it takes place in the credit system. It is understood that in addition to *moral* guarantees the creditor also has the guarantee of *judicial* force and more or less *real* guarantees for his man. If the debtor is himself affluent, *credit* becomes merely a facilitating *medium* of exchange, and *money* itself acquires an *ideal* form. Credit is the *economic* judgment of man's morality. In credit, *man* himself instead of metal and paper has become the *medium* of exchange, but not as man, but rather as the *existence of capital* and interest. The medium of exchange is thus returned from its material form to man, but only because man has been externalized and has himself become a material form. Within the credit relationship, money is not transcended in man, but man is transformed into *money,* and money is *incorporated* in him. *Human individuality* and human *morality* have become an article of trade and the *material* in which money exists. Instead of money and paper, my very personal existence, my flesh and blood, my social virtue and reputation is the matter and the substance of the *monetary spirit.* Credit no longer reduces monetary value to money, but to human flesh and the human heart. All the progress and inconsequence of a false system thus constitute the extreme regression and consequence of ignominy.

The nature of the credit system as alienated from man is confirmed in the following manner under the appearance of the economic recognition of man: (1) The contrast between the capitalist and the laborer—between the big and the small capitalist—becomes even greater as credit is given only to the one who already has and is a new chance for accumulation for the wealthy, or as the poor person sees his *entire* existence confirmed or denied, and completely dependent upon the accidental caprice and judgment of the wealthy man. (2) Mutual dissimulation, hypocrisy, and sanctimoniousness are carried to the point that a moral judgment is added to the simple statement that a man without credit is poor, a judgment that he is untrustworthy and unworthy of recognition, a social pariah and bad man. On top of suffering from his destitution the poor man suffers from having to make a debasing *plea* to the rich for credit. (3) With this completely *ideal* existence of money, man must *counterfeit* his own person and must obtain credit by sneaking and lying. The credit relationship—for the creditor as well as for the debtor—becomes an object of trade, an object of mutual betrayal and misuse. Here *mistrust* is brilliantly apparent as the basis of economic trust; in the distrustful weighing as to whether credit should or should not be given; in the spying into the secrets of the private life of the one seeking credit; in the revealing of a rival's temporary misfortunes in order to wreck him by shaking his credit, etc.; the entire system of bankruptcy, pseudo-enterprises, etc. . . . In the *credit system on the state level* the state occupies completely the same position as shown above for man . . . The game with governmental bonds shows how far the state has become the plaything of men of commerce.

(4) The *credit system* is perfected in *banking.* The creation of the banker's position, state regulation of banking, concentration of fortunes in these hands—this economic *areopagus* of the nation—is the lauded perfection of the monetary system. As the *moral recognition of a man* and the *confidence in the state* has the form of *credit* in the credit system, the secret involved in the deception of that moral recognition, the *amoral ignominy* of that morality as well as the sanctimoniousness and egoism in the confidence in the state become apparent—and all this reveals itself for what it actually is.

The *exchange* of human activity within production itself as well as the exchange of *human products* with one another is equivalent to the *generic activity* and generic spirit whose actual, conscious, and authentic existence is *social* activity and *social* satisfaction. As *human* nature is the *true common life* [*Gemeinwesen*] of man, men through the activation of their *nature create* and produce a human *common life*, a social essence which is no abstractly universal power opposed to the single individual, but is the essence or nature of every single individual, his own activity, his own life,

[margin, handwritten: Public Shame]

his own spirit, his own wealth. *Authentic common life* arises not through reflection; rather it comes about from the *need* and *egoism* of individuals, that is, immediately from the activation of their very existence. It is not up to man whether this common life exists or not. However, so long as man does not recognize himself as man and does not organize the world humanly, this *common life* appears in the form of *alienation,* because its *subject,* man, is a being alienated from itself. Men as actual, living, particular individuals, not in an abstraction, *constitute* this common life. It is, therefore, *what* men are. To say that *man* alienates himself is the same as saying that the *society* of this alienated man is the caricature of his *actual common life,* of his true generic life. His activity, therefore, appears as torment, his own creation as a force alien to him, his wealth as poverty, the *essential bond* connecting him with other men as something unessential so that the separation from other men appears as his true existence. His life appears as the sacrifice of his life, the realization of his nature as the diminution of his life, his production as the production of his destruction, his power over the object as the power of the object over him; the master of his creation appears as its slave.

Political economy understands the *common life of man,* the self-activating *human* essence and mutual reintegration toward generic and truly human life, in the form of *exchange* and *commerce. Society,* says Destutt de Tracy, is a *series of multilateral exchanges.* It is constituted by this movement of multilateral integration. *Society,* says Adam Smith, is a *commercial enterprise.* Each of its members is a *merchant.* It is evident that political economy *establishes* an *alienated* form of social intercourse as the *essential, original,* and definitive human form.

Economics—like the actual process itself—proceeds from the *relationship of man to man* and from the relationship of one *property owner to another.* Let us presuppose man as *property owner,* that is, as exclusive possessor who maintains his personality and distinguishes himself from other men and relates himself to them through this exclusive possession. Private property is his personal existence, his *distinguishing* and hence essential existence. The *loss* or *relinquishing* of private property, then, is an *externalization of man* as well as of *private property.* We are concerned here only with the latter. When I yield my private property to another person, it ceases being mine. It becomes something independent of me and *outside* my sphere, something external to me. I externalize my private property. So far as I am concerned, it is *externalized* private property. I see it only as something generally *externalized;* I only transcend my *personal* relationship to it; and I return it to the *elemental* forces of nature when I externalize it only in relation to myself. It only becomes externalized *private property* as it ceases being *my* private property without ceasing to be *private property* in general, that is, when it acquires the same relationship to *another* man *outside* of me, as it had to me—in a word, when it becomes the *private property* of *another* man. Apart from the situation of *force*, what causes me to externalize *my* private property to another person? Economics answers correctly: *need* and *want*. The other person is also a property owner, but of *another* object which I lack and which I neither can nor want to be without, an object which to me seems to be something *needed* for the reintegration of my existence and the realization of my nature.

The bond relating the two property owners to each other is the *specific nature of the object*. The fact that either property owner desires and wants objects makes him aware that he has another *essential* relationship to objects outside of property and that he is not the particular being he takes himself to be but rather a *total* being whose wants have a relationship of *inner* property to the products of the labor of the other person. For the need of an object is the most evident and irrefutable proof that the object belongs to *my* nature and that the existence of the object for me and its *property* are the property appropriate to my essence. Both owners are thus impelled to relinquish their property, but in such a way that at the same time they reaffirm that property; or they are impelled to relinquish that property within the relationship of private property. Each thus externalizes a part of his property in the other person.

The *social* relationship of both owners is thus the *mutuality of externalization*, the relationship of externalization on both sides—or *externalization* as the relationship of both owners—while in simple private property *externalization* takes place only one-sidedly, in relationship to itself.

Exchange or *barter*, therefore, is the social, generic act, the common essence, the social intercourse and integration of man within *private property*, and the external, the *externalized* generic act. For that very reason it appears as *barter*. And hence it is likewise the opposite of the *social* relationship.

Through the mutual externalization or alienation of private property, *private property* itself has been determined as *externalized* private property. First of all it has ceased being the product of labor and being the exclusive, distinctive personality of its owner because the owner has externalized it; it has been removed from the owner whose product it was and has acquired a personal significance for the person who did *not* produce it. It has lost its personal significance for the owner. In the second place it has been related to and equated with another private property. A private property of a *different* nature has taken its place, just as it itself takes the position of a private property of a *different* nature. On both sides, then, private property appears as a representative of private property of a different nature, as the *equivalence* of another natural product. Both sides are so related that each represents the existence of the *other* and they mutually serve as *substitutes* for themselves and the other. The existence of private property as such has thus become a *substitute,* an *equivalent.* Instead of its immediate self-unity it exists only in relationship to *something else.* As an *equivalent* its existence is no longer something peculiarly appropriate to it. It has become *value* and immediately *exchange value.* Its existence as *value* is a determination of *itself,* different from its immediate existence, outside of its specific nature, and *externalized*—only a *relative* existence.

It will be shown elsewhere how this *value* is more precisely determined and how it becomes *price.*

The relationship of exchange being presupposed, *labor immediately* becomes *wage-labor.* This relationship of alienated labor reaches its apex only by the fact (1) that on the one side *wage-labor,* the product of the laborer, stands in no *immediate* relationship to his need and to his *status* but is rather determined in both directions through social combinations alien to the laborer; (2) that the *buyer* of the product is not himself productive but exchanges what has been produced by others. In the crude form of *externalized* private property, *barter,* each of the two private owners produces what his need, his inclination, and the existing raw material induces him to produce. They exchange only the surplus of their production. To be sure, labor was for each one the immediate *source of his subsistence;* at the same time, however, it was also the confirmation of his *individual existence.* Through exchange, his *labor* has partly become his *source of income.* The purpose and existence of labor have changed. The product is created as *value, exchange value,* and an *equivalent* and no longer because of its immediate personal relationship to the producer. The more varied production becomes—in other words, the more varied the needs become on the one hand and the more one-sided the producer's output becomes on the other—the more does his labor fall into the category of *wage-labor,* until it is eventually nothing but wage-labor and until it becomes entirely *incidental* and *unessential* whether the producer immediately enjoys and needs his product and whether the *activity,* the action of labor itself, is his self-satisfaction and the realization of his natural dispositions and spiritual aims.

The following elements are contained in *wage-labor.* (1) the chance relationship and alienation of labor from the laboring subject; (2) the chance relationship and alienation of labor from its object; (3) the determination of the laborer through social needs which are an alien compulsion to him, a compulsion to which he submits out of egoistic need and distress—these social needs are merely a source of providing the necessities of life for him, just as he is merely a slave for them; (4) the maintenance of his individual existence appears to the worker as the *goal* of his activity and his real action is only a means; he lives to acquire the means of *living.*

The greater and the more articulated the social power is within the relationship of private property, the more *egoistic* and asocial man becomes, the more he becomes alienated from his own nature.

Just as the mutual exchange of products of *human activity* appears as *trading* and *bargaining,* so does the mutual reintegration and exchange of the activity itself appear as the *division of labor* making man as far as possible an abstract being, an automaton, and transforming him into a spiritual and physical monster.

Precisely the unity of human labor is regarded as being its *division* because its social nature comes into being only as its opposite, in the form of alienation. The *division of labor* increases with civilization.

Within the presupposition of the division of labor, the product and material of private property gradually acquire for the individual the significance of an *equivalent.* He no longer exchanges his *surplus,* and he can become *indifferent* to the object of his production. He no longer immediately exchanges his product for the product he *needs.* The equivalent becomes an equivalent in *money* which is the immediate result of wage-labor and the *medium* of exchange. (See above.)

The complete domination of the alienated object *over* man is evident in *money* and the complete disregard of the nature of the material, the specific nature of private property as well as the personality of the proprietor.

What formerly was the domination of one person over another has now become the general domination of the *thing* over the *person,* the domination of the product over the producer. Just as the determination of the *externalization* of private property lay in the *equivalent* and in value, so is *money* the sensuous, self-objectified existence of this *externalization.*

It is clear that economics can grasp this entire development only as a *factum* and as the offspring of chance need.

The separation of labor from itself = separation of laborer from capitalist = separation of labor from capital whose original form can be divided into *real property* and *chattel property* . . . The original determination of private property is monopoly; as soon as it acquires a political constitution, it is that of monopoly. Monopoly perfected is competition.—The economist distinguishes *production* and *consumption,* and as media of both he refers to *exchange* or *distribution.* The separation of production from consumption, and of activity from mind in various individuals and within the same individual is the *separation of labor* from its *object* and from itself as one mind. *Distribution* is the self-active power of private property.—The mutual separation of labor, capital, and real property as well as the separation of labor from labor, of capital from capital, of real property from real property, and finally the separation of labor from wages, of capital from profit, of profit from interest, and of real property from rent makes self-alienation appear in the form of self-alienation as well as in the form of mutual alienation.

Free Human Production

It is the basic presupposition of private property that man *produces* only in order to *own*. The purpose of production is to *own*. It not only has such a *useful* purpose; it also has a *selfish* purpose. Man only produces in order to *own* something for himself. The object of his production is the objectification of his *immediate*, selfish *need*. Man—in his wild, barbaric condition—determines his production by the *extent* of his immediate need whose content is the *immediately* produced object itself.

In that condition man produces *no more* than he immediately needs. The *limit of his need* is the *limit of his production*. Demand and supply coincide. Production is *determined* by need. Either no exchange takes place or the exchange is reduced to the exchange of man's labor for the product of his labor, and this exchange is the latent form (the germ) of real exchange.

As soon as exchange occurs, there is an overproduction beyond the immediate boundary of ownership. But this overproduction does not exceed selfish need. Rather it is only an *indirect* way of satisfying a need which finds its objectification in the production of another person. Production has become a *source of income*, labor for profit. While formerly need determined the extent of production, now production, or rather the *owning of the product*, determines how far needs can be satisfied.

I have produced for myself and not for you, just as you have produced for yourself and not for me. The result of my production as such has as little direct connection with you as the result of your production has with me, that is, our production is not production of man for man as man, not *socialized* production. No one is gratified by the production of another. Our mutual production means nothing for us as human beings. Our exchange, therefore, cannot be the mediating movement in which it would be acknowledged that my product means anything for you because it is an *objectification* of your being, your need. *Human nature* is not the bond of our production for each other. Exchange can only set in *motion* and confirm the *relationship* which each of us has to his own product and

[margin note: exchange only occurs if overproduction]

to the production of the other person. Each of us sees in his product
only his *own* objectified self-interest and in the product of another person, *another* self-interest which is independent, alien, and objectified.

As a human being, however, you do have a human relation to my
product; you *want* my product. It is the object of your desire and your
will. But your want, desire, and will for my product are impotent. In
other words, your *human* nature, necessarily and intimately related to my
human production, is not your *power*, not your sharing in this production,
because the *power* of human nature is not acknowledged in my production. Rather it is the *bond* which makes you dependent upon me because
it makes you dependent on my product. It is far from being the *means* of
giving you *power* over my production; rather it is the *means* of giving me
power over you.

When I produce *more* than I can consume, I subtly *reckon* with your
need. I produce only the *semblance* of a surplus of the object. In truth I
produce a *different* object, the object of your production which I plan to
exchange for this surplus, an exchange already accomplished in thought.
My *social* relationship with you and my labor for your want is just plain
deception and our mutual reintegration is *deception* just as well. Mutual
pillaging is its base. Its background is the intent to pillage, to defraud.
Since our exchange is selfish on your side as well as mine and since every
self-interest attempts to surpass that of another person, we necessarily
attempt to defraud each other. The power I give my object over yours,
however, requires your *acknowledgment* to become real. Our mutual acknowledgment of the mutual power of our objects is a battle and the one
with more insight, energy, power, and cleverness is the winner. If my
physical strength suffices, I pillage you directly. If there is no physical
power, we mutually dissemble and the more adroit comes out on top. It
makes no difference for the *entire* relationship who the winner is, for the
ideal and *intended* victory takes place on both sides; in his own judgment
each of the two has overcome the other.

On both sides exchange necessarily requires the *object* of mutual production and mutual ownership. The ideal relationship to the mutual
objects of our production is our mutual need. But the *real* and *truly
effective* relationship is only the mutually *exclusive ownership* of mutual
production. It is your *object*, the *equivalent* of my object, that gives your
want for my object *value*, *dignity*, and *efficacy* for me. Our mutual product, therefore, is the *means*, the *intermediary*, the *instrument*, the *acknowledged power* of our mutual needs. Your *demand* and the *equivalent of your
property* are terms which for me are *synonymous* and equally valid, and
your demand is effective only when it has an effect on me. Without this
effect your demand is merely an unsatisfied effort on your part and

without consequence for me. You have no relationship to my object as a human being because I *myself* have no human relation to it. But the *means* is the *real power* over an object, and we mutually regard our product as the *power* each one has over the other and over himself. In other words, our own product is turned against us. It appeared to be our property, but actually we are its property. We ourselves are excluded from *true* property because our *property* excludes the other human being.

(Our objects in their relation to one another constitute the only intelligible language we use with one another. We would not understand a human language, and it would remain without effect. On the one hand, it would be felt and spoken as a plea, as begging, and as *humiliation* and hence uttered with shame and with a feeling of supplication; on the other hand, it would be heard and rejected as *effrontery* or *madness*. We are so much mutually alienated from human nature that the direct language of this nature is an *injury to human dignity* for us, while the alienated language of objective values appears as justified, self-confident, and self-accepted human dignity.)

To be sure, from your point of view your product is an *instrument*, a *means* for the appropriation of my product and for the satisfaction of your need. But from my point of view it is the *goal* of our exchange. I regard you as a means and instrument for the production of this object, that is, my goal, and much more so than I regard you as related to my object. But (1) each of us actually *does* what the other thinks he is doing. You actually made yourself the means, the instrument, and the producer of *your* own object in order to appropriate mine; (2) for you, your own object is only the *sensuous shell* and *concealed form* of my object; its production *means* and *expressly* is the *acquisition* of my object. You indeed become the *means* and *instrument* of your object; your greed is the *slave* of this object, and you performed slavish services so that the object is never again a remission of your greed. This mutual servitude to the object is actually manifested to us at the beginning of its development as the relationship of *lordship* and *slavery*, and is only the *crude* and *frank* expression of our essential relationship.

Our *mutual* value is the *value* of our mutual objects for us. Man himself, therefore, is mutually *valueless* for us.

Suppose we had produced things as human beings: in his production each of us would have *twice affirmed* himself and the other. (1) In my *production* I would have objectified my *individuality* and its *particularity*, and in the course of the activity I would have enjoyed an individual *life;* in viewing the object I would have experienced the individual joy of knowing my personality as an *objective, sensuously perceptible,* and *indubitable* power. (2) In your satisfaction and your use of my product I would have had the *direct* and conscious satisfaction that my work satisfied a *human* need, that it objectified *human* nature, and that it created an object appropriate to the need of another *human* being. (3) I would have been the *mediator* between you and the species and you would have experienced me as a reintegration of your own nature and a necessary part of your self; I would have been affirmed in your thought as well as your love. (4) In my individual life I would have directly created your life; in my individual activity I would have immediately *confirmed* and *realized* my true *human* and *social* nature.

Our productions would be so many mirrors reflecting our nature.

What happens so far as I am concerned would also apply to you.

Let us summarize the various factors in the supposition above:

My labor would be a *free manifestation of life* and an *enjoyment* of *life*. Under the presupposition of private property it is an *externalization* of *life* because I work *in order to live* and provide for myself the *means* of living. Working *is not* living.

Furthermore, in my labor the *particularity* of my individuality would be affirmed because my *individual* life is affirmed. Labor then would be *true, active property*. Under the presupposition of private property my individuality is externalized to the point where I *hate* this *activity* and where it is a *torment* for me. Rather it is then only the *semblance* of an activity, only a *forced* activity, imposed upon me only by *external* and accidental necessity and *not* by an *internal* and *determined* necessity.

My labor can appear in my object only according to its nature; it cannot appear as something *different* from itself. My labor, therefore, is manifested as the objective, sensuous, perceptible, and indubitable expression of my *self-loss* and my *powerlessness.*

Economic and Philosophic Manuscripts (selections)

Karl Marx

During the summer of 1844, Marx wrote a rough draft of a work on themes in political economy. Four manuscripts have survived. The first contains for the most part copied passages from various of the texts in political economy that Marx had been studying. The last section of it, given below, includes some of Marx's most famous remarks on alienation and, in particular, alienated labor. The second manuscript is a fragment on the conflict between capital and labor and is omitted here. The major portion of the third manuscript is a discussion of private property, labor, and communism and is given below, as is a discussion of Hegel's dialectic, also from the third manuscript. The fourth manuscript is a summary of the final chapter of Hegel's Phenomenology *and is included in the section on Hegel. In many ways, these manuscripts represent the first attempt by Marx to develop in a systematic way the themes that would occupy him in all of his work on the philosophical foundations and presuppositions of political economy.*

The Economic and Philosophic Manuscripts *was first published in 1932. Its influence on the understanding of Marx's philosophical outlook was and continues to be dramatic. Some have seen in these manuscripts the most important philosophical writing that Marx produced. Others dismiss them as the product of a young Marx who was still a Feuerbachian humanist and not yet a true scientific Marxist. In particular, attention has centered on the centrality of the concept of alienation in these manuscripts; as a result, there has been a rethinking of how that concept relates to Marx's later writings, especially* Capital. *These manuscripts are also seen as crucial to an understanding of Marx's relation to Hegel. Some find in these early writings evidence of a humanist young Marx who is still very influenced by Hegel and who is to be sharply differentiated from the later, scientific Marx. Others see the concepts of alienation and emancipation as continuing through all of Marx's work and providing his ongoing philosophical focus. The latter interpretation stresses the continuity in Marx's own development and in his relation to Hegel.*

These selections, beginning on p. 56, are translated from the German by Loyd D. Easton and Kurt H. Guddat.

The *"Alienated Labor"* essay contains what is perhaps Marx's most explicit discussion of his philosophical anthropology. Labor is the central category. "The animal is its life activity. Man makes his life activity itself into an object of will and consciousness." A human being is a Homo faber in essence. We are beings who can labor in a unique way, capable of making both the object of our labor and the process of laboring intentional objects that we can control. The manner in which we labor expresses what we are. In particular, the relations with others that we have in our labor are a central factor determining the nature of our concrete being. "In the treatment of the objective world, therefore, man proves himself to be genuinely a species-being. This production is his active species-life." When the labor process is controlled by someone other than the worker, when the worker is deprived of control over the object of labor, the result is that the worker is alienated from that very activity that is central to being a fully realized human. A sense of meaninglessness, a lack of true flourishing, and a difficulty in establishing truly human relationships with others follow. At the core of the problem is the alienated labor caused by the practice of wage labor. The alienation due to private property and market relations discussed in earlier writings is now seen to be a consequence of the more basic form of alienation in the process of production.

In *"Private Property and Communism,"* Marx continues his investigation of the effects of alienated labor in relation to private property and its abolition in communism. Communism, he writes, "is the genuine resolution of the antagonism between man and nature and between man and man; it is the true resolution of the conflict between existence and essence, objectification and self-affirmation, freedom and necessity, individual and species. It is the riddle of history solved and knows itself as this solution." Marx goes on in this section to explore the implications of overcoming alienation for our relation to nature and natural science.

"Critique of Hegelian Dialectic and Philosophy in General" is Marx's most extensive attempt to come to terms with Hegel's logic and general philosophical approach, especially in light of Feuerbach's materialist critique of Hegel. While accusing Hegel of serious errors and misunderstandings, Marx does credit Hegel with grasping "the self-development of man as a process, objectification as loss of the object, as alienation and transcendence of this alienation; that he thus grasps the nature of work and comprehends objective man, authentic because actual, as the result of his own work." That is, Hegel, in however a distorted or inverse way, had true insight into what Marx takes as the major fact of human history and self-making.

Preface

In the *Deutsch-Französische Jahrbücher* I announced a critique of jurisprudence and political science in the form of a critique of the *Hegelian*
philosophy of law. Preparing this for publication, I found that the combination of criticism directed solely against speculation with criticism of
various subjects would be quite unsuitable; it would impede the development of the argument and render comprehension difficult. Moreover,
the wealth and diversity of the subjects to be dealt with could have been
accommodated in a *single* work only in a very aphoristic style, and such
aphoristic presentation would have given the *impression* of arbitrary sys-
tematization. Therefore, I shall issue the critique of law, morals, politics,
etc., in separate, independent brochures, and finally attempt to give in a
separate work the unity of the whole, the relation of the separate parts,
and eventually a critique of the speculative treatment of the material.
Hence in the present work the relationships of political economy with
the state, law, morals, civil life, etc., are touched upon only insofar as
political economy itself, ex professo, deals with these subjects.

It is hardly necessary to assure the reader familiar with political economy that my conclusions have been obtained through an entirely empirical analysis, based on a thorough, critical study of political economy.

((The uninformed reviewer, however, who tries to hide his complete
ignorance and poverty of thought by hurling *"utopian phrase"* at the
positive critic's head or such phrases as "the entirely pure, entirely decisive, entirely critical criticism," the "not merely legal but social, entirely
social society," the "compact, massy mass," the "outspoken spokesman of
the massy mass"—this reviewer [Bruno Bauer] has yet to furnish the first
proof that outside his theological family affairs he has anything to contribute to *worldly* matters.))[*]

It is a matter of course that in addition to the French and English
socialists I have also used German socialist works. The significant and
original German contributions on this subject—apart from Weitling's
writings—amount to no more than the essays by Hess in *Twenty-one
Sheets [from Switzerland]* and Engels' "Outlines of a Critique of Political
Economy" in the *Deutsch-Französische Jahrbücher* where I indicated the
basic elements of the present work in a very general way.

((Besides the criticism concerned with political economy, positive criticism in general, and thus also German positive criticism of political
economy, is really founded on the discoveries of *Feuerbach* against whose

[*Material within double parentheses, from here on, vertically crossed out by
Marx.]

Philosophy of the Future and "Theses on the Reform of Philosophy" in the *Anekdota* the petty envy of some and the loud rage of others seem to have instigated an organized conspiracy of *silence*, despite the tacit use that is made of Feuerbach's works.))

Positive humanistic and naturalistic criticism begins with *Feuerbach.* The less vociferous *Feuerbach's* writings are, the more certain, profound, extensive, and lasting is their influence—the only writings since Hegel's *Phenomenology* [*of Spirit*] and *Logic* containing a real theoretical revolution.

In contrast to the *critical theologians* of our time [Bruno Bauer and followers] I have regarded the concluding chapter of the present work—the discussion of the *Hegelian dialectic* and philosophy in general—to be absolutely necessary because such a task has not yet been accomplished. This lack of *thoroughness* is inevitable because even the *critical* theologian remains a *theologian.* Either he must proceed from certain presuppositions of philosophy, accepting them as authoritative, or else, if in the course of criticism and as a result of other persons' discoveries doubts arise in his mind about the philosophical presuppositions, he abandons them in a cowardly, indefensible manner, *abstracts* from them, and manifests his servitude to these very presuppositions and his vexation over this servitude in a negative, unconscious, and sophistical way.

((manifests this only negatively and unconsciously, on the one hand, in constantly repeating the assurance of the *purity* of his own criticism, and on the other hand, in trying to present the appearance that criticism only has to do with a limited form of the criticism outside—say that of the eighteenth century—and with the obtuseness of the *mass,* in order to divert the observer's eyes as well as his own from the *necessary* clash between *criticism* and its birthplace—Hegelian *dialectic* and German philosophy in general—and from the necessary advancement of modern criticism beyond its own narrowness and natural origin. Finally, however, when discoveries such as *Feuerbach's* are made about the nature of his own philosophical presuppositions, the critical theologian may claim to have made the discovery *himself* and pretend this by hurling *catch phrases,* the results of the discovery which he was not able to develop, at writers who are still caught in philosophy. He may even manage to secure the sense of his superiority to that discovery, not by attempting, even if he could, to bring into their proper relations the elements of Hegelian *dialectic* which he still finds missing in the criticism of Hegelian dialectic not yet served up to him, but rather by employing those elements in veiled, mischievous, and sceptical ways, in a secretive manner, against the criticism of Hegelian dialectic—such as the category of mediating proof against the category of positive, self-originating truth, the [. . . ?], etc.—

in the form *peculiar* to Hegelian dialectic. The theological critic finds it quite natural that everything is to *be done* by philosophy so that he can *chatter* about purity, resoluteness, about the very critical criticism. He fancies himself the true *conqueror of philosophy* whenever he happens to *feel* that some moment in Hegel is lacking in relation to Feuerbach—for however much the theological critic practices the spiritualistic idolatry of *"Self-Consciousness"* and "Spirit," he can not go beyond feeling and achieve consciousness.))

Considered closely, *theological criticism*—while in the beginning of the movement an actual factor of progress—in the final analysis is nothing but the culmination and consequence of the old *philosophical* transcendence, particularly *Hegelian transcendence*, distorted into a *theological caricature*. On another occasion [subsequently in *The Holy Family*] I shall describe in detail this interesting historical justice, this historical nemesis, which is inducing theology, ever the sore point of philosophy, to exhibit in itself the negative dissolution of philosophy—that is, its decomposition process.

((To what extent *Feuerbach's* discoveries about the nature of philosophy still require—at least for their *proof*—a critical analysis of philosophical dialectic will be learned from my exposition itself.))

Alienated Labor

We have proceeded from the presuppositions of political economy. We have accepted its language and its laws. We presupposed private property, the separation of labor, capital and land, hence of wages, profit of capital and rent, likewise the division of labor, competition, the concept of exchange value, etc. From political economy itself, in its own words, we have shown that the worker sinks to the level of a commodity, the most miserable commodity; that the misery of the worker is inversely proportional to the power and volume of his production; that the necessary result of competition is the accumulation of capital in a few hands and thus the revival of monopoly in a more frightful form; and finally that the distinction between capitalist and landowner, between agricultural laborer and industrial worker, disappears and the whole society must divide into the two classes of *proprietors* and propertyless *workers*.

Political economy proceeds from the fact of private property. It does not explain private property. It grasps the actual, *material* process of private property in abstract and general formulae which it then takes as *laws*. It does not *comprehend* these laws, that is, does not prove them as proceeding from the nature of private property. Political economy does not disclose the reason for the division between capital and labor, between capital and land. When, for example, the relation of wages to profits is determined, the ultimate basis is taken to be the interest of the capitalists; that is, political economy assumes what it should develop. Similarly, competition is referred to at every point and explained from external circumstances. Political economy teaches us nothing about the extent to which these external, apparently accidental circumstances are simply the expression of a necessary development. We have seen how political economy regards exchange itself as an accidental fact. The only wheels which political economy puts in motion are *greed* and the *war among the greedy, competition.*

Just because political economy does not grasp the interconnections within the movement, the doctrine of competition could stand opposed to the doctrine of monopoly, the doctrine of freedom of craft to that of the guild, the doctrine of the division of landed property to that of the great estate. Competition, freedom of craft, and division of landed property were developed and conceived only as accidental, deliberate, forced consequences of monopoly, the guild, and feudal property, rather than necessary, inevitable, natural consequences.

We now have to grasp the essential connection among private property, greed, division of labor, capital and landownership, and the connection of exchange with competition, of value with the devaluation of men, of monopoly with competition, etc., and of this whole alienation with the money-system.

Let us not put ourselves in a fictitious primordial state like a political economist trying to clarify things. Such a primordial state clarifies nothing. It merely pushes the issue into a gray, misty distance. It acknowledges as a fact or event what it should deduce, namely, the necessary relation between two things for example, between division of labor and exchange. In such a manner theology explains the origin of evil by the fall of man. That is, it asserts as a fact in the form of history what it should explain.

We proceed from a *present* fact of political economy.

The worker becomes poorer the more wealth he produces, the more his production increases in power and extent. The worker becomes a cheaper commodity the more commodities he produces. The *increase in value* of the world of things is directly proportional to the *decrease in value* of the human world. Labor not only produces commodities. It also produces itself and the worker as a *commodity,* and indeed in the same proportion as it produces commodities in general.

This fact simply indicates that the object which labor produces, its product, stands opposed to it as an *alien thing,* as a *power independent* of the producer. The product of labor is labor embodied and made objective in a thing. It is the *objectification* of labor. The realization of labor is its objectification. In the viewpoint of political economy this realization

of labor appears as the *diminution of the worker*, the objectification as
the *loss of and subservience to the object*, and the appropriation as *alienation [Entfremdung]*, as externalization [*Entäusserung*].

So much does the realization of labor appear as diminution that the
worker is diminished to the point of starvation. So much does objectification appear as loss of the object that the worker is robbed of the
most essential objects not only of life but also of work. Indeed, work
itself becomes a thing of which he can take possession only with the
greatest effort and with the most unpredictable interruptions. So much
does the appropriation of the object appear as alienation that the more
objects the worker produces, the fewer he can own and the more he falls
under the domination of his product, of capital.

All these consequences follow from the fact that the worker is related
to the *product of his labor* as to an *alien* object. For it is clear according to
this premise: The more the worker exerts himself, the more powerful
becomes the alien objective world which he fashions against himself, the
poorer he and his inner world become, the less there is that belongs to
him. It is the same in religion. The more man attributes to God, the less
he retains in himself. The worker puts his life into the object; then it no
longer belongs to him but to the object. The greater this activity, the
poorer is the worker. What the product of his work is, he is not. The
greater this product is, the smaller he is himself. The *externalization* of
the worker in his product means not only that his work becomes an
object, an *external* existence, but also that it exists *outside him* independently, alien, an autonomous power, opposed to him. The life he has
given to the object confronts him as hostile and alien.

Let us now consider more closely the *objectification*, the worker's production and with it the *alienation* and *loss* of the object, his product.

The worker can make nothing without *nature*, without the *sensuous
external world*. It is the material wherein his labor realizes itself, wherein
it is active, out of which and by means of which it produces.

But as nature furnishes to labor the *means of life* in the sense that labor
cannot *live* without objects upon which labor is exercised, nature also
furnishes the *means of life* in the narrower sense, namely, the means of
physical subsistence of the *worker* himself.

The more the worker *appropriates* the external world and sensuous
nature through his labor, the more he deprives himself of the *means of
life* in two respects: first, that the sensuous external world gradually
ceases to be an object belonging to his labor, a *means of life* of his work;
secondly, that it gradually ceases to be a *means of life* in the immediate
sense, a means of physical subsistence of the worker.

In these two respects, therefore, the worker becomes a slave to his objects; first, in that he receives an *object of labor*, that is, he receives *labor*, and secondly that he receives the *means of subsistence*. The first enables him to exist as a *worker* and the second as a *physical subject*. The terminus of this slavery is that he can only maintain himself as a *physical subject* so far as he is a *worker*, and only as a *physical subject* is he a worker.

(The alienation of the worker in his object is expressed according to the laws of political economy as follows: the more the worker produces, the less he has to consume; the more values he creates the more worthless and unworthy he becomes; the better shaped his product, the more misshapen is he; the more civilized his product, the more barbaric is the worker; the more powerful the work, the more powerless becomes the worker; the more intelligence the work has, the more witless is the worker and the more he becomes a slave of nature.)

Political economy conceals the alienation in the nature of labor by ignoring the direct relationship between the worker (labor) *and production*. To be sure, labor produces marvels for the wealthy but it produces deprivation for the worker. It produces palaces, but hovels for the worker. It produces beauty, but mutilation for the worker. It displaces labor through machines, but it throws some workers back into barbarous labor and turns others into machines. It produces intelligence, but for the worker it produces imbecility and cretinism.

The direct relationship of labor to its products is the relationship of the worker to the objects of his production. The relationship of the rich to the objects of production and to production itself is only a *consequence* of this first relationship and confirms it. Later we shall observe the latter aspect.

Thus, when we ask, What is the essential relationship of labor? we ask about the relationship of the *worker* to production.

Up to now we have considered the alienation, the externalization of the worker only from one side: his *relationship to the products of his labor*. But alienation is shown not only in the result but also in the *process of production*, in the *producing activity* itself. How could the worker stand in an alien relationship to the product of his activity if he did not alienate himself from himself in the very act of production? After all, the product is only the résumé of activity, of production. If the product of work is externalization, production itself must be active externalization, externalization of activity, activity of externalization. Only alienation—and externalization in the activity of labor itself—is summarized in the alienation of the object of labor.

What constitutes the externalization of labor?

First is the fact that labor is *external* to the laborer—that is, it is not part of his nature—and that the worker does not affirm himself in his work but denies himself, feels miserable and unhappy, develops no free physical and mental energy but mortifies his flesh and ruins his mind. The worker, therefore feels at ease only outside work, and during work he is outside himself. He is at home when he is not working and when he is working he is not at home. His work, therefore, is not voluntary, but coerced, *forced labor.* It is not the satisfaction of a need but only a *means* to satisfy other needs. Its alien character is obvious from the fact that as soon as no physical or other pressure exists, labor is avoided like the plague. External labor, labor in which man is externalized, is labor of self-sacrifice, of penance. Finally, the external nature of work for the worker appears in the fact that it is not his own but another person's, that in work he does not belong to himself but to someone else. In religion the spontaneity of human imagination, the spontaneity of the human brain and heart, acts independently of the individual as an alien, divine or devilish activity. Similarly, the activity of the worker is not his own spontaneous activity. It belongs to another. It is the loss of his own self.

The result, therefore, is that man (the worker) feels that he is acting freely only in his animal functions—eating, drinking, and procreating, or at most in his shelter and finery—while in his human functions he feels only like an animal. The animalistic becomes the human and the human the animalistic.

To be sure, eating, drinking, and procreation are genuine human functions. In abstraction, however, and separated from the remaining sphere of human activities and turned into final and sole ends, they are animal functions.

We have considered labor, the act of alienation of practical human activity, in two aspects: (1) the relationship of the worker to the *product of labor* as an alien object dominating him. This relationship is at the same time the relationship to the sensuous external world, to natural objects as an alien world hostile to him; (2) the relationship of labor to the *act of production* in *labor.* This relationship is that of the worker to his own activity as alien and not belonging to him, activity as passivity, power as weakness, procreation as emasculation, the worker's *own* physical and spiritual energy, his personal life—for what else is life but activity—as an activity turned against him, independent of him, and not belonging to him. *Self-alienation,* as against the alienation of the *object,* stated above.

We have now to derive a third aspect of *alienated labor* from the two previous ones.

Man is a species-being [*Gattungswesen*] not only in that he practically and theoretically makes his own species as well as that of other things his object, but also—and this is only another expression for the same thing—in that as present and living species he considers himself to be a *universal* and consequently free being.

The life of the species in man as in animals is physical in that man, (like the animal) lives by inorganic nature. And as man is more universal than the animal, the realm of inorganic nature by which he lives is more universal. As plants, animals, minerals, air, light, etc., in theory form a part of human consciousness, partly as objects of natural science, partly as objects of art—his spiritual inorganic nature or spiritual means of life which he first must prepare for enjoyment and assimilation—so they also form in practice a part of human life and human activity. Man lives physically only by these products of nature; they may appear in the form of food, heat, clothing, housing, etc. The universality of man appears in practice in the universality which makes the whole of nature his *inorganic* body: (1) as a direct means of life, and (2) as the matter, object, and instrument of his life activity. Nature is the *inorganic body* of man, that is, nature insofar as it is not the human body. Man *lives* by nature. This means that nature is his *body* with which he must remain in perpetual process in order not to die. That the physical and spiritual life of man is tied up with nature is another way of saying that nature is linked to itself, for man is a part of nature.

In alienating (1) nature from man, and (2) man from himself, his own active function, his life activity, alienated labor also alienates the *species* from him; it makes *species-life* the means of individual life. In the first place it alienates species-life and the individual life, and secondly it turns the latter in its abstraction into the purpose of the former, also in its abstract and alienated form.[7]

For labor, *life activity*, and *productive life* appear to man at first only as a *means* to satisfy a need, the need to maintain physical existence. Productive life, however, is species-life. It is life begetting life. In the mode of life activity lies the entire character of a species, its species-character; and free conscious activity is the species-character of man. Life itself appears only as a *means of life.*[8]

The animal is immediately one with its life activity, not distinct from it. The animal is *its life activity.* Man makes his life activity itself into an object of will and consciousness. He has conscious life activity. It is not a determination with which he immediately identifies. Conscious life activity distinguishes man immediately from the life activity of the animal. Only thereby is he a species-being. Or rather, he is only a conscious being—that is, his own life is an object for him—since he is a species-being. Only on that account is his activity free activity. Alienated labor reverses the relationship in that man, since he is a conscious being, makes his life activity, his *essence*, only a means for his *existence*.

The practical creation of an *objective world*, the *treatment* of inorganic nature, is proof that man is a conscious species-being, that is, a being which is related to its species as to its own essence or is related to itself as a species-being. To be sure animals also produce. They build themselves nests, dwelling places, like the bees, beavers, ants, etc. But the animal produces only what is immediately necessary for itself or its young. It produces in a one-sided way while man produces universally. The animal produces under the domination of immediate physical need while man produces free of physical need and only genuinely so in freedom from such need. The animal only produces itself while man reproduces the whole of nature. The animal's product belongs immediately to its physical body while man is free when he confronts his product. The animal builds only according to the standard and need of the species to which it belongs while man knows how to produce according to the standard of any species and at all times knows how to apply an intrinsic standard to the object. Thus man creates also according to the laws of beauty.

In the treatment of the objective world, therefore, man proves himself to be genuinely a *species-being.* This production is his active species-life. Through it nature appears as *his* work and his actuality. The object of labor is thus the *objectification of man's species-life:* he produces himself not only intellectually, as in consciousness, but also actively in a real sense and sees himself in a world he made. In taking from man the object of his production, alienated labor takes from his *species-life,* his actual and objective existence as a species. It changes his superiority to the animal to inferiority, since he is deprived of nature, his inorganic body.

By degrading free spontaneous activity to the level of a means, alienated labor makes the species-life of man a means of his physical existence.

The consciousness which man has from his species is altered through alienation, so that species-life becomes a means for him.

(3) Alienated labor hence turns the *species-existence of man,* and also nature as his mental species-capacity, into an existence *alien* to him, into the *means* of his *individual existence.* It alienates his spiritual nature, his *human essence,* from his own body and likewise from nature outside him.

(4) A direct consequence of man's alienation from the product of his work, from his life activity, and from his species-existence, is the *alienation of man* from *man.* When man confronts himself, he confronts *other* men. What holds true of man's relationship to his work, to the product of his work, and to himself, also holds true of man's relationship to other men, to their labor, and the object of their labor.

In general, the statement that man is alienated from his species-existence means that one man is alienated from another just as each man is alienated from human nature.

The alienation of man, the relation of man to himself, is realized and expressed in the relation between man and other men.

Thus in the relation of alienated labor every man sees the others according to the standard and the relation in which he finds himself as a worker.

We began with an economic fact, the alienation of the worker and his product. We have given expression to the concept of this fact: *alienated, externalized* labor. We have analyzed this concept and have thus analyzed merely a fact of political economy.

Let us now see further how the concept of alienated, externalized labor must express and represent itself in actuality.

If the product of labor is alien to me, confronts me as an alien power, to whom then does it belong?

If my own activity does not belong to me, if it is an alien and forced activity, to whom then does it belong?

To a being *other* than myself.

Who is this being?

Gods? To be sure, in early times the main production, for example, the building of temples in Egypt, India, and Mexico, appears to be in the service of the gods, just as the product belongs to the gods. But gods alone were never workmasters. The same is true of *nature*. And what a contradiction it would be if the more man subjugates nature through his work and the more the miracles of gods are rendered superfluous by the marvels of industry, man should renounce his joy in producing and the enjoyment of his product for love of these powers.

The *alien* being who owns labor and the product of labor, whom labor serves and whom the product of labor satisfies can only be *man* himself.

That the product of labor does not belong to the worker and an alien power confronts him is possible only because this product belongs to *a man other than the worker*. If his activity is torment for him, it must be the *pleasure* and the life-enjoyment for another. Not gods, not nature, but only man himself can be this alien power over man.

Let us consider the statement previously made, that the relationship of man to himself is *objective* and *actual* to him only through his relationship to other men. If man is related to the product of his labor, to his objectified labor, as to an *alien*, hostile, powerful object independent of him, he is so related that another alien, hostile, powerful man independent of him is the lord of this object. If he is unfree in relation to his own activity, he is related to it as bonded activity, activity under the domination, coercion, and yoke of another man.

Every self-alienation of man, from himself and from nature, appears in the relationship which he postulates between other men and himself and nature. Thus religious self-alienation appears necessarily in the relation of laity to priest, or also to a mediator, since we are here now concerned with the spiritual world. In the practical real world self-alienation can appear only in the practical real relationships to other men. The means whereby the alienation proceeds is a *practical* means. Through alienated labor man thus not only produces his relationship to the object and to the act of production as an alien man at enmity with him. He also creates the relation in which other men stand to his production and product, and the relation in which he stands to these other men. Just as he begets his own production as loss of his reality, as his punishment; just as he begets his own product as a loss, a product not belonging to him, so he begets the domination of the non-producer over production and over product. As he alienates his own activity from himself, he confers upon the stranger an activity which is not his own.

Up to this point, we have investigated the relationship only from the side of the worker and will later investigate it also from the side of the non-worker.

Thus through *alienated externalized labor* does the worker create the relation to this work of man alienated to labor and standing outside it. The relation of the worker to labor produces the relation of the capitalist to labor, or whatever one wishes to call the lord of labor. *Private property* is thus product, result, and necessary consequence of *externalized labor*, of the external relation of the worker to nature and to himself.

Private property thus is derived, through analysis, from the concept of *externalized labor*, that is, *externalized man*, alienated labor, alienated life, and *alienated* man.

We have obtained the concept of *externalized labor* (*externalized life*) from political economy as a result of the *movement of private property*. But the analysis of this idea shows that though private property appears to be the ground and cause of externalized labor, it is rather a consequence of externalized labor, just as gods are *originally* not the cause but the effect of an aberration of the human mind. Later this relationship reverses.

Only at the final culmination of the development of private property does this, its secret, reappear—namely, that on the one hand it is the *product* of externalized labor and that secondly it is the *means* through which labor externalizes itself, the *realization of this externalization.*

This development throws light on several conflicts hitherto unresolved.

(1) Political economy proceeds from labor as the very soul of production and yet gives labor nothing, private property everything. From this contradiction Proudhon decided in favor of labor and against private property. We perceive, however, that this apparent contradiction is the contradiction of *alienated labor* with itself and that political economy has only formulated the laws of alienated labor.

Therefore we also perceive that *wages* and *private property* are identical: for when the product, the object of labor, pays for the labor itself, wages are only a necessary consequence of the alienation of labor. In wages labor appears not as an end in itself but as the servant of wages. We shall develop this later and now only draw some conclusions.

An enforced *raising of wages* (disregarding all other difficulties, including that this anomaly could only be maintained forcibly) would therefore be nothing but a *better slave-salary* and would not achieve either for the worker or for labor human significance and dignity.

Even the *equality of wages,* as advanced by Proudhon, would only convert the relation of the contemporary worker to his work into the relation of all men to labor. Society would then be conceived as an abstract capitalist.

Wages are a direct result of alienated labor, and alienated labor is the direct cause of private property. The downfall of one is necessarily the downfall of the other.

(2) From the relation of alienated labor to private property it follows further that the emancipation of society from private property, etc., from servitude, is expressed in its *political* form as the *emancipation of workers*, not as though it is only a question of their emancipation but because in their emancipation is contained universal human emancipation. It is contained in their emancipation because the whole of human servitude is involved in the relation of worker to production, and all relations of servitude are only modifications and consequences of the worker's relation to production.

As we have found the concept of *private property* through *analysis* from the concept of *alienated, externalized labor,* so we can develop all the *categories* of political economy with the aid of these two factors, and we shall again find in each category—for example, barter, competition, capital, money—only a *particular* and *developed expression* of these primary foundations.

Before considering this configuration, however, let us try to solve two problems.

(1) To determine the general *nature of private property* as a result of alienated labor in its relation to *truly human* and *social property*.

(2) We have taken the *alienation of labor* and its *externalization* as a fact and analyzed this fact. How, we ask now, does it happen that *man externalizes* his *labor,* alienates it? How is this alienation rooted in the nature of human development? We have already achieved much in resolving the problem by *transforming* the question concerning the *origin of private property* into the question concerning the relationship of *externalized labor* to evolution of humanity. In talking about *private property*

one believes he is dealing with something external to man. Talking of
labor, one is immediately dealing with man himself. This new formulation of the problem already contains its solution.

On (1) *The general nature of private property and its relation to truly
human property.*

We have resolved alienated labor into two parts which mutually determine each other or rather are only different expressions of one and the
same relationship. *Appropriation appears as alienation, as externalization;
externalization as appropriation; alienation as the true naturalization.*

We considered the one side, *externalized* labor, in relation to the *worker*
himself, that is, the *relation of externalized labor to itself.* We have found
the *property relation of the non-worker* to the *worker* and *labor* to be the
product, the necessary result, of this relationship. *Private property* as the
material, summarized expression of externalized labor embraces both
relationships—the *relationship of worker to labor, the product of his work,
and the non-worker;* and the relationship of the *non-worker to the worker*
and *the product of his labor.*

As we have seen that in relation to the worker who *appropriates* nature
through his labor the appropriation appears as alienation—self-activity as
activity for another and of another, living as the sacrifice of life, production of the object as loss of it to an alien power, an *alien* man—we now
consider the relationship of this *alien* man to the worker, to labor and its
object.

It should be noted first that everything which appears with the worker
as an *activity of externalization* and an *activity of alienation* appears with
the non-worker as a *condition of externalization,* a *condition of alienation.*

Secondly, that the *actual, practical attitude* of the worker in production
and to his product (as a condition of mind) appears as a *theoretical*
attitude in the non-worker confronting him.

Thirdly, the non-worker does everything against the worker which the
worker does against himself, but he does not do against his own self what
he does against the worker.

Let us consider more closely these three relationships. [Here the
manuscript breaks off, unfinished.]

Private Property and Communism

The antithesis between *propertylessness* and *property,* however, still remains indifferent, not grasped in its *active connection* with its *internal*
relationship as *contradiction,* so long as it is not understood as the antithesis of *labor* and *capital.* This antithesis can be expressed in the *first*
form even without the advanced development of private property as in

ancient Rome, in Turkey, etc. It does not yet *appear* as instituted by private property itself. But labor, the subjective essence of private property as exclusion of property, and capital, objective labor as the exclusion of labor, is *private property* as its developed relation of contradiction, hence a dynamic relation driving toward resolution.

The overcoming [*Aufhebung*] of self-alienation follows the same course as self-alienation. *Private property* is first considered only in its objective aspect—but still with labor as its essence. Its form of existence is therefore *capital* which is to be overcome "as such" (Proudhon). Or the *particular form* of labor—leveled down, parceled, and thus unfree labor—is taken as the source of the *perniciousness* of private property and its humanly alienated existence. *Fourier*, agreeing with the physiocrats, thus regards *agricultural labor* as being at least *exemplary*, while *Saint-Simon* on the other hand holds *industrial labor* as such to be the essence of labor and thus seeks the *exclusive* predominance of the industrialists and the improvement of the workers' condition. *Communism* is ultimately the *positive* expression of private property as overcome [*aufgehoben*]. Immediately it is *universal* private property. In taking this relation in its *universality* communism is: (1) In its first form only a *universalization* and *completion* of this relationship. As such it appears in a double pattern: On the one hand the domination of *material* property bulks so large that it wants to destroy *everything* which cannot be possessed by everyone as *private property*. It wants to abstract from talent, etc., by *force*. Immediate, physical *possession* is for it the sole aim of life and existence. The condition of the *laborer* is not overcome but extended to all men. The relationship of private property remains the relationship of the community to the world of things. Ultimately this movement which contrasts universal private property to private property is expressed in the animalistic form that *marriage* (surely a *form* of *exclusive private property*) is counterposed to the *community of women* where they become *communal* and *common* property. We might say that this idea of the *community of women* is the *open secret* of this still very crude, unthinking communism. As women go from marriage into universal prostitution, so the whole world of wealth—that is, the objective essence of man—passes from the relationship of exclusive marriage with the private owner into the relationship of universal prostitution with the community. This communism—in that it negates man's *personality* everywhere—is only the logical expression of the private property which is this negation. Universal *envy* establishing itself as a power is only the disguised form in which *greed* reestablishes and satisfies itself in *another* way. The thought of every piece of private property as such is *at the very least* turned against *richer* private property as envy and the desire to level so that envy and the desire to level in fact constitute the essence of competition. Crude communism is only the fulfillment of this envy and leveling on the basis of a *preconceived* minimum. It has a *definite delimited* measure. How little this overcoming of private property is an actual appropriation is shown precisely by the abstract negation of the entire world of culture and civilization, the reversion to the *unnatural* simplicity of the *poor* and wantless man who has not gone beyond private property, has not yet even achieved it.

The community is only a community of *labor* and an equality of *wages* which the communal capital, the *community* as universal capitalist, pays out. Both sides of the relationship are raised to a *supposed* universality—*labor* as the condition in which everyone is put, *capital* as the recognized universality and power of the community.

In the relationship with *woman*, as the spoil and handmaid of communal lust, is expressed the infinite degradation in which man exists for himself since the secret of this relationship has its *unambiguous*, decisive, *plain*, and revealed expression in the relationship of *man* to *woman* and in the way in which the *immediate, natural* species-relationship is conceived. The immediate, natural, necessary relationship of human being to human being is the *relationship* of *man* to *woman*. In this *natural* species-relationship man's relationship to nature is immediately his relationship to man, as his relationship to man is immediately his relationship to nature, to his own *natural* condition. In this relationship the extent to which the human essence has become nature for man or nature has become the human essence of man is *sensuously manifested*, reduced to a perceptible *fact*. From this relationship one can thus judge the entire level of mankind's development. From the character of this relationship follows the extent to which *man* has become and comprehended himself as a *generic being*, as *man;* the relationship of man to woman is the *most natural* relationship of human being to human being. It thus indicates the extent to which man's *natural* behavior has become *human* or the extent to which his *human* essence has become a *natural* essence for him, the extent to which his *human nature* has become *nature* to him. In this relationship is also apparent the extent to which man's *need* has become *human*, thus the extent to which the *other* human being, as human being, has become a need for him, the extent to which he in his most individual existence is at the same time a social being.

The first positive overcoming of private property—*crude* communism—is thus only an *apparent form* of the vileness of private property trying to set itself up as the *positive community*.

(2) Communism (a) still of political nature, democratic or despotic; (b) with the overcoming of the state, but still incomplete and influenced by private property, that is, by the alienation of man. In both forms commu-

nism already knows itself as the reintegration or return of man to himself, as the overcoming of human self-alienation, but since it has not yet understood the positive essence of private property and just as little the *human* nature of needs, it still remains captive to and infected by private property. It has, indeed, grasped its concept but still not its essence.

(3) *Communism* as *positive* overcoming of *private property* as *human self-alienation,* and thus as the actual *appropriation of the human* essence through and for man; therefore as the complete and conscious restoration of man to himself within the total wealth of previous development, the restoration of man as a *social,* that is, human being. This communism as completed naturalism is humanism, as completed humanism it is naturalism. It is the *genuine* resolution of the antagonism between man and nature and between man and man; it is the true resolution of the conflict between existence and essence, objectification and self-affirmation, freedom and necessity, individual and species. It is the riddle of history solved and knows itself as this solution.

The entire movement of history is therefore both its *actual* genesis—the birth of its empirical existence—and also for its thinking awareness the *conceived* and *conscious* movement of its *becoming* whereas the other yet undeveloped communism seeks in certain historical forms opposed to private property a *historical* proof, a proof in what explicitly exists. It thereby tears particular moments out of the movement (Cabet, Villegardelle, etc., particularly ride this horse) and marks them as proofs of its historical pedigree. Thus it makes clear that the far greater part of this movement contradicts its claims and that if it once existed, its *past* existence refutes the pretension of its *essence.*

It is easy to see the necessity that the whole revolutionary movement finds both its empirical as well as theoretical basis in the development of *private property*—in the economy, to be exact.

This *material,* immediately *perceptible* private property is the material, sensuous expression of *alienated human* life. Its movement—production and consumption—is the *sensuous* manifestation of the movement of all previous production, that is, the realization or actuality of man. Religion, family, state, law, morality, science, art, etc., are only *particular* forms of production and fall under its general law. The positive overcoming of *private property* as the appropriation of *human* life is thus the positive overcoming of all alienation and the return of man from religion, family, state, etc., to his *human,* that is, *social* existence. Religious alienation as such occurs only in the sphere of the inner human *consciousness,* but economic alienation belongs to *actual life*—its overcoming thus includes both aspects. It is obvious that the movement has its *first* beginning among different peoples depending on whether their true *acknowledged* life proceeds more in consciousness or in the external world, is more ideal or real. Communism thus begins (*Owen*) with atheism, but atheism is at the beginning still far from being *communism* since it is mostly an *abstraction.**—The philanthropy of atheism is at first therefore only a *philosophical,* abstract philanthropy; that of communism is at once *real* and immediately bent toward *action.*

On the assumption that private property has been positively overcome we have seen how man produces man, himself, and other men; how the object, the immediate activity of his individuality, is at the same time his own existence for other men, their existence, and their existence for him. Similarly, however, both the material of labor and man as subject are equally the result and beginning of the movement (and the historical *necessity* of private property lies precisely in the fact that they must be this *beginning*). Thus is the *social* character the general character of the whole movement; *as* society itself produces *man* as *man,* so it is *produced* by him. Activity and satisfaction [*Genuss*], both in their content and *mode of existence,* are *social, social* activity and *social* satisfaction. The *human* essence of nature primarily exists only for *social* man, because only here is nature a *link* with *man,* as his existence for others and their existence for him, as the life-element of human actuality—only here is nature the *foundation* of man's own *human* existence. Only here has the *natural* existence of man become his *human* existence and nature become human. Thus *society* is the completed, essential unity of man with nature, the true resurrection of nature, the fulfilled naturalism of man and humanism of nature.

Social activity and satisfaction by no means exist *merely* in the form of an *immediate* communal activity and immediate *communal* satisfaction. Nevertheless such activity and satisfaction, expressed and confirmed immediately in *actual association* with other men, will occur wherever that *immediate* expression of sociality is essentially grounded in its content and adequate to its nature.

Even as I am *scientifically* active, etc.—an activity I can seldom pursue in direct community with others—I am *socially* active because I am active as a *man.* Not only is the material of my activity—such as the language in which the thinker is active—given to me as a social product, but my *own* existence *is* social activity; what I make from myself I make for society, conscious of my nature as social.

---

*Prostitution is only a *particular* expression of the *general* prostitution of the *laborer,* and since prostitution is a relationship which includes not only the prostituted but also the prostitutor—whose vileness is still greater—so also the capitalist, etc. falls in this category [Marx's footnote].

My *general* consciousness is only the *theoretical* form of that whose *living* form is the *real* community, the social essence, although at present *general* consciousness is an abstraction from actual life and antagonistically opposed to it. Consequently the *activity* of my general consciousness is thus, as activity, my *theoretical* existence as a social being.

To be avoided above all is establishing "society" once again as an abstraction over against the individual. The individual *is* the *social being.* The expression of his life—even if it does not appear immediately in the form of a *communal* expression carried out together with others—is therefore an expression and assertion of *social life.* The individual and generic life of man are not *distinct,* however much—and necessarily so—the mode of existence of individual life is either a more *particular* or more *general* mode of generic life, or generic life a more *particular* or *universal* mode of individual life.

As *generic consciousness* man asserts his real *social life* and merely repeats his actual existence in thought just as, conversely, generic existence asserts itself in generic consciousness and in its universality exists explicitly as a thinking being. Though man is therefore a *particular* individual—and precisely his particularity makes him an individual, an actual *individual* communal being—he is equally the *totality,* the ideal totality, the subjective existence of society explicitly thought and experienced. Likewise he also exists in actuality both as perception and actual satisfaction of social existence and as a totality of human expression of life.

Thinking and being, to be sure, are thus *distinct* but at the same time in *unity* with one another.

Death seems to be a harsh victory of the species over the particular individual and to contradict the species' unity, but the particular individual is only a *particular generic being* and as such mortal.

(((4) Just as *private property* is only the sensuous expression of the fact that man becomes *objective* for himself and at the same time becomes an alien and inhuman object for himself, that his expression of life is his externalization of life and his realization a loss of reality, an *alien* actuality, so the positive overcoming of private property—that is, the *sensuous* appropriation of the human essence and life, of objective man and of human *works* by and for man—is not to be grasped only as *immediate,* exclusive *satisfaction* or as *possession,* as *having.* Man appropriates to himself his manifold essence in an all-sided way, thus as a whole man. Every one of his *human* relations to the world—seeing, hearing, smelling, tasting, feeling, thinking, perceiving, sensing, wishing, acting, loving—in short, all the organs of his individuality, which are immediately communal in form, are an appropriation of the object in their *objective* relation

[*Verhalten*] or their *relation to it*. This appropriation of *human* actuality and its relation to the object is the *confirmation of human actuality*. It is therefore as varied as are the *determinations* of the human *essence* and *activities.*(It is human *efficacy* and human *suffering*, for suffering, humanly conceived, is a satisfaction of the self in man.)

Private property has made us so stupid and one-sided that an object is *ours* only if we have it, if it exists for us as a capital or is immediately possessed by us, eaten, drunk, worn, lived in, etc., in short, *used;* but private property grasps all these immediate forms of possession only as *means of living*, and the life they serve is the *life* of *private property*, labor, and capitalization.

Hence *all* the physical and spiritual senses have been replaced by the simple alienation of them *all*, the sense of *having*. Human nature had to be reduced to this absolute poverty so that it could give birth to its inner wealth. (On the category of *having*, see *Hess* in *Twenty-one Sheets*.)

The overcoming of private property means therefore the complete *emancipation* of all human senses and aptitudes [*Eigenschaften*], but it means this emancipation precisely because these senses and aptitudes have become *human* both subjectively and objectively. The eye has become a *human* eye, just as its *object* has become a social, *human* object derived from and for man. The *senses* have therefore become *theoreticians* immediately in their *praxis*. They try to relate themselves to their *subject matter* [*Sache*] for its own sake, but the subject matter itself is an *objective human* relation to itself and to man,* and vice versa. Need or satisfaction have thus lost their *egoistic* nature, and nature has lost its mere *utility* by use becoming *human* use.

Similarly the senses and satisfactions of other men have become my *own* appropriation. Besides these immediate organs, *social* organs are therefore developed in the *form* of society; for example, activity in direct association with others, etc., has become an organ of a *life-expression* and a way of appropriating *human* life.

It is obvious that the *human* eye appreciates differently from the crude, inhuman eye, the human *ear* differently from the crude ear, etc.

Only if man's object, we have seen, becomes for him a *human* object or objective man, is he not lost in it. This is possible only when the object becomes *social* and he himself becomes social just as society becomes essential for him in this object.

On the one hand, therefore, it is only when objective actuality generally becomes for man in society the actuality of essential human capacities, human actuality, and thus the actuality of his *own* capacities that all

---

*I can practically relate myself to the subject matter in a human way only if it is itself humanly related to man [Marx's footnote].

objects become for him the *objectification* of himself, become objects which confirm and realize his individuality as *his* objects, that is, *he himself* becomes the object. *How* they become his depends on the *nature* of the *object* and the nature of the *essential capacity* corresponding to *it*, for it is precisely the *determinateness* of this relationship which shapes the particular, *actual* mode of affirmation. For the *eye* an object is different than for the *ear*, and the object of the eye *is* another object than that of the *ear*. The peculiarity of each essential capacity is precisely its *characteristic essence* and thus also the characteristic mode of its objectification, of its *objectively actual*, living *being*. Thus man is affirmed in the objective world not only in thought but with *all* his senses.

On the other hand and from the subjective point of view, as music alone awakens man's musical sense and the most beautiful music has *no* meaning for the unmusical ear—is no object for it, because my object can only be the confirmation of one of my essential capacities and can therefore only be so for me insofar as my essential capacity exists explicitly as a subjective capacity, because the meaning of an object for me reaches only as far as *my* senses go (only makes sense for a corresponding sense)—for this reason the *senses* of social man *differ* from those of the unsocial. Only through the objectively unfolded wealth of human nature is the wealth of the subjective *human* sensibility either cultivated or created—a musical ear, an eye for the beauty of form, in short, *senses* capable of human satisfaction, confirming themselves as essential *human* capacities. For not only the five senses but also the so-called spiritual and moral senses (will, love, etc.), in a word, *human* sense and the humanity of the senses come into being only through the existence of *their* object, through nature *humanized*. The *development* of the five senses is a labor of the whole previous history of the world. *Sense* subordinated to crude, practical need has only a *narrow* meaning.)) For the starving man food does not exist in its human form but only in its abstract character as food. It could be available in its crudest form and one could not say wherein the starving man's eating differs from that of *animals*. The care-laden, needy man has no mind for the most beautiful play. The dealer in minerals sees only their market value but not their beauty and special nature; he has no mineralogical sensitivity. Hence the objectification of the human essence, both theoretically and practically, is necessary to *humanize* man's *senses* and also create a *human sense* corresponding to the entire wealth of humanity and nature.

((Just as the coming society finds at hand all the material for this *cultural development* [*Bildung*] through the movement of *private property*, its wealth as well as its poverty both material and spiritual, *so* the fully *constituted* society produces man in this entire wealth of his being, produces the *rich*, deep, and *entirely sensitive* man as its enduring actuality.))

It is apparent how subjectivism and objectivism, spiritualism and materialism, activity and passivity lose their opposition and thus their existence as antitheses only in the social situation; ((it is apparent how the resolution of *theoretical* antitheses is possible *only* in a *practical* way, only through man's practical energy, and hence their resolution is in no way merely a problem of knowledge but a *real* problem of life which *philosophy* could not solve because it grasped the problem as *only* theoretical.))

((It is apparent how the history of *industry*, industry as *objectively* existing, is the *open* book of *man's essential powers*, the observably present human *psychology*, which has not been thus far grasped in its connection with man's *essential* nature but only in an external utilitarian way because in the perspective of alienation only the general existence of man—religion or history in its abstract-general character as politics, art, literature, etc.—was grasped as the actuality of man's essential powers and his *human generic action*. We have before us the *objectified essential powers* of man in the form of *sensuous, alien, useful objects*—in the form of alienation—in *ordinary material industry* (which can be conceived as a part of that general movement just as that movement can be grasped as a *particular* part of industry since all human activity up to the present has been labor, industry, activity alienated from itself). A *psychology* for which this book, that is, the most observably present and accessible part of history, remains closed cannot become an actual, substantial, and *real* science.)) What indeed should one think of a science which *arbitrarily* abstracts from this large area of human labor and is unaware of its own incompleteness while such an extended wealth of human activity means no more to it than can be expressed in one word—*"need," "common need"*?

The *natural sciences* have become enormously active and have accumulated an ever growing subject-matter. But philosophy has remained as alien to them as they have to it. Their momentary unity was only a *fantastic illusion*. The will was there, but the means were missing. Historiography itself only occasionally takes account of natural science as a moment of enlightenment, utility, some particular great discoveries. But natural science has penetrated and transformed human life all the more *practically* through industry, preparing for human emancipation however much it immediately had to accentuate dehumanization. *Industry* is the *actual* historical relationship of nature, and thus of natural science, to man. If it is grasped as the *exoteric* manifestation of man's *essential powers*, the *human* essence of nature or the *natural* essence of man can also be understood. Hence, natural science will lose its abstract material—or rather idealistic—tendency and become the basis of *human* science as it has already become, though in an alienated form, the basis of actual human life. One basis for life and *another* for *science* is in itself a lie.

((Nature developing in human history—the creation of human society— is the *actual* nature of man; hence nature as it develops through industry, though in an *alienated* form, is true *anthropological* nature.))

Sense perception (see Feuerbach) must be the basis of all science. Science is only *actual* when it proceeds from sense perception in the twofold form of both *sensuous* awareness and *sensuous* need, that is, from nature. The whole of history is a preparation for *"man"* to become the object of *sensuous* awareness and for the needs of "man as man" to become sensuous needs. History itself is an *actual* part of *natural history*, of nature's development into man. Natural science will in time include the science of man as the science of man will include natural science: There will be *one* science.

Man is the immediate object of natural science because immediately *perceptible nature* is for man, immediately, human sense perception (an identical statement) as the *other* man immediately perceptible for him. His own sense perception only exists as human sense perception for himself through the *other* man. But *nature* is the direct object of the *science of man*. The first object for man—man himself—is nature, sense perception; and the particular, perceptible, and essential powers of man can attain self-knowledge only in natural science because they are objectively developed only in *natural* objects. The element of thought itself, the element of the life-expression of thought, *language*, is perceptible nature. The *social* actuality of nature and *human* natural science or the *natural science of man* are identical expressions.

((It is apparent how the *rich man* and wide *human* need appear in place of economic *wealth* and *poverty*. The rich man is simultaneously one who *needs* a totality of human manifestations of life and in whom his own realization exists as inner necessity, as *need*. Not only the *wealth* but also the *poverty* of man equally acquire—under the premise of socialism—a *human* and thus social meaning. It is the passive bond which lets man experience the greatest wealth, the *other* human being, as need. The domination of the objective essence within me, the sensuous eruption of my essential activity, is *emotion* which thereby becomes the *activity* of my nature.))

(5) A *being* only regards himself as independent when he stands on his own feet, and he stands on his own feet only when he owes his *existence* to himself. A man who lives by the favor of another considers himself dependent. But I live entirely by the favor of another if I owe him not only the maintenance of my life but also its *creation*, its *source*. My life necessarily has such an external ground if it is not my own creation. The notion of *creation* is thus very difficult to expel from popular consciousness. For such consciousness the self-subsistence of nature and man is *inconceivable* because it contradicts all the *palpable facts* of practical life.

The creation of the *earth* has been severely shaken by *geognosy* [rather: by *geogony*], the science which presents the formation and development of the earth as a self-generative process. Generatio aequivoca is the only practical refutation of the theory of creation.

It is easy indeed to tell a particular individual what Aristotle said: You were begotten by your father and mother, so in you the mating of two human beings, a generic act of mankind, produced another. You see therefore that man owes even his physical existence to another. Here you must not keep in view only *one* of the two aspects, the *infinite* progression, and ask further, Who begot my father? Who his grandfather? etc. You must also keep in mind the *circular movement* sensibly apparent in that process whereby man reproduces himself in procreation; thus *man* always remains the subject. But you will answer: I grant this circular movement but you must allow the progression which leads even further until I ask, Who created the first man and nature as a whole? I can only answer: Your question is itself a product of abstraction. Ask yourself how you arrive at that question, whether it does not arise from a standpoint to which I cannot reply because it is twisted. Ask yourself whether that progression exists as such for rational thought. If you ask about the creation of nature and man, you thus abstract from man and nature. You assert them as *non-existent* and yet want me to prove them to you as *existing.* I say to you: Give up your abstraction and you will also give up your question. Or if you want to maintain your abstraction, be consistent and if you think of man and nature as *non-existent,* think of yourself as non-existent as you too are nature and man. Do not think, do not question me, for as soon as you think and question, your *abstraction* from the existence of nature and man makes no sense. Or are you such an egoist that you assert everything as nothing and yet want yourself to exist?

You may reply to me: I do not want to assert the nothingness of nature, etc. I only ask about its *genesis* as I ask the anatomist about the formation of bones, etc.

Since for socialist man, however, the *entire so-called world history* is only the creation of man through human labor and the development of nature for man, he has evident and incontrovertible proof of his *self-creation,* his own *formation process.* Since the *essential dependence* of man in nature—man for man as the existence of nature and nature for man as the existence of man—has become practical, sensuous and perceptible, the question about an *alien* being beyond man and nature (a question which implies the unreality of nature and man) has become impossible in practice. *Atheism* as a denial of this unreality no longer makes sense because it is a *negation of God* and through this negation asserts the *existence of man.* But socialism as such no longer needs such mediation. It begins with the *sensuous perception, theoretically and practically,* of man and nature as *essential beings*. It is man's *positive self-consciousness*, no longer attained through the overcoming of religion, just as *actual life* is positive actuality no longer attained through the overcoming of private property, through *communism*. The position of communism is the negation of the negation and hence, for the next stage of historical development, the necessary *actual* phase of man's emancipation and rehabilitation. *Communism* is the necessary form and dynamic principle of the immediate future but not as such the goal of human development—the form of human society.

Critique of Hegelian Dialectic and Philosophy in General

This is perhaps the place at which to make some comments explaining and justifying what has been said about Hegel's dialectic in general, particularly its exposition in the *Phenomenology* [*of Spirit*] and *Logic*, and finally about its relation to the modern critical movement.

Modern German criticism has been so much preoccupied with the past, so much restricted by the development of its subject matter, that it has had a completely uncritical attitude toward methods of criticism and has been completely oblivious to the *seemingly formal* but actually *essential* question: How do we now stand in relation to the Hegelian *dialectic*? This lack of awareness concerning the relation of modern criticism to Hegel's philosophy in general and his dialectic in particular has been so great that critics like *Strauss* and *Bruno Bauer* have been completely entrapped in the Hegelian logic—the former completely and the latter at least implicitly in his [*Critique of the Gospel History of the*] *Synoptics* (where he substitutes the "self-consciousness" of abstract man for the substance of "abstract nature," in opposition to Strauss) and even in his *Revealed Christianity*, where you find, for example: "As though self-consciousness in producing the world did not produce its difference and thereby produce itself in what it produced since it again transcends the distinction between what is produced and itself, since it exists only in this production and movement—as though it should not have its purpose in this movement," etc. Or again: "They (the French materialists) could not yet see that the movement of the universe has only become actual for itself and unified with itself as the movement of self-consciousness." Such expressions not only verbally agree with the Hegelian perspective but reproduce it literally.

How little awareness there was in relation to the Hegelian dialectic during the act of criticism (Bauer, *Synoptics*) and how little this awareness appeared even after the act of substantial criticism is shown by Bauer in his *Good Cause of Freedom* [*and My Own Concern*] when he discusses Herr Gruppe's impertinent question—"What about logic now?"—and refers it to future critics.

But now that *Feuerbach* in his "Theses" appearing in the *Anekdota* and more fully in his [*Principles of the*] *Philosophy of the Future* has destroyed the inner principle of the old dialectic and philosophy, the school of criticism which was unable to do this by itself but has seen it done has proclaimed itself pure, decisive, absolute, and entirely clear with itself. In its spiritual pride it has reduced the entire process of history to the relation between the rest of the world—which falls under the category of "the Mass"—and itself and has reduced dogmatic antitheses into the one between its own cleverness and the stupidity of the world, between the critical Christ and "Humanity" as the *"rabble."* Daily and hourly it has demonstrated its own excellence against the stupidity of the masses and has finally announced the critical *last judgment* to the effect that the day is at hand when the whole of fallen humanity will assemble before it and be divided into groups with each particular mob receiving its testimonium paupertatis. Now that this school of criticism has publicized its superiority to human feelings as well as to the whole world, above which it sits enthroned in sublime solitude, from time to time letting fall from its sarcastic lips the laughter of the Olympian gods—even now after all these entertaining antics of idealism (of Young Hegelianism) expiring in the form of criticism—even now it has not once expressed the suspicion that there must be a reckoning with its own source, the Hegelian dialectic. It has not even indicated a critical relation to Feuerbach's dialectic. This is a procedure with a completely uncritical attitude toward itself.

Feuerbach is the only one who has a *serious, critical* relation to Hegel's dialectic, who has made genuine discoveries in this field, and who above all is the true conqueror of the old philosophy. The magnitude of Feuerbach's achievement and the unpretentious simplicity with which he presents it to the world stand in a strikingly opposite inverse ratio.

Feuerbach's great achievement is: (1) proof that philosophy is nothing more than religion brought to and developed in reflection, and thus is equally to be condemned as another form and mode of the alienation of man's nature;

(2) the establishment of *true materialism* and *real science* by making the social relationship of "man to man" the fundamental principle of his theory;

(3) opposing to the negation of the negation, which claims to be the absolute positive, the self-subsistent positive positively grounded on itself.

Feuerbach explains Hegel's dialectic (and thereby justifies starting out from the positive, from sense certainty) in the following way:

Hegel proceeds from the alienation of substance (logically, from the infinite, abstract universal), from absolute and fixed abstraction—that is, in popular language, he proceeds from religion and theology.

Secondly, he transcends [*hebt auf*] the infinite and posits the actual, the perceptible, the real, the finite, the particular (philosophy, the transcendence of religion and theology).

Thirdly, he then transcends the positive and re-establishes abstraction, the infinite. Re-establishment of religion and theology.

Feuerbach thus views the negation of the negation as *merely* a contradiction of philosophy with itself, as philosophy which affirms theology (the transcendent, etc.) after having denied it, thus affirming it in opposition to itself.

The positing or self-affirmation and self-confirmation in the negation of the negation is taken to be a positing which is still not sure of itself and hence is burdened with its opposite, is still doubtful of itself and hence is in need of proof, and is thus not demonstrated by its own existence and not grasped as a self-justifying position and hence directly and immediately confronts the self-grounded position of sense certainty.

Because Hegel conceived the negation of the negation from the aspect of the positive relation inherent in it as the only true positive, and from the aspect of the negative relation inherent in it as the only true and self-confirming act of all being, he found only the *abstract, logical, speculative* expression of the movement of history, not the *actual* history of man as a given subject but only man's *genesis,* the *history of his origin.* We shall explain both the abstract form of this movement and the difference between this movement as conceived by Hegel and, in contrast, by modern criticism in Feuerbach's *Essence of Christianity,* or rather the *critical* form of this movement which is still uncritical with Hegel.

Let us take a look at Hegel's system. We must begin with his *Phenomenology,* the true birthplace and secret of his philosophy.

Phenomenology

A. Self-consciousness

I. *Consciousness.* (α) Sense certainty or the "this" and *meaning.* (β) *Perception* or the thing with its properties and *illusion.* (γ) Force and understanding, phenomenon and supersensible world.

II. *Self-consciousness.* The truth of self-certainty. (a) Independence and dependence of self-consciousness, lordship and bondage. (b) Freedom of self-consciousness. Stoicism, scepticism, the unhappy consciousness.

III. *Reason.* Certainty and truth of reason. (a) Observational reason; observation of nature and self-consciousness. (b) The realization of rational self-consciousness through itself. Pleasure and necessity. The law of the heart and the frenzy of vanity. Virtue and the way of the world. (c) Individuality which is real in and for itself. The spiritual animal kingdom and deception or the real fact. Law-giving reason. Law-testing reason.

B. Spirit [Geist]

I. True spirit, ethicality. II. Self-alienated spirit, culture. III. Spirit certain of itself, morality.

C. Religion

Natural religion, *religion as art, revealed* religion.

D. Absolute Knowledge

Since Hegel's *Encyclopedia* begins with logic, with *pure speculative thought,* and ends with *absolute knowledge*—with self-consciousness, self-comprehending or absolute, that is, superhuman, abstract mind [*Geist*]— it is altogether nothing but the *expanded essence* of the philosophical mind, its self-objectification. And the philosophical mind is only the alienated world-mind thinking within its self-alienation, that is, comprehending itself abstractly. *Logic*—the *currency* of mind, the speculative *thought-value* of man and nature, their essence indifferent to any actual determinate character and hence unreal—is *thought externalized* and hence *thought* abstracting from nature and actual men. It is *abstract* thinking. The *externality of this abstract thinking . . . nature* as it exists for this abstract thought. Nature is external to it, its self-loss, and is also conceived as something external, as abstract thought but as externalized abstract thought. Finally, [there is] *mind,* thinking which returns to its own birthplace and which as anthropological, phenomenological, psychological, ethical, and artistic-religious is not valid for itself until ultimately it finds itself and relates itself to itself as *absolute* knowledge in the absolute (i.e. abstract) mind containing its conscious and corresponding local existence. For its actual existence is *abstraction.*

Hegel makes a double mistake.

The first appears most clearly in the *Phenomenology,* the birthplace of the Hegelian philosophy. Where Hegel, to be specific, conceives wealth, state power, etc. as entities alienated from *man's* nature, this only happens in their thought form . . . They are thought-entities and hence merely an alienation of *pure,* that is, abstract, philosophical thinking. The whole movement, accordingly, ends with absolute knowledge. It is precisely abstract thought from which these objects are alienated and which they confront with their presumption of actuality. The *philosopher*—himself an abstract form of alienated man—sets himself up as the *measuring rod* of the alienated world. The entire *history of externalization* and the *withdrawal* from externalization is therefore nothing but the *history of the production* of abstract, that is, of absolute, logical, speculative thought. The *alienation* thus forming the real interest and transcendence of this externalization is the opposition of *in itself* and *for itself,* of *consciousness* and *self-consciousness,* of *object and subject*—that is, the opposition within thought itself between abstract thinking and sensuous actuality or actual sensibility. All other contradictions and their movements are only the *appearance,* the *cloak,* the *exoteric* form of these uniquely interesting opposites which constitute the *meaning* of the other profane contradictions. It is not that the human being *objectifies* himself *inhumanly* in opposition to himself, but that he *objectifies* himself by *distinction* from and in *opposition* to abstract thought—this is the essence of alienation as given and as to be transcended. The appropriation of man's essential capacities which have become things, even alien things, is thus primarily only an *appropriation* taking place in *consciousness,* in *pure thought,* that is, in *abstraction.* It is the appropriation of these objects as *thoughts* and *thought processes.* Hence there is already implicit in the *Phenomenology* as a germ, potentiality, and secret—despite its thoroughly negative and critical appearance and despite the actual criticism it contains which often anticipates later developments—the uncritical positivism and equally uncritical idealism of Hegel's later works, the philosophical dissolution and restoration of the existing empirical world.

Secondly, the vindication of the objective world for man—for example, the recognition that *sense* perception is no *abstract* sense perception but *human* sense perception, that religion, wealth, etc., are only the alienated actuality of *human* objectification, of *man's* essential capacities put to work, and therefore are only the *path* to genuine *human* actuality—this appropriation or insight into this process appears in Hegel as the affirmation that *sensuousness, religion,* state power, etc., are *mental* entities since *spirit* alone is the *genuine* essence of man and the true form of spirit is the thinking spirit, the logical, speculative mind. The *human quality* of nature, of nature produced through history, and of man's products appears in their being *products* of abstract spirit and hence phases of *mind, thought-entities.* The *Phenomenology* is thus concealed and mystifying criticism, unclear to itself, but inasmuch as it firmly grasps the *alienation* of man—even though man appears only as mind—*all* the elements of criticism are implicit in it, already *prepared* and *elaborated* in a manner far surpassing the Hegelian standpoint. The sections on the "unhappy consciousness," the "honest consciousness," the struggle between the "noble and base consciousness," etc., etc., contain the *critical* elements—though still in an alienated form—of whole spheres such as religion, the state, civil life, etc. Just as the *entity* or *object* appears as a thought-entity, so is the *subject* always *consciousness* or *self-consciousness;* or rather the object appears only as *abstract* consciousness, man only as *self-consciousness*, and the diverse forms of alienation which make their appearance are therefore only different forms of consciousness and self-consciousness. Since abstract consciousness—the form in which the object is conceived—is *in itself* only a moment of distinction in self-consciousness, the result of the movement is the identity of self-consciousness with consciousness (absolute knowledge) or the movement of abstract thought no longer directed outward but proceeding only within itself. That is to say, the dialectic of pure thought is the result.

The great thing in Hegel's *Phenomenology* and its final result—the dialectic of negativity as the moving and productive principle—is simply that Hegel grasps the self-development of man as a process, objectification as loss of the object, as alienation and transcendence of this alienation; that he thus grasps the nature of *work* and comprehends objective man, authentic because actual, as the result of his *own work.* The *actual,* active relation of man to himself as a species-being or the confirmation of his species-being as an actual, that is, human, being is only possible so far as he actually brings forth all his *species-powers*—which in turn is only possible through the collective effort of mankind, only as the result of history—and treats them as objects, something which immediately is again only possible in the form of alienation.

We shall now indicate in detail Hegel's one-sidedness and limitations in the closing chapter of the *Phenomenology* on absolute knowledge—a chapter containing the pervasive spirit of the whole book, its relation to speculative dialectic, and Hegel's *consciousness* of both and their interrelationship.

Provisionally, let us say this much in advance: Hegel's standpoint is that of modern political economy. He views *labor* as the *essence,* the self-confirming essence of man; he sees only the positive side of labor, not its negative side. Labor is *man's coming-to-be for himself* within *externalization* or as *externalized* man. The only labor Hegel knows and recognizes is *abstract, mental* labor. So that which above all constitutes the *essence* of philosophy—the *externalization of man knowing himself* or *externalized* knowledge *thinking itself*—Hegel grasps as its essence. Therefore, he is able to collect the separate elements of preceding philosophy and present his own as *the* philosophy. What other philosophers did—grasp separate phases of nature and human life as phases of self-consciousness, indeed, abstract self-consciousness—Hegel *knows* from *doing* philosophy. Hence his science is absolute.

Let us now proceed to our subject

Absolute knowledge. The last chapter of the Phenomenology.

The main point is that the *object* of *consciousness* is nothing else but *self-consciousness,* or that the object is only *objectified self-consciousness,* self-consciousness as object. (Assume man = self-consciousness.)

It is a question, therefore, of surmounting the *object of consciousness.* *Objectivity* as such is regarded as an *alienated* human relationship which does not correspond to the *essence of man,* to self-consciousness. *Reappropriation* of the objective essence of man, developed as something alien and determined by alienation, means not only the overcoming of *alienation* but also of *objectivity*—that is, man is regarded as a *non-objective, spiritual* being.

The process of *surmounting the object of consciousness* is described by Hegel as follows:

The *object* does not reveal itself as *returning* into the *self* (for Hegel that is a *one-sided* view of the movement, grasping only one aspect). Man is assumed as equivalent to self. But the self is only man conceived *abstractly,* derived through abstraction. Man is a *self.* His eye, his ear, etc., belong to a *self;* every one of his essential capacities has the quality of *selfhood.* But on that account it is quite false to say that *self-consciousness* has eyes, ears, essential capacities. Self-consciousness is rather a quality of human nature, of the human eye, etc.; human nature is not a quality of *self-consciousness.*

The self, abstracted and fixed for itself, is man as *abstract egoist,* purely abstract *egoism* raised to the level of thought. (We shall return to this later.)

For Hegel *human nature, man,* is equivalent to *self-consciousness.* All alienation of human nature is thus *nothing* but the *alienation of self-consciousness.* The alienation of self-consciousness is not taken to be an expression of the *actual* alienation of human nature reflected in knowledge and thought. *Actual* alienation, that which appears real, is rather in its *innermost* and concealed character (which philosophy only brings to light) only the *appearance* of the alienation of actual human nature, of *self-consciousness.* The science which grasps this is therefore called *phenomenology.* All reappropriation of that alienated objective nature thus appears as an incorporation into self-consciousness. The man who takes possession of his nature is *only* self-consciousness taking possession of its objective nature. Hence the return of the object into the self is its reappropriation.

Expressed *comprehensively*, the *surmounting* of the *object of consciousness* amounts to this: (1) that the object as such presents itself to consciousness as something vanishing; (2) that it is the externalization of self-consciousness which establishes thinghood; (3) that this externalization has not only a *negative* but a *positive* significance as well; (4) that it has this significance not only *for us* or in itself but *for self-consciousness itself;* (5) *for self-consciousness* the negative of the object or its self-transcendence thereby has *positive* significance—*self-consciousness* thus *knows* this negativity of the object—since self-consciousness externalized itself and in this externalization establishes *itself* as object or establishes the object as itself on behalf of the indivisible unity of *being-for-self;* (6) on the other hand, there is also present this other moment in the process, that self-consciousness has transcended and reabsorbed into itself this externalization, this objectivity, and is thus at one with itself in *its* other-being *as such;* (7) this is the movement of consciousness, and consciousness is therefore the totality of its phases; (8) consciousness must similarly have related itself to the object in all its aspects and have grasped the object in terms of each of them. This totality of its aspects gives the object *implicitly* a *spiritual nature,* and it truly becomes this nature for consciousness through the apprehension of every one of these aspects as belonging to the *self* or through what was earlier called the *spiritual* relation to them.

ad (1) that the object as such presents itself to consciousness as something vanishing—this is the *return of the object into the self* mentioned above.

ad (2) the *externalization of self-consciousness* establishes *thinghood.* Since man equals self-consciousness, his externalized objective nature or *thinghood* is equivalent to externalized *self-consciousness* and *thinghood* is established through this externalization. (Thinghood is that which is *an object for man* and an object is truly only for him if it is essential to him and thus his *objective* essence. Since it is not *actual man* and therefore also not *nature*—man being *nature as human*—who as such becomes a subject but only the abstraction of man, self-consciousness, thinghood can only be externalized self-consciousness.) It is entirely to be expected that a living, natural being endowed with objective (i.e. material) capacities should have *real natural objects* corresponding to its nature and also that its self-externalization should establish an *actual* objective world but a world in the form of *externality,* one which does not belong to such a being's nature, an overpowering world. There is nothing incomprehensible or mysterious in this. The contrary, rather, would be mysterious.

But it is equally clear that a *self-consciousness*, that is, its externalization, can only establish *thinghood*, that is, only an abstract thing, a thing of abstraction and no *actual* thing. It is further clear that thinghood thus completely lacks *independence, essentiality*, over and against self-consciousness but is a mere artifice *established* by self-consciousness. And what is established, instead of confirming itself, is only a confirmation of the act of establishing which for a moment, but only a moment, fixes its energy as product and *apparently* gives it the role of an independent, actual nature.

When actual, corporeal *man* with his feet firmly planted on the solid ground, inhaling and exhaling all of nature's energies *establishes* his actual, objective *essential capacities* as alien objects through his externalization, the *establishing* is not the subject but the subjectivity of *objective* capacities whose action must therefore also be *objective*. An objective being acts objectively and would not act objectively if objectivity did not lie in its essential nature. It creates and establishes *only objects because* it is established through objects, because it is fundamentally part of *nature*. In the act of establishing, this objective being does not therefore descend from its "pure activity" to the *creation* of the *object*, but its *objective* product merely confirms its *objective activity*, its activity as that of an objective, natural being.

We see here how a consistent naturalism or humanism is distinguished from both idealism and materialism as well, and at the same time is the unifying truth of both. We also see how only naturalism is able to comprehend the act of world history.

((Immediately, *man* is a *natural being*. As a living natural being he is, in one aspect, endowed with the *natural capacities* and *vital powers* of an *active* natural being. These capacities exist in him as tendencies and capabilities, as *drives*. In another aspect as a natural, living, sentient and objective being man is a *suffering*, conditioned, and limited creature like an animal or plant. The *objects* of his drives, that is to say, exist outside him as independent, yet they are *objects* of his *need*, essential and indispensable to the exercise and confirmation of his *essential capacities*. The fact that man is a *corporeal*, actual, sentient, objective being with natural capacities means that he has *actual, sensuous objects* for his nature as objects of his life-expression, or that he can only *express* his life in actual sensuous objects. *To be* objective, natural, sentient and at the same time have an object, nature, and sense outside oneself or be oneself object, nature, and sense for a third person is one and the same thing.)) *Hunger* is a natural *need;* it thus requires *nature* and an *object* outside itself to be satisfied and quieted. Hunger is the objective need of a body for an *object* existing outside itself, indispensable to its integration and the expression of its nature. The sun is the *object* of the plant, indispensable to it and confirming its life, just as the plant is object for the sun *expressing* its life-awakening, its *objective* and essential power.

A being which does not have its nature outside itself is not a *natural* one and has no part in the system of nature. A being which has no object outside itself is not objective. A being which is not itself an object for a third being has no being for its *object*, that is, is not related objectively, its being is not objective.

An unobjective being is a *nonentity*.

Suppose there is a being which is not an object itself and does not have one. First of all, such a being would be the *only* being; no other being would exist outside of it; it would be solitary and alone. For as soon as there are objects outside of me, as soon as I am not *alone*, I am *another, another actuality* from the object outside me. For this third object I am thus an *other actuality* than it, that is, *its* object. To assume a being which is not the object of another is thus to suppose that *no* objective being exists. As soon as I have an object, it has me for its object. But a *non-objective* being is an unactual, non-sensuous, merely conceived being. It is merely imagined, an abstraction. To be *sensuous* or actual is to be an object of sense or *sensuous* object and thus to have sensuous objects outside oneself, objects of sensibility. To be sentient is to *suffer*.

As an objective sentient being man is therefore a *suffering* being, and since he feels his suffering, he is a *passionate* being. Passion is man's essential capacity energetically bent on its object.

((But man is not only a natural being; he is a *human* natural being. That is, he is a being for himself and hence a *species-being;* as such he must confirm and express himself as much in his being as in his knowing. Accordingly, *human* objects are not natural objects as they immediately present themselves nor is *human* sense immediately and objectively *human* sensibility, human objectivity. Neither objective nor subjective nature is immediately presented in a form adequate to the *human* being.)) And as everything natural must *have its genesis, man* too has his genetic act, *history*, which is for him, however, known and hence consciously self-transcending. History is the true natural history of mankind. (We shall return to this later.)

Thirdly, since this establishment of thinghood is itself only an appearance, an act contradicting the essence of pure activity, it must again be transcended and thinghood must be denied.

ad 3, 4, 5, 6. (3) This externalization of consciousness has not only a *negative* significance but a *positive* significance as well, and (4) it has this positive significance not only *for us* or in itself but for consciousness itself. (5) *For consciousness* the negative of the object or its transcendence of its own self thereby has the *positive* significance or thereby *knows* the nullity of the object by the fact that it externalizes its *own self,* because in this externalization it *knows* itself as object or the object as its own self, serving the indivisible unity of *being-for-self.* (6) On the other hand there is equally present here the other moment or aspect, that consciousness has also transcended and reabsorbed this externalization and objectivity and is thus *at one with itself* in its *other-being as such.*

As we have already seen, the appropriation of alienated, objective being or the transcendence of objectivity in the mode of *alienation*—which must proceed from indifferent otherness to actual, antagonistic alienation—for Hegel means also or primarily the transcendence of *objectivity* since the *objective* character of the object for self-consciousness, not its *determinateness,* is the scandal of alienation. Hence the object is something negative, a self-transcendence, a *nullity.* This nullity of the object has not merely a negative but also a *positive* meaning for consciousness because it is precisely the self-*confirmation* of non-objectivity, of the *abstraction* of itself. For *consciousness itself* this nullity therefore has a positive significance in that it *knows* this nullity, objective being, as its *self-externalization* and knows that it exists only as a result of its self-externalization. . . .

The way in which consciousness is and the way in which something is for it is *knowing.* Knowing is its only act. Hence something comes to exist for consciousness insofar as consciousness *knows* that *something.* Knowing is its sole objective relation. Consciousness knows, then, the nullity of the object (i.e. knows the non-existence of the distinction between object and itself, the non-existence of the object for it) because it knows the object is its *self-externalization;* that is, it knows itself—knowing as object—in that the object is only the *appearance* of an object, a deception, which essentially is nothing but knowing itself which has confronted itself with itself and hence with a *nullity,* with a something which has *no* objectivity outside the knowing. Or, knowing knows that in relating itself to an object it is merely *outside* itself externalized, that *it* only *appears* to *itself* as object or that what appears to it as object is only itself.

On the other hand, says Hegel, there is equally present here the other moment or aspect, that consciousness has also transcended and reabsorbed this externalization and objectivity and thus is *at one with itself* in its *other-being as such.*

All the illusions of speculation are assembled in this discussion.

First, consciousness—self-consciousness—is *at one with itself* in *its other-being as such.* Hence if we here abstract from Hegel's abstraction and replace consciousness with the self-consciousness of man, it is *at one with itself* in its *other-being as such.* This means, for one thing, that consciousness—knowing as knowing, thinking as thinking—claims to be immediately the *other* of itself, sensibility, actuality, life—thought surpassing itself in thought. (Feuerbach.) This aspect is present inasmuch as consciousness as mere consciousness is offended at *objectivity as such,* not alienated objectivity.

Secondly, this implies that self-conscious man, insofar as he has recognized and transcended the spiritual world—or the general spiritual existence of his world—as self-externalization, then reaffirms it in this externalized form and presents it as his authentic existence, reestablishes it, and pretends to be *at one in his other-being as such.* Thus after transcending religion, for example, and recognizing it as a product of self-externalization, he yet finds confirmation of himself in *religion as religion.* Here *is* the root of Hegel's *false* positivism or of his merely *apparent* criticism which Feuerbach noted as the positing, negation, and reestablishment of religion or theology—but which has to be conceived in more general terms. Thus reason is at one with itself in unreason as unreason. Having recognized that man leads an externalized life in law, politics, etc., man leads in this externalized life as such his truly human life. Self-affirmation and self-confirmation in *contradiction* with itself and with the knowledge and essence of the object is thus authentic *knowledge* and authentic *life.*

There can thus no longer be any question about Hegel's accommodation in regard to religion, the state, etc., since this lie is the lie of his principle.

If I *know* that religion is the *externalized* self-consciousness of man, what I know in it as religion is not my self-consciousness but my externalized self-consciousness confirmed in it. Then I know my own self and its essential self-consciousness not as confirmed in *religion* but rather in the *suppression* and *transcendence* of religion.

Thus with Hegel the negation of the negation is not the confirmation of my authentic nature even through the negation of its appearance. It is the confirmation of the apparent or self-alienated nature in its denial— the denial of the apparent nature as objective, as existing outside and independent of man—and its transformation into a subject. *Transcendence,* therefore, has a special role in which *denial* and preservation, denial and affirmation, are bound together.

Thus in Hegel's philosophy of law, for example, *private right* transcended is *morality,* morality transcended is the *family,* the family transcended is *civil society,* civil society transcended is the *state,* and the state transcended is *world history.* In *actuality* private right, morality, the family, civil society, the state, etc., remain in existence only as they have become *moments* or aspects, modes of the particular existence of man, which are meaningless in isolation but mutually dissolve and generate one another. They are *moments of process.*

In their actual existence their *process*-nature is hidden. It first appears and becomes manifest in thought, in philosophy. Hence my authentic religious existence is my existence in *philosophy of religion*, my authentic political existence is my existence in *philosophy of law*, my authentic natural existence is my existence in *philosophy of nature*, my authentic aesthetic existence is my existence in *philosophy of art*, and my authentic human existence is my existence in *philosophy*. Likewise the authentic existence of religion, the state, nature, and art is the *philosophy* of religion, of the state, of nature, and of art. But if the philosophy of religion, etc., is for me the only authentic existence of religion, I am only truly religious as a *philosopher of religion* and hence I deny *actual* religious feeling and the actually *religious* man. But at the same time I *assert* them, partly in my own particular existence or in the alien existence which I oppose to them—for this *is* only their *philosophical* expression—and partly in their particular original form, since for me they mean only the *apparent* other-being as allegories, forms of their own authentic existence concealed in sensuous coverings, that is, forms of my *philosophical* existence.

In the same way, *quality* transcended is *quantity*, quantity transcended is *magnitude*, magnitude transcended is *essence*, essence transcended is *phenomenon*, phenomenon transcended is *actuality*, actuality transcended is the *concept*, the concept transcended is *objectivity*, objectivity transcended is *absolute Idea*, the absolute Idea transcended is *nature*, nature transcended is *subjective* spirit, subjective spirit transcended is the *ethical* objective Spirit, the ethical objective Spirit transcended is *art*, art transcended is *religion*, and religion transcended is *absolute Knowledge*.

On the one hand this transcendence is transcendence of a thought-entity; thus private property as *thought* is transcended in the *thought* of morality. And because thought imagines itself to be immediately the other of itself or *sensuous actuality*—thus taking its own action for *actual, sensuous* action—this transcendence in thought which leaves its object intact in actuality believes it has actually overcome it. On the other hand, the object, having become a moment of thought for this transcendence, hence also becomes in its actuality a self-confirmation of the same transcendence, of self-consciousness, of abstraction.

From one aspect, the particular existence which Hegel *transcends* in philosophy is therefore not *actual* religion, not the *actual* state, and not *actual* nature but religion as already an object of knowledge, that is, *dogmatics*. (Similarly with *jurisprudence*, *political science*, and *natural science*.) In this respect he thus opposes both the *actual* nature of the object and the immediate unphilosophical *knowledge*—the unphilosophical concepts—of that nature. He therefore contradicts conventional *concepts.*

From the other aspect, the religious man, etc., can find his ultimate justification in Hegel.

Now the *positive* moments or aspects of the Hegelian dialectic—within the category of alienation—must be considered.

(a) *Transcendence* as an objective movement *reabsorbing* externalization into itself.—((This is the insight into the *appropriation* of objective being, expressed within alienation, through the transcendence of its alienation. It is the alienated insight into the *actual objectification* of man and into the actual appropriation of his objective nature by the destruction of the *alienated* character of the objective world, by the transcendence of the objective world in its alienated existence, just as atheism which transcends God is the emergence of theoretical humanism, and communism which transcends private property is the vindication of actual human life as man's property, the emergence of practical humanism. Or, atheism is humanism mediated through itself by the transcendence of religion, and communism is humanism mediated through itself by the transcendence of private property. Only through the transcendence of this mediation—which is, however, a necessary presupposition—emerges *positive* humanism, humanism emerging positively from itself.))

But atheism and communism are no flight from, no abstraction from, no loss of the objective world created by man as his essential capacities objectified. They are no impoverished return to unnatural, primitive simplicity. Rather they are primarily the actual emergence and the actual, developed realization of man's nature as something actual.

In grasping the *positive* significance of self-referring negation—even if again in an alienated way—Hegel thus grasps man's self-alienation, the externalization of his nature, his loss of objectivity and actualization as finding of self, expression of his nature, objectification, and realization. ((In short, he grasps labor, within the realm of abstraction, as man's *act of self-creation,* his relation to himself as something alien, and the manifestation of his developing *species-consciousness* and *species-life* as something alien.))

(b) But in Hegel—apart from or rather as a result of the inversion already described—this act of self-creation appears, first, as *merely formal* because it is abstract and because human nature itself is viewed only as *abstract,* as *thinking,* as self-consciousness.

Secondly, since the conception is *formal* and *abstract,* the transcendence of externalization affirms the externalization. Or, for Hegel the process of *self-creation* and *self-objectification* in the form of *self-externalization and self-alienation* is the *absolute* and hence final *expression of human life* which has itself as its goal, is at peace with itself, and is at one with its essence.

This movement in its abstract form as dialectic is therefore regarded as *authentic human life*, and since it is still an abstraction, an alienation of human life, it is regarded as a *divine process* and hence the divine process of mankind—a process carried out by man's abstract, pure, absolute nature as distinguished from himself.

Thirdly: This process must have a bearer, a subject. But the subject only emerges as a result—namely, the subject knowing itself as absolute self-consciousness which is therefore *God, Absolute Spirit, the self-knowing and self-manifesting Idea.* Actual man and actual nature become merely predicates or symbols of this concealed, unreal man and nature. Hence subject and predicate are absolutely inverted in relation to each other. There is a *mystical subject-object* or a *subjectivity passing beyond the object,* the *absolute subject* as a *process* of self-*externalization* and returning from this externalization into itself but at the same time reabsorbing it into itself. And there is the subject as this process—a pure, restless revolving within itself.

First, the *formal and abstract* conception of man's act of self-creation or self-objectification.

With Hegel's identification of man and self-consciousness, the alienated object or alienated essence of man is nothing but *consciousness,* merely the thought of alienation, its *abstract* and hence empty and unreal expression, *negation.* The transcendence of externalization is thus also nothing but an abstract, empty transcendence of that empty abstraction, the *negation of the negation.* The rich, living, sensuous, concrete activity of self-objectification therefore becomes its mere abstraction, *absolute negativity,* an abstraction fixed as such and regarded as independent activity, as activity itself. Since this so-called negativity is only the *abstract, empty* form of that real living act, its content can only be *formal,* derived by abstraction from all content. Hence there are general, abstract *forms of abstraction*—thought forms and logical categories detached from *actual* spirit and *actual* nature—pertaining to any content and indifferent to all and valid for every content. (We shall develop the *logical* content of absolute negativity later.)

Hegel's positive achievement here (in his speculative logic) is his view that *determinate concepts,* universal *fixed thought-forms* independent of nature and spirit, are a necessary result of the universal alienation of human nature and human thought. Hegel has collated and presented

them as moments of the abstraction process. For example, Being transcended is Essence, Essence transcended is Concept, Concept transcended . . . Absolute Idea. But what, then, is the Absolute Idea? It must
again transcend its own self unless it wants to go through once more
from the beginning the whole movement of abstraction and remain content with being a collection of abstractions or a self-comprehending
abstraction. But a self-comprehending abstraction knows itself to be
nothing; it must abandon itself as abstraction to arrive at something
which is its exact opposite, *nature*. Hence the entire Logic is proof that
abstract thought is nothing for itself, that the Absolute Idea is nothing for
itself, and only *nature* is something.

The Absolute Idea, the *Abstract Idea* which "considered in its unity
with itself is *intuiting*" [*Anschauen*] (Hegel's *Encyclopedia*, 3rd ed., p. 222
[¶ 244]) and which "in its own absolute truth *decides* to let the moment
of its particularity or of initial determination and other-being, the *immediate idea* as its reflection, freely *proceed from itself* as *nature*" (*ibid.*)—this
entire Idea which behaves in such a peculiar and extravagant way and has
given the Hegelians such terrible headaches is from beginning to end
nothing but *abstraction*, that is, the abstract thinker. It is abstraction
which, wise from experience and enlightened concerning its truth, decides under various conditions, themselves false and still abstract, to
release itself and establish its other-being, the particular, and the determinate, in place of its oneness with itself, non-being, universality, and
indeterminateness. It decides to let *nature*, which it hid within itself as a
mere abstraction or thought entity, *proceed freely from itself*—that is, it
decides to forsake abstraction and for once pay attention to nature *free* of
abstraction. The abstract idea which becomes unmediated *intuiting* is
through and through nothing but abstract thought abandoning itself and
deciding on *intuition*. This entire transition from Logic to Philosophy of
Nature is nothing but the transition from *abstracting* to *intuiting*, very
difficult for the abstract thinker and hence so quixotically described by
him. The *mystical* feeling which drives a philosopher from abstract
thinking to intuiting is *boredom*, the longing for a content.

(Man alienated from himself is also the thinker alienated from his
nature, that is, from his natural and human essence. Hence his thoughts
are fixed, ghostly spirits outside nature and man. Hegel has imprisoned
all these spirits together in his Logic, conceiving each of them first as
negation, as *externalization* of *human* thought, and then as the negation
of the negation, the transcendence of this externalization as *actual* externalization of human thought. But since this negation of the negation is
still itself imprisoned in alienation, it partly re-establishes these fixed

spirits in their alienation and partly halts at the last step of alienation, self-reference, as their authentic existence.* Insofar as this abstraction apprehends itself and experiences an infinite boredom with itself, Hegel abandons abstract thinking moving solely within thinking—without eyes, teeth, ears, everything—as he decides to recognize *nature* as essential being and devote himself to intuition.)

But *nature* too, taken abstractly, for itself, and fixedly isolated from man, is *nothing* for man. It is obvious that the abstract thinker who has committed himself to intuiting, intuits nature abstractly. As nature lay enclosed in the thinker as absolute Idea, as a *thought-entity* in a form hidden and mysterious to the thinker himself, what he has in truth let proceed from himself was only this *abstract nature*, only nature as a thought-entity, but now with the significance of the other-being of thought, actual and perceived nature distinguished from abstract thought. Or, to speak in human terms, the abstract thinker perceives in his intuition of nature that the entities he thought he was creating out of nothing from pure abstraction, in a divine dialectic as pure products of the labor of thought weaving within itself and never perceiving outward actuality—these entities he thought he was creating are merely *abstractions* from *nature's characteristics*. The whole of nature thus only repeats logical abstractions to him in a sensuous, external form.—He again *analyzes* nature and these abstractions. His intuition of nature is thus only the act of confirming his abstraction by the intuition of nature, his conscious re-enactment of the process of producing his abstraction. Thus, for example, Time is its own self-related Negativity (*loc. cit.*, p. 238). To Becoming transcended as particular Being there corresponds, in natural form, Movement transcended as Matter. In *natural* form Light is *Reflection-in-itself.* Body as *Moon* and *Comet* is the *natural*

---

*That is, Hegel puts in place of these fixed abstractions the act of abstraction revolving within itself. He has thereby performed the service, in the first place, of having indicated the source of all these inappropriate concepts originally belonging to different philosophies, of having brought them together, and of having created the entire range of abstraction rather than some specific abstraction as the object of criticism. (Later we shall see why Hegel separates thinking from *subject.* But now it is already clear that if man is not human, his characteristic externalization cannot exist and hence thinking itself could not be viewed as the characteristic externalization of man as a human and natural subject with eyes, ears, etc., living in society, the world, and nature.) [Marx's parenthetical remark within the paragraph of the manuscript.]

form of the *opposition* which the Logic on one side calls the *positive grounded on itself* and on the other, the *negative* grounded on itself. The Earth is the *natural* form of the logical *ground* as the negative unity of the opposition, etc.

Nature as nature, that is, so far as it is sensuously distinguished from that secret meaning hidden within it, nature separated and distinguished from these abstractions, is *nothing*, a *nothing proving* itself to be *nothing*. It is *meaningless* or only means an externality which has been transcended.

"In the finite-*teleological* point of view is to be found the correct premise that nature does not contain in itself the absolute end or purpose" (p. 225 [¶ 245]). Its purpose is the confirmation of abstraction. "Nature has revealed itself as the Idea in the *form* of *other-being*. Since the *Idea* in this form is the negative of itself or *outside itself,* nature is not just relatively outside this Idea [. . .] but *externality* determines how it exists as nature" (p. 227 [¶ 247]).

Externality is not to be understood here as *self-externalizing sensuousness* open to the light and to the *sensibility* of sensuous man. It is here to be taken as externalization, error, a defect which ought not be. For what is true is still the Idea. Nature is only the *form* of the *other-being* of the Idea. And since abstract thought is the *essence* of things, something external to it is in essence merely *external.* The abstract thinker also recognizes that *sensuousness, externality* as distinguished from thought weaving *within itself,* is the essence of nature. But at the same time he expresses this distinction in such a way as to make this *externality of nature*, its *contrast* to thought, its *defect.* And inasmuch as nature is distinct from abstraction it is something defective. Something which is defective not only for me, in my eyes, but also in itself has something outside itself which it lacks. That is to say, its essence is something other than itself. For the abstract thinker nature must consequently transcend itself since it is already promulgated by him as a potentially *transcended* existence.

"For us, Spirit has *nature* as its *presupposition* since it is nature's *truth* and hence its *absolute prius.* In this truth nature has *disappeared* and Spirit has yielded to the Idea as Being-for-itself whose *object* as well as *subject* is the *Concept.* This identity is *absolute negativity* because in nature the Concept has its complete external objectivity but here its externalization has been transcended and in this transcendence the Concept has become self-identical. It is this identity only in being a return from nature" (p. 392 [¶ 381]).

"Revelation, as the *abstract* idea, is unmediated transition, the *becoming*

of nature; as revelation of Spirit which is free it *establishes* nature as *its own* world. This establishing as reflection is likewise the *presupposition* of the world as independently existing nature. Revelation conceptually is the creation of nature as Spirit's own being in which Spirit gives itself the *affirmation* and *truth* of its freedom." "The *Absolute is Spirit;* this is the highest definition of the Absolute" [¶ 384].

Theses on Feuerbach

Karl Marx

For those who see a sharp rupture between the young, still Feuerbachian pre-Marxism Marx and the mature Marx of historical materialism, the crucial period is from the summer of 1844 to the spring of 1845. The document that is taken as the indication of the final break with his Hegelian and Feuerbachian past is the "Theses on Feuerbach." For those who tend to see a more continuous line of development in Marx, the theses are seen as a statement of the final integration of Hegel's idealism and Feuerbach's materialism that Marx had been working towards. These notes in the form of eleven aphorisms were written down around March or April of 1845, after Marx had left Paris for Brussels. Engels later described the theses as containing "the brilliant germ of a new world-view." They were first published by Engels in 1888 as an appendix to his Ludwig Feuerbach and the End of Classical German Philosophy.

The theses represent Marx's attempt to distance himself from Feuerbachian materialism and to articulate a form of materialism that is distinctively different from "all previous materialism," which he finds wanting. Prior materialism has been too passive and ahistorical. What needs to be done is infuse materialism with the central Hegelian insight discussed in the Economic and Philosophic Manuscripts, *namely, the notion of human history as a process of active self-making. That is, humans have to be understood in terms of "sensuous human activity," the chief form of which is, of course, labor. As Marx says, "The coincidence of the change of circumstances and of human activity or self-change can be comprehended and rationally understood only as revolutionary practice."*

The philosophical problems of freedom and the self that reside at the core of Hegelian idealism can be resolved only by properly understanding the materialist basis of human self-making. "All mysteries which lead theory to mysticism find their rational solution in human practice and the comprehension of this practice." Once we realize this point, we can see that the solution to the philosophical problem of freedom lies in controlling the material conditions under which we make our history and ourselves. Marx concludes these thoughts, then, with what may be his most famous thought. "The philosophers have only interpreted the world in various ways; the point is, to change it."

The following theses are translated from the German by Loyd D. Easton and Kurt H. Guddat.

(1)

The chief defect of all previous materialism (including Feuerbach's) is that the object, actuality, sensuousness is conceived only in the form of the *object or perception* [*Anschauung*], but not as *sensuous human activity, practice* [*Praxis*], not subjectively. Hence in opposition to materialism the *active* side was developed by idealism—but only abstractly since idealism naturally does not know actual, sensuous activity as such. Feuerbach wants sensuous objects actually different from thought objects: but he does not comprehend human activity itself as *objective*. Hence in *The Essence of Christianity* he regards only the theoretical attitude as the truly human attitude, while practice is understood and fixed only in its dirtily Jewish form of appearance. Consequently he does not comprehend the significance of "revolutionary," of "practical-critical" activity.

(2)

The question whether human thinking can reach objective truth—is not a question of theory but a *practical* question. In practice man must prove the truth, that is, actuality and power, this-sidedness of his thinking. The dispute about the actuality or non-actuality of thinking—thinking isolated from practice—is a purely *scholastic* question.

(3)

The materialistic doctrine concerning the change of circumstances and education forgets that circumstances are changed by men and that the educator must himself be educated. Hence this doctrine must divide society into two parts—one of which towers above [as in Robert Owen, Engels added].

The coincidence of the change of circumstances and of human activity or self-change can be comprehended and rationally understood only as *revolutionary practice*.

(4)

Feuerbach starts out from the fact of religious self-alienation, the duplication of the world into a religious and secular world. His work consists in resolving the religious world into its secular basis. But the fact that the secular basis becomes separate from itself and establishes an independent realm in the clouds can only be explained by the cleavage and self-contradictoriness of the secular basis. Thus the latter must itself be both understood in its contradiction and revolutionized in practice. For instance, after the earthly family is found to be the secret of the holy family, the former must then be theoretically and practically nullified.

(5)

Feuerbach, not satisfied with *abstract thinking,* wants *perception;* but he does not comprehend sensuousness as *practical,* human-sensuous activity.

(6)

Feuerbach resolves the religious essence into the *human* essence. But the essence of man is no abstraction inhering in each single individual. In its actuality it is the ensemble of social relationships.

Feuerbach, who does not go into the criticism of this actual essence, is hence compelled

1. to abstract from the historical process and to establish religious feeling as something self-contained, and to presuppose an abstract— *isolated*—human individual;

2. to view the essence of man merely as "species," as the inner, dumb generality which unites the many individuals *naturally.*

(7)

Feuerbach does not see, consequently, that "religious feeling" is itself a social product and that the abstract individual he analyzes belongs to a particular form of society.

(8)

All social life is essentially *practical.* All mysteries which lead theory to mysticism find their rational solution in human practice and the comprehension of this practice.

(9)

The highest point attained by perceptual materialism, that is, materialism that does not comprehend sensuousness as practical activity, is the view of separate individuals and civil society.

(10)

The standpoint of the old materialism is civil society; the standpoint of the new is human society or socialized humanity.

(11)

The philosophers have only *interpreted* the world in various ways; the point is, to *change* it.

II.

WRITINGS ON
HISTORICAL
MATERIALISM

The German Ideology

Part I

(selections)

Karl Marx and Friedrich Engels

In April of 1845, Engels moved to Brussels to join Marx. That summer the two travelled to England to study economic theory and to make connections with German workers' groups in London. Upon their return to Brussels, they undertook a joint work, their first, which had two chief aims: negatively, to criticize and "settle accounts with" various of their erstwhile Young Hegelian colleagues and clarify how their newly emerging views differed from the "ideologies" of these others; and positively, to develop their own materialist theory of history. Their main targets were Bauer, Feuerbach, Max Stirner, and Karl Grun and the so-called true or utopian socialists. The result of their efforts, which lasted through the summer of 1846, was a manuscript of about five hundred pages. The long second and third parts of the work consist largely of satirical polemics against their opponents, especially Stirner, who had recently published The Ego and Its Own, *in which Marx and Engels had been criticized. These parts are little read today. The first part, however, which ostensibly is a critique of Feuerbach but, more important, is the first systematic exposition of historical materialism, is one of the most influential of all of Marx's writings. The work was never published in their lifetimes, however. As Marx wrote in the Preface to "A Contribution to the Critique of Political Economy,"[1] the second and third parts of the manuscript had "reached the publishers in Westphalia when we were informed that owing to changed circumstances it could not be printed. We abandoned the manuscript to the gnawing criticism of the mice all the more willingly since we had achieved our main purpose—self-clarification." It was published for the first time in 1932.*

In Part I of The German Ideology, *Marx and Engels attempt to clarify at greater length than previously how their theory of history differs from that of Feuerbachian materialism, on the one hand, and Hegelian idealism, on the other. Their view "is not devoid of premises. It proceeds from real premises and does not abandon them for a moment. These premises are men, not in any fantastic isolation and fixation, but in their real, empirically perceptible process of development under certain conditions. . . . Where speculation ends, namely in actual life, there real, positive science begins as the representation of*

1. See p. 209 below.

*the practical activity and practical process of the development of men." From
this beginning point, they describe the theoretical process of accounting for
the development of social institutions, including the state and the realm of
culture and ideas, and outline the nature of historical evolution. All social
institutions and practices are to be understood in terms of the prevailing
material conditions. Consciousness, or ideology, is a reflection of material
relations, in particular, the relations of production. Thus, to understand
contemporary German philosophy and law, one must understand the rise of
manufacturing, the division of labor, trade relations, and other factors shaping economic life. Important remarks about communism are also scattered
through the manuscript.*

Part I of The German Ideology *was never finished and was put aside
when the plans for publishing the second and third parts fell through. It
does not, then, represent a polished work, and important themes are not systematically developed. Also, compared to later writings of Marx on history,
this work clearly suffers from a lack of the detailed knowledge of history
that Marx would acquire in the 1850's. Nonetheless, all of the major points
of historical materialism are in* The German Ideology, *if not in a fully
worked-out form, and the importance of the document cannot be denied.*

Preface

Until now men have constantly had false conceptions of themselves,
about what they are or what they ought to be. They have related themselves to one another in conformity with their ideas of God, of normal
man, etc. The phantoms of their imagination have gotten too big for
them. They, the creators, have been bowing to their creations. Let us
liberate them from their chimeras, from their ideas, dogmas, imaginary
beings, under whose yoke they are languishing. Let us rebel against the
rule of thoughts. Let us teach man, says one person, to exchange these
imaginings for thoughts that correspond to man's essence; let us teach
man to be critical toward them, says another; let us teach man to get rid
of them altogether, says a third. Then—existing reality will collapse.

Such innocent and childlike fantasies make up the core of recent
Young-Hegelian philosophy which not only is received with horror and
awe by the German public, but is also propounded by the *philosophic*

This selection is the first part of *The German Ideology* as translated from the
German by Loyd D. Easton and Kurt H. Guddat.

heroes themselves with a ceremonious consciousness of its cataclysmic dangerousness and criminal disregard. The first volume of the present publication attempts to unmask these sheep who consider themselves and are taken to be wolves, to show how their bleating only follows in philosophy the conceptions of the average German citizen, to indicate how the boasting of these philosophic exegetes simply mirrors the wretchedness of actual conditions in Germany. This publication aims to debunk and discredit that philosophic struggle with shadows of reality which so appeals to the dreamy, drowsy German people.

A clever fellow once got the idea that people drown because they are possessed by the *idea of gravity*. If they would get this notion out of their heads by seeing it as religious superstition, they would be completely safe from all danger of water. For his entire life he fought against the illusion of gravity while all statistics gave him new and abundant evidence of its harmful effects. That kind of fellow is typical of the new revolutionary philosophers in Germany.

I. *Feuerbach: Opposition of Materialistic and Idealistic Outlook*[*]

German ideologists say that Germany experienced an unprecedented revolution during the past few years. The decomposition of the Hegelian philosophy that began with Strauss developed into a ferment of worldwide proportions affecting all "powers of the past." Gigantic empires grew in the general chaos, only to decline again. Heroes emerged momentarily, only to be hurled back again into obscurity by bolder and mightier rivals. The French Revolution was child's play in comparison with this revolution which dwarfs even that of the Diadochi [successors of Alexander the Great]. Principles ousted one another with unprecedented speed. Heroes of the mind speedily overthrew one another, and in three years, 1842–45, more of the past was swept away in Germany than in three centuries at other periods.

All this is said to have happened in the realm of pure thought.

We are certainly dealing with an interesting phenomenon: the rotting away of absolute Spirit. Its last spark having failed, the various components of this caput mortuum began to decompose, entered into new compounds, and formed new substances. The industrialists of philosophy, having lived off the exploitation of absolute Spirit, then seized on the compounds. Each of them retailed his share with all possible zeal.

[*Title in the elder Engels's handwriting on the last manuscript page of Part I.]

Competition had to arise, and in the beginning it was rather bourgeois and traditional. Later when the German market was glutted and the commodity could not be sold on the world market despite all efforts, business was spoiled in typically German fashion by mass production or pseudo-production, by a lowering of quality, adulteration of raw materials, falsification of labels, fictitious purchases, bill-jobbing, and a credit system lacking any real basis. The competition turned into bitter fighting, which is now interpreted and extolled as a revolution of world-historical significance and as producing the most tremendous results and achievements. If we are to recognize fully this philosophical charlatanry which awakens even in the breast of the honest German citizen a warm feeling of national pride, and if we are to point out the pettiness, the parochial narrow-mindedness of the entire Young-Hegelian movement, and particularly the tragicomical contrast between the actual accomplishments of these heroes and the illusions they have about their achievements, we have to examine the whole spectacle from a standpoint outside of Germany.

A. Ideology in General, Particularly German Ideology

Right up to its most recent efforts, German criticism never left the realm of philosophy. Far from examining its general philosophic premises, all of its inquiries were based on one philosophical system, that of Hegel. There was mystification not only in the answers but also even in the questions themselves. This dependence on Hegel is the reason why none of these modern critics even attempted a comprehensive criticism of the Hegelian system, though each of them claimed to have gone beyond Hegel. Their polemics against Hegel and against one another are rather limited. Each critic picks one aspect of the Hegelian system and applies it to the entire system as well as to the aspects chosen by other critics. In the beginning they took up pure and unfalsified Hegelian categories such as "Substance" or "Self-consciousness." Later they desecrated such categories by giving them more mundane names such as "Species," "the Unique," "Man," etc.

All German philosophical criticism from Strauss to Stirner is confined to criticism of *religious* conceptions. The critics proceeded from real religion and actual theology. As they went on, they determined in various ways what constitutes religious consciousness and religious conceptions. Their progress consisted of their subsuming the allegedly dominant metaphysical, political, juridical, moral, and other concepts under the class of religious or theological concepts. Similarly, they declared political, juridical, and moral consciousness to be religious or theological consciousness, and the political, juridical, and moral man, *"Man"* in the last resort, to be religious. They presupposed the governance of religion. Gradually every dominant relationship was held to be religious and made into a cult, such as the cult of law, the cult of state, etc. Eventually there was nothing but dogmas and belief in dogmas. The world was more and more sanctified until our honorable Saint Max [Stirner] was able to sanctify it en bloc and dismiss it once for all.

The Old Hegelians had *comprehended* everything once they reduced it to a Hegelian logical category. The Young Hegelians *criticized* everything by imputing religious conceptions to it or declaring everything to be theological. The Young Hegelians are in agreement with the Old Hegelians in believing in the governance of religion, concepts, a universal principle in the existing world. But one party attacks this governance as usurpation while the other party praises it as legitimate.

Since the Young Hegelians regard concepts, thoughts, ideas, and all products of consciousness, to which they give independent existence, as the real fetters of man—while the Old Hegelians pronounced them the true bonds of human society—it is obvious that the Young Hegelians have to fight only against the illusions of consciousness. In the Young Hegelians' fantasies the relationships of men, all their actions, their chains, and their limitations are products of their consciousness. Consequently they give men the moral postulate of exchanging their present consciousness for human, critical or egoistic consciousness to remove their limitations. This amounts to a demand to interpret what exists in a different way, that is, to recognize it by means of a different interpretation. The Young-Hegelian ideologists are the staunchest conservatives, despite their allegedly "world-shaking" statements. The most recent among them have found the correct expression for their doings in saying they are fighting only against *"phrases."* They forget, however, that they fight them only with phrases of their own. In no way are they attacking the actual existing world; they merely attack the phrases of this world. The only results this philosophic criticism could achieve were some elucidations on Christianity, one-sided as they are, from the point of view of religious history. All their other assertions are only further embellishments of their basic claim that these unimportant elucidations are discoveries of world-historical significance.

Not one of these philosophers ever thought to look into the connection between German philosophy and German reality, between their criticism and their own material environment.

1. Ideology in General, Especially German Philosophy.[*] ((We know only one science, the science of history. History can be viewed from two sides: it can be divided into the history of nature and that of man. The two sides, however, are not to be seen as independent entities. As long as man has existed, nature and man have affected each other. The history of nature, so-called natural history, does not concern us here at all. But we will have to discuss the history of man, since almost all ideology amounts to either a distorted interpretation of this history or a complete abstraction from it. Ideology itself is only one of the sides of this history.))

The premises from which we start are not arbitrary; they are no dogmas but rather actual premises from which abstraction can be made only in imagination. They are the real individuals, their actions, and their material conditions of life, those which they find existing as well as those which they produce through their actions. These premises can be substantiated in a purely empirical way.

The first premise of all human history, of course, is the existence of living human individuals. ((The first *historical* act of these individuals, the act by which they distinguish themselves from animals is not the fact that they think but the fact that they begin to *produce their means of subsistence*.)) The first fact to be established, then, is the physical organization of these individuals and their consequent relationship to the rest of nature. Of course, we cannot discuss here the physical nature of man or the natural conditions in which man finds himself—geological, orohydrographical, climatic, and others. ((These relationships affect not only the original and natural organization of men, especially as to race, but also his entire further development or non-development up to the present.)) All historiography must proceed from these natural bases and their modification in the course of history through the actions of men.

Man can be distinguished from the animal by consciousness, religion, or anything else you please. He begins to distinguish himself from the animal the moment he begins to *produce* his means of subsistence, a step required by his physical organization. By producing food, man indirectly produces his material life itself.

The way in which man produces his food depends first of all on the nature of the means of subsistence that he finds and has to reproduce. This mode of production must not be viewed simply as reproduction of the physical existence of individuals. Rather it is a definite form of their activity, a definite way of expressing their life, a definite *mode of life*. As

[*This heading and subsequent material within double parentheses crossed out in the manuscript.]

individuals express their life, so they are. What they are, therefore, coincides with what they produce, with *what* they produce and *how* they produce. The nature of individuals thus depends on the material conditions which determine their production.

This production begins with *population growth* which in turn presupposes *interaction* [*Verkehr*] among individuals. The form of such interaction is again determined by production.[*]

The relations of various nations with one another depend upon the extent to which each of them has developed its productive forces, the division of labor, and domestic commerce. This proposition is generally accepted. But not only the relation of one nation to others, but also the entire internal structure of the nation itself depends on the stage of development achieved by its production and its domestic and international commerce. How far the productive forces of a nation are developed is shown most evidently by the degree to which the division of labor has been developed. Each new productive force, insofar as it is not only a quantitative extension of productive forces already known (e.g. cultivation of land) will bring about a further development of the division of labor.

The division of labor in a nation leads first of all to the separation of industrial-commercial labor from agricultural labor and consequently to the separation of *town* and *country* and to a clash of their interests. Its further development leads to the separation of commercial from industrial labor. At the same time, within these various branches, there develop through the division of labor further various divisions among the individuals cooperating in specific kinds of labor. The relative position of these individual groups is determined by the methods employed in agricultural, industrial, and commercial labor (patriarchalism, slavery, estates, classes). The same conditions can be observed in the relations of various nations if commerce has been further developed.

The different stages of development in the division of labor are just so many different forms of ownership; that is, the stage in the division of labor also determines the relations of individuals to one another so far as the material, instrument, and product of labor are concerned.

The first form of ownership is tribal ownership. It corresponds to the undeveloped stage of production where people live by hunting and fishing, by breeding animals or, in the highest stage, by agriculture. Great areas of uncultivated land are required in the latter case. The division of

[*Break in manuscript text indicated by triple indentation of first line of the following paragraph. In all the text to follow some long paragraphs have been divided to facilitate reading, but in such cases the first lines of the new paragraphs have ordinary indentations.]

labor at this stage is still very undeveloped and confined to extending the natural division of labor in the family. The social structure thus is limited to an extension of the family: patriarchal family chieftains, below them the members of the tribe, finally the slaves. The slavery latent in the family develops only gradually with the increase in population, the increase of wants, and the extension of external relations in war as well as in barter.

(The second form is the ancient communal and state ownership which proceeds especially from the union of several tribes into a *city* by agreement or by conquest; this form is still accompanied by slavery. Alongside communal ownership there already develops movable, and later even immovable, private property, but as an abnormal form subordinate to communal ownership.) The citizens hold power over their laboring slaves only in community and are therefore bound to the form of communal ownership. The communal private property of the active citizens compels them to remain in this natural form of association over against their slaves. Hence the whole social structure based on communal ownership and with it the power of the people decline as immovable private property develops. The division of labor is developed to a larger extent. We already find antagonism between town and country and later antagonism between states representing urban interests and those representing rural interests. Within the cities themselves we find the antagonism between industry and maritime commerce. The class relation between citizens and slaves is then fully developed.

With the development of private property we encounter for the first time those conditions which we shall find again with modern private property, only on a larger scale. On the one hand, there is the concentration of private property which began very early in Rome (as proved by the Licinian agrarian law) and proceeded very rapidly from the time of the civil wars and particularly under the emperors. On the other hand, there is linked to this the transformation of the plebeian small peasantry into a proletariat that never achieved an independent development because of its intermediate position between propertied citizens and slaves.

The third form is feudal or estate ownership. Antiquity started out from the *town* and the small territory around it; the Middle Ages started out from the *country*. This different starting-point was caused by the sparse population at that time, scattered over a large area and receiving no large population increase from the conquerors. In contrast to Greece and Rome, the feudal development began in a much larger area, prepared by the Roman conquests and the spreading of agriculture initially connected with these conquests. The last centuries of the declining Roman Empire and its conquest by the barbarians destroyed many

[margin note: land communal land → owned]

productive forces. Agriculture had declined, trade had come to a stand-still or had been interrupted by force, and the rural and urban population had decreased. These conditions and the mode of organization of the conquest determined by them developed feudal property under the influ-ence of the Germanic military constitution. Like tribal and communal ownership, it is based again on a community. While the slaves stood in opposition to the ancient community, here the serfs as the direct produc-ing class stand in opposition. As soon as feudalism is fully developed, there also emerges antagonism to the towns. The hierarchical system of land ownership and the armed bodies of retainers gave the nobility power over the serfs. Like the ancient communal ownership this feudal organization was an association directed against a subjected producing class. But the form of association and the relation to the direct producers were different because of the different conditions of production.

This feudal organization of land ownership had its counterpart in the *towns* in the form of corporate property, the feudal organization of the trades. Property consisted mainly in the labor of each individual. The necessity for association against the organized robber nobility, the need for communal markets in an age when the industrialist was at the same time a merchant, the growing competition of escaped serfs pouring into the rising cities, and the feudal structure of the whole country gave rise to *guilds*. The gradually accumulated capital of individual craftsmen and their stable number in comparison to the growing population produced the relationship of journeyman and apprentice. In the towns, this led to a hierarchy similar to that in the country.

The main form of property during the feudal times consisted on the one hand of landed property with serf labor and on the other hand, individual labor with small capital controlling the labor of journeymen. The organization of both was determined by the limited conditions of production: small-scale, primitive cultivation of land and industry based on crafts. There was little division of labor when feudalism was at its peak. Every district carried in itself the antagonism of town and country. Though division into estates was strongly marked, there was no division of importance apart from the differentiation of princes, nobility, clergy, and peasants in the country, and masters, journeymen, apprentices, and soon the mob of day laborers in the cities. The strip-system hindered such a division in agriculture; cottage industry of the peasants them-selves emerged; and in industry there was no division of labor at all within particular trades, and very little among them. The separation of industry and commerce occurred in older towns, and in newer towns it developed later when they entered into mutual relations.

The merger of larger territories into feudal kingdoms was a necessity for the landed nobility as well as for the cities. The organization of the ruling class, the nobility, had a monarch at its head in all instances.

The fact is, then, that definite individuals who are productively active in a specific way enter into these definite social and political relations. In each particular instance, empirical observation must show empirically, without any mystification or speculation, the connection of the social and political structure with production. The social structure and the state continually evolve out of the life-process of definite individuals, but individuals not as they may appear in their own or other people's imagination but rather as they *really* are, that is, as they work, produce materially, and act under definite material limitations, presuppositions, and conditions independent of their will.

((The ideas which these individuals form are ideas either about their relation to nature, their mutual relations, or their own nature. It is evident that in all these cases these ideas are the conscious expression—real or illusory—of their actual relationships and activities, of their production and commerce, and of their social and political behavior. The opposite assumption is possible only if, in addition to the spirit of the actual and materially evolved individuals, a separate spirit is presupposed. If the conscious expression of the actual relations of these individuals is illusory, if in their imagination they turn reality upside down, this in turn is a result of their limited mode of activity and their limited social relations arising from it.))

The production of ideas, of conceptions, of consciousness is directly interwoven with the material activity and the material relationships of men; it is the language of actual life. Conceiving, thinking, and the intellectual relationships of men appear here as the direct result of their material behavior. The same applies to intellectual production as manifested in a people's language of politics, law, morality, religion, metaphysics, etc. Men are the producers of their conceptions, ideas, etc., but these are real, active men, as they are conditioned by a definite development of their productive forces and of the relationships corresponding to these up to their highest forms. Consciousness can never be anything else except conscious existence, and the existence of men is their actual life-process. If men and their circumstances appear upside down in all ideology as in a camera obscura, this phenomenon is caused by their historical life-process, just as the inversion of objects on the retina is caused by their immediate physical life.

In direct contrast to German philosophy, which descends from heaven to earth, here one ascends from earth to heaven. In other words, to arrive at man in the flesh, one does not set out from what men say, imagine, or conceive, nor from man as he is described, thought about, imagined, or conceived. Rather one sets out from real, active men and their actual life-process and demonstrates the development of ideological reflexes and echoes of that process. The phantoms formed in the human brain, too, are necessary sublimations of man's material life-process which is empirically verifiable and connected with material premises. Morality, religion, metaphysics, and all the rest of ideology and their corresponding forms of consciousness no longer seem to be independent. They have no history or development. Rather, men who develop their material production and their material relationships alter their thinking and the products of their thinking along with their real existence. Consciousness does not determine life, but life determines consciousness. In the first view the starting point is consciousness taken as a living individual; in the second it is the real living individuals themselves as they exist in real life, and consciousness is considered only as *their* consciousness.

(This view is not devoid of premises. It proceeds from real premises and does not abandon them for a moment. These premises are men, not in any fantastic isolation and fixation, but in their real, empirically perceptible process of development under certain conditions. When this active life-process is presented, history ceases to be a collection of dead facts as it is with the empiricists who are themselves still abstract, or an imagined activity of imagined subjects, as with the idealists.) vs · 107

Where speculation ends, namely in actual life, there real, positive science begins as the representation of the practical activity and practical process of the development of men. Phrases about consciousness cease and real knowledge takes their place. With the description of reality, independent philosophy loses its medium of existence. At best, a summary of the most general results, abstractions derived from observation of the historical development of men, can take its place. Apart from actual history, these abstractions have in themselves no value whatsoever. They can only serve to facilitate the arrangement of historical material and to indicate the sequence of its particular strata. By no means do they give us a recipe or schema, as philosophy does, for trimming the epochs of history. On the contrary, the difficulties begin only when we start the observation and arrangement of the material, the real description, whether of a past epoch or of the present. The removal of these difficulties is governed by premises we cannot state here. Only the study of the real life-process and the activity of the individuals of any given epoch will yield them. We shall select here some of these abstractions which we use in opposing ideology, and we shall illustrate them by historical examples.

⟨⟨*Feuerbach*⟩⟩[*] [. . . (at least two manuscript pages missing)] in reality and for the *practical* materialist, that is, the *communist*, it is a question of revolutionizing the world as it is, of practically tackling and changing existing things. Though we sometimes find such views with Feuerbach, they never go beyond isolated surmises and have much too little influence on his general outlook to be considered here as anything but embryos capable of development. Feuerbach's "conception" of the sensuous world is confined to mere perception [*Anschauung*] of it on the one hand and to mere sensation [*Empfindung*] on the other. He speaks of "Man" instead of "real historical men." "Man" is actually "the German." In the first case, in the *perception* of the sensuous world, he necessarily encounters things which contradict his consciousness and feeling and disturb the harmony he presupposes of all parts of the sensuous world and especially of man with nature. ⟨Feuerbach's mistake is not that he subordinates the flatly obvious, the sensuous *appearance*, to the sensuous reality established by closer examination of the sensuous facts, but that he cannot, after all, cope with sensuousness except by looking at it with the "eyes," that is, through the "eyeglasses" of the *philosopher.*⟩[*] To remove this disturbance, he must take refuge in a dual perception: a profane one which apprehends only the "flatly obvious" and a higher, philosophical one which gets at the "true essence" of things. He does not see that the world surrounding him is not something directly given and the same from all eternity but the product of industry and of the state of society in the sense that it is a historical product, the result of the activity of a whole succession of generations, each standing on the shoulders of the preceding one, developing further its industry and commerce, and modifying its social order according to changed needs. Even the objects of the simplest "sensuous certainty" are given to him only through social development, industry, and commercial relationships. The cherry tree, like almost all fruit trees, was transplanted into our zone by *commerce* only a few centuries ago, as we know, and only *by* this action of a particular society in a particular time has it become "sensuous certainty" for Feuerbach.

Incidentally, when we conceive things as they really are and happened, any profound philosophical problem is resolved quite simply into an

[*Double pointed brackets for adjacent addenda in Marx's handwriting in the right column of the manuscript page. Each manuscript page is halved lengthwise into two columns, the left filled with most of the text in Engels's script—he wrote more smoothly and quickly than Marx—from joint dictation.]

[*Single pointed brackets for adjacent addenda in Engels's writing in the right column of the manuscript page.]

empirical fact, as will be seen even more clearly below. For example, the important question of the relation of man to nature (Bruno [Bauer] even goes so far as to speak of the "antitheses in nature and history" as if these were two separate "things" and man did not always have before him a historical nature and a natural history) from which all the "unfathomably lofty works" on "Substance" and "Self-consciousness" were born, collapses when we understand that the celebrated "unity of man with nature" has always existed in industry in varying forms in every epoch according to the lesser or greater development of industry, just like the "struggle" of man with nature, right up to the development of his productive forces on a corresponding basis. Industry and commerce, production and the exchange of the necessities of life, determine distribution and the structure of the various social classes, and are in turn determined as to the mode in which they are carried on. And so it happens that in Manchester, for instance, Feuerbach sees only factories and machines, where a hundred years ago only spinning wheels and weaving looms could be seen, or in the Campagna di Roma he discovers only pasture and swamps, where in the time of Augustus he would have found nothing but the vineyards and villas of Roman capitalists.

Feuerbach speaks in particular of the viewpoint of natural science. He mentions secrets disclosed only to the eye of the physicist and chemist. But where would natural science be without industry and commerce? Even this "pure" natural science receives its aim, like its material, only through commerce and industry, through the sensuous activity of men. So much is this activity, this continuous sensuous working and creating, this production, the basis of the whole sensuous world as it now exists, that, were it interrupted for only a year, Feuerbach would find not only a tremendous change in the natural world but also would soon find missing the entire world of men and his own perceptual faculty, even his own existence. Of course, the priority of external nature remains, and all this has no application to the original men produced by generatio aequivoca [spontaneous generation]. But this differentiation has meaning only insofar as man is considered distinct from nature. And after all, the kind of nature that preceded human history is by no means the nature in which Feuerbach lives, the nature which no longer exists anywhere, except perhaps on a few Australian coral islands of recent origin, and which does not exist for Feuerbach either.

Feuerbach admittedly has a great advantage over the "pure" materialists because he realizes that man too is "sensuous object"; but he sees man only as "sensuous object," not as "sensuous activity," because he remains in the realm of theory and does not view men in their given social connection, not under their existing conditions of life which have made them what they are. He never arrives at the really existing active men, but stops at the abstraction "Man" and gets only to the point of recognizing the "true, individual, corporeal man" emotionally, that is, he knows no other "human relationships" "of man to man" than love and friendship, and these idealized. He gives no criticism of the present conditions of life. He never manages to view the sensuous world as the total living sensuous *activity* of the individuals composing it. When he sees, for example, a crowd of scrofulous, over-worked, and consumptive wretches instead of healthy men, he is compelled to take refuge in the "higher perception" and "ideal compensation in the species." Thus he relapses into idealism at the very point where the communistic materialist sees the necessity and at the same time the condition of transforming industry as well as the social structure.

As far as Feuerbach is a materialist he does not deal with history, and as far as he deals with history he is not a materialist. Materialism and history completely diverge with him, a fact which should already be obvious from what has been said.

⟨⟨*History*⟩⟩ In dealing with Germans devoid of premises, we must begin by stating the first premise of all human existence, and hence of all history, the premise, namely, that men must be able to live in order to be able "to make history." ⟨⟨*Hegel.* Geological, hydrographical, etc., conditions. Human bodies. Needs, labor.⟩⟩ But life involves above all eating and drinking, shelter, clothing, and many other things. The first historical act is thus the production of the means to satisfy these needs, the production of material life itself. This is a historical act, a fundamental condition of all history which must be fulfilled in order to sustain human life every day and every hour, today as well as thousands of years ago. Even when sensuousness is reduced to a minimum, to a stick as with Saint Bruno [Bauer], it presupposes the activity of producing the stick. The first principle therefore in any theory of history is to observe this fundamental fact in its entire significance and all its implications and to attribute to this fact its due importance. The Germans have never done this, as we all know, so they have never had an *earthly* basis for history and consequently have never had a historian. Though the French and the English grasped the connection of this fact with so-called history only in an extremely one-sided way, particularly so long as they were involved in political ideology, they nevertheless made the first attempts to give historiography a materialistic basis by writing histories of civil society, commerce, and industry.

The second point is that once a need is satisfied, which requires the action of satisfying and the acquisition of the instrument for this purpose, new needs arise. The production of new needs is the first historical act. Here we see immediately where the great historical wisdom of the Germans comes from. When they run out of positive material and are not dealing with theological, political, or literary nonsense, they do not think of history at all but of "prehistoric times," without explaining how we can get from the nonsense of "prehistory" to history proper. With their historical speculation, on the other hand, they seize upon "prehistory" because they believe that there they are safe from interference by "crude facts" and can give full rein to their speculative impulses to establish and tear down hypotheses by the thousand.

The third circumstance entering into historical development from the very beginning is the fact that men who daily remake their own lives begin to make other men, begin to propagate: the relation between husband and wife, parents and children, the *family*. The family, initially the only social relationship, becomes later a subordinate relationship (except in Germany) when increased needs produce new social relations and an increased population creates new needs. It must then be treated and developed in accordance with the existing empirical data and not according to the "concept of the family" as is customary in Germany. These three aspects of social activity are not to be taken as three different stages, but just for what they are, three aspects. To make it clear for the Germans we might call them three "moments" which have existed simultaneously ever since the dawn of history and the first men and still exist today.

The production of life, of one's own life in labor and of another in procreation, now appears as a double relationship: on the one hand as a natural relationship, on the other as a social one. The latter is social in the sense that individuals cooperate, no matter under what conditions, in what manner, and for what purpose. Consequently a certain mode of production or industrial stage is always combined with a certain mode of cooperation or social stage, and this mode of cooperation is itself a "productive force." We observe in addition that the multitude of productive forces accessible to men determines the nature of society and that the "history of mankind" must always be studied and treated in relation to the history of industry and exchange. It is also clear, however, why it is impossible in Germany to write such a history. The Germans lack not only the power of comprehension required and the material but also "sensuous certainty." On the other side of the Rhine people cannot have any experience of these matters because history has come to a standstill there. It is obvious at the outset that there is a materialistic connection among men determined by their needs and their modes of production and as old as men themselves. This connection is forever assuming new forms and thus presents a "history" even in absence of any political or religious nonsense which might hold men together in addition.

Having considered four moments, four aspects of the primary historical relationships, we now find that man also possesses "consciousness." ⟨⟨Men have history because they must *produce* their life, and [. . . ?] in a *certain* way: this is determined by their physical organization; their consciousness is determined in the same way.⟩⟩ But this consciousness is not inherent, not "pure." From the start the "spirit" bears the curse of being "burdened" with matter which makes its appearance in the form of agitated layers of air, sounds, in short, in the form of language. Language is as old as consciousness. It *is* practical consciousness which exists also for other men and hence exists for me personally as well. Language, like consciousness, only arises from the need and necessity of relationships with other men. ((My relationship to my surroundings is my consciousness.)) Where a relationship exists, it exists for me. The animal has no *"relations"* with anything, no relations at all. Its relation to others does not exist as a relation. Consciousness is thus from the very beginning a social product and will remain so as long as men exist. At first consciousness is concerned only with the *immediate* sensuous environment and a limited relationship with other persons and things outside the individual who is becoming conscious of himself. At the same time it is consciousness of nature which first appears to man as an entirely alien, omnipotent, and unassailable force. Men's relations with this consciousness are purely animal, and they are overawed by it like beasts. Hence it is a purely animal consciousness of nature (natural religion)—for the very reason that nature is not yet modified historically. On the other hand it is consciousness of the necessity to come in contact with other individuals; it is the beginning of man's consciousness of the fact that he lives in a society. This beginning is as animalistic as social life itself at this stage. It is the mere consciousness of being a member of a flock, and the only difference between sheep and man is that man possesses consciousness instead of instinct, or in other words his instinct is more conscious.

⟨⟨We here see immediately that this natural religion or particular relation to nature is determined by the form of society and vice versa. As it is the case everywhere, the identity of nature and man appears in such a way that the restricted behavior of men toward nature determines their restricted behavior to one another, and their restricted behavior to one another determines their restricted behavior to nature.⟩⟩ This sheeplike or tribal consciousness receives further development and formation through increased productivity, the increase of needs, and what is fundamental to both, the increase of population. Along with these, division of labor develops which originally was nothing but the division of labor in the sexual act, then that type of division of labor which comes about spontaneously or "naturally" because of natural predisposition (e.g. physical strength), needs, accidents, etc., etc. The division of labor is a true division only from the moment a division of material and mental labor appears. ⟨⟨The first form of ideologists, *priests*, is concurrent.⟩⟩ From this moment on consciousness can really boast of being something other than consciousness of existing practice, of *really* representing something without representing something real. From this moment on consciousness can emancipate itself from the world and proceed to the formation of "pure" theory, theology, philosophy, ethics, etc. But even if this theory, theology, philosophy, ethics, etc., comes into conflict with existing relations, this can only occur because existing social relations have come into conflict with the existing force of production. Incidentally this can also occur in national relationships through a conflict not within the nation but between a particular national consciousness and the practice of other nations, that is, between the national and the general consciousness of a nation (as we observe now in Germany). ⟨⟨*Religion.* The Germans and *ideology* as such.⟩⟩ Since this contradiction appears only as a contradiction within national consciousness, and since the struggle seems to be limited to this na⟨⟨tional crap just because this nation is crap in and for itself.⟩⟩

Moreover it does not make any difference what consciousness starts to do on its own. The only result we obtain from all such muck is that these three moments—the force of production, the state of society, and consciousness—can and must come into conflict with one another because the *division of labor* implies the possibility, indeed the necessity, that intellectual and material activity ⟨⟨activity and thinking, that is, thoughtless activity and inactive thought [later deleted.]⟩⟩—enjoyment and labor, production and consumption—are given to different individuals, and the only possibility of their not coming into conflict lies in again transcending the division of labor. It is self-evident that words such as "specters," "bonds," "higher being," "concept," "scruple," are only the idealistic, spiritual expression, the apparent conception of the isolated individual, the image of very empirical fetters and restrictions within which the mode of production of life and the related form of interaction move. ⟨⟨This idealistic expression of existing economic restrictions is present not only in pure theory but also in practical consciousness; that is to say, having emancipated itself and having entered into conflict with the existing mode of production, consciousness shapes not only religions and philosophies but also states.⟩⟩

With the division [*Teilung*] of labor, in which all these conflicts are implicit and which is based on the natural division of labor in the family and the partition of society into individual families opposing one another, there is at the same time distribution [*Verteilung*], indeed *unequal* distribution, both quantitative and qualitative, of labor and its products, hence property which has its first form, its nucleus, in the family where wife and children are the slaves of the man. The latent slavery in the family, though still very crude, is the first property. Even at this initial stage, however, it corresponds perfectly to the definition of modern economists who call it the power of controlling the labor of others. ⟨Division of labor and private property are identical expressions. What is said in the former in regard to activity is expressed in the latter in regard to the product of the activity.⟩

Furthermore, the division of labor implies the conflict between the interest of the individual or the individual family and the communal interest of all individuals having contact with one another. The communal interest does not exist only in the imagination, as something "general," but first of all in reality, as a mutual interdependence of those individuals among whom the labor is divided. And finally, the division of labor offers us the first example for the fact that man's own act becomes an alien power opposed to him and enslaving him instead of being controlled by him—as long as man remains in natural society, as long as a split exists between the particular and the common interest, and as long as the activity is not voluntarily but naturally divided. For as soon as labor is distributed, each person has a particular, exclusive area of activity which is imposed on him and from which he cannot escape. He is a hunter, a fisherman, a herdsman, or a critical critic, and he must remain so if he does not want to lose his means of livelihood. (In communist society, however, where nobody has an exclusive area of activity and each can train himself in any branch he wishes, society regulates the general production, making it possible for me to do one thing today and another tomorrow, to hunt in the morning, fish in the afternoon, breed cattle in the evening, criticize after dinner, just as I like, without ever becoming a hunter, a fisherman, a herdsman, or a critic. This fixation of social activity, this consolidation of our own products into an objective power above us, growing out of our control, thwarting our expectations, and nullifying our calculations, is one of the chief factors in historical development so far, [. . . (nine lines deleted and illegible)]

⟨[beside previous paragraph] Out of this very contradiction between the interest of the individual and that of the community the latter takes an independent form as the *State*, separated from the real interests of individual and community, and at the same time as an illusory communal life, but always based on the real bonds present in every family and every tribal conglomeration, such as flesh and blood, language, division of labor on a larger scale, and other interests, and particularly based, as we intend to show later, on the classes already determined by the division of labor, classes which form in any such mass of people and of which one dominates all the others. It follows from this that all struggles within the State, the struggle between democracy, aristocracy and monarchy, the struggle for franchise, etc., etc., are nothing but the illusory forms in which the real struggles of different classes are carried out among one another (the German theoreticians do not have the faintest inkling of this fact, although they have had sufficient information in the *Deutsch-Französische Jahrbücher* and *The Holy Family*). Furthermore, it follows that every class striving to gain control—even when such control means the transcendence of the entire old form of society and of control itself, as is the case with the proletariat—must first win political power in order to represent its interest in turn as the universal interest, something which the class is forced to do immediately.⟩ ⟨⟨Just because individuals seek *only* their particular interest, which for them does not coincide with their communal interest, the latter will be imposed on them as something "alien" and "independent," as a "universal" interest of a particular and peculiar nature in its turn. Otherwise they themselves must remain within this discord, as in democracy. On the other hand, the *practical* struggle of these particular interests, which constantly *really* run counter to the communal and illusory communal interests, necessitates *practical* intervention and control through the illusory "universal" interest in the form of the State.

Communism is for us not a *state of affairs* still to be established, not an *ideal* to which reality [will] have to adjust. We call communism the *real* movement which abolishes the present state of affairs. The conditions of this movement result from premises now in existence.⟩⟩ The social power, that is, the multiplied productive force from the cooperation of different individuals determined by the division of labor, appears to these individuals not as their own united power but as a force alien and outside them because their cooperation is not voluntary but has come about naturally. They do not know the origin and the goal of this alien force, and they cannot control it. On the contrary, it passes through a peculiar series of phases and stages independent of the will and the action of men, even directing their will. X [Insertion mark for paragraph to follow] How else could property, for example, have a history at all and assume various forms? How else could landed property, according to different premises, have changed in France from parcellation to centralization in the hands of a few, and in England from centralization in the hands of a few to parcellation, as is actually the case today? Or how does it happen that trade, which after all is nothing more than the exchange of products of various individuals and countries, rules the entire world through supply and demand—a relation, as an English economist says, which hovers over the earth like the fate of antiquity, distributing fortune and misfortune with invisible hand, establishing and overthrowing empires, causing nations to rise and to disappear? How could this go on, while with the abolition of the basis of private property, with communistic regulation of production and hence with abolition of the alienation between men and their own products, the power of supply and demand is completely dissolved and men regain control of exchange, production, and the mode of their mutual relationships?

⟨⟨X This *"alienation,"* to use a term which the philosophers will understand, can be abolished only on the basis of two *practical* premises. To become an "intolerable" power, that is, a power against which men make a revolution, it must have made the great mass of humanity "propertyless" and this at the same time in contradiction to an existing world of wealth and culture, both of which presuppose a great increase in productive power and a high degree of its development. On the other hand, this development of productive forces (which already implies the actual empirical existence of men on a *world-historical* rather than local scale) is an absolutely necessary practical premise because, without it, *want* is merely made general, and with *destitution* the struggle for necessities and all the old muck would necessarily be reproduced; and furthermore, because only with this universal development of productive forces is a *universal* commerce among men established which produces in all nations simultaneously the phenomenon of a "propertyless" mass (universal competition), makes each nation dependent on the revolutions of the others, and finally replaces local individuals with *world-historical*, empirically universal individuals. Without this, (1) communism could only exist locally; (2) the *forces* of interaction themselves could not have developed as *universal* and thus intolerable powers, but would have remained homebred, superstitious "conditions"; (3) any extension of interaction would abolish local communism. Empirically, communism is only possible as the act of dominant peoples "all at once" and simultaneously, which presupposes the universal development of productive

Communism

power and worldwide interaction linked with communism. Besides, the mass of *propertyless* workers—labor power on a mass scale cut off from capital or even limited satisfaction, and hence no longer just temporarily deprived of work as a secure source of life—presupposes a *world market* through competition. The proletariat can thus only exist *world-historically*, just as communism, its activity, can only have a "world-historical" existence. World-historical existence of individuals means existence of individuals which is directly bound up with world history.⟩⟩

The form of interaction determined by and in turn determining the existing productive forces at all previous historical stages is *civil society.* It is clear from what has been said above, that civil society has as its premise and basis the simple family and the multiple family, the so-called tribe. More detailed definitions are contained in our remarks above. Already we see here how civil society is the true focus and scene of all history. We see how nonsensical is the old conception of history which neglects real relationships and restricts itself to high-sounding dramas of princes and states.

So far we have concerned ourselves mainly with one aspect of human activity, how man *affects nature.* ⟨⟨Interaction and productive power.⟩⟩ The other aspect, how *man affects man*—origin of the state and the relation of the state to civil society [. . .]

History is nothing but the succession of separate generations, each of which exploits the materials, capital, and productive forces handed down to it by all preceding generations. On the one hand, it thus continues the traditional activity in completely changed circumstances and, on the other, modifies the old circumstances with a completely changed activity. This can be speculatively distorted so that later history is made the goal of earlier history, for example, the goal ascribed to the discovery of America is to assure the outbreak of the French Revolution. History then obtains its own aims and becomes a "person ranking with other persons" (to wit: "Self-consciousness, Criticism, the Unique," etc.), while what is designated with the words "destiny," "goal," "germ," or "idea" of earlier history is nothing more than an abstraction formed from later history, an abstraction from the active influence which earlier history exercises on later history.

The further the separate spheres that interact on one another extend in the course of this development, the more the original isolation of separate nationalities is destroyed by the developed mode of production, commerce, and division of labor between various nations naturally brought forth by these and the more does history become world history. For instance, when a machine is invented in England to deprive countless workers of bread in India and China and revolutionize the entire life of these empires, it becomes a world-historical fact. Sugar and coffee proved their world-historical importance in the nineteenth century when the lack of these products, occasioned by the Napoleonic Continental System, caused the Germans to rise against Napoleon. Lack of sugar and coffee thus became the real basis of the glorious Wars of Liberation of 1813. Hence the transformation of history into world history is not a mere abstract act of the "Self-consciousness," the world spirit, or of any other metaphysical specter, but a completely material, empirically verifiable act, an act for which every individual furnishes proof as he comes and goes, eats, drinks, and clothes himself.

⟨⟨*On the Production of Consciousness*⟩⟩ In history up to the present it is certainly an empirical fact that separate individuals, with the broadening of their activity into world-historical activity, have become more and more enslaved to a power alien to them (a hardship they conceive as chicanery on the part of the so-called World Spirit, etc.), a power which has become increasingly great and finally turns out to be the *world market*. But it is just as empirically established that by the overthrow of the existing state of society by the communist revolution (more about this below) and the abolition of private property which is identical with it, this alien power so baffling to German theoreticians will be dissolved. Then the liberation of each single individual will be accomplished to the extent that history becomes world history. Hence it is clear that the real intellectual wealth of the individual depends entirely on the wealth of his real connections. Only in this way will separate individuals be liberated from the various national and local barriers, be brought into practical connection with the material and intellectual production of the whole world, and be able to enjoy this all-sided production of the whole earth (the creations of man). *All-around* dependence, that natural form of the *world-historical* cooperation of individuals, will be transformed by the communist revolution into the control and conscious governance of these powers, which, born of the interaction of men, have until now overawed and governed men as powers completely alien to them. Now this view can be expressed again speculatively and idealistically, that is, fantastically, as "self-generation of the species" ("society as the subject"), and thereby the consecutive series of interrelated individuals can be conceived as a single individual which accomplishes the mystery of generating itself. It is clear here that individuals certainly generate *one another*, physically and mentally, but do not generate themselves either in the nonsense of Saint Bruno [Bauer] ((or in the sense of the "Unique," of "made" Man)).

Finally, from the conception of history as developed above we obtain these further conclusions: (1) In the development of productive forces there comes a stage when productive forces and means of interaction are achieved which under the existing relationships cause nothing but mischief and are no longer productive forces but rather destructive ones (machinery and money). Connected with this is a class which has to bear all the burdens of society without enjoying its advantages. It is excluded from society and forced into extreme opposition to all other classes. It constitutes the majority of all members of society, and from it arises a consciousness of the necessity of fundamental revolution, communist consciousness, which may of course arise also in the other classes perceiving the situation of this class. (2) The conditions under which definite productive forces can be applied are the conditions of the rule of a definite class of society whose social power, deriving from its property, has its *practical*-idealistic expression in the form of the state as it happens to exist then. Therefore, every revolutionary struggle is directed against a class which until then has been in power. ⟨⟨The people are interested in maintaining the present state of production.⟩⟩ (3) In all revolutions up till now the mode of activity remained unchanged, and it was only a question of a different distribution of this activity, a new distribution of labor to other persons. But the communist revolution is directed against the preceding *mode* of activity, does away with *labor*, and abolishes the rule of all classes along with the classes themselves, because it is accomplished by the class which society no longer recognizes as a class and is itself the expression of the dissolution of all classes, nationalities, etc. (4) For the production of this communist consciousness on a mass scale and for the success of the cause itself, the alteration of men on a mass scale is required. This can only take place in a practical movement, in a *revolution*. A revolution is necessary, therefore, not only because the *ruling* class cannot be overthrown in any other way but also because the class *overthrowing* it can succeed only by revolution in getting rid of all the traditional muck and become capable of establishing society anew.

This conception of history depends on our ability to set forth the real process of production, starting out from the material production of life itself, and to comprehend the form of interaction connected with this and created by this mode of production, that is, by civil society in its various stages, as the basis of all history. We have to show civil society in action as State and also explain all the different theoretical products and forms of consciousness, religion, philosophy, ethics, etc., and trace their genesis from that basis. The whole thing can be depicted in its totality (and thus the reciprocal action of these various sides too). Unlike the idealistic view of history this conception does not look for a category in every historical period; rather it remains constantly on the real *ground* of history. It does not explain practice from the idea but explains the formation of ideas from material practice. Consequently it arrives at the conclusion that all forms and products of consciousness cannot be dissolved by mental criticism, by resolution into "Self-consciousness" or transformation into "apparitions," "specters," "fancies," etc., but only by the practical overthrow of the actual social relations which gave rise to this idealistic trickery. Not criticism but revolution is the driving force of history and also of religion, philosophy, and all other types of theory. It shows that history does not end by being resolved into "Self-consciousness" as "spirit of the Spirit," but that there is a material result at each historical stage, a sum of productive forces, a historically created relation of individuals to nature and to one another which is handed down to each generation from its predecessor—a mass of productive forces, capital funds, and conditions which on the one hand is modified by the new generation but on the other hand also prescribes its conditions of life, giving it a definite development and a special character. It shows, therefore, that circumstances make men just as much as men make circumstances.

The sum of productive forces, capital funds, and social forms of interaction which every individual and every generation finds existing is the real basis of what the philosophers have conceived as "Substance" and "essence of Man," what they have apotheosized and attacked, that is, a real basis which is not in the least disturbed in its effect and influence on the development of men by the fact that these philosophers revolt against it as "Self-consciousness" and the "Unique." These conditions of life which the various generations find in existence also decide whether periodical and recurring revolutionary tremors will be strong enough to overthrow the basis of the entire existing system. If these material elements of total revolution are not present (namely, the existing productive forces on the one hand and the formation of a revolutionary mass on the other, a mass which revolts not only against particular conditions of the prevailing society but against the prevailing "production of life" itself, the "total activity" on which it was based) then it is absolutely immaterial, so far as practical development is concerned, whether the *idea* of this revolution has already been expressed a hundred times, as the history of communism proves.

In the whole conception of history up to the present this actual basis of history has been either totally neglected or considered as a minor matter irrelevant to the course of history. Thus history must always be written according to an extraneous standard. The actual production of life appears as something unhistorical, while the historical appears as something separated from ordinary life, something extra-superterrestrial. Thus the relation of man to nature is excluded from history and the antithesis of nature and history is created. The exponents of this conception of history have only been able to see in history political action and religious or other theoretical struggles. In each historical epoch they have had to *share the illusion of that epoch.* For example, if an epoch imagines itself to be determined by purely "political" or "religious" motives, even though "religion" and "politics" are only forms of its actual motives, the historian accepts this opinion. The "notion" [*Einbildung*], the "conception" of the people about their real practice, is transformed into the sole determining and active force controlling and determining their practice. When the crude form in which the division of labor appears with the Indians and Egyptians brings about the caste system in their states and in their religions, the historian believes that the caste system is the power which produced this social form. While the French and the English at least adhere to a political illusion moderately close to reality, the Germans move in the realm of the "pure Spirit" and make religious illusion the driving force of history.

The Hegelian philosophy of history is the last consequence, the "purest expression," of all this German historiography which does not deal with real interests, not even political ones, but with pure thoughts which consequently must appear to Saint Bruno [Bauer] as a series of "thoughts" devouring one another and perishing in "Self-consciousness." The Blessed Max Stirner, who does not know a thing about real history, goes even farther. He sees history as a mere tale of "knights," robbers, and ghosts from whose visions he can escape only by "unholiness." ⟨⟨So-called *objective* historiography has just consisted in treating historical conditions as separate from activity. Reactionary character.⟩⟩ This conception is truly religious. It postulates religious man as the original man, the starting point of all history. In its imagination it puts the religious production of fancies in the place of the real production of the means of subsistence and of life itself. This whole conception of history together with its dissolution and the scruples and qualms resulting from it is a purely *national* affair of the Germans and has only *local* interest for Germany, as for example the important question which has been treated several times of late: How does one "pass from the realm of God to the realm of Man"? As if this realm of God had ever existed anywhere except in the imagination, and the learned gentlemen, without being aware of it, were not constantly living in the "realm of Man" which they are now seeking. As if the learned pastime, for it is nothing more, of explaining the mystery of this theoretical cloud-formation did not on the contrary lie in demonstrating its origin in actual earthly conditions. For these Germans it is always simply a matter of resolving some nonsense at hand into some other freak. In other words, they presuppose that all this nonsense has a special *sense* which can be discovered, while actually they should explain this theoretical talk from the actual existing conditions. The real, practical dissolution of these phrases, the removal of these notions from the consciousness of men will be effected by altered circumstances, not by theoretical deduction, as we have already said. Such theoretical notions do not exist and need not be explained to the mass of men, that is, the proletariat. If this mass ever had any theoretical notions, for example, religion, these have now long been dissolved by circumstances.

The purely national character of these questions and answers is shown also in the way these theorists believe in all seriousness that phantoms like "the God-Man," "Man," etc., have presided over individual epochs of history—Saint Bruno [Bauer] even goes so far as to assert that only "criticism and critics make history." When they construct historical systems, they skip over all earlier periods with greatest haste and jump immediately from "Mongoldom" to history "with meaningful content," to the history of the [young Hegelian] *Hallische* and *Deutsche Jahrbücher* [edited by Arnold Ruge] and the dissolution of the Hegelian school in a general squabble. They forget all other nations, all real events, and the theatrum mundi is confined to the Leipzig Book Fair and the mutual quarrels of "criticism," "Man," and the "Unique." When these theorists attempt to treat really historical subjects, as for example the eighteenth century, they merely give a history of the ideas of the times, torn away from the facts and practical developments fundamental to them. They give such a history only with the intention of representing that period as an imperfect preliminary stage, as the limited forerunner of the real historical age, that is, the period of the German philosophical struggle from 1840 to 1844. When the history of an earlier period is written with the aim of bringing out the fame of an unhistoric person and his fantasies, the really historical events, even the really historic invasions of politics into history, receive no mention. Instead we get a narrative based not on studies but on conjectures and literary gossip such as Saint Bruno presented in his now forgotten history of the eighteenth century. These pompous and haughty idea-peddlers who believe they are far above all national prejudices are actually far more national than the beer-philistines who dream of a united Germany. They do not recognize the deeds of other nations as historical. They turn the Rhine Song into a religious hymn and conquer Alsace-Lorraine by robbing French philosophy instead of the French state, by Germanizing French ideas instead of French provinces. Venedey is a cosmopolitan compared with the Saints Bruno [Bauer] and Max [Stirner] who in the universal domination of theory proclaim the universal domination of Germany.

It is also clear from this discussion how grossly Feuerbach deceives himself when he declares himself a communist (*Wigand's Vierteljahrsschrift*, II, 1845) by virtue of the qualification "common man" converted into a predicate "*of*" Man, and thus he believes it possible to change the word communist, which actually means the follower of a definite revolutionary party, into a mere category. Feuerbach's whole deduction concerning the relation of men to one another goes only so far as to prove that men need and *always have needed* one another. He wants to establish consciousness of this fact. Like other theorists he wants to bring about a correct awareness of an *existing* fact, whereas the real communist aims to overthrow the existing state of things. We appreciate fully that Feuerbach, trying to produce consciousness of just *this* fact, goes as far as a theorist possibly can without ceasing being a theorist and philosopher. It is characteristic, however, that Saint Bruno and Saint Max take Feuerbach's conception of the communist and substitute it for the real communist, partly so that they too can combat communism as "spirit of the Spirit," as a philosophical category, as an equal opponent— and in the case of Saint Bruno also for pragmatic reasons. As an example of Feuerbach's acceptance and at the same time misunderstanding of existing reality, something he still shares with our opponents, we recall the passage in his *Philosophy of the Future* where he develops the view that the existence of a thing or a man is at the same time its or his essence, that the conditions of existence, the mode of life, and the activity of an animal or human individual are those in which its or his "essence" feels satisfied. Here every exception is expressly conceived as an unfortunate accident and unalterable abnormality. If millions of proletarians in no way feel contented with their conditions of life, if their "existence"[*] does not in the least correspond to their "essence," this is an unavoidable misfortune which must be borne quietly. The millions of proletarians and communists, however, think differently and will prove this when they bring their "existence" into harmony with their "essence" in a practical way, by means of revolution. Feuerbach never speaks of the human world in such cases but always takes refuge in external nature, in nature *as such*, not yet subdued by men. But every new invention and every advance made by industry removes another portion of this domain so the ground which produces examples to illustrate Feuerbach's propositions is steadily shrinking. The "essence" of the fish is its "existence," water—to go no further than this one proposition. The "essence" of the freshwater fish is the water of a river. But this ceases to be the "essence" of the fish and is no longer a suitable medium of existence as soon as the river is made to serve industry, as soon as it is polluted by dyes and other waste products and navigated by steamboats, when its water is diverted into canals and the fish is deprived of its medium of existence by simple drainage. The explanation that all such contradictions are inevitable abnormalities does not essentially differ from the consolation which the Blessed Max Stirner offers [in *The Ego and Its Own*] to the discontented, saying that this contradiction is their own contradiction and this predicament their own predicament, that they should relax, or keep their disgust to themselves, or revolt against it in some fantastic way. It differs just as

[*From here to paragraph below ending ". . . language of reality.))" are translated hitherto missing pages found in the International Institute of Social History, Amsterdam.]

little from Saint Bruno's allegation [*op. cit.*] that these unfortunate circumstances arose because those concerned are stuck in the muck of
"Substance," have not advanced to "absolute Self-consciousness," and
do not realize that these adverse conditions are spirit of their spirit.

Of course, we shall not take the trouble to enlighten our wise philosophers by explaining to them that the "liberation" of "man" is not advanced a single step by their reducing Philosophy, Theology, Substance,
and all that trash to "Self-consciousness" and by their liberating man
from the domination of these phrases which have never held him in
thrall. ⟨⟨Feuerbach. Philosophic and real liberation. *Man*. The *Unique*.
The individual. Geological, hydrographical, etc., conditions. The human
body. Need and labor.⟩⟩ Nor will we explain to them that real liberation
can be achieved only in the real world and with real means, that slavery
cannot be abolished without the steam engine and the spinning jenny,
that serfdom cannot be abolished without improved agriculture, and that
people on the whole cannot be liberated so long as they are unable to
obtain food and drink, shelter and clothing in adequate quality and
quantity. "Liberation" is a historical and not a mental act. It is effected
by historical conditions, by the development of industry, commerce, agriculture, transportation [manuscript page damaged, unreadable]

In Germany, a country where only a shabby historical development is
occurring, these mental developments, these glorified and ineffective
trivialities, naturally serve as a substitute for the lack of historical development, and they take root and have to be combated. But this is a fight of
local significance. ⟨⟨Phrases and real movement. The importance of
phrases in Germany. Language is the language of reality.⟩⟩

In every epoch the ideas of the ruling class are the ruling ideas, that is,
the class that is the ruling *material* power of society is at the same time
its ruling *intellectual* power. The class having the means of material
production has also control over the means of intellectual production, so
that it also controls, generally speaking, the ideas of those who lack the
means of intellectual production. The ruling ideas are nothing more
than the ideal expression of the dominant material relationships grasped
as ideas, hence of the relationships which make the one class the ruling
one and therefore the ideas of its domination. The individuals who
comprise the ruling class possess among other things consciousness and
thought. Insofar as they rule as a class and determine the extent of a
historical epoch, it is self-evident that they do it in its entire range.
Among other things they rule also as thinkers and producers of ideas
and regulate the production and distribution of the ideas of their age.
Their ideas are the ruling ideas of the epoch. For example, in an age and
in a country where royal power, aristocracy, and bourgeoisie are contend-

ing for domination and where control is shared, the doctrine of the separation of powers proves to be the dominant idea and is expressed as an "eternal law."

The division of labor, which we saw above (pp. [424–25]) as one of the chief forces of history up till now, is expressed also in the ruling class as the division of mental and material labor, so that within this class one part appears as the thinkers of the class (its active, conceptive ideologists who make perfecting the illusion of this class about itself their main source of livelihood), while the others' attitude toward these ideas and illusions is more passive and receptive because they are really the active members of this class and have less time to make up illusions and ideas about themselves. Within this class this split can even develop into opposition and hostility between the two parts, which disappears, however, in the case of a practical collision where the class itself is in danger. In this case the appearance that the ruling ideas were not ideas of the ruling class with a power distinct from the power of this class also vanishes. The existence of revolutionary ideas in a particular epoch presupposes the existence of a revolutionary class. About the premises for the latter we have made sufficient comment above (pp. [427–28]).

If in considering the course of history we detach the ideas of the ruling class from the ruling class itself and attribute to them an independent existence, if we confine ourselves to saying that these or those ideas prevailed in a certain epoch without bothering ourselves about their conditions of production or producers, if we ignore the individuals and world conditions which are the source of the ideas, we can say, for example, that during the time when aristocracy was dominant the concepts of honor, loyalty, etc., prevailed, during the dominion of the bourgeoisie, the concepts of freedom, equality, etc. The ruling class itself generally imagines this to be the case. This conception of history, common to all historians particularly since the eighteenth century, will necessarily come up against the phenomenon that increasingly the abstract ideas prevail, that is, ideas that increasingly take on the form of universality. Each new class which displaces the one previously dominant is forced, simply to be able to carry out its aim, to represent its interest as the common interest of all members of society, that is, ideally expressed. It has to give its ideas the form of universality and represent them as the only rational, universally valid ones. The class making revolution emerges at the outset simply because it is opposed to a *class* not as a class but as a representative of the whole of society. It appears as the whole mass of society confronting one ruling class. ⟨⟨Universality corresponds to (1) class versus estate, (2) competition, world trade, etc., (3) the great numerical strength of the ruling class, (4) the illusion of *common* interests (in the beginning this illusion is true), (5) the delusion of ideologists and the division of labor.⟩⟩ It can do this because in the beginning its interest really is more attached to the common interest of all other non-ruling classes and because under the pressure of prevailing conditions its interest has not yet been able to develop as the particular interest of a particular class. Its victory, therefore, benefits also many individuals of other classes which do not win power but only insofar as it now puts these individuals in a position to raise themselves into the ruling class. When the French bourgeoisie overthrew the power of the aristocracy, it permitted many proletarians to raise themselves above the proletariat, but only insofar as they became bourgeois. Every new class, therefore, achieves dominance only on a broader basis than that of the previous class ruling, whereas the opposition of the non-ruling class against the new ruling class later develops all the more sharply and deeply. Both these factors mean that the struggle to be waged against this new ruling class aims at a more decided and more radical negation of the previous conditions of society than could all previous classes striving for dominance.

This entire appearance, that the rule of a certain class is only the rule of certain ideas, comes to a natural end as soon as class rule in general ceases to be the form in which society is organized, as soon as it is no longer necessary to represent a particular interest as general or "the general interest" as dominant.

When ruling ideas are separated from ruling individuals and above all from relationships resulting from a given level of the mode of production and the conclusion has been reached that ideas are always ruling history, it is very easy to abstract from these various ideas "*the* ideas," the Idea, etc., as the dominant force in history and thus understand all these separate ideas and concepts as "Self-determinations" of *the* Concept developing in history. It follows, of course, that all the relationships of men can be derived from the concept of man, man as conceived, the essence of man, *Man.* This has been done in speculative philosophy. ⟨⟨Hegel himself admits at the end of the *Philosophy of History* that he "has considered the progress of the *Concept* only" and has presented the "true *theodicy*" in history (p. 446).⟩⟩ Now one can go back again to the producers of "the Concept," to the theorists, ideologists, and philosophers, and one comes to the conclusion that the philosophers, the thinkers as such, have always been dominant in history—a conclusion, as we see, already advanced by Hegel. Thus the whole trick of proving the hegemony (Stirner calls it hierarchy) of Spirit in history is confined to the following three efforts.

No. 1. One must separate the ideas of those ruling for empirical reasons, under empirical conditions, and as material individuals from the actual rulers; one must recognize the rule of ideas or illusions in history.

No. 2. One must put order into this rule of ideas, prove a mystical connection among the successive ruling ideas, which is managed by seeing them as "self-determinations of the Concept" (this is possible because these ideas are actually connected with one another by virtue of their empirical basis and because as *mere* ideas they become self-distinctions, distinctions made by thought).

No. 3. To remove the mystical appearance of this "self-determining Concept" one changes it into a person—"Self-Consciousness"—or, to make it appear thoroughly materialistic, into a series of persons who represent "the Concept" in history, into "the thinkers," "philosophers," ideologists who again are understood as the manufacturers of history, "the council of guardians," the rulers. ⟨⟨Man = the "rational human spirit."⟩⟩ Thus all materialistic elements have been removed from history and full rein can be given to one's speculative steed.

This historical method which prevailed in Germany and particularly the reason why it prevailed must be explained from its connection with the illusion of ideologists in general, for example, the illusions of jurists, politicians (even of the practical statesmen among them), and from the dogmatic dreamings and distortions of these fellows. It is very simply explained from their practical position in life, their employment, and the division of labor.

While in ordinary life every shopkeeper is very well able to distinguish between what somebody professes to be and what he really is, our historians have not yet achieved this trivial insight. They take every epoch at its word and believe everything it says and imagines about itself. [Pages 36 through 39 in Marx's pagination missing here.]

[Division of Labor][. . .] are found. From the first, there follows the premise of a highly developed division of labor and extensive commerce; from the second, the locality. In the first case, individuals must be brought together; in the second, they find themselves alongside the given instrument of production as instruments of production themselves. Here arises the difference between natural instruments of production and those created by civilization. The *land* (water, etc.) can be regarded as a natural instrument of production. In the first case, with the natural instrument of production, individuals are subservient to nature; in the second, to a product of labor. In the first case, property (landed property) appears as direct natural domination; in the second, as domination of labor, particularly of accumulated labor, capital. The first case presupposes

that the individuals are united by some bond: family, tribe, the land itself, etc. The second case presupposes that they are independent of one another and are only held together by exchange. In the first case, the exchange is mainly an exchange between men and nature in which the labor of men is exchanged for the products of nature; in the second, it is predominantly an exchange of men among themselves. In the first case, average human common sense suffices; physical activity is not as yet separated from mental activity. In the second, the division between physical and mental labor already must be practically completed. In the first case, the domination of the proprietor over non-proprietors may be based on a personal relationship or kind of community; in the second, it must have taken on physical shape in a third party: money. In the first case, small industry exists, but determined by the utilization of the natural instrument of production and hence without distribution of labor among various individuals; in the second, industry exists only in and through division of labor.

We started from instruments of production and showed that private property was a necessity for certain industrial stages. In *industrie extractive* private property still coincides with labor. In small industry and agriculture up till now property is the necessary consequence of the existing instruments of production. Only with big industry does the contradiction between the instrument of production and private property appear; it is the product of big industry. In addition, big industry must be highly developed to produce it. Only with big industry is the abolition of private property possible.

The greatest division of material and intellectual labor is the separation of town and country. The opposition between the two begins with the transition from barbarism to civilization, from the tribe to the state, from locality to nation, and runs through the whole history of civilization to the present day (the Anti-Corn-Law League). With the existence of towns there is the necessity of administration, police, taxes, etc., in short of municipal life and thus politics in general. Here first became apparent the division of the population into two great classes directly based on the division of labor and the instruments of production. The town already shows in actual fact a concentration of population, of instruments of production, of capital, satisfactions, and needs, while the country demonstrates the opposite, isolation and separation. The antagonism between town and country can exist only with private property. It is the crassest expression of the subsumption of the individual under the division of labor, under a definite activity forced upon him, a subsumption making one man into a narrow town animal, the other into a narrow country animal, and every day creates anew the conflict between their interests.

Labor is again the main thing here, power *over* individuals, and as long as this power exists, private property must exist. The overcoming of the antagonism between town and country is one of the first conditions of communal life, a condition depending on a mass of material premises. Mere will, as anyone can see at first glance, cannot fulfill this condition. (We will have to discuss these conditions.) Separation of town and country can also be understood as the separation of capital and landed property, as the beginning of capital's existence and development independent of landed property, the beginning of property based only on labor and exchange.

In towns that had not existed before but were newly built by freed serfs in the Middle Ages, each man's particular labor was his only property except for the small capital he brought with him consisting only of the most necessary tools of his craft. The competition of serfs constantly taking refuge in the towns, the constant war of the country against the town, and thus the necessity of an organized municipal military force, the bond of common ownership in a particular kind of labor, the necessity of sharing buildings for the sale of their wares when craftsmen were also traders, and consequently the exclusion of unauthorized persons from these buildings, the conflict of interests among various crafts, the necessity of protecting their laboriously acquired skill, and the feudal organization of the entire country—all these were causes of the union of workers of each craft into guilds. At this point we need not go further into the numerous modifications of the guild system with later historical developments. The flight of serfs into the towns continued without interruption through the entire Middle Ages. These serfs, persecuted by their lords in the country, came separately into the towns where they found an organized community against which they were powerless and in which they had to adjust to the station which their organized urban competitors assigned to them according to their need of labor and their interest. Arriving separately, these workers were never able to gain any power because if their labor was of the guild type and had to be learned, the guild masters put them in subjection and organized them according to their interest. If their labor was not of this type but rather day labor, they never managed to organize themselves and remained unorganized rabble. The need for day labor in the towns created the rabble.

These towns were true "associations" created by a direct need to provide for protection of property, multiply the means of production, and defend the individual members. The rabble of these towns was deprived of all power. It was composed of individuals who were strange to one another, had arrived separately, were unorganized, and faced an organized power armed for war and jealously supervising them. In each craft journeymen and apprentices were organized as best suited their master's interest. Their patriarchal relationship with their masters gave the masters a double power, first because of their direct influence on all aspects of life of the journeymen and secondly because there was a real bond uniting the journeymen who worked for the same master, a bond separating them from journeymen working for other masters. And finally the journeymen were bound to the existing order by their interest in becoming masters themselves. While the rabble at least carried out some revolts against the whole municipal order, revolts that remained completely ineffective because of their impotence, the journeymen had only insignificant squabbles within their guild and such as pertain to the nature of the system. The great revolts of the Middle Ages all started in the country. They, too, remained totally ineffective because of the dispersal and resulting cruelty of the peasants.

Capital in these towns consisted of a house, tools of the craft, and natural hereditary customers; it was natural capital. Since it was unrealizable because of the primitive form of commerce and lack of circulation, it had to descend from father to son. Unlike modern capital which can be appraised monetarily and invested in this thing or that, this natural capital was directly tied up with the particular work of the owner, was inseparable from it, and was thus *estate* capital.

In the towns the division of labor between the various guilds was quite natural; in the guilds themselves it was not all carried out among the individual workers. Every worker had to be well versed in a whole round of tasks and had to be able to make all things that could be made with his tools. The limited commerce and the lack of good communications between individual towns, the lack of population, and limited needs did not permit a higher division of labor. Every man who set out to become a master craftsman had to be proficient in the whole of his craft. The medieval craftsmen still exhibited an interest in their special work and their skill in it which could develop to a certain limited artistic talent. For that very reason, however, every medieval craftsman was completely absorbed in his work, had a contented slavish relationship to it, and was subjected to it to a far greater extent than is the modern worker for whom his work is a matter of indifference.

The next extension of the division of labor was the separation of production and commerce and the formation of a special class of merchants, a separation which had been handed down (as for example with the Jews) in established towns and soon appeared in new ones. With this there was the possibility of commerce transcending the immediate neighborhood, and the realization of this possibility depended on existing means of communication, the state of public safety in the countryside determined by political conditions (throughout the Middle Ages the merchants traveled in armed caravans, as is well known), and on the cruder or more developed needs of the area accessible to commerce as determined by the stage of culture. With commerce as the proper business of a particular class and extension of trade through the merchants beyond the immediate surroundings of the town, an immediate reciprocal action between production and commerce appeared. The towns entered into relations *with one another.* New tools were brought from one town into the other. The division between production and commerce soon created a new division of production among individual towns, each exploiting a predominant branch of industry. Earlier local restrictions gradually broke down.

It depends entirely on the extension of commerce whether the productive forces, especially inventions, in a locality are lost for later development or not. As long as there is no commerce beyond the immediate neighborhood, every invention must be separately made in each locality. Pure accidents such as eruptions of barbaric peoples and even ordinary wars are enough to cause a country with advanced productive forces and needs to start all over again from the beginning. In primitive history every invention had to be made anew, independently, every day and in each locality. That well-developed productive forces are not safe from complete destruction even with relatively extensive commerce is proved by the Phoenicians ⟨⟨and glass painting in the Middle Ages⟩⟩ whose inventions were largely lost for a long time through the displacement of this nation from commerce, its conquest by Alexander, and its consequent decline. Glass painting in the Middle Ages had a similar fate. Only when commerce has become worldwide and is based on large-scale industry, when all nations are drawn into the competitive struggle, will the permanence of the acquired productive forces be assured.

[Manufacturing] A direct consequence of the division of labor between the various towns was the rise of manufactures, branches of production that had developed from the guild system. They first flourished in Italy and later in Flanders because of the historical condition of trade with foreign nations. In other countries, for example, England and France, manufacturing was at first confined to the domestic market. Besides the conditions already mentioned, manufacturing depends on an advanced concentration of population—particularly in the country—and of capital which began to accumulate in the hands of individuals, partly in the guilds despite their regulations, and partly among the merchants.

That kind of labor which from the beginning required a machine, even of the crudest kind, soon turned out to be most capable of development. Weaving, previously done by peasants in the country as a secondary job to provide clothing, was the first labor to receive an impetus and a further development through the extension of commerce. Weaving was the first and remained the main manufacturing. The rising demand for clothing materials from the growth of the population, the growing accumulation and mobilization of natural capital through accelerated circulation, the demand for luxuries caused by the accelerated circulation and generally facilitated by the gradual extension of commerce, gave weaving a quantitative and qualitative impetus which removed it from the prevailing form of production. Beside the peasants who continued, and still continue, to weave for their own use, a new class of weavers emerged in the towns whose fabrics were destined for the entire domestic market and usually also foreign markets. Weaving, a job usually requiring little skill, soon branched out into various kinds of jobs and resisted the restrictions of a guild. For this reason weaving was done mostly in villages and marketplaces, without guild organization. Villages grew into towns, and indeed the most flourishing ones in each country.

With guild-free manufacturing, property relations changed rapidly. The first advance beyond natural-estate capital was provided by the emergence of merchants whose capital was from the start movable, capital in the modern sense as far as we can speak of it in considering the circumstances of those times. The second advance came with manufacturing which again mobilized a great deal of natural capital and altogether increased the mass of movable capital as compared to that of natural capital. At the same time manufacturing became a refuge of the peasants from the guilds which excluded them or paid them poorly, just as earlier the guild towns had served as a refuge for the peasants from the landlords.

With the beginning of manufacturing there was immediately a period of vagrancy caused by the abolition of feudal retainers, the disbanding of armies which had served the kings against their vassals, the improvement of agriculture, and the transformation of large strips of arable land into pasture land. It is clear from this alone how this vagrancy coincides with the disintegration of the feudal system. Isolated epochs of this kind occurred as early as the thirteenth century. Only at the end of the fifteenth and beginning of the sixteenth centuries is it generally present and for quite some duration. These vagabonds were so numerous that, to give one example, Henry VIII of England had 72,000 of them hanged. They could be put to work only with the greatest difficulty and through most extreme destitution, and then after long resistance. The rapid rise of manufacturing, particularly in England, gradually absorbed them.

With the rise of manufacturing, the various nations entered into a competitive relationship, the fight for trade, which was fought out in wars, protective duties, and prohibitions, while the nations formerly had carried on an inoffensive exchange if they were in contact at all. From then on trade assumed political significance.

The relationship between worker and employer also changed. In the guilds the patriarchal relationship between journeyman and master continued to exist; in manufacturing the monetary relation between worker and capitalist took its place, a relationship which retained a patriarchal tinge in the country and the small towns but quite early lost almost all patriarchal coloration in the larger, the real manufacturing towns.

Manufacturing and the movement of production in general received an enormous stimulus through the extension of commerce with the discovery of America and a sea route to the East Indies. The new products imported from America and the Indies and particularly the large quantities of gold and silver which came into circulation completely changed the position of classes toward each other and dealt a hard blow to feudal landed property and laborers. The expeditions of adventurers, colonization, and above all the extension of markets into a world market, now possible and becoming more and more a fact with each day, called forth a new phase of historical development which we cannot further discuss here. Through the colonization of newly discovered lands, the commercial struggle of nations against one another received new fuel and thus became bigger and more bitter.

Expansion of trade and manufacturing accelerated the accumulation of movable capital while natural capital in the guilds remained stable or even decreased without any stimulus for increased production. Trade and manufacturing created the big bourgeoisie; the petty bourgeoisie was concentrated in the guilds, no longer a prevailing power in the cities but bowing to the power of big merchants and manufacturers. ⟨⟨[vertically] The petty bourgeois—Middle class—Big bourgeoisie⟩⟩ As soon as the guilds came into contact with manufacturing, they declined.

During the epoch under discussion the relationships of the nations to one another took on two different forms. In the beginning the small quantity of gold and silver in circulation brought about the ban on the export of these metals. Industry, mostly imported from abroad and needed to employ the increasing urban population, required those privileges which could be granted not only against competition at home but mainly against foreign competition. In the original prohibitions the local guild privilege was extended over the whole nation. Customs duties originated from levies which feudal lords exacted as protection money from merchants passing through their territories and from levies later imposed by towns as the most convenient method of raising money for their treasury. The appearance of American gold and silver on the European markets, the gradual development of industry, the rapid expansion of trade, and the consequent rise of the non-guild bourgeoisie and of money gave these measures a different significance. Being from day to day less able to do without money, the state now upheld the ban on the export of gold and silver for fiscal reasons. The bourgeois for whom these masses of money on the market became the chief object of speculation were thoroughly pleased. Privileges became a source of income for the government and were sold for money. In customs legislation export duties appeared which had a purely fiscal aim and were only a hindrance to industry.

The second period began in the middle of the seventeenth century and lasted almost to the end of the eighteenth. Commerce and navigation had expanded more rapidly than manufacturing which played a secondary role. Colonies were becoming important consumers. After long struggles the individual nations shared the opening world market. This period begins with the Navigation Laws and colonial monopolies. Competition of the nations among themselves was excluded so far as possible by tariffs, prohibitions, and treaties. In the last resort the competitive struggle was carried out and decided in wars (particularly in naval wars). The most powerful maritime nation, the English, held pre-eminence in trade and manufacturing. Here we already have concentration in one country.

Manufacturing was constantly protected at home by tariffs, in the colonial market by monopolies, and abroad as much as possible by differential duties. The processing of domestic raw materials was encouraged (wool and linen in England, silk in France); the export of raw materials was forbidden (wool in England); and the processing of important material was neglected or suppressed (cotton in England). The nation ruling in sea trade and colonial power naturally secured for itself also the greatest quantitative and qualitative expansion of manufacturing. Manufacturing could not do without protection. Through the slightest change taking place in other countries, it could lose its market and be ruined. It can be easily introduced into a country under reasonably favorable conditions and for this reason can be easily destroyed. Through the mode in which manufacturing was carried on particularly in rural areas of the eighteenth century, it was so much interwoven with the vital relationships of a great mass of individuals that no country dared jeopardize its existence by permitting free competition. When a country manages to export, this depends entirely on the extension or restriction of commerce and exercises a relatively small effect. [Corner of manuscript damaged.] Hence the secondary [importance] and influence of [the merchants] in the eighteenth century. More than anyone else the merchants and especially the shippers insisted on protection and monopolies. The manufacturers also demanded and received protection but were inferior in political importance at all times. The commercial towns, particularly the maritime towns, became to some degree civilized and big-bourgeois, but an extreme petty bourgeois outlook persisted in the factory towns. See Aikin [*Description of the Country from Thirty to Forty Miles round Manchester*, London, 1795], etc. The eighteenth century was a century of trade. Pinto says this expressly [*Traité de la circulation et du crédit*, Amsterdam, 1771]: "Commerce is the rage of the century," and: "for some time now people have been talking only about commerce, navigation, and the navy."

The movement of capital, although significantly accelerated, remained relatively slow. The splitting of the world market into separate parts, each of which was exploited by a particular nation, the exclusion of nations' competition among themselves, the clumsiness of production itself, and the fact that the financial system was only developing from its early stages—all this greatly impeded circulation. The consequence was a haggling, shabby, petty spirit which still clung to all merchants and the whole mode of carrying on trade. Compared with manufacturers and particularly craftsmen, they were certainly big bourgeois; compared with the merchants and industrialists of the next period they remain petty bourgeois. Cf. Adam Smith [*The Wealth of Nations*].

This period is also characterized by the cancellation of bans on the export of gold and silver, and the beginning of trade in money; by banks, national debts, paper money, speculation in stocks and shares, and jobbing in all articles; by the development of finance in general. Capital again lost a great part of the national character which it had still possessed.

The concentration of trade and manufacturing in one country, England, developed irresistibly in the seventeenth century and gradually created for that country a relative world market and thus a demand for its manufactured products which could no longer be met by the prevailing industrial forces of production. The demand outgrew the productive forces and was the motive power to bring about the third period of private ownership since the Middle Ages by producing big industry—the application of elemental forces to industrial purposes, machinery, and a very extensive division of labor. There already existed in England the remaining conditions for this new phase: freedom of competition within the nation and the development of theoretical mechanics (as perfected by Newton, the most popular science in France and England in the eighteenth century). (Free competition within the nation itself everywhere had to be obtained by revolution—1640 and 1688 in England, 1789 in France.) Competition soon forced every country that wanted to retain its historical role to protect its manufacturers by renewed customs regulations (the old duties were of little help against big industry) and soon introduce big industry under protective duties. Big industry universalized competition (practical free trade; the protective duty is only a palliative, a measure of defense *within* free trade) despite protective measures, established means of communication and the modern world market, subordinated trade to itself, transformed all capital into industrial capital, and thus produced the rapid circulation (development of finance) and centralization of capital funds. ⟨By universal competition it forced all individuals to strain their energy to the extreme. So far as possible, big industry destroyed ideology, religion, morality, etc., and where it could not, made them into a plain lie.⟩ It produced world history for the first time in that it made every civilized nation and every individual member of the nation dependent for the satisfaction of his wants on the whole world, thus destroying the former natural exclusiveness of separate nations. It subsumed natural science under capital and took from the division of labor the last semblance of its natural character. It destroyed natural growth in general, so far as this is possible in labor, and resolved all natural relationships into money relationships. In the place of naturally grown towns it created overnight modern, large industrial cities. Wherever big industry prevailed, it destroyed the crafts and all earlier stages of industry. It completed the victory [of the town] over the country. [Its premise] was the automatic system. [Its development] resulted in a mass of productive forces for which private property became just as much a fetter as the guild had been for manufacturer and the small rural shop for the developing craft. Under the system of private property these productive forces receive only a one-sided development and become destructive forces for the majority. A great multitude of such forces cannot find application at all under the system of private ownership. In general, big industry created everywhere the same relation between the classes of society and thus destroyed the particularity of each nationality. And finally, while the bourgeoisie of each nation still retained separate national interests, big industry created a class having the same interests in all nations and for which nationality is already destroyed; a class which is really rid of the entire old world and stands opposed to it. Big industry makes unbearable for the worker not only his relation to the capitalist but even labor itself.

It is clear that big industry does not develop equally in all districts of a country. However, this does not hinder the class movement of the proletariat, because the proletarians created by big industry assume leadership of this movement and carry the crowd with them, and because the workers excluded from big industry are put in a worse situation than the workers in big industry itself. Countries with big industries affect in a similar manner the more or less non-industrial countries, if the latter are swept by global commerce into universal competitive struggle. These different forms are only so many forms of the organization of labor and hence of property. In each period a unification of the existing productive forces takes place insofar as this has been made necessary by needs.

This contradiction between the productive forces and the form of commerce, which we observe occurring several times in past history without endangering the basis of history, had to burst out in a revolution each time, taking on at the same time various secondary forms, such as comprehensive collisions, collisions of various classes, contradictions of consciousness, battle of ideas, etc., political struggle, etc. From a narrow point of view one can isolate one of these secondary forms and consider it the basis of these revolutions. This is all the more easy as the individuals who started the revolutions had illusions about their own activity according to their degree of education and stage of historical development.

In our view all collisions in history have their origin in the contradiction between the productive forces and the form of interaction [*Verkehrsform*]. Incidentally, this contradiction does need to have reached its extreme in a particular country to lead to collisions in that country. Competition with industrially more developed countries brought about by expanded international commerce is sufficient to produce a similar contradiction in countries where industry is lagging behind (e.g. the latent proletariat in Germany brought out by the competition of English industry).

Competition isolates individuals, not only the bourgeois but even more the proletarians, despite the fact that it brings them together. It takes a long time before these individuals can unite, apart from the fact that for this union—if it is not to be merely local—big industry must first produce the necessary means, the big industrial cities and inexpensive, quick communications. Therefore, every organized power standing in opposition to these isolated individuals, who live in relationships daily reproducing this isolation, can be conquered only after long struggles. To demand the opposite would be tantamount to demanding that competition should not exist in this definite historical period, or that the individuals should banish from their minds relationships over which they, the isolated, have no control.

[Community] The building of houses. With savages every family has its own cave or hut, just as with the nomads each family has a separate tent. This separate domestic economy is made even more necessary by the

further development of private property. With agricultural people a communal domestic economy is just as impossible as is a communal cultivation of the soil. The building of towns was a great advance. In all previous periods, however, the abolition of individual economy, which cannot be separated from the abolition of private property, was impossible for the simple reason that the material conditions were not present. To establish a communal domestic economy presupposes the development of machinery, of the use of natural forces and of many other productive forces—for example, of water supplies, of gaslighting, steam heating, etc., the removal [of the antagonism] of town and country. Without these conditions a communal economy could not form a new productive force. Lacking any material basis and resting on a purely theoretical foundation, it would be only a freak and would not achieve more than a monastic economy achieves.—What was possible can be seen in the formation of cities which started when people moved close together and in the erection of communal buildings for various definite purposes (prisons, barracks, etc.). It is self-evident that the transcendence of individual economy cannot be separated from the transcendence of the family.

Saint Max's frequent statement that everyone is all that he is through the state is basically the same as the statement that the bourgeois is only a specimen of the bourgeois species, a statement presupposing that the *class* of the bourgeois existed before the individuals constituting it. ⟨⟨With the philosophers, *pre-existence* of a class.⟩⟩ In the Middle Ages the citizens of each town were compelled to unite against the landed nobility to save their skins. Extension of trade and establishment of communication acquainted separate towns with others which had asserted the same interests in the fight against the same opponent. Out of the many local corporations of burghers there gradually but very slowly arose the burgher *class.* The conditions of life of the individual burghers became conditions which were common to them all and independent of each individual because of their contradiction to the existing relationships and because of the mode of labor determined by these. The burghers had created these conditions insofar as they had freed themselves from feudal ties and had been created by them insofar as they were determined by their opposition to the existing feudal system. When the individual towns began to enter into associations, these common conditions developed into class conditions. These same conditions, the same antagonism, and the same interests had to call forth generally similar customs everywhere. With its conditions, the bourgeoisie itself develops only gradually, splits into various fractions according to the division of labor, ⟨⟨It absorbs, first of all, the branches of labor belonging directly to the state, then all more or less ideological estates.⟩⟩ and finally absorbs all existing propertied classes (while it develops most of the formerly propertyless class and part of the previously propertied class into a new class, the proletariat) to the extent that all existing property is transformed into industrial or commercial capital. Various individuals form a class only insofar as they have to carry on a joint battle against another class. Otherwise they are hostile, competing with each other. On the other hand, a class in turn achieves independent existence in relation to individuals so that they find their conditions of life predestined, have their position in life and their personal development assigned, and are subsumed under the class. This is the same phenomenon as the subsumption of particular individuals under the division of labor and can only be removed by the transcendence of private property and of labor itself. We have already indicated several times, how this subsuming of individuals under the class is accompanied by their subsumption under all kinds of ideas, etc.

If one considers this evolution of individuals *philosophically* in the common conditions of existence of estates and classes following one another and in the accompanying general conceptions forced on those individuals, it is certainly very easy to imagine that in these individuals the species or Man has evolved, or that they evolved Man. In this way one can give history some hard blows in the head. One can conceive these various estates and classes as specific terms of a general expression, as subordinate varieties of the species, as evolutionary phases of Man.

This subsuming of individuals under definite classes cannot be abolished until a class has taken shape which no longer has any particular class interest to assert against the ruling class.

The transformation of personal into material powers (relationships) through the division of labor cannot be transcended by dismissing the general idea of it from one's mind but only by individuals again controlling these material powers and transcending the division of labor. ⟨(Feuerbach: being and essence)⟩ This is not possible without the community. Only in community do the means exist for every individual to cultivate his talents in all directions. Only in the community is personal freedom possible. In previous substitutes for the community, in the state, etc., personal freedom has existed only for the individuals who developed within the ruling class and only insofar as they belonged to this class. The illusory community, in which individuals have come together up till now, always took on an independent existence in relation to them and was at the same time not only a completely illusory community but also a new fetter because it was the combination of one class against another. In a real community individuals obtained their freedom in and through their association.

Individuals have always started with themselves though within their given historical conditions and relationships, not with the "pure" individual in the sense of the ideologists. But in the course of historical development and precisely through the inevitable fact that in the division of labor social relationships assume an independent existence, there occurs a division in the life of each individual, insofar as it is personal and determined by some branch of labor and by the conditions pertaining to it. (This does not mean that, for example, the rentier, the capitalist, etc., cease to be persons; but their personality is conditioned and determined by very definite class relationships, and the differentiation appears only in their opposition to another class and, for themselves, only when they go bankrupt.) In the estate (and even more in the tribe) this is as yet concealed. A nobleman, for instance, will always remain a nobleman and a commoner always a commoner apart from his other relationships, a quality inseparable from his individuality. The differentiation between the personal and class individual and the accidental nature of the conditions of life for the individual appears only with the rise of the class which itself is a product of the bourgeoisie. Competition and the struggle of individuals among themselves engender and develop this accidental character. In imagination, individuals seem freer under the rule of the bourgeoisie than before because their conditions of life seem accidental to them. In reality they are less free, because they are more subjected to the domination of things. The difference from the estate is brought out particularly in the antagonism between the bourgeoisie and the proletariat.

When the estate of urban burghers, the corporations, etc., emerged in opposition to the landed nobility, their condition of existence, namely, movable property and craft labor already existing latently before their separation from feudal ties, appeared as something positive which was asserted against feudal landed property and hence at first took on a feudal form. Certainly the escaped serfs considered their previous servitude as something accidental to their personality. But they were only doing what every class freeing itself from a fetter does. And they did not free themselves as a class but as separate individuals. They did not rise above the system of estates, but merely formed a new estate and retained their previous mode of labor even in their new situation, developing it further by freeing it from its earlier fetters which no longer corresponded to the development already attained.

For the proletarians, on the other hand, the condition of their existence, labor, and thus all the conditions governing modern society have become something accidental, something over which they, as separate proletarians, have no control and over which no *social* organization can give them control. The contradiction between the personality of each separate proletarian and labor, the condition of life forced upon him, is very evident to him, for he is sacrificed from his youth on and within his class has no chance of arriving at conditions which would place him in another class.

N.B. It must not be forgotten that the serf's very need to exist and the impossibility of large-scale economy with distribution of allotments among the serfs soon reduced the duties of the serfs to an average of payments in kind and statute-labor for their lord. This enabled the serf to accumulate movable property, facilitated his escape from the possession of his lord, and gave him the prospect of making his way as a burgher. It also created gradations among the serfs; the runaway serfs were already half burghers. It is obvious that the serfs who were trained in a craft had the best chance of acquiring movable property.

While the runaway serfs only wished to become free in order to develop and assert those conditions of existence already present and hence in the end only arrived at free labor, the proletarians, if they are to assert themselves as individuals, must abolish the very condition of their existence which has been that of all society up to the present: labor. Thus they find themselves directly opposed to the form in which individuals composing society have given themselves collective expression, the state: and they must overthrow the state in order to realize their personality.

It is clear from what has been said that the communal relationship, into which the individuals of a class entered and which was determined by their common interests over against a third party, was always a community to which these individuals belonged only as average individuals, only insofar as they lived within the conditions of existence of their class—a relationship in which they participated not as individuals but as members of a class. On the other hand, it is just the reverse with the community of revolutionary proletarians who take their conditions of existence and those of all members of society under their control. The individuals participate in this community as individuals. It is this combination of individuals (assuming the present stage of productive forces, of course) which puts the conditions of the free development and movement of individuals under their control, conditions which were previously abandoned to chance and had acquired independent existence over against separate individuals because of their separation as individuals and because of the necessity of their combination which had been determined by the division of labor and through their separation had become a bond alien to them. Up till now the combination, by no means an arbitrary one as expounded in the *Contrat social* but a necessary one, was an agreement on these conditions within which the individuals were free to enjoy accidents of fortune (compare, for example, the formation of the North American state and the South American republics). This right to the undisturbed enjoyment of accidents of fortune, though within certain conditions, has been called personal freedom.—These conditions of existence are, of course, only the productive forces and forms of interaction of the particular time.

[Communism: Production of the Form of Interaction Itself] Communism differs from all previous movements because it overturns the basis of all previous relations of production and interaction, and for the first time consciously treats all natural premises as creations of men, strips them of their national character, and subjects them to the power of united individuals. Its organization, therefore, is essentially economic, the material production of the conditions of this unity. It turns existing conditions into conditions of unity. The reality that communism creates is the actual basis for making it impossible that anything should exist independently of individuals, insofar as this reality is only a product of the preceding interaction of individuals themselves. Communists in practice treat the conditions created until now by production and interaction as inorganic conditions, without imagining, however, that it was the plan or the destiny of previous generations to provide them material and without believing that these conditions were inorganic for the individuals creating them.

The difference between the individual as a person and what is accidental to him is not a conceptual difference but a historical fact. This distinction has a different significance in different periods, for example, the estate as something accidental to the individual in the eighteenth century and the family more or less accidental too. We do not have to make this distinction for each age; rather, each age itself makes it from the different elements which it finds in existence, not according to a concept but compelled by material collisions of life. Elements which appear accidental to a later age in comparison with an earlier one, including those handed down by the earlier age, constitute a form of interaction which corresponded to a particular stage of productive forces. The relation of the productive forces to the form of interaction is the relation of the form of interaction to the occupation or activity of the individuals. (Of course, the fundamental form of this activity is material; all other forms, intellectual, political, religious, etc., depend on it. The diverse shaping of material life is always dependent on needs already developed, and the production as well as satisfaction of these needs is itself a historical process not found with a sheep or a dog (the perverse principal argument of Stirner's *adversus* hominem) though sheep and dogs in their present form and in spite of themselves are products of a historical process.)

The conditions under which individuals interact so long as contradiction is still absent are nothing external to them but are conditions pertaining to their individuality, conditions under which these particular individuals living in particular circumstances can produce their material life and what is connected with it. They are the conditions of their self-activity and are produced by this self-activity. ⟨⟨Production of the form of interaction itself.⟩⟩ In the absence of contradiction the particular condition under which they produce thus corresponds to the actuality of their conditioned nature, their one-sided existence, the one-sidedness of which shows only when contradiction enters and thus only exists for later individuals. Then this condition appears as an accidental fetter, and the consciousness that it is a fetter is imputed to the earlier age.

These various conditions, which appear first as conditions of self-activity and later as fetters upon it, form in the whole evolution of history a coherent series of forms of interaction. The coherence consists of the fact that in the place of an earlier form of interaction, which has become a fetter, is put a new one corresponding to the more developed productive forces and thus to an advanced mode of the self-activity of individuals, a form which in turn becomes a fetter to be replaced by another. Since these conditions correspond at every stage to the simultaneous development of productive forces, their history is at the same time the history of the evolving productive forces taken over by each new generation and hence the history of the development of the forces of the individuals themselves.

Since this evolution proceeds naturally and is not subordinated to a general plan of freely united individuals, it starts out from various localities, tribes, nations, branches of labor, etc., each of which develops independently of the others and only gradually enters into relationship with the others. It proceeds only very slowly. The various stages and interests are never completely overcome but only subordinated to the winning interest and drag along with it for centuries. Thus we see that even within a nation the individuals, apart from their pecuniary circumstances, have quite different developments. We see that an earlier interest, whose peculiar form of interaction has already been supplanted by a form belonging to a later interest, remains for a long time afterwards in possession of a traditional power in the illusory community (state, law) which has become independent of individuals, a power that can only be broken by revolution. This explains why, with reference to particular points which permit a more general summary, consciousness can sometimes appear further advanced than contemporary empirical relationships so one can quote earlier theoreticians as authorities in the struggles of a later epoch.

In countries like North America which begin in an already advanced historical epoch, development proceeds very rapidly. Such countries have no other natural premises than the individuals who settled there and were induced to do so because the forms of interaction in the old countries did not correspond to their wants. Thus they begin with the most advanced individuals of the old countries and with the correspondingly most advanced form of interaction, even before this form of interaction has been established in the old countries. This is the case with all colonies which are not military or trading stations. Carthage, the Greek colonies, and Iceland in the eleventh and twelfth centuries are examples of this. A similar relationship is established by conquest when a form of interaction which has evolved elsewhere is introduced complete into the conquered country. While it was still encumbered with interests and relationships from earlier periods at home, it can and must be established completely and without hindrance in the conquered country to assure the conquerors' lasting power. (England and Naples after the Norman Conquest, when they received the most perfect form of feudal organization.)

This whole interpretation of history appears to be contradicted by the fact of conquest. Violence, war, pillage, murder, etc., have been seen as the motive force of history. We must limit ourselves here to the chief points and take up only the most striking example, the destruction of an old civilization by a barbarous people and the resulting formation of an entirely new organization of society (Rome and the barbarians; feudalism and Gaul; the Byzantine Empire and the Turks). As indicated above, with the conquering barbarian people, war is still a regular form of interaction which is the more eagerly exploited as the population increases and requires new means of production to take the place of the traditional and the only possible crude mode of production. In Italy, however, concentration of landed property (caused not only by purchases and indebtedness, but also by inheritance, since the old families died out from loose living and rare marriages and their possessions fell into the hands of a few) and its conversion into grazing land (caused not only by common economic forces still existing today but also by the importation of plundered and tribute grain and the resultant lack of demand for Italian grain) made the free population disappear almost completely. Slaves died out again and again and constantly had to be replaced by new ones. Slavery remained the basis of the entire productive system. The plebeians standing between freemen and slaves never succeeded in becoming more than proletarian rabble. Indeed, Rome never became more than a city. Its connection with the provinces was almost exclusively political and could easily be broken by political events.

Nothing is more common than the notion that in history up till now *taking* has been the thing that counts. The barbarians *take* the Roman Empire, and the transition from the old world to the feudal system is explained with this fact of taking. In this taking by barbarians it is important whether the conquered nation has industrial productive forces, as is the case with modern peoples, or whether its productive forces are based for the most part merely on association and community. Taking is further determined by the object taken. A banker's fortune consisting of paper cannot be taken without the taker's submitting to the conditions of production and interaction in the country taken. It is similar with the total industrial capital of a modern industrial country. Finally, taking very soon comes to an end, and when there is nothing more to take, one must begin to produce. From this necessity of producing, which comes about very soon, it follows that the form of community adopted by the settling conquerors must correspond to the stage of development of the productive forces they find in existence; or, if this is not the case from the start, it must change to accord with the productive forces. This explains what people say they have noticed everywhere in the period after the Great Migration, namely, that the servant was master and that the conquerors very soon adopted the language, culture, and manners of the conquered.

The feudal system was by no means brought complete from Germany. As far as the conquerors were concerned, it had its origin in the organization of the army during the conquest itself and developed after the conquest into the feudal system proper through the action of the productive forces found in the conquered countries. To what extent this form was determined by the productive forces is shown by the abortive attempts to institute other forms derived from reminiscences of ancient Rome (Charlemagne, etc.). To be continued.

In big industry and competition all the conditions of existence, the determining factors, and the biases of individuals are fused together into the two simplest forms: private property and labor. With money every form of interaction, and interaction itself, is considered accidental for individuals. Money implies that all previous interaction was only commerce of individuals under particular conditions, not of individuals as individuals. These conditions are reduced to two: accumulated labor of private property, and actual labor. Even if only one of these ceases, interaction comes to a standstill. The modern economists themselves, for example, Sismondi, Cherbuliez, etc., juxtapose "association of individuals" and "association of capital." On the other hand, the individuals themselves are completely subsumed under the division of labor and brought into complete dependence on one another. Private property, insofar as it is opposed to labor within labor itself, evolves out of the necessity of accumulation and has at first the form of community. But in its further development it approaches more and more the modern form of private property. From the outset, the division of labor implies division of the *conditions of labor*, of tools and materials, and the splitting up of accumulated capital into the hands of various owners, and thus the division between capital and labor and different forms of capital itself. The further division of labor proceeds and the more accumulation grows, the more pronounced does the fragmentation become. Labor itself can exist only under the premise of this fragmentation.

Personal energy of the individuals of various nations—Germans and Americans—energy generated already through crossbreeding— hence the cretinism of the Germans—in France, England, etc., foreign peoples transplanted to a land already developed, in America to virgin land—in Germany the native population quietly remained in its locale.

Thus two facts become clear. First, the productive forces appear as a world by themselves independent of, removed from, and alongside individuals because the individuals whose forces they are, exist as split up and opposed to one another. On the other hand these forces are only real forces in the interaction and association of the individuals. Thus we have, on the one hand, a totality of productive forces which, so to speak, have assumed material form and are for the individuals no longer the forces of individuals but of private property—of individuals only insofar as they are owners of private property. Never before have the productive forces taken on a form so indifferent to the interaction of individuals *as* individuals, because their interaction was still restricted. On the other hand, opposing the productive forces, there is the majority of the individuals from whom these forces have been wrested away and who have become abstract individuals deprived of all real life content. Only through this fact, however, are they enabled to enter into relation with one another *as individuals.* The only connection still linking them with the productive forces and with their own existence, labor, has lost all semblance of self-activity and sustains their life only by stunting it. While in earlier periods self-activity and the production of material life were separated by the fact that they devolved on different persons and because the production of material life was considered a subordinate mode of self-activity due to the narrowness of the individuals themselves, they now diverge to such an extent that material life appears as the end, and labor, the producer of this material life (now the only possible but negative form of self-activity, as we see), appears as means.

Things have come to the point where individuals must appropriate the existing totality of productive forces not merely to achieve self-activity but to secure their very existence. This appropriation is determined by the object to be appropriated—the productive forces developed to a totality and existing only within a universal interaction. From this aspect alone, this appropriation must have a universal character corresponding to the productive forces and interaction. The appropriation of these forces is itself nothing more than the development of individual capacities corresponding to the material instruments of production. For this very reason, the appropriation of a totality of instruments of production is the development of a totality of capabilities in the individuals themselves. It is further determined by the appropriating individuals. Only the proletarians of the present, completely deprived of any self-activity, can achieve a complete and unrestricted self-activity involving the appropriation of a totality of productive forces and consequently the development of a totality of capacities. All previous revolutionary appropriations were restricted. Individuals, whose self-activity was restricted by a crude instrument of production and limited interaction, appropriated this crude instrument of production and merely attained a new plateau of limitation. Their instrument of production became their property, but they themselves remained subject to the division of labor and their own instrument of production. In all appropriations up to now a mass of individuals remained subservient to a single instrument of production. In the appropriation by the proletarians, a mass of instruments of production must be subservient to each individual and the property of all. The only way for individuals to control modern universal interaction is to make it subject to the control of all.

The appropriation is further determined by the manner in which it must be carried through. It can only be accomplished by a union, universal because of the character of the proletariat itself, and through a revolution in which the power of the social organization and of earlier modes of production and interaction is overthrown and the proletariat's universal character and energy for the act of appropriation is developed. Furthermore, the proletariat must get rid of everything still clinging to it from its earlier position in society.

Not until this stage is reached will self-activity coincide with material life, will individuals become complete individuals. Only then will the shedding of all natural limitations be accomplished. The transformation of labor into self-activity corresponds to the transformation of the previous restricted interaction into the interaction of individuals as such. With the appropriation of the total productive forces through united individuals, private property ceases to exist. While in previous history a particular condition always appeared as accidental, now the isolation of individuals and the particular private gain of any individual have become accidental.

Individuals who are no longer subjected to the division of labor have been conceived by the philosophers as an ideal under the name of "Man." They have grasped the whole process described as the evolutionary process of "Man," so at every historical stage "Man" was substituted for individuals and presented as the motive force of history. The whole process was seen as a process of the self-alienation of "Man," essentially because the average individual of the later stage was always foisted on the earlier stage and the consciousness of a later period on the individuals of an earlier. ⟨⟨Self-alienation⟩⟩ Through this inversion, which from the beginning has been an abstraction of the actual conditions, it was possible to transform all history into an evolutionary process of consciousness.

Civil society comprises the entire material interaction among individuals at a particular evolutionary stage of the productive forces. It comprises the entire commercial and industrial life of a stage and hence transcends the state and the nation even though that life, on the other hand, is manifested in foreign affairs as nationality and organized within a state. The term "civil society" emerged in the eighteenth century when property relations had already evolved from the community of antiquity and medieval times. Civil society as such only develops with the bourgeoisie. The social organization, however, which evolves directly from production and commerce and in all ages forms the basis of the state and the rest of the idealistic superstructure, has always been designated by the same name.

Relation of the State and Law to Property

The first form of property in antiquity as in the Middle Ages is tribal property, determined with the Romans chiefly by war and with the Germanic peoples by cattle breeding. Since several tribes lived together in one town in the ancient world, tribal property was state property and the right of the individual to it was mere Possessio, confined like tribal property as a whole to landed property only. With the ancients as with modern nations, real private property began with movable property— (slavery and community) (*dominium ex jure Quiritum* [ownership from the law of full Roman citizenship]). In nations evolving from the Middle Ages, tribal property developed through several stages—feudal landed property, corporative movable property, manufacturing capital—to modern capital determined by big industry and universal competition, pure private property free of all semblance of a communal institution and excluding the state from any influence on its development.

To such modern private property corresponds the modern state which has been gradually bought by property owners through taxes, has fallen entirely into their hands through the national debt, and has become completely dependent on the commercial credit they, the bourgeois, extend to it in the rise and fall of government bonds on the stock exchange. Being a *class* and no longer an *estate*, the bourgeoisie is forced to organize itself nationally rather than locally and give a general form to its averaged interest. Through the emancipation of private property from the community, the state has become a separate entity beside and outside civil society. But the state is nothing more than the form of organization which the bourgeois by necessity adopts for both internal and external purposes as a mutual guarantee of their property and interests. The independence of the state is found today only in countries where estates have not fully developed into classes, where estates, having disappeared in more advanced countries, still have a role to play, and where a mixture exists—countries where no one section of the population can attain control over the others. This is the case particularly in Germany. The perfect example of the modern state is North America. The modern French, English, and American writers all express the opinion that the state exists only for the sake of private property; this fact has entered into the consciousness of the ordinary man.

Since the state is the form in which the individuals of a ruling class assert their common interests and the entire civil society of an epoch is epitomized, the state acts as an intermediary in the formation of all communal institutions and gives them a political form. Hence there is the illusion that law is based on will, that is, on will divorced from its real basis, on *free* will. In a similar fashion, right in turn is reduced to statute law.

Civil law develops simultaneously with private property from the disintegration of the natural community. With the Romans the development of private property and civil law had no further industrial and commercial consequences because their whole mode of production remained unchanged. ⟨⟨Usury!⟩⟩ In modern nations where the feudal community was eliminated by industry and trade, there began with the rise of private property and civil law a new phase capable of further development. The very first town with extensive sea trade in the Middle Ages, Amalfi, also developed maritime law. As soon as industry and trade developed private property further, first in Italy and then in other countries, Roman civil law was adopted in a perfected form and made authoritative. When later the bourgeoisie had acquired so much power that princes took up the interests of the bourgeoisie in order to topple feudal nobility through the bourgeoisie, the real development of law began in all countries—in France in the sixteenth century. With the exception of England, it proceeded everywhere on the basis of the Roman Codex. Even in England, Roman legal principles had to be adopted to further the development of civil law, particularly in regard to movable property. (It must not be forgotten that law has just as little independent history as religion.)

In civil law the existing property relationships are declared to be the result of a general will. The *jus utendi et abutendi* [right of using and consuming] itself expresses, on the one hand, the fact that private property has become entirely independent of the community, and on the other the illusion that private property itself is based simply on private will, on the arbitrary disposition of the thing. In practice, the *abuti* has very definite economic limitations for the owner of private property if he does not wish to see his property and thus his *jus abutendi* pass into the hands of another person, because the thing, considered only with reference to his will, is not a thing at all but only becomes actual property through interaction and independently of the right to the thing (a *relationship* which the philosophers call an idea). ⟨⟨*Relationship for the philosophers = idea.* They only know the relationship "*of* Man" to himself, and thus all actual relationships become ideas for them.⟩⟩ This juridical illusion, which reduces law to mere will, in further development of property relationships necessarily leads to one's having legal title to a thing without actually having it. If for example the income from a piece of land is lost due to competition, the owner, to be sure, has his legal title to it along with the *jus utendi et abutendi.* But he cannot do anything with it. If he does not have enough capital to cultivate his land he owns nothing as a landed proprietor. This illusion of lawyers also explains why for them, as for every code, it is altogether accidental that individuals enter into relationships with one another, for example, make contractual agreements; why they hold the view that these relationships [can] be entered into or not at will and that their content [re]sts entirely on the individual free [will] of the contracting parties. Every time new forms of [com]merce evolved through the develop[ment] of industry and trade, for [example] insurance companies, etc., the law was compelled to admit thcm among the modes of acquiring property. [The continuous text in Engels' script ends here; directly below, in the left column, Marx added the following notes.]

Influence of division of labor on science.
Repression in state, law, morality, etc.
[In] law the bourgeois must present themselves as universal just

because they rule as a class ⟨⟨⟨(Catholic) religious conceptions particularly correspond to the "community," to this bond, as it appears in the state of antiquity, in the feudal system, in absolute monarchy⟩⟩.

Natural science and history.

There is no history of politics, law, science, etc., of art, religion, etc.

Why ideologists turn everything upside down.

Religionists, lawyers, politicians.

Lawyers, politicians (government officials in general), moralists, religionists.

For this ideological subdivision within a class, 1. *Occupation becomes independent through the division of labor;* everybody thinks of his craft as the true one. Because it is determined by the nature of the craft itself, one necessarily has illusions about the connection of his craft with reality. In jurisprudence, politics, etc., relationships turn into concepts in consciousness. Since they do not transcend these relationships, the concepts become fixations. A judge, for example, applies the code. For him legislation is the true, active force. Respect for their goods because their occupation involves the universal.

Idea of law. Idea of state. In *ordinary* consciousness, the matter is turned upside down.

Religion from the outset is consciousness of *transcendence* [which] arises from a *real* necessity.

This in a more popular manner.

Tradition, in regard to law, religion, etc.

Individuals have always begun, always begin, with themselves. Their relationships are relationships of their actual life-process. How does it happen that their relationships become something independent over against them, that the forces of their own life overpower them?

Briefly: *the division of labor,* whose level depends on the productive power developed at the time.

Communal property.

Landed property, feudal, modern.

Estate property. Manufacturing property. Industrial capital.

The Communist Manifesto

Karl Marx and Friedrich Engels

The Communist Manifesto *is the most widely read of all of Marx's writings and arguably the most influential piece of political writing of modern times. It was written by Marx and Engels at the end of 1847 and the beginning of 1848 at the request of a radical and conspiratorial German workers' party, the League of the Just. Marx and Engels began having increased contact with the League, then headquartered in London, in the mid-1840's. In 1847, the League dropped its conspiratorial orientation, changed its name to the Communist League, and approached Marx and Engels to draft a statement of principles, in effect, a party platform, for it. They accepted, and the* Manifesto *was published in London in February, 1848.*

The Manifesto *is a combination of theoretical summary and revolutionary polemic and succeeds brilliantly on both levels. Its central point was perhaps best summarized by Engels in the "Preface" to the 1883 German edition of the work.*

> The basic thought running through the Manifesto—that economic production and the structure of society of every historical epoch necessarily arising therefrom constitute the foundation for the political and intellectual history of that epoch; that consequently (ever since the dissolution of the primeval communal ownership of land) all history has been a history of class struggles, of struggles between exploited and exploiting, between dominated and dominating classes at various stages of social development; that this struggle, however, has now reached a stage where the exploited and oppressed class (the proletariat) can no longer emancipate itself from the class which exploits and oppresses it (the bourgeoisie), without at the same time for ever freeing the whole of society from exploitation, oppression and class struggles—this basic thought belongs solely and exclusively to Marx.[1]

The Manifesto *is divided into four sections. The first sketches a history of class struggle from the Middle Ages through the rise of the bourgeoisie to the present class situation of modern capitalist society and the struggle between the bourgeoisie and the proletariat. In the second section, the position of the communist movement in relation to the working class is put forward and defended against a variety of criticisms. At the end of this section, Marx and Engels list some of the measures to be put into effect by the communists once*

1. Karl Marx, Friedrich Engels, *The Communist Manifesto*, with an Introduction by A.J.P. Taylor (Harmondsworth, England: Penguin Books Inc., 1967), p. 57.

the proletariat rises to power. It is interesting to note that, in the light of subsequent history, some items on the list, such as a graduated income tax, have lost their revolutionary appearance. In the third section, Marx and Engels argue with various other socialist positions, indicating ways in which theirs is the correct form of socialism. The final, short section discusses the relation of the communists to parties in other countries and ends with the famous exhortation, "The proletarians have nothing to lose but their chains. They have a world to win. WORKING MEN OF ALL COUNTRIES, UNITE!"

A spectre is haunting Europe—the spectre of Communism. All the Powers of old Europe have entered into a holy alliance to exorcise this spectre: Pope and Czar, Metternich and Guizot, French Radicals and German police-spies.

Where is the party in opposition that has not been decried as Communistic by its opponents in power? Where the Opposition that has not hurled back the branding reproach of Communism, against the more advanced opposition parties, as well as against its reactionary adversaries?

Two things result from this fact:

I. Communism is already acknowledged by all European Powers to be itself a Power.

II. It is high time that Communists should openly, in the face of the whole world, publish their views, their aims, their tendencies, and meet this nursery tale of the Spectre of Communism with a Manifesto of the party itself.

To this end, Communists of various nationalities have assembled in London, and sketched the following Manifesto, to be published in the English, French, German, Italian, Flemish and Danish languages.

I
BOURGEOIS AND PROLETARIANS*

The history of all hitherto existing society** is the history of class struggles.

The edition used here is the standard English edition of 1888.

*By bourgeoisie is meant the class of modern Capitalists, owners of the means of social production and employers of wage-labour. By proletariat, the class of modern wage-labourers who, having no means of production of their own, are reduced to selling their labour-power in order to live. [*Note by Engels to the English edition of 1888.*]

**That is, all *written* history. In 1847, the pre-history of society, the social organisation existing previous to recorded history, was all but unknown. Since

Freeman and slave, patrician and plebeian, lord and serf, guild-master*
and journeyman, in a word, oppressor and oppressed, stood in constant
opposition to one another, carried on an uninterrupted, now hidden, now
open fight, a fight that each time ended, either in a revolutionary re-
constitution of society at large, or in the common ruin of the contending
classes.

In the earlier epochs of history, we find almost everywhere a complicated arrangement of society into various orders, a manifold gradation of
social rank. In ancient Rome we have patricians, knights, plebeians,
slaves; in the Middle Ages, feudal lords, vassals, guild-masters, journeymen, apprentices, serfs; in almost all of these classes, again, subordinate
gradations.

The modern bourgeois society that has sprouted from the ruins of
feudal society has not done away with class antagonisms. It has but
established new classes, new conditions of oppression, new forms of
struggle in place of the old ones.

Our epoch, the epoch of the bourgeoisie, possesses, however, this
distinctive feature: it has simplified the class antagonisms. Society as a
whole is more and more splitting up into two great hostile camps, into
two great classes directly facing each other: Bourgeoisie and Proletariat.

From the serfs of the Middle Ages sprang the chartered burghers of
the earliest towns. From these burgesses the first elements of the bourgeoisie were developed.

The discovery of America, the rounding of the Cape, opened up fresh
ground for the rising bourgeoisie. The East-Indian and Chinese markets, the colonisation of America, trade with the colonies, the increase in
the means of exchange and in commodities generally, gave to commerce,
to navigation, to industry, an impulse never before known, and thereby, to

---

then, Haxthausen discovered common ownership of land in Russia, Maurer
proved it to be the social foundation from which all Teutonic races started in
history, and by and by village communities were found to be, or to have been the
primitive form of society everywhere from India to Ireland. The inner organisation of this primitive Communistic society was laid bare, in its typical form, by
Morgan's crowning discovery of the true nature of the *gens* and its relation to the
tribe. With the dissolution of these primeval communities society begins to be
differentiated into separate and finally antagonistic classes. I have attempted to
retrace this process of dissolution in *Der Ursprung der Familie, des Pri-
vateigenthums und des Staats,* 2nd edition, Stuttgart, 1886. [*Note by Engels to the
English edition of 1888, and—less the last sentence—to the German edition of
1890.*]

*Guild-master, that is, a full member of a guild, a master within, not a head of a
guild. [*Note by Engels to the English edition of 1888.*]

the revolutionary element in the tottering feudal society, a rapid development.

The feudal system of industry, under which industrial production was monopolised by closed guilds, now no longer sufficed for the growing wants of the new markets. The manufacturing system took its place. The guild-masters were pushed on one side by the manufacturing middle class; division of labour between the different corporate guilds vanished in the face of division of labour in each single workshop.

Meantime the markets kept ever growing, the demand ever rising. Even manufacture no longer sufficed. Thereupon, steam and machinery revolutionised industrial production. The place of manufacture was taken by the giant, Modern Industry, the place of the industrial middle class, by industrial millionaires, the leaders of whole industrial armies, the modern bourgeois.

Modern industry has established the world market, for which the discovery of America paved the way. This market has given an immense development to commerce, to navigation, to communication by land. This development has, in its turn, reacted on the extension of industry; and in proportion as industry, commerce, navigation, railways extended, in the same proportion the bourgeoisie developed, increased its capital, and pushed into the background every class handed down from the Middle Ages.

We see, therefore, how the modern bourgeoisie is itself the product of a long course of development, of a series of revolutions in the modes of production and of exchange.

Each step in the development of the bourgeoisie was accompanied by a corresponding political advance of that class. An oppressed class under the sway of the feudal nobility, an armed and self-governing association in the medieval commune;* here independent urban republic (as in Italy and Germany), there taxable "third estate" of the monarchy (as in France), afterwards, in the period of manufacture proper, serving either

---

*"Commune" was the name taken, in France, by the nascent towns even before they had conquered from their feudal lords and masters local self-government and political rights as the "Third Estate." Generally speaking, for the economical development of the bourgeoisie, England is here taken as the typical country; for its political development, France. [*Note by Engels to the English edition of 1888.*]

This was the name given their urban communities by the townsmen of Italy and France, after they had purchased or wrested their initial rights of self-government from their feudal lords. [*Note by Engels to the German edition of 1890.*]

the semi-feudal or the absolute monarchy as a counterpoise against the nobility, and, in fact, cornerstone of the great monarchies in general, the bourgeoisie has at last, since the establishment of Modern Industry and of the world market, conquered for itself, in the modern representative State, exclusive political sway. The executive of the modern State is but a committee for managing the common affairs of the whole bourgeoisie.

The bourgeoisie, historically, has played a most revolutionary part.

The bourgeoisie, wherever it has got the upper hand, has put an end to all feudal, patriarchal, idyllic relations. It has pitilessly torn asunder the motley feudal ties that bound man to his "natural superiors," and has left remaining no other nexus between man and man than naked self-interest, than callous "cash payment." It has drowned the most heavenly ecstasies of religious fervour, of chivalrous enthusiasm, of philistine sentimentalism, in the icy water of egotistical calculation. It has resolved personal worth into exchange value, and in place of the numberless indefeasible chartered freedoms, has set up that single, unconscionable freedom—Free Trade. In one word, for exploitation, veiled by religious and political illusions, it has substituted naked, shameless, direct, brutal exploitation.

The bourgeoisie has stripped of its halo every occupation hitherto honoured and looked up to with reverent awe. It has converted the physician, the lawyer, the priest, the poet, the man of science, into its paid wage-labourers.

The bourgeoisie has torn away from the family its sentimental veil, and has reduced the family relation to a mere money relation.

The bourgeoisie has disclosed how it came to pass that the brutal display of vigour in the Middle Ages, which Reactionists so much admire, found its fitting complement in the most slothful indolence. It has been the first to show what man's activity can bring about. It has accomplished wonders far surpassing Egyptian pyramids, Roman aqueducts, and Gothic cathedrals; it has conducted expeditions that put in the shade all former Exoduses of nations and crusades.

The bourgeoisie cannot exist without constantly revolutionising the instruments of production, and thereby the relations of production, and with them the whole relations of society. Conservation of the old modes of production in unaltered form, was, on the contrary, the first condition of existence for all earlier industrial classes. Constant revolutionising of production, uninterrupted disturbance of all social conditions, everlasting uncertainty and agitation distinguish the bourgeois epoch from all earlier ones. All fixed, fast-frozen relations, with their train of ancient and venerable prejudices and opinions, are swept away, all new-formed ones become antiquated before they can ossify. All that is solid melts into air, all that is holy is profaned, and man is at last compelled to face with sober senses, his real conditions of life, and his relations with his kind.

The need of a constantly expanding market for its products chases the bourgeoisie over the whole surface of the globe. It must nestle everywhere, settle everywhere, establish connexions everywhere.

The bourgeoisie has through its exploitation of the world market given a cosmopolitan character to production and consumption in every country. To the great chagrin of Reactionists, it has drawn from under the feet of industry the national ground on which it stood. All old-established national industries have been destroyed or are daily being destroyed. They are dislodged by new industries, whose introduction becomes a life and death question for all civilised nations, by industries that no longer work up indigenous raw material, but raw material drawn from the remotest zones; industries whose products are consumed, not only at home, but in every quarter of the globe. In place of the old wants, satisfied by the productions of the country, we find new wants, requiring for their satisfaction the products of distant lands and climes. In place of the old local and national seclusion and self-sufficiency, we have intercourse in every direction, universal interdependence of nations. And as in material, so also in intellectual production. The intellectual creations of individual nations become common property. National one-sidedness and narrow-mindedness become more and more impossible, and from the numerous national and local literatures, there arises a world literature.

The bourgeoisie, by the rapid improvement of all instruments of production, by the immensely facilitated means of communication, draws all, even the most barbarian, nations into civilisation. The cheap prices of its commodities are the heavy artillery with which it batters down all Chinese walls, with which it forces the barbarians' intensely obstinate hatred of foreigners to capitulate. It compels all nations, on pain of extinction, to adopt the bourgeois mode of production; it compels them to introduce what it calls civilisation into their midst, i.e., to become bourgeois themselves. In one word, it creates a world after its own image.

The bourgeoisie has subjected the country to the rule of the towns. It has created enormous cities, has greatly increased the urban population as compared with the rural, and has thus rescued a considerable part of the population from the idiocy of rural life. Just as it has made the country dependent on the towns, so it has made barbarian and semibarbarian countries dependent on the civilised ones, nations of peasants on nations of bourgeois, the East on the West.

The bourgeoisie keeps more and more doing away with the scattered state of the population, of the means of production, and of property. It has agglomerated population, centralised means of production, and has concentrated property in a few hands. The necessary consequence of this was political centralisation. Independent, or but loosely connected provinces with separate interests, laws, governments and systems of taxation, became lumped together into one nation, with one government, one code of laws, one national class-interest, one frontier and one customs-tariff.

The bourgeoisie, during its rule of scarce one hundred years, has created more massive and more colossal productive forces than have all preceding generations together. Subjection of Nature's forces to man, machinery, application of chemistry to industry and agriculture, steam-navigation, railways, electric telegraphs, clearing of whole continents for cultivation, canalisation of rivers, whole populations conjured out of the ground—what earlier century had even a presentiment that such productive forces slumbered in the lap of social labour?

We see then: the means of production and of exchange, on whose foundation the bourgeoisie built itself up, were generated in feudal society. At a certain stage in the development of these means of production and of exchange, the conditions under which feudal society produced and exchanged, the feudal organisation of agriculture and manufacturing industry, in one word, the feudal relations of property became no longer compatible with the already developed productive forces; they became so many fetters. They had to be burst asunder; they were burst asunder.

Into their place stepped free competition, accompanied by a social and political constitution adapted to it, and by the economical and political sway of the bourgeois class.

A similar movement is going on before our own eyes. Modern bourgeois society with its relations of production, of exchange and of property, a society that has conjured up such gigantic means of production and of exchange, is like the sorcerer, who is no longer able to control the powers of the nether world whom he has called up by his spells. For many a decade past the history of industry and commerce is but the history of the revolt of modern productive forces against modern conditions of production, against the property relations that are the conditions for the existence of the bourgeoisie and of its rule. It is enough to mention the commercial crises that by their political return put on its trial, each time more threateningly, the existence of the entire bourgeois society. In these crises a great part not only of the existing products, but also of the previously created productive forces, are periodically destroyed. In these crises there breaks out an epidemic that, in all earlier epochs, would have seemed an absurdity—the epidemic of over-production. Society suddenly finds itself put back into a state of momentary barbarism; it appears as if a famine, a universal war of devastation had cut off the supply of every means of subsistence; industry and commerce seem to be destroyed; and why? Because there is too much civilisation, too much means of subsistence, too much industry, too much commerce. The productive forces at the disposal of society no longer tend to further the development of the conditions of bourgeois property; on the contrary, they have become too powerful for these conditions, by which they are fettered, and so soon as they overcome these fetters, they bring disorder into the whole of bourgeois society, endanger the existence of bourgeois property. The conditions of bourgeois society are too narrow to comprise the wealth created by them. And how does the bourgeoisie get over these crises? On the one hand by enforced destruction of a mass of productive forces; on the other, by the conquest of new markets, and by the more thorough exploitation of the old ones. That is to say, by paving the way for more extensive and more destructive crises, and by diminishing the means whereby crises are prevented.

The weapons with which the bourgeoisie felled feudalism to the ground are now turned against the bourgeoisie itself.

But not only has the bourgeoisie forged the weapons that bring death to itself; it has also called into existence the men who are to wield those weapons—the modern working class—the proletarians.

In proportion as the bourgeoisie, *i.e.*, capital, is developed, in the same proportion is the proletariat, the modern working class, developed—a class of labourers, who live only so long as they find work, and who find work only so long as their labour increases capital. These labourers, who must sell themselves piecemeal, are a commodity, like every other article of commerce, and are consequently exposed to all the vicissitudes of competition, to all the fluctuations of the market.

Owing to the extensive use of machinery and to division of labour, the work of the proletarians has lost all individual character, and, consequently, all charm for the workman. He becomes an appendage of the machine, and it is only the most simple, most monotonous, and most easily acquired knack, that is required of him. Hence, the cost of production of a workman is restricted, almost entirely, to the means of subsistence that he requires for his maintenance, and for the propagation of his race. But the price of a commodity, and therefore also of labour, is equal to its cost of production. In proportion, therefore, as the repulsiveness of the work increases, the wage decreases. Nay more, in proportion as the use of machinery and division of labour increases, in the same proportion the burden of toil also increases, whether by prolongation of the working hours, by increase of the work exacted in a given time or by increased speed of the machinery, etc.

Modern industry has converted the little workshop of the patriarchal

master into the great factory of the industrial capitalist. Masses of labourers, crowded into the factory, are organised like soldiers. As privates
of the industrial army they are placed under the command of a perfect
hierarchy of officers and sergeants. Not only are they slaves of the
bourgeois class, and of the bourgeois State; they are daily and hourly
enslaved by the machine, by the overlooker, and, above all, by the individual bourgeois manufacturer himself. The more openly this despotism
proclaims gain to be its end and aim, the more petty, the more hateful
and the more embittering it is.

The less the skill and exertion of strength implied in manual labour,
in other words, the more modern industry becomes developed, the more
is the labour of men superseded by that of women. Differences of age
and sex have no longer any distinctive social validity for the working
class. All are instruments of labour, more or less expensive to use,
according to their age and sex.

No sooner is the exploitation of the labourer by the manufacturer, so
far, at an end, and he receives his wages in cash, than he is set upon by
the other portions of the bourgeoisie, the landlord, the shopkeeper, the
pawnbroker, etc.

The lower strata of the middle class—the small tradespeople, shopkeepers, and retired tradesmen generally, the handicraftsmen and peasants—all these sink gradually into the proletariat, partly because their
diminutive capital does not suffice for the scale on which Modern Industry is carried on, and is swamped in the competition with the large
capitalists, partly because their specialised skill is rendered worthless by
new methods of production. Thus the proletariat is recruited from all
classes of the population.

The proletariat goes through various stages of development. With its
birth begins its struggle with the bourgeoisie. At first the contest is
carried on by individual labourers, then by the workpeople of a factory,
then by the operatives of one trade, in one locality, against the individual
bourgeois who directly exploits them. They direct their attacks not
against the bourgeois conditions of production, but against the instruments of production themselves; they destroy imported wares that com-
pete with their labour, they smash to pieces machinery, they set factories
ablaze, they seek to restore by force the vanished status of the workman
of the Middle Ages.

At this stage the labourers still form an incoherent mass scattered over
the whole country, and broken up by their mutual competition. If anywhere they unite to form more compact bodies, this is not yet the consequence of their own active union, but of the union of the bourgeoisie,
which class, in order to attain its own political ends, is compelled to set

the whole proletariat in motion, and is moreover yet, for a time, able to do so. At this stage, therefore, the proletarians do not fight their enemies, but the enemies of their enemies, the remnants of absolute monarchy, the landowners, the non-industrial bourgeois, the petty bourgeoisie. Thus the whole historical movement is concentrated in the hands of the bourgeoisie; every victory so obtained is a victory for the bourgeoisie.

But with the development of industry the proletariat not only increases in number; it becomes concentrated in greater masses, its strength grows, and it feels that strength more. The various interests and conditions of life within the ranks of the proletariat are more and more equalised, in proportion as machinery obliterates all distinctions of labour, and nearly everywhere reduces wages to the same low level. The growing competition among the bourgeois, and the resulting commercial crises, make the wages of the workers ever more fluctuating. The unceasing improvement of machinery, ever more rapidly developing, makes their livelihood more and more precarious; the collisions between individual workmen and individual bourgeois take more and more the character of collisions between two classes. Thereupon the workers begin to form combinations (Trades' Unions) against the bourgeois; they club together in order to keep up the rate of wages; they found permanent associations in order to make provision beforehand for these occasional revolts. Here and there the contest breaks out into riots.

Now and then the workers are victorious, but only for a time. The real fruit of their battles lies, not in the immediate result, but in the ever-expanding union of the workers. This union is helped on by the improved means of communication that are created by modern industry and that place the workers of different localities in contact with one another. It was just this contact that was needed to centralise the numerous local struggles, all of the same character, into one national struggle between classes. But every class struggle is a political struggle. And that union, to attain which the burghers of the Middle Ages, with their miserable highways, required centuries, the modern proletarians, thanks to railways, achieve in a few years.

This organisation of the proletarians into a class, and consequently into a political party, is continually being upset again by the competition between the workers themselves. But it ever rises up again, stronger, firmer, mightier. It compels legislative recognition of particular interests of the workers, by taking advantage of the divisions among the bourgeoisie itself. Thus the ten-hours' bill in England was carried.

Altogether collisions between the classes of the old society further, in many ways, the course of development of the proletariat. The bourgeoisie finds itself involved in a constant battle. At first with the aristocracy; later on, with those portions of the bourgeoisie itself, whose interests have become antagonistic to the progress of industry; at all times, with the bourgeoisie of foreign countries. In all these battles it sees itself compelled to appeal to the proletariat, to ask for its help, and thus, to drag it into the political arena. The bourgeoisie itself, therefore, supplies the proletariat with its own elements of political and general education, in other words, it furnishes the proletariat with weapons for fighting the bourgeoisie.

Further, as we have already seen, entire sections of the ruling classes are, by the advance of industry, precipitated into the proletariat, or are at least threatened in their conditions of existence. These also supply the proletariat with fresh elements of enlightenment and progress.

Finally, in times when the class struggle nears the decisive hour, the process of dissolution going on within the ruling class, in fact within the whole range of old society, assumes such a violent, glaring character, that a small section of the ruling class cuts itself adrift, and joins the revolutionary class, the class that holds the future in its hands. Just as, therefore, at an earlier period, a section of the nobility went over to the bourgeoisie, so now a portion of the bourgeoisie goes over to the proletariat, and in particular, a portion of the bourgeois ideologists, who have raised themselves to the level of comprehending theoretically the historical movement as a whole.

Of all the classes that stand face to face with the bourgeoisie today, the proletariat alone is a really revolutionary class. The other classes decay and finally disappear in the face of Modern Industry; the proletariat is its special and essential product.

The lower middle class, the small manufacturer, the shopkeeper, the artisan, the peasant, all these fight against the bourgeoisie, to save from extinction their existence as fractions of the middle class. They are therefore not revolutionary, but conservative. Nay more, they are reactionary, for they try to roll back the wheel of history. If by chance they are revolutionary, they are so only in view of their impending transfer into the proletariat, they thus defend not their present, but their future interests, they desert their own standpoint to place themselves at that of the proletariat.

The "dangerous class," the social scum, that passively rotting mass thrown off by the lowest layers of old society may, here and there, be swept into the movement by a proletarian revolution; its conditions of life, however, prepare it far more for the part of a bribed tool of reactionary intrigue.

In the conditions of the proletariat, those of old society at large are already virtually swamped. The proletarian is without property; his relation to his wife and children has no longer anything in common with the bourgeois family relations; modern industrial labour, modern subjection to capital, the same in England as in France, in America as in Germany, has stripped him of every trace of national character. Law, morality, religion, are to him so many bourgeois prejudices, behind which lurk in ambush just as many bourgeois interests.

All the preceding classes that got the upper hand, sought to fortify their already acquired status by subjecting society at large to their conditions of appropriation. The proletarians cannot become masters of the productive forces of society, except by abolishing their own previous mode of appropriation, and thereby also every other previous mode of appropriation. They have nothing of their own to secure and to fortify; their mission is to destroy all previous securities for, and insurances of, individual property.

All previous historical movements were movements of minorities, or in the interest of minorities. The proletarian movement is the self-conscious, independent movement of the immense majority, in the interest of the immense majority. The proletariat, the lowest stratum of our present society, cannot stir, cannot raise itself up, without the whole superincumbent strata of official society being sprung into the air.

Though not in substance, yet in form, the struggle of the proletariat with the bourgeoisie is at first a national struggle. The proletariat of each country must, of course, first of all settle matters with its own bourgeoisie.

In depicting the most general phases of the development of the proletariat, we traced the more or less veiled civil war, raging within existing society, up to the point where that war breaks out into open revolution, and where the violent overthrow of the bourgeoisie lays the foundation for the sway of the proletariat.

Hitherto, every form of society has been based, as we have already seen, on the antagonism of oppressing and oppressed classes. But in order to oppress a class, certain conditions must be assured to it under which it can, at least, continue its slavish existence. The serf, in the period of serfdom, raised himself to membership in the commune, just as the petty bourgeois, under the yoke of feudal absolutism, managed to develop into a bourgeois. The modern labourer, on the contrary, instead of rising with the progress of industry, sinks deeper and deeper below the conditions of existence of his own class. He becomes a pauper, and pauperism develops more rapidly than population and wealth. And here it becomes evident, that the bourgeoisie is unfit any longer to be the ruling class in society, and to impose its conditions of existence upon society as an over-riding law. It is unfit to rule because it is incompetent to assure an existence to its slave within his slavery, because it cannot help letting him sink into such a state, that it has to feed him, instead of being fed by him. Society can no longer live under this bourgeoisie, in other words, its existence is no longer compatible with society.

The essential condition for the existence, and for the sway of the bourgeois class, is the formation and augmentation of capital; the condition for capital is wage-labour. Wage-labour rests exclusively on competition between the labourers. The advance of industry, whose involuntary promoter is the bourgeoisie, replaces the isolation of the labourers, due to competition, by their revolutionary combination, due to association. The development of Modern Industry, therefore, cuts from under its feet the very foundation on which the bourgeoisie produces and appropriates products. What the bourgeoisie, therefore, produces, above all, is its own grave-diggers. Its fall and the victory of the proletariat are equally inevitable.

II
PROLETARIANS AND COMMUNISTS

In what relation do the Communists stand to the proletarians as a whole?

The Communists do not form a separate party opposed to other working-class parties.

They have no interests separate and apart from those of the proletariat as a whole.

They do not set up any sectarian principles of their own, by which to shape and mould the proletarian movement.

The Communists are distinguished from the other working-class parties by this only: 1. In the national struggles of the proletarians of the different countries, they point out and bring to the front the common interests of the entire proletariat, independently of all nationality. 2. In the various stages of development which the struggle of the working class against the bourgeoisie has to pass through, they always and everywhere represent the interests of the movement as a whole.

The Communists, therefore, are on the one hand, practically, the most advanced and resolute section of the working-class parties of every country, that section which pushes forward all others; on the other hand, theoretically, they have over the great mass of the proletariat the advantage of clearly understanding the line of march, the conditions, and the ultimate general results of the proletarian movement.

The immediate aim of the Communists is the same as that of all the other proletarian parties: formation of the proletariat into a class, overthrow of the bourgeois supremacy, conquest of political power by the proletariat.

The theoretical conclusions of the Communists are in no way based on ideas or principles that have been invented, or discovered by this or that would-be universal reformer.

They merely express, in general terms, actual relations springing from an existing class struggle, from a historical movement going on under our very eyes. The abolition of existing property relations is not at all a distinctive feature of Communism.

All property relations in the past have continually been subject to historical change consequent upon the change in historical conditions.

The French Revolution, for example, abolished feudal property in favour of bourgeois property.

The distinguishing feature of Communism is not the abolition of property generally, but the abolition of bourgeois property. But modern bourgeois private property is the final and most complete expression of the system of producing and appropriating products, that is based on class antagonisms, on the exploitation of the many by the few.

In this sense, the theory of the Communists may be summed up in the single sentence: Abolition of private property.

We Communists have been reproached with the desire of abolishing the right of personally acquiring property as the fruit of a man's own labour, which property is alleged to be the groundwork of all personal freedom, activity and independence.

Hard-won, self-acquired, self-earned property! Do you mean the property of the petty artisan and of the small peasant, a form of property that preceded the bourgeois form? There is no need to abolish that; the development of industry has to a great extent already destroyed it, and is still destroying it daily.

Or do you mean modern bourgeois private property?

But does wage-labour create any property for the labourer? Not a bit. It creates capital, *i.e.*, that kind of property which exploits wage-labour, and which cannot increase except upon condition of begetting a new supply of wage-labour for fresh exploitation. Property, in its present form, is based on the antagonism of capital and wage-labour. Let us examine both sides of this antagonism.

To be a capitalist is to have not only a purely personal, but a social *status* in production. Capital is a collective product, and only by the united action of many members, nay, in the last resort, only by the united action of all members of society, can it be set in motion.

Capital is, therefore, not a personal, it is a social power.

When, therefore, capital is converted into common property, into the property of all members of society, personal property is not thereby transformed into social property. It is only the social character of the property that is changed. It loses its class character.

Let us now take wage-labour.

The average price of wage-labour is the minimum wage, *i.e.,* that quantum of the means of subsistence, which is absolutely requisite to keep the labourer in bare existence as a labourer. What, therefore, the wage-labourer appropriates by means of his labour, merely suffices to prolong and reproduce a bare existence. We by no means intend to abolish this personal appropriation of the products of labour, an appropriation that is made for the maintenance and reproduction of human life, and that leaves no surplus wherewith to command the labour of others. All that we want to do away with is the miserable character of this appropriation, under which the labourer lives merely to increase capital, and is allowed to live only in so far as the interest of the ruling class requires it.

In bourgeois society, living labour is but a means to increase accumulated labour. In Communist society, accumulated labour is but a means to widen, to enrich, to promote the existence of the labourer.

In bourgeois society, therefore, the past dominates the present; in Communist society, the present dominates the past. In bourgeois society capital is independent and has individuality, while the living person is dependent and has no individuality.

And the abolition of this state of things is called by the bourgeois abolition of individuality and freedom! And rightly so. The abolition of bourgeois individuality, bourgeois independence, and bourgeois freedom is undoubtedly aimed at.

By freedom is meant, under the present bourgeois conditions of production, free trade, free selling and buying.

But if selling and buying disappears, free selling and buying disappears also. This talk about free selling and buying, and all the other "brave words" of our bourgeoisie about freedom in general, have a meaning, if any, only in contrast with restricted selling and buying, with the fettered traders of the Middle Ages, but have no meaning when opposed to the Communistic abolition of buying and selling, of the bourgeois conditions of production, and of the bourgeoisie itself.

You are horrified at our intending to do away with private property. But in your existing society, private property is already done away with for nine-tenths of the population; its existence for the few is solely due to its non-existence in the hands of those nine-tenths. You reproach us, therefore, with intending to do away with a form of property, the necessary condition for whose existence is the non-existence of any property for the immense majority of society.

In one word, you reproach us with intending to do away with your property. Precisely so; that is just what we intend.

From the moment when labour can no longer be converted into capital, money, or rent, into a social power capable of being monopolised, *i.e.*, from the moment when individual property can no longer be transformed into bourgeois property, into capital, from that moment, you say, individuality vanishes.

You must, therefore, confess that by "individual" you mean no other person than the bourgeois, than the middle-class owner of property. This person must, indeed, be swept out of the way, and made impossible.

Communism deprives no man of the power to appropriate the products of society; all that it does is to deprive him of the power to subjugate the labour of others by means of such appropriation.

It has been objected that upon the abolition of private property all work will cease, and universal laziness will overtake us.

According to this, bourgeois society ought long ago to have gone to the dogs through sheer idleness; for those of its members who work, acquire nothing, and those who acquire anything, do not work. The whole of this objection is but another expression of the tautology: that there can no longer be any wage-labour when there is no longer any capital.

All objections urged against the Communistic mode of producing and appropriating material products, have, in the same way, been urged against the Communistic modes of producing and appropriating intellectual products. Just as, to the bourgeois, the disappearance of class property is the disappearance of production itself, so the disappearance of class culture is to him identical with the disappearance of all culture.

That culture, the loss of which he laments, is, for the enormous majority, a mere training to act as a machine.

But don't wrangle with us so long as you apply, to our intended abolition of bourgeois property, the standard of your bourgeois notions of freedom, culture, law, &c. Your very ideas are but the outgrowth of the conditions of your bourgeois production and bourgeois property, just as your jurisprudence is but the will of your class made into a law for all, a will, whose essential character and direction are determined by the economical conditions of existence of your class.

The selfish misconception that induces you to transform into eternal laws of nature and of reason, the social forms springing from your present mode of production and form of property—historical relations that rise and disappear in the progress of production—this misconception you share with every ruling class that has preceded you. What you see clearly in the case of ancient property, what you admit in the case of feudal property, you are of course forbidden to admit in the case of your own bourgeois form of property.

Abolition of the family! Even the most radical flare up at this infamous proposal of the Communists.

On what foundation is the present family, the bourgeois family, based? On capital, on private gain. In its completely developed form this family exists only among the bourgeoisie. But this state of things finds its complement in the practical absence of the family among the proletarians, and in public prostitution.

The bourgeois family will vanish as a matter of course when its complement vanishes, and both will vanish with the vanishing of capital

Do you charge us with wanting to stop the exploitation of children by their parents? To this crime we plead guilty.

But, you will say, we destroy the most hallowed of relations, when we replace home education by social.

And your education! Is not that also social, and determined by the social conditions under which you educate, by the intervention, direct or indirect, of society, by means of schools, &c? The Communists have not invented the intervention of society in education; they do but seek to alter the character of that intervention, and to rescue education from the influence of the ruling class.

The bourgeois clap-trap about the family and education, about the hallowed co-relation of parent and child, becomes all the more disgusting, the more, by the action of Modern Industry, all family ties among the proletarians are torn asunder, and their children transformed into simple articles of commerce and instruments of labour.

But you Communists would introduce community of women, screams the whole bourgeoisie in chorus.

The bourgeois sees in his wife a mere instrument of production. He hears that the instruments of production are to be exploited in common, and, naturally, can come to no other conclusion than that the lot of being common to all will likewise fall to the women.

He has not even a suspicion that the real point aimed at is to do away with the status of women as mere instruments of production.

For the rest, nothing is more ridiculous than the virtuous indignation of our bourgeois at the community of women which, they pretend, is to be openly and officially established by the Communists. The Communists have no need to introduce community of women; it has existed almost from time immemorial.

Our bourgeois, not content with having the wives and daughters of their proletarians at their disposal, not to speak of common prostitutes, take the greatest pleasure in seducing each other's wives.

Bourgeois marriage is in reality a system of wives in common and thus, at the most, what the Communists might possibly be reproached with, is that they desire to introduce, in substitution for a hypocritically concealed, an openly legalised community of women. For the rest, it is self-evident that the abolition of the present system of production must bring with it the abolition of the community of women springing from that system, *i.e.*, of prostitution both public and private.

The Communists are further reproached with desiring to abolish countries and nationality.

The working men have no country. We cannot take from them what they have not got. Since the proletariat must first of all acquire political supremacy, must rise to be the leading class of the nation, must constitute itself *the* nation, it is so far, itself national, though not in the bourgeois sense of the word.

National differences and antagonisms between peoples are daily more and more vanishing, owing to the development of the bourgeoisie, to freedom of commerce, to the world market, to uniformity in the mode of production and in the conditions of life corresponding thereto.

The supremacy of the proletariat will cause them to vanish still faster. United action, of the leading civilised countries at least, is one of the first conditions for the emancipation of the proletariat.

In proportion as the exploitation of one individual by another is put an end to, the exploitation of one nation by another will also be put an end to. In proportion as the antagonism between classes within the nation vanishes, the hostility of one nation to another will come to an end.

The charges against Communism made from a religious, a philosophical, and, generally, from an ideological standpoint, are not deserving of serious examination.

Does it require deep intuition to comprehend that man's ideas, views and conceptions, in one word, man's consciousness, changes with every change in the conditions of his material existence, in his social relations and in his social life?

What else does the history of ideas prove, than that intellectual production changes its character in proportion as material production is changed? The ruling ideas of each age have ever been the ideas of its ruling class.

When people speak of ideas that revolutionise society, they do but express the fact, that within the old society, the elements of a new one have been created, and that the dissolution of the old ideas keeps even pace with the dissolution of the old conditions of existence.

When the ancient world was in its last throes, the ancient religions were overcome by Christianity. When Christian ideas succumbed in the 18th century to rationalist ideas, feudal society fought its death battle with the then revolutionary bourgeoisie. The ideas of religious liberty and freedom of conscience merely gave expression to the sway of free competition within the domain of knowledge.

"Undoubtedly," it will be said, "religious, moral, philosophical and juridical ideas have been modified in the course of historical development. But religion, morality, philosophy, political science, and law, constantly survived this change.

"There are, besides, eternal truths, such as Freedom, Justice, etc., that are common to all states of society. But Communism abolishes eternal truths, it abolishes all religion and all morality, instead of constituting them on a new basis; it therefore acts in contradiction to all past historical experience."

What does this accusation reduce itself to? The history of all past society has consisted in the development of class antagonisms, antagonisms that assumed different forms at different epochs.

But whatever form they may have taken, one fact is common to all past ages, *viz.*, the exploitation of one part of society by the other. No wonder, then, that the social consciousness of past ages, despite all the multiplicity and variety it displays, moves within certain common forms, or general ideas, which cannot completely vanish except with the total disappearance of class antagonisms.

The Communist revolution is the most radical rupture with traditional property relations; no wonder that its development involves the most radical rupture with traditional ideas.

But let us have done with the bourgeois objections to Communism.

We have seen above, that the first step in the revolution by the working class is to raise the proletariat to the position of ruling class, to win the battle of democracy.

The proletariat will use its political supremacy to wrest, by degrees, all capital from the bourgeoisie, to centralise all instruments of production in the hands of the State, *i.e.*, of the proletariat organised as the ruling class; and to increase the total of productive forces as rapidly as possible.

Of course, in the beginning, this cannot be effected except by means of despotic inroads on the rights of property, and on the conditions of bourgeois production; by means of measures, therefore, which appear economically insufficient and untenable, but which, in the course of the movement, outstrip themselves, necessitate further inroads upon the old social order, and are unavoidable as a means of entirely revolutionising the mode of production.

These measures will of course be different in different countries.

Nevertheless in the most advanced countries, the following will be pretty generally applicable.

1. Abolition of property in land and application of all rents of land to public purposes.
2. A heavy progressive or graduated income tax.

3. Abolition of all right of inheritance.
4. Confiscation of the property of all emigrants and rebels.
5. Centralisation of credit in the hands of the State, by means of a national bank with State capital and an exclusive monopoly.
6. Centralisation of the means of communication and transport in the hands of the State.
7. Extension of factories and instruments of production owned by the State; the bringing into cultivation of waste-lands, and the improvement of the soil generally in accordance with a common plan.
8. Equal liability of all to labour. Establishment of industrial armies, especially for agriculture.
9. Combination of agriculture with manufacturing industries; gradual abolition of the distinction between town and country, by a more equable distribution of the population over the country.
10. Free education for all children in public schools. Abolition of children's factory labour in its present form. Combination of education with industrial production, &c, &c.

When, in the course of development, class distinctions have disappeared, and all production has been concentrated in the hands of a vast association of the whole nation, the public power will lose its political character. Political power, properly so called, is merely the organised power of one class for oppressing another. If the proletariat during its contest with the bourgeoisie is compelled, by the force of circumstances, to organise itself as a class, if, by means of a revolution, it makes itself the ruling class, and, as such, sweeps away by force the old conditions of production, then it will, along with these conditions, have swept away the conditions for the existence of class antagonisms and of classes generally, and will thereby have abolished its own supremacy as a class.

In place of the old bourgeois society, with its classes and class antagonisms, we shall have an association, in which the free development of each is the condition for the free development of all.

III
SOCIALIST AND COMMUNIST LITERATURE

1. Reactionary Socialism

a. Feudal Socialism Owing to their historical position, it became the vocation of the aristocracies of France and England to write pamphlets against modern bourgeois society. In the French revolution of July 1830, and in the English reform agitation, these aristocracies again succumbed to the hateful upstart. Thenceforth, a serious political contest was altogether out of question. A literary battle alone remained possible. But even in the domain of literature the old cries of the restoration period* had become impossible.

In order to arouse sympathy, the aristocracy were obliged to lose sight, apparently, of their own interests, and to formulate their indictment against the bourgeoisie in the interest of the exploited working class alone. Thus the aristocracy took their revenge by singing lampoons on their new master, and whispering in his ears sinister prophecies of coming catastrophe.

In this way arose feudal Socialism; half lamentation, half lampoon; half echo of the past, half menace of the future; at times, by its bitter, witty and incisive criticism, striking the bourgeoisie to the very heart's core; but always ludicrous in its effect, through total incapacity to comprehend the march of modern history.

The aristocracy, in order to rally the people to them, waved the proletarian alms-bag in front for a banner. But the people, so often as it joined them, saw on their hindquarters the old feudal coats of arms, and deserted with loud and irreverent laughter.

One section of the French Legitimists and "Young England" exhibited this spectacle.

In pointing out that their mode of exploitation was different to that of the bourgeoisie, the feudalists forget that they exploited under circumstances and conditions that were quite different, and that are now antiquated. In showing that, under their rule, the modern proletariat never existed, they forget that the modern bourgeoisie is the necessary offspring of their own form of society.

For the rest, so little do they conceal the reactionary character of their criticism that their chief accusation against the bourgeoisie amounts to this, that under the bourgeois *régime* a class is being developed, which is destined to cut up root and branch the old order of society.

What they upbraid the bourgeoisie with is not so much that it creates a proletariat, as that it creates a *revolutionary* proletariat.

In political practice, therefore, they join in all coercive measures against the working class; and in ordinary life, despite their high-falutin phrases, they stoop to pick up the golden apples dropped from the tree of industry, and to barter truth, love, and honour for traffic in wool, beetroot-sugar, and potato spirits.**

---

*Not the English Restoration 1660 to 1689, but the French Restoration 1814 to 1830. [*Note by Engels to the Eglish edition of 1888.*]

**This applies chiefly to Germany where the landed aristocracy and squirearchy have large portions of their estates cultivated for their own account by stewards, and are, moreover, extensive beetroot-sugar manufacturers and distillers of

As the parson has ever gone hand in hand with the landlord, so has Clerical Socialism with Feudal Socialism.

Nothing is easier than to give Christian asceticism a Socialist tinge. Has not Christianity declaimed against private property, against marriage, against the State? Has it not preached in the place of these, charity and poverty, celibacy and mortification of the flesh, monastic life and Mother Church? Christian Socialism is but the holy water with which the priest consecrates the heart-burnings of the aristocrat.

b. Petty-Bourgeois Socialism The feudal aristocracy was not the only class that was ruined by the bourgeoisie, not the only class whose conditions of existence pined and perished in the atmosphere of modern bourgeois society. The medieval burgesses and the small peasant proprietors were the precursors of the modern bourgeoisie. In those countries which are but little developed, industrially and commercially, these two classes still vegetate side by side with the rising bourgeoisie.

In countries where modern civilisation has become fully developed, a new class of petty bourgeois has been formed, fluctuating between proletariat and bourgeoisie and ever renewing itself as a supplementary part of bourgeois society. The individual members of this class, however, are being constantly hurled down into the proletariat by the action of competition, and, as modern industry develops, they even see the moment approaching when they will completely disappear as an independent section of modern society, to be replaced, in manufactures, agriculture and commerce, by overlookers, bailiffs and shopmen.

In countries like France, where the peasants constitute far more than half of the population, it was natural that writers who sided with the proletariat against the bourgeoisie, should use, in their criticism of the bourgeois *régime*, the standard of the peasant and petty bourgeois, and from the standpoint of these intermediate classes should take up the cudgels for the working class. Thus arose petty-bourgeois Socialism. Sismondi was the head of this school, not only in France but also in England.

This school of Socialism dissected with great acuteness the contradictions in the conditions of modern production. It laid bare the hypocritical apologies of economists. It proved, incontrovertibly, the disastrous effects of machinery and division of labour; the concentration of capital

---

potato spirits. The wealthier British aristocracy are, as yet, rather above that; but they, too, know how to make up for declining rents by lending their names to floaters of more or less shady joint-stock companies. [*Note by Engels to the English edition of 1888.*]

and land in a few hands; over-production and crises; it pointed out the inevitable ruin of the petty bourgeois and peasant, the misery of the proletariat, the anarchy in production, the crying inequalities in the distribution of wealth, the industrial war of extermination between nations, the dissolution of old moral bonds, of the old family relations, of the old nationalities.

In its positive aims, however, this form of Socialism aspires either to restoring the old means of production and of exchange, and with them the old property relations, and the old society, or to cramping the modern means of production and of exchange, within the framework of the old property relations that have been, and were bound to be, exploded by those means. In either case, it is both reactionary and Utopian.

Its last words are: corporate guilds for manufacture; patriarchal relations in agriculture.

Ultimately, when stubborn historical facts had dispersed all intoxicating effects of self-deception, this form of Socialism ended in a miserable fit of the blues.

c. German, or "True," Socialism The Socialist and Communist literature of France, a literature that originated under the pressure of a bourgeoisie in power, and that was the expression of the struggle against this power, was introduced into Germany at a time when the bourgeoisie, in that country, had just begun its contest with feudal absolutism.

German philosophers, would-be philosophers, and *beaux esprits*, eagerly seized on this literature, only forgetting, that when these writings immigrated from France into Germany, French social conditions had not immigrated along with them. In contact with German social conditions, this French literature lost all its immediate practical significance, and assumed a purely literary aspect. Thus, to the German philosophers of the Eighteenth Century, the demands of the first French Revolution were nothing more than the demands of "Practical Reason" in general, and the utterance of the will of the revolutionary French bourgeoisie signified in their eyes the laws of pure Will, of Will as it was bound to be, of true human Will generally.

The work of the German *literati* consisted solely in bringing the new French ideas into harmony with their ancient philosophical conscience, or rather, in annexing the French ideas without deserting their own philosophic point of view.

This annexation took place in the same way in which a foreign language is appropriated, namely, by translation.

It is well known how the monks wrote silly lives of Catholic Saints *over* the manuscripts on which the classical works of ancient heathendom had been written. The German *literati* reversed this process with the profane French literature. They wrote their philosophical nonsense beneath the French original. For instance, beneath the French criticism of the economic functions of money, they wrote "Alienation of Humanity," and beneath the French criticism of the bourgeois State they wrote, "Dethronement of the Category of the General," and so forth.

The introduction of these philosophical phrases at the back of the French historical criticisms they dubbed "Philosophy of Action," "True Socialism," "German Science of Socialism," "Philosophical Foundation of Socialism," and so on.

The French Socialist and Communist literature was thus completely emasculated. And, since it ceased in the hands of the German to express the struggle of one class with the other, he felt conscious of having overcome "French one-sidedness" and of representing, not true requirements, but the requirements of Truth; not the interests of the proletariat, but the interests of Human Nature, of Man in general, who belongs to no class, has no reality, who exists only in the misty realm of philosophical fantasy.

This German Socialism, which took its schoolboy task so seriously and solemnly, and extolled its poor stock-in-trade in such mounte-bank fashion, meanwhile gradually lost its pedantic innocence.

The fight of the German, and, especially, of the Prussian bourgeoisie, against feudal aristocracy and absolute monarchy, in other words, the liberal movement, became more earnest.

By this, the long wished-for opportunity was offered to "True" Socialism of confronting the political movement with the Socialist demands, of hurling the traditional anathemas against liberalism, against representative government, against bourgeois competition, bourgeois freedom of the press, bourgeois legislation, bourgeois liberty and equality, and of preaching to the masses that they had nothing to gain, and everything to lose, by this bourgeois movement. German Socialism forgot, in the nick of time, that the French criticism, whose silly echo it was, presupposed the existence of modern bourgeois society, with its corresponding economic conditions of existence, and the political constitution adapted thereto, the very things whose attainment was the object of the pending struggle in Germany.

To the absolute governments, with their following of parsons, professors, country squires and officials, it served as a welcome scarecrow against the threatening bourgeoisie.

It was a sweet finish after the bitter pills of floggings and bullets with which these same governments, just at that time, dosed the German working-class risings.

While this "True" Socialism thus served the governments as a weapon for fighting the German bourgeoisie, it, at the same time, directly represented a reactionary interest, the interest of the German Philistines. In Germany the *petty-bourgeois* class, a relic of the sixteenth century, and since then constantly cropping up again under various forms, is the real social basis of the existing state of things.

To preserve this class is to preserve the existing state of things in Germany. The industrial and political supremacy of the bourgeoisie threatens it with certain destruction; on the one hand, from the concentration of capital; on the other, from the rise of a revolutionary proletariat. "True" Socialism appeared to kill these two birds with one stone. It spread like an epidemic.

The robe of speculative cobwebs, embroidered with flowers of rhetoric, steeped in the dew of sickly sentiment, this transcendental robe in which the German Socialists wrapped their sorry "eternal truths," all skin and bone, served to wonderfully increase the sale of their goods amongst such a public.

And on its part, German Socialism recognised, more and more, its own calling as the bombastic representative of the petty-bourgeois Philistine.

It proclaimed the German nation to be the model nation, and the German petty Philistine to be the typical man. To every villainous meanness of this model man it gave a hidden, higher, Socialistic interpretation, the exact contrary of its real character. It went to the extreme length of directly opposing the "brutally destructive" tendency of Communism, and of proclaiming its supreme and impartial contempt of all class struggles. With very few exceptions, all the so-called Socialist and Communist publications that now (1847) circulate in Germany belong to the domain of this foul and enervating literature.*

2. Conservative, or Bourgeois, Socialism

A part of the bourgeoisie is desirous of redressing social grievances, in order to secure the continued existence of bourgeois society.

To this section belong economists, philanthropists, humanitarians, improvers of the condition of the working class, organisers of charity, members of societies for the prevention of cruelty to animals, temperance fanatics, hole-and-corner reformers of every imaginable kind.

---

*The revolutionary storm of 1848 swept away this whole shabby tendency and cured its protagonists of the desire to dabble further in Socialism. The chief representative and classical type of this tendency is Herr Karl Grün. [*Note by Engels to the German edition of 1890.*]

This form of Socialism has, moreover, been worked out into complete systems.

We may cite Proudhon's *Philosophie de la Misère* as an example of this form.

The Socialistic bourgeois want all the advantages of modern social conditions without the struggles and dangers necessarily resulting therefrom. They desire the existing state of society minus its revolutionary and disintegrating elements. They wish for a bourgeoisie without a proletariat. The bourgeoisie naturally conceives the world in which it is supreme to be the best; and bourgeois Socialism develops this comfortable conception into various more or less complete systems. In requiring the proletariat to carry out such a system, and thereby to march straightway into the social New Jerusalem, it but requires in reality, that the proletariat should remain within the bounds of existing society, but should cast away all its hateful ideas concerning the bourgeoisie.

A second and more practical, but less systematic, form of this Socialism sought to depreciate every revolutionary movement in the eyes of the working class, by showing that no mere political reform, but only a change in the material conditions of existence, in economical relations, could be of any advantage to them. By changes in the material conditions of existence, this form of Socialism, however, by no means understands abolition of the bourgeois relations of production, an abolition that can be effected only by a revolution, but administrative reforms, based on the continued existence of these relations; reforms, therefore, that in no respect affect the relations between capital and labour, but, at the best, lessen the cost, and simplify the administrative work, of bourgeois government.

Bourgeois Socialism attains adequate expression, when, and only when, it becomes a mere figure of speech.

Free trade: for the benefit of the working class. Protective duties: for the benefit of the working class. Prison Reform: for the benefit of the working class. This is the last word and the only seriously meant word of bourgeois Socialism.

It is summed up in the phrase: the bourgeois is a bourgeois—for the benefit of the working class.

3. Critical-Utopian Socialism and Communism

We do not here refer to that literature which, in every great modern revolution, has always given voice to the demands of the proletariat, such as the writings of Babeuf and others.

The first direct attempts of the proletariat to attain its own ends, made in times of universal excitement, when feudal society was being over-thrown, these attempts necessarily failed, owing to the then undeveloped state of the proletariat, as well as to the absence of the economic condi-tions for its emancipation, conditions that had yet to be produced, and could be produced by the impending bourgeois epoch alone. The revolu-tionary literature that accompanied these first movements of the pro-letariat had necessarily a reactionary character. It inculcated universal asceticism and social levelling in its crudest form.

The Socialist and Communist systems properly so called, those of Saint-Simon, Fourier, Owen and others, spring into existence in the early undeveloped period, described above, of the struggle between pro-letariat and bourgeoisie (see Section I. Bourgeois and Proletarians).

The founders of these systems see, indeed, the class antagonisms, as well as the action of the decomposing elements in the prevailing form of society. But the proletariat, as yet in its infancy, offers to them the spectacle of a class without any historical initiative or any independent political movement.

Since the development of class antagonism keeps even pace with the development of industry, the economic situation, as they find it, does not as yet offer to them the material conditions for the emancipation of the proletariat. They therefore search after a new social science, after new social laws, that are to create these conditions.

Historical action is to yield to their personal inventive action, histor-ically created conditions of emancipation to fantastic ones, and the grad-ual, spontaneous class organisation of the proletariat to an organisation of society specially contrived by these inventors. Future history resolves itself, in their eyes, into the propaganda and the practical carrying out of their social plans.

In the formation of their plans they are conscious of caring chiefly for the interests of the working class, as being the most suffering class. Only from the point of view of being the most suffering class does the pro-letariat exist for them.

The undeveloped state of the class struggle, as well as their own surroundings, causes Socialists of this kind to consider themselves far superior to all class antagonisms. They want to improve the condition of every member of society, even that of the most favoured. Hence, they habitually appeal to society at large, without distinction of class; nay, by preference, to the ruling class. For how can people, when once they understand their system, fail to see in it the best possible plan of the best possible state of society?

Hence, they reject all political, and especially all revolutionary, action; they wish to attain their ends by peaceful means, and endeavour, by small experiments, necessarily doomed to failure, and by the force of example, to pave the way for the new social Gospel.

Such fantastic pictures of future society, painted at a time when the proletariat is still in a very undeveloped state and has but a fantastic conception of its own position, correspond with the first instinctive yearnings of that class for a general reconstruction of society.

But these Socialist and Communist publications contain also a critical element. They attack every principle of existing society. Hence they are full of the most valuable materials for the enlightenment of the working class. The practical measures proposed in them—such as the abolition of the distinction between town and country, of the family, of the carrying on of industries for the account of private individuals, and of the wage system, the proclamation of social harmony, the conversion of the functions of the State into a mere superintendence of production, all these proposals point solely to the disappearance of class antagonisms which were, at that time, only just cropping up, and which, in these publications, are recognised in their earliest indistinct and undefined forms only. These proposals, therefore, are of a purely Utopian character.

The significance of Critical-Utopian Socialism and Communism bears an inverse relation to historical development. In proportion as the modern class struggle develops and takes definite shape, this fantastic standing apart from the contest, these fantastic attacks on it, lose all practical value and all theoretical justification. Therefore, although the originators of these systems were, in many respects, revolutionary, their disciples have, in every case, formed mere reactionary sects. They hold fast by the original views of their masters, in opposition to the progressive historical development of the proletariat. They, therefore, endeavour, and that consistently, to deaden the class struggle and to reconcile the class antagonisms. They still dream of experimental realisation of their social Utopias, of founding isolated "phalanstères," of establishing "Home Colonies," of setting up a "Little Icaria"*—duodecimo editions of the New Jerusalem—and to realise all these castles in the air, they are compelled to appeal to the feelings and purses of the bourgeois. By degrees they sink into the category of the reactionary [or] conservative

---

Phalanstères were Socialist colonies on the plan of Charles Fourier; *Icaria* was the name given by Cabet to his Utopia and, later on, to his American Communist colony. [*Note by Engels to the English edition of 1888.*]

"Home Colonies" were what Owen called his Communist model societies. *Phalanstères* was the name of the public palaces planned by Fourier. *Icaria* was the name given to the Utopian land of fancy, whose Communist institutions Cabet portrayed. [*Note by Engels to the German edition of 1890.*]

Socialists depicted above, differing from these only by more systematic pedantry, and by their fanatical and superstitious belief in the miraculous effects of their social science.

They, therefore, violently oppose all political action on the part of the working class; such action, according to them, can only result from blind unbelief in the new Gospel.

The Owenites in England, and the Fourierists in France, respectively oppose the Chartists and the *Réformistes*.

IV
POSITION OF THE COMMUNISTS IN RELATION TO THE VARIOUS EXISTING OPPOSITION PARTIES

Section II has made clear the relations of the Communists to the existing working-class parties, such as the Chartists in England and the Agrarian Reformers in America.

The Communists fight for the attainment of the immediate aims, for the enforcement of the momentary interests of the working class; but in the movement of the present, they also represent and take care of the future of that movement. In France the Communists ally themselves with the Social-Democrats,* against the conservative and radical bourgeoisie, reserving, however, the right to take up a critical position in regard to phrases and illusions traditionally handed down from the great Revolution.

In Switzerland they support the Radicals, without losing sight of the fact that this party consists of antagonistic elements, partly of Democratic Socialists, in the French sense, partly of radical bourgeois.

In Poland they support the party that insists on an agrarian revolution as the prime condition for national emancipation, that party which fomented the insurrection of Cracow in 1846.

In Germany they fight with the bourgeoisie whenever it acts in a

---

*The party then represented in Parliament by Ledru-Rollin, in literature by Louis Blanc, in the daily press by the *Réforme*. The name of Social-Democracy signified, with these its inventors, a section of the Democratic or Republican party more or less tinged with Socialism. [*Note by Engels to the English edition of 1888.*]

The party in France which at that time called itself Socialist-Democratic was represented in political life by Ledru-Rollin and in literature by Louis Blanc; thus it differed immeasurably from present-day German Social-Democracy. [*Note by Engels to the German edition of 1890.*]

revolutionary way, against the absolute monarchy, the feudal squirearchy, and the petty bourgeoisie.

But they never cease, for a single instant, to instil into the working class the clearest possible recognition of the hostile antagonism between bourgeoisie and proletariat, in order that the German workers may straightway use, as so many weapons against the bourgeoisie, the social and political conditions that the bourgeoisie must necessarily introduce along with its supremacy, and in order that, after the fall of the reactionary classes in Germany, the fight against the bourgeoisie itself may immediately begin.

The Communists turn their attention chiefly to Germany, because that country is on the eve of a bourgeois revolution that is bound to be carried out under more advanced conditions of European civilisation, and with a much more developed proletariat, than that of England was in the seventeenth, and of France in the eighteenth century, and because the bourgeois revolution in Germany will be but the prelude to an immediately following proletarian revolution.

In short, the Communists everywhere support every revolutionary movement against the existing social and political order of things.

In all these movements they bring to the front, as the leading question in each, the property question, no matter what its degree of development at the time.

Finally, they labour everywhere for the union and agreement of the democratic parties of all countries.

The Communists disdain to conceal their views and aims. They openly declare that their ends can be attained only by the forcible overthrow of all existing social conditions. Let the ruling classes tremble at a Communistic revolution. The proletarians have nothing to lose but their chains. They have a world to win.

WORKING MEN OF ALL COUNTRIES, UNITE!

The Eighteenth Brumaire
of Louis Bonaparte
(excerpts)

Karl Marx

The year 1848 witnessed a wave of revolutionary activity across Europe; Marx and Engels had responded by returning to Germany to participate in the unrest there. The revolutionary momentum was short-lived, however, and reaction soon set in. In France, the Bourbon Restoration was overthrown in 1848 and the Second Republic established; Louis Napoleon Bonaparte, the nephew of Napoleon I, was elected President. Consolidating his power with the aid of conservative forces, Louis Bonaparte staged a coup d'état on December 2, 1851, and seized power, establishing himself as Napoleon III, Emperor of the Second Empire. Marx, by then living in London, wrote a series of articles between December, 1851, and March, 1852, analyzing Louis Bonaparte's rise to power. They were published in a German-language journal, Die Revolution, *in New York in 1852.*

The title refers to the seizure of power and the creation of the First Empire by Louis Bonaparte's uncle on November 9, 1799, the eighteenth Brumaire according to the calendar introduced during the First Republic. But as Marx sarcastically remarks at the beginning of the essay, enlarging on an observation by Hegel, while historical events may happen twice, the first time they occur "as tragedy, the second as farce." The second Napoleon would prove to be but a shadow of the first. Marx's purpose in the piece is to trace the events that culminated in the 1851 coup, setting them especially in the context of class politics. Most commentators agree that this essay is his most successful attempt to apply his theoretical perspective to analyze a course of actual political developments. The lesson to be learned is, as he announces at the start, that "Men make their own history, but they do not make it just as they please; they do not make it under circumstances chosen by themselves, but under circumstance directly encountered, given and transmitted from the past."

This selection is sections I and VII of the 1869 second edition of the essay, taken from *Karl Marx/Friedrich Engels: Collected Works*, published by International Publishers.

In an earlier work written in 1850, The Class Struggles in France, *Marx had analyzed the 1848 revolution and its aftermath. After summarizing that material in* The Eighteenth Brumaire, *he continues his account of the subsequent events. The final section of the work contains important points about the development of the state and its relation to civil society, remarks which have formed the starting point of Marxist attempts in the twentieth century to analyze fascism.*

But under the absolute monarchy, during the first revolution, under Napoleon, bureaucracy was only the means of preparing the class rule of the bourgeoisie. Under the Restoration, under Louis Philippe, under the parliamentary republic, it was the instrument of the ruling class, however much it strove for power of its own.

Only under the second Bonaparte does the state seem to have made itself completely independent. . . .

And yet the state power is not suspended in mid air. Bonaparte represents a class, and the most numerous class of French society at that, the *small-holding peasantry.*

Yet Bonaparte must maintain an awkward relationship to the bourgeoisie. And in this contradictory situation, the army as the instrument of order looms large, a situation not uncommon in the contemporary world.

I

Hegel remarks somewhere that all facts and personages of great importance in world history occur, as it were, twice. He forgot to add: the first time as tragedy, the second as farce. Caussidière for Danton, Louis Blanc for Robespierre, the Montagne of 1848 to 1851 for the Montagne of 1793 to 1795, the Nephew for the Uncle. And the same caricature occurs in the circumstances attending the second edition of the eighteenth Brumaire!

Men make their own history, but they do not make it just as they please; they do not make it under circumstances chosen by themselves, but under circumstances directly encountered, given and transmitted from the past. The tradition of all the dead generations weighs like a nightmare on the brain of the living. And just when they seem engaged in revolutionising themselves and things, in creating something that has never yet existed, precisely in such periods of revolutionary crisis they anxiously conjure up the spirits of the past to their service and borrow from them names, battle-cries and costumes in order to present the new scene of world history in this time-honoured disguise and this borrowed language. Thus Luther donned the mask of the Apostle Paul, the revolution of 1789 to 1814 draped itself alternately as the Roman Republic and the Roman Empire, and the revolution of 1848 knew nothing better to do than to parody, now 1789, now the revolutionary tradition of 1793 to 1795. In like manner a beginner who has learnt a new language always translates it back into his mother tongue, but he has assimilated the spirit of the new language and can freely express himself in it only when he finds his way in it without recalling the old and forgets his native tongue in the use of the new.

Consideration of this world-historical necromancy reveals at once a salient difference. Camille Desmoulins, Danton, Robespierre, Saint-Just, Napoleon, the heroes as well as the parties and the masses of the old French Revolution, performed the task of their time in Roman costume and with Roman phrases, the task of unchaining and setting up modern *bourgeois* society. The first ones knocked the feudal basis to pieces and mowed off the feudal heads which had grown on it. The other created inside France the conditions under which free competition could first be developed, parcelled landed property exploited and the unchained industrial productive forces of the nation employed; and beyond the French borders he everywhere swept the feudal institutions away, so far as was necessary to furnish bourgeois society in France with a suitable up-to-date environment on the European Continent. The new social formation once established, the antediluvian Colossi disappeared and with them resurrected Romanity—the Brutuses, Gracchi, Publicolas, the tribunes, the senators, and Caesar himself. Bourgeois society in its sober reality had begotten its true interpreters and mouthpieces in the Says, Cousins, Royer-Collards, Benjamin Constants and Guizots; its real commanders sat behind the counter, and the hogheaded Louis XVIII was its political chief. Wholly absorbed in the production of wealth and in peaceful competitive struggle, it no longer comprehended that ghosts from the days of Rome had watched over its cradle. But unheroic as bourgeois society is, it nevertheless took heroism, sacrifice, terror, civil war and battles of peoples to bring it into being. And in the classically austere traditions of the Roman Republic its gladiators found the ideals and the art forms, the self-deceptions that they needed in order to conceal from themselves the bourgeois limitations of the content of their struggles and to maintain their passion on the high plane of great historical tragedy. Similarly, at another stage of development, a century earlier, Cromwell and the English people had borrowed speech, passions and illusions from the Old Testament for their bourgeois revolution. When the real aim had been achieved, when the bourgeois transformation of English society had been accomplished, Locke supplanted Habakkuk.

Thus the resurrection of the dead in those revolutions served the purpose of glorifying the new struggles, not of parodying the old; of magnifying the given task in imagination, not of fleeing from its solution in reality; of finding once more the spirit of revolution, not of making its ghost walk about again.

From 1848 to 1851 only the ghost of the old revolution walked about, from Marrast, the *républicain en gants jaunes*, who disguised himself as the old Bailly, down to the adventurer who hides his commonplace repulsive features under the iron death mask of Napoleon. An entire people, which had imagined that by means of a revolution it had imparted to itself an accelerated power of motion, suddenly finds itself set back into a defunct epoch and, in order that no doubt as to the relapse may be possible, the old dates arise again, the old chronology, the old names, the old edicts, which had long become a subject of antiquarian erudition, and the old myrmidons of the law, who had seemed long decayed. The nation feels like that mad Englishman in Bedlam who fancies that he lives in the times of the ancient Pharaohs and daily bemoans the hard labour that he must perform in the Ethiopian mines as a gold digger, immured in this subterranean prison, a dimly burning lamp fastened to his head, the overseer of the slaves behind him with a long whip, and at the exits a confused welter of barbarian mercenaries, who understand neither the forced labourers in the mines nor one another, since they speak no common language. "And all this is expected of me," sighs the mad Englishman, "of me, a freeborn Briton, in order to make gold for the old Pharaohs." "In order to pay the debts of the Bonaparte family," sighs the French nation. The Englishman, so long as he was in his right mind, could not get rid of the fixed idea of making gold. The French, so long as they were engaged in revolution, could not get rid of the memory of Napoleon, as the election of December 10 proved. They hankered to return from the perils of revolution to the fleshpots of Egypt, and December 2, 1851 was the answer. They have not only a caricature of the old Napoleon, they have the old Napoleon himself, caricatured as he must appear in the middle of the nineteenth century.

The social revolution of the nineteenth century cannot draw its poetry from the past, but only from the future. It cannot begin with itself before it has stripped off all superstition about the past. Earlier revolutions required recollections of past world history in order to dull themselves to their own content. In order to arrive at its own content, the revolution of the nineteenth century must let the dead bury their dead. There the words went beyond the content; here the content goes beyond the words.

The February revolution was a surprise attack, a *taking* of the old society *unawares*, and the people proclaimed this unexpected *coup de main* as a deed of historic importance, ushering in the new epoch. On

December 2 the February revolution is conjured away by a cardsharper's trick, and what seems overthrown is no longer the monarchy but the liberal concessions that were wrung from it by centuries of struggle. Instead of *society* having conquered a new content for itself, it seems that the *state* only returned to its oldest form, to the shamelessly simple domination of the sabre and the cowl. This is the answer to the *coup de main* of February 1848, given by the *coup de tête* of December 1851. Easy come, easy go. Meanwhile the intervening time has not passed by unused. During the years 1848 to 1851 French society made up, and that by an abbreviated because revolutionary method, for the studies and experiences which, in a regular, so to speak, textbook course of development, would have had to precede the February revolution, if it was to be more than a ruffling of the surface. Society now seems to have fallen back behind its point of departure; it has in truth first to create for itself the revolutionary point of departure, the situation, the relations, the conditions under which alone modern revolution becomes serious.

Bourgeois revolutions, like those of the eighteenth century, storm swiftly from success to success, their dramatic effects outdo each other, men and things seem set in sparkling brilliants, ecstasy is the everyday spirit, but they are short-lived, soon they have attained their zenith, and a long crapulent depression seizes society before it learns soberly to assimilate the results of its storm-and-stress period. On the other hand, proletarian revolutions, like those of the nineteenth century, criticise themselves constantly, interrupt themselves continually in their own course, come back to the apparently accomplished in order to begin it afresh, deride with unmerciful thoroughness the inadequacies, weaknesses and paltrinesses of their first attempts, seem to throw down their adversary only in order that he may draw new strength from the earth and rise again, more gigantic, before them, and recoil again and again from the indefinite prodigiousness of their own aims, until a situation has been created which makes all turning back impossible, and the conditions themselves cry out:

Hic Rhodus, hic salta!
Here is the rose, here dance!

For the rest, every fairly competent observer, even if he had not followed the course of French development step by step, must have had a presentiment that an unheard-of fiasco was in store for the revolution. It was enough to hear the self-complacent howl of victory with which Messieurs the Democrats congratulated each other on the beneficial consequences of the second Sunday in May 1852. In their minds the second Sunday in May 1852 had become a fixed idea, a dogma, like the day on which Christ should reappear and the millennium begin, in the minds of the Chiliasts. As ever, weakness had taken refuge in a belief in miracles, fancied the enemy overcome when it had only conjured him away in imagination, and lost all understanding of the present in a passive glorification of the future in store for it and of the deeds it had *in petto* but which it merely did not want as yet to make public. Those heroes who seek to disprove their proven incapacity by offering each other their sympathy and getting together in a crowd had tied up their bundles, collected their laurel wreaths in advance and were just then engaged in discounting on the exchange market the republics *in partibus* for which they had already providently organised the government personnel with all the calm of their unassuming disposition. December 2 struck them like a thunderbolt from a clear sky, and the peoples that in periods of pusillanimous depression gladly let their inward apprehension be drowned out by the loudest bawlers will have perhaps convinced themselves that the times are past when the cackle of geese could save the Capitol.

The Constitution, the National Assembly, the dynastic parties, the blue and the red republicans, the heroes of Africa, the thunder from the platform, the sheet lightning of the daily press, the entire literature, the political names and the intellectual reputations, the civil law and the penal code, the *liberté, égalité, fraternité* and the second Sunday in May 1852—all has vanished like a phantasmagoria before the spell of a man whom even his enemies do not make out to be a magician. Universal suffrage seems to have survived only for a moment, in order that with its own hand it may make its last will and testament before the eyes of all the world and declare in the name of the people itself: "All that comes to birth is fit for overthrow, as nothing worth."

It is not enough to say, as the French do, that their nation was taken unawares. A nation and a woman are not forgiven the unguarded hour in which the first adventurer that came along could violate them. The riddle is not solved by such turns of speech, but merely formulated differently. It remains to be explained how a nation of thirty-six million can be surprised and delivered unresisting into captivity by three swindlers.

Let us recapitulate into general outline the phases that the French Revolution went through from February 24, 1848 to December 1851.

Three main periods are unmistakable: *the February period;* May 4, 1848 to May 28, 1849: *the period of the constitution of the republic* or *of the Constituent National Assembly;* May 28, 1849 to December 2, 1851: *the period of the constitutional republic* or *of the Legislative National Assembly.*

The *first period,* from February 24, or the overthrow of Louis

Philippe, to May 4, 1848, the meeting of the Constituent Assembly, the *February period* proper, may be described as the *prologue* to the revolution. Its character was officially expressed in the fact that the government improvised by it declared itself that it was *provisional* and, like the government, everything that was mooted, attempted or enunciated during this period proclaimed itself to be only *provisional.* Nothing and nobody ventured to lay claim to the right of existence and of real action. All the elements that had prepared or determined the revolution, the dynastic opposition, the republican bourgeoisie, the democratic-republican petty bourgeoisie and the Social-Democratic workers, provisionally found their place in the February *government.*

It could not be otherwise. The February days originally aimed at an electoral reform, by which the circle of the politically privileged among the possessing class itself was to be widened and the exclusive domination of the finance aristocracy overthrown. When it came to the actual conflict, however, when the people mounted the barricades, the National Guard maintained a passive attitude, the army offered no serious resistance and the monarchy ran away, the republic appeared to be a matter of course. Every party construed it in its own way. Having secured it arms in hand, the proletariat impressed its stamp upon it and proclaimed it to be a *social republic.* There was thus indicated the general content of the modern revolution, a content which was in most singular contradiction to everything that, with the material available, with the degree of education attained by the masses, under the given circumstances and relations, could be immediately realised in practice. On the other hand, the claims of all the remaining elements that had collaborated in the February revolution were recognised by the lion's share that they obtained in the government. In no period do we, therefore, find a more confused mixture of high-flown phrases and actual uncertainty and clumsiness, of more enthusiastic striving for innovation and more thorough domination of the old routine, of more apparent harmony of the whole of society and more profound estrangement of its elements. While the Paris proletariat still revelled in the vision of the wide prospects that had opened before it and indulged in earnest discussions on social problems, the old forces of society had grouped themselves, rallied, reflected and found unexpected support in the mass of the nation, the peasants and petty bourgeois, who all at once stormed on to the political stage, after the barriers of the July monarchy had fallen.

The *second period,* from May 4, 1848 to the end of May 1849, is the period of the *constitution,* the *foundation, of the bourgeois republic.* Directly after the February days not only had the dynastic opposition been surprised by the republicans and the republicans by the Socialists, but all

France by Paris. The National Assembly, which met on May 4, 1848, had emerged from the national elections and represented the nation. It was a living protest against the aspirations of the February days and was to reduce the results of the revolution to the bourgeois scale. In vain the Paris proletariat, which immediately grasped the character of this National Assembly, attempted on May 15, a few days after it met, forcibly to negate its existence, to dissolve it, to disintegrate again into its constituent parts the organic form in which the proletariat was threatened by the reacting spirit of the nation. As is known, May 15 had no other result save that of removing Blanqui and his comrades, that is, the real leaders of the proletarian party, from the public stage for the entire duration of the cycle we are considering.

The *bourgeois monarchy* of Louis Philippe can be followed only by a *bourgeois republic,* that is to say, whereas a limited section of the bourgeoisie ruled in the name of the king, the whole of the bourgeoisie will now rule on behalf of the people. The demands of the Paris proletariat are utopian nonsense, to which an end must be put. To this declaration of the Constituent National Assembly the Paris proletariat replied with the *June insurrection,* the most colossal event in the history of European civil wars. The bourgeois republic triumphed. On its side stood the finance aristocracy, the industrial bourgeoisie, the middle class, the petty bourgeois, the army, the lumpenproletariat organised as the Mobile Guard, the intellectuals, the clergy and the rural population. On the side of the Paris proletariat stood none but itself. More than 3,000 insurgents were butchered after the victory, and 15,000 were deported without trial. With this defeat the proletariat recedes into the *background* of the revolutionary stage. It attempts to press forward again on every occasion, as soon as the movement appears to make a fresh start, but with ever decreased expenditure of strength and always slighter results. As soon as one of the social strata situated above it gets into revolutionary ferment, the proletariat enters into an alliance with it and so shares all the defeats that the different parties suffer, one after another. But these subsequent blows become the weaker, the greater the surface of society over which they are distributed. The more important leaders of the proletariat in the Assembly and in the press successively fall victim to the courts, and ever more equivocal figures come to head it. In part it throws itself into *doctrinaire experiments, exchange banks and workers' associations, hence into a movement in which it renounces the revolutionising of the old world by means of the latter's own great, combined resources, and seeks, rather, to achieve its salvation behind society's back, in private fashion, within its limited conditions of existence, and hence necessarily suffers shipwreck.* It seems to be unable either to rediscover revolutionary greatness in itself or to win new energy from the connections newly entered into, until *all classes* with which it contended in June themselves lie prostrate beside it. But at least it succumbs with the honours of the great, world-historic struggle; not only France, but all Europe trembles at the June earthquake, while the ensuing defeats of the upper classes are so cheaply bought that they require barefaced exaggeration by the victorious party to be able to pass for events at all, and become the more ignominious the further the defeated party is from the proletarian party.

The defeat of the June insurgents, to be sure, had indeed prepared and levelled the ground on which the bourgeois republic could be founded and built up, but it had shown at the same time that in Europe the questions at issue are other than that of "republic or monarchy." It had revealed that here *bourgeois republic* signifies the unlimited despotism of one class over other classes. It had proved that in countries with an old civilisation, with a developed formation of classes, with modern conditions of production and with an intellectual consciousness in which all traditional ideas have been dissolved by the work of centuries, *the republic* signifies in *general only the political form of the revolutionising of bourgeois society* and not its *conservative form of life*, as, for example, in the United States of North America, where, though classes already exist, they have not yet become fixed, but continually change and interchange their component elements in constant flux, where the modern means of production, instead of coinciding with a stagnant surplus population, rather compensate for the relative deficiency of heads and hands, and where, finally, the feverish, youthful movement of material production, which has to make a new world its own, has left neither time nor opportunity for abolishing the old spirit world.

During the June days all classes and parties had united in the *Party of Order* against the proletarian class as the *Party of Anarchy*, of socialism, of communism. They had "saved" society from "*the enemies of society.*" They had given out the watch-words of the old society, "*property, family, religion, order,*" to their army as passwords and had proclaimed to the counter-revolutionary crusaders: "By this sign thou shalt conquer!" From this moment, as soon as one of the numerous parties which had gathered under this sign against the June insurgents seeks to hold the revolutionary battlefield in its own class interest, it goes down before the cry: "Property, family, religion, order." Society is saved just as often as the circle of its rulers contracts, as a more exclusive interest is maintained against a wider one. Every demand of the simplest bourgeois financial reform, of the most ordinary liberalism, of the most formal republicanism, of the most shallow democracy, is simultaneously castigated as an "attempt on society" and stigmatised as "socialism." And, finally, the high priests of "religion and order" themselves are driven with kicks from their Pythian tripods, hauled out of their beds in the darkness of night, put in prison-vans, thrown into dungeons or sent into exile; their temple is razed to the ground, their mouths are sealed, their pens broken, their law torn to pieces in the name of religion, of property, of the family, of order. Bourgeois fanatics for order are shot down on their balconies by mobs of drunken soldiers, their domestic sanctuaries profaned, their houses bombarded for amusement—in the name of property, of the family, of religion and of order. Finally, the scum of bourgeois society forms the *holy phalanx of order* and the hero Krapülinski installs himself in the Tuileries as the *"savior of society."*

VII

On the threshold of the February revolution, the *social republic* appeared as a phrase, as a prophecy. In the June days of 1848, it was drowned in the blood of the *Paris proletariat,* but it haunts the subsequent acts of the drama like a ghost. The *democratic republic* announces its arrival. On June 13, 1849 it is dissipated together with its *petty bourgeois,* who have taken to their heels, but in its flight it blows its own trumpet with redoubled boastfulness. The *parliamentary republic,* together with the bourgeoisie, takes possession of the entire stage; it enjoys its existence to the full, but December 2, 1851 buries it to the accompaniment of the anguished cry of the coalitioned royalists: "Long live the Republic!"

The French bourgeoisie balked at the power of the working proletariat; it has brought the lumpenproletariat to power, with the chief of the Society of December 10 at the head. The bourgeoisie kept France in breathless fear of the future terrors of red anarchy; Bonaparte discounted this future for it when, on December 4, he had the eminent bourgeois of the Boulevard Montmartre and the Boulevard des Italiens shot down at their windows by the liquor-inspired army of order. The bourgeoisie apotheosised the sword; the sword rules it. It destroyed the revolutionary press; its own press has been destroyed. It placed popular meetings under police supervision; its salons are under the supervision of the police. It disbanded the democratic National Guards; its own National Guard is disbanded. It imposed a state of siege; a state of siege is imposed upon it. It supplanted the juries by military commissions; its juries are supplanted by military commissions. It subjected public education to the sway of the priests; the priests subject it to their own education. It transported people without trial; it is being transported without trial. It repressed every stirring in society by means of the state power; every stirring in its society is suppressed by the state power. Out of enthusiasm for its purse, it rebelled against its own politicians and men of letters; its politicians and men of letters are swept aside, but its purse is being plundered now that its mouth has been gagged and its pen broken. The bourgeoisie never wearied of crying out to the revolution what Saint Arsenius cried out to the Christians: *"Fuge, tace, quiesce!* Flee, be silent, keep still!"* Bonaparte cries to the bourgeoisie: *"Fuge, tace, quiesce!* Flee, be silent, keep still!"*

The French bourgeoisie had long ago found the solution to Napoleon's dilemma: *"Dans cinquante ans, l'Europe sera républicaine ou cosaque."* It had found the solution to it in the *"république cosaque."* No Circe, by means of black magic, has distorted that work of art, the bourgeois republic, into a monstrous shape. That republic has lost nothing but the semblance of respectability. Present-day France was contained in a finished state within the parliamentary republic. It only requires a bayonet thrust for the abcess to burst and the monster to spring forth before our eyes.

Why did the Paris proletariat not rise in revolt after December 2?

The overthrow of the bourgeoisie had as yet been only decreed: the decree had not been carried out. Any serious insurrection of the proletariat would at once have put fresh life into the bourgeoisie, would have reconciled it with the army and ensured a second June defeat for the workers.

On December 4 the proletariat was incited by bourgeois and *épicier* to fight. On the evening of that day several legions of the National Guard promised to appear, armed and uniformed, on the scene of battle. For the bourgeois and the *épicier* had got wind of the fact that in one of his decrees of December 2 Bonaparte abolished the secret ballot and enjoined them to record their "yes" or "no" in the official registers after their names. The resistance of December 4 intimidated Bonaparte. During the night he caused placards to be posted on all the street corners of Paris, announcing the restoration of the secret ballot. The bourgeois and the *épicier* believed that they had gained their end. Those who failed to appear next morning were the bourgeois and the *épicier.*

By a *coup de main* during the night of December 1 to 2, Bonaparte had robbed the Paris proletariat of its leaders, the barricade commanders. An army without officers, averse to fighting under the banner of the Montagnards because of the memories of June 1848 and 1849 and May 1850, it left to its vanguard, the secret societies, the task of saving the insurrectionary honour of Paris, which the bourgeoisie had so unresistingly surrendered to the soldiery that, later on, Bonaparte could sneeringly give as his motive for disarming the National Guard—his fear that its arms would be turned against itself by the anarchists!

"*C'est le triomphe complet et définitif du socialisme!*" Thus Guizot characterised December 2. But if the overthrow of the parliamentary republic contains within itself the germ of the triumph of the proletarian revolution, its immediate and palpable result was *the victory of Bonaparte over parliament, of the executive power over the legislative power, of force without words over the force of words.* In parliament the nation made its general will the law, that is, it made the law of the ruling class its general will. Before the executive power it renounces all will of its own and submits to the superior command of an alien will, to authority. The executive power, in contrast to the legislative power, expresses the heteronomy of a nation, in contrast to its autonomy. France, therefore, seems to have escaped the despotism of a class only to fall back beneath the despotism of an individual, and, what is more, beneath the authority of an individual without authority. The struggle seems to be settled in such a way that all classes, equally impotent and equally mute, fall on their knees before the rifle butt.

But the revolution is thorough. It is still journeying through purgatory. It does its work methodically. By December 2, 1851 it had completed one half of its preparatory work; it is now completing the other half. First it perfected the parliamentary power, in order to be able to overthrow it. Now that it has attained this, it perfects the *executive power*, reduces it to its purest expression, isolates it, sets it up against itself as the sole target, in order to concentrate all its forces of destruction against it. And when it has done this second half of its preliminary work, Europe will leap from its seat and exultantly exclaim: Well burrowed, old mole!

This executive power with its enormous bureaucratic and military organisation, with its extensive and artificial state machinery, with a host of officials numbering half a million, besides an army of another half million, this appalling parasitic body, which enmeshes the body of French society like a net and chokes all its pores, sprang up in the days of the absolute monarchy, with the decay of the feudal system, which it helped to hasten. The seignorial privileges of the landowners and towns became transformed into so many attributes of the state power, the feudal dignitaries into paid officials and the motley pattern of conflicting medieval plenary powers into the regulated plan of a state authority whose work is divided and centralised as in a factory. The first French Revolution, with its task of breaking all separate local, territorial, urban and provincial powers in order to create the civil unity of the nation, was bound to develop what the absolute monarchy had begun: the centralisation, but at the same time the extent, the attributes and the agents of governmental power. Napoleon perfected this state machinery. The Legitimist monarchy and the July monarchy added nothing but a greater division of labour, growing in the same measure as the division of labour within bourgeois society created new groups of interests, and, therefore, new material for state administration. Every *common* interest was straightway severed from society, counterposed to it as a higher, *general* interest, snatched from the activity of society's members themselves and made an object of government activity, whether it was a bridge, a schoolhouse and the communal property of a village community, or the railways, the national wealth and the national university of France. Finally, in its struggle against the revolution, the parliamentary republic found itself compelled to strengthen, along with the repressive measures, the resources and centralisation of governmental power. All revolutions perfected this machine instead of breaking it. The parties that contended in turn for domination regarded the possession of this huge state edifice as the principal spoils of the victor.

But under the absolute monarchy, during the first revolution, under Napoleon, bureaucracy was only the means of preparing the class rule of the bourgeoisie. Under the Restoration, under Louis Philippe, under the parliamentary republic, it was the instrument of the ruling class, however much it strove for power of its own.

Only under the second Bonaparte does the state seem to have made itself completely independent. As against civil society, the state machine has consolidated its position so thoroughly that the chief of the Society of December 10 suffices for its head, a casual adventurer from abroad, raised up as leader by a drunken soldiery, which he has bought with liquor and sausages, and which he must continually ply with more sausage. Hence the downcast despair, the feeling of most dreadful humiliation and degradation that oppresses the breast of France and makes her catch her breath. She feels dishonoured.

And yet the state power is not suspended in mid air. Bonaparte represents a class, and the most numerous class of French society at that, the *small-holding peasantry*.

Just as the Bourbons were the dynasty of big landed property and just as the Orleans were the dynasty of money, so the Bonapartes are the dynasty of the peasants, that is, the mass of the French people. Not the Bonaparte who submitted to the bourgeois parliament, but the Bonaparte who dispersed the bourgeois parliament is the chosen man of the peasantry. For three years the towns had succeeded in falsifying the meaning of the election of December 10 and in cheating the peasants out of the restoration of the empire. The election of December 10, 1848 has been consummated only by the coup d'état of December 2, 1851.

The small-holding peasants form a vast mass, the members of which live in similar conditions but without entering into manifold relations with one another. Their mode of production isolates them from one another instead of bringing them into mutual intercourse. The isolation is increased by France's bad means of communication and by the poverty of the peasants. Their field of production, the smallholding, admits of no division of labour in its cultivation, no application of science and, therefore, no diversity of development, no variety of talent, no wealth of social relationships. Each individual peasant family is almost self-sufficient; it itself directly produces the major part of its consumption and thus acquires its means of life more through exchange with nature than in intercourse with society. A smallholding, a peasant and his family; alongside them another smallholding, another peasant and another family. A few score of these make up a village, and a few score of villages make up a department. In this way, the great mass of the French nation is formed by simple addition of homologous magnitudes, much as potatoes in a sack form a sack of potatoes. Insofar as millions of families live under economic conditions of existence that separate their mode of life, their interests and their culture from those of the other classes, and put them in hostile opposition to the latter, they form a class. Insofar as there is merely a local interconnection among these small-holding peasants, and the identity of their interests begets no community, no national bond and no political organisation among them, they do not form a class. They are consequently incapable of enforcing their class interests in their own name, whether through a parliament or through a convention. They cannot represent themselves, they must be represented. Their representative must at the same time appear as their master, as an authority over them, as an unlimited governmental power that protects them against the other classes and sends them rain and sunshine from above. The political influence of the small-holding peasants, therefore, finds its final expression in the executive power subordinating society to itself.

Historical tradition gave rise to the belief of the French peasants in the miracle that a man named Napoleon would bring all the glory back to them. And an individual turned up who gives himself out as the man because he bears the name of Napoleon, as a result of the *Code Napoléon*, which lays down that *la recherche de la paternité est interdite*. After a vagabondage of twenty years and after a series of grotesque adventures, the legend finds fulfillment and the man becomes Emperor of the French. The fixed idea of the Nephew was realised, because it coincided with the fixed idea of the most numerous class of the French people.

But, it may be objected, what about the peasant risings in half of France, the raids on the peasants by the army, the mass incarceration and transportation of peasants?

Since Louis XIV, France has experienced no similar persecution of the peasants "for demagogic practices."

But let there be no misunderstanding. The Bonaparte dynasty represents not the revolutionary, but the conservative peasant; not the peasant that strikes out beyond the condition of his social existence, the small-holding, but rather the peasant who wants to consolidate this holding; not the country folk who, linked up with the towns, want to overthrow the old order through their own energies, but on the contrary those who, in stupefied seclusion within this old order, want to see themselves and their smallholdings saved and favoured by the ghost of the empire. It represents not the enlightenment, but the superstition of the peasant; not his judgment, but his prejudice; not his future, but his past; not his modern Cévennes, but his modern Vendée.

The three years' rigorous rule of the parliamentary republic had freed a part of the French peasants from the Napoleonic illusion and had revolutionised them, even if only superficially; but the bourgeoisie violently repressed them whenever they set themselves in motion. Under the parliamentary republic the modern and the traditional consciousness of the French peasant contended for mastery. This progress took the form of an incessant struggle between the schoolmasters and the priests. The bourgeoisie struck down the schoolmasters. For the first time the peasants made efforts to behave independently in the face of the activity of the government. This was shown in the continual conflict between the *maires* and the prefects. The bourgeoisie deposed the *maires.* Finally, during the period of the parliamentary republic, the peasants of different localities rose against their own offspring, the army. The bourgeoisie punished them with states of siege and punitive expeditions. And this same bourgeoisie now cries out about the stupidity of the masses, the *vile multitude,* that has betrayed it to Bonaparte. It has itself forcibly strengthened the imperial sentiments of the peasant class, it conserved the conditions that form the birthplace of this peasant religion. The bourgeoisie, to be sure, is bound to fear the stupidity of the masses as long as they remain conservative, and the insight of the masses as soon as they become revolutionary.

In the risings after the coup d'état, a part of the French peasants protested, arms in hand, against their own vote of December 10, 1848. The school they had gone through since 1848 had sharpened their wits. But they made themselves over to the underworld of history; history held them to their word, and the majority was still so prejudiced that in precisely the reddest departments the peasant population voted openly for Bonaparte. In its view, the National Assembly had hindered his progress. He had now merely broken the fetters that the towns had imposed on the will of the countryside. In some parts the peasants even entertained the grotesque notion of a convention side by side with Napoleon.

After the first revolution had transformed the peasants from semivilleins into freeholders, Napoleon confirmed and regulated the conditions on which they could exploit undisturbed the soil of France which had only just fallen to their lot and slake their youthful passion for property. But what is now causing the ruin of the French peasant is his smallholding itself, the division of the land, the form of property which Napoleon consolidated in France. It is precisely the material conditions which made the French feudal peasant a small-holding peasant and Napoleon an emperor. Two generations have sufficed to produce the inevitable result: progressive deterioration of agriculture, progressive indebtedness of the agriculturist. The "Napoleonic" form of property, which at the beginning of the nineteenth century was the condition for the liberation and enrichment of the French country folk, has developed in the course of this century into the law of their enslavement and pauperisation. And precisely this law is the first of the *"idées napoléoniennes"* which the second Bonaparte has to uphold. If he still shares with the peasants the illusion that the cause of their ruin is to be sought, not in this small-holding property itself, but outside it, in the influence of secondary circumstances, his experiments will burst like soap bubbles when they come in contact with the relations of production.

The economic development of small-holding property has radically changed the relation of the peasants to the other classes of society. Under Napoleon, the fragmentation of the land in the countryside supplemented free competition and the beginning of big industry in the towns. The peasant class was the ubiquitous protest against the landed aristocracy which had just been overthrown. The roots that smallholding property struck in French soil deprived feudalism of all nutriment. Its landmarks formed the natural fortifications of the bourgeoisie against any *coup de main* on the part of its old overlords. But in the course of the nineteenth century the feudal lords were replaced by urban usurers; the feudal obligation that went with the land was replaced by the mortgage; aristocratic landed property was replaced by bourgeois capital. The smallholding of the peasant is now only the pretext that allows the capitalist to draw profits, interest and rent from the soil, while leaving it to the tiller of the soil himself to see how he can extract his wages. The mortgage debt burdening the soil of France imposes on the French peasantry payment of an amount of interest equal to the annual interest on the entire British national debt. Small-holding property, in this enslavement by capital to which its development inevitably pushes forward, has transformed the mass of the French nation into troglodytes. Sixteen million peasants (including women and children) dwell in hovels, a large number of which have but one opening, others only two and the most favoured only three. And windows are to a house what the five senses are to the head. The bourgeois order, which at the beginning of the century set the state to stand guard over the newly arisen smallholding and manured it with laurels, has become a vampire that sucks out its blood and brains and throws them into the alchemist's cauldron of capital. The *Code Napoléon* is now nothing but a *codex* of distraints, forced sales and compulsory auctions. To the four million (including children, etc.) officially recognised paupers, vagabonds, criminals and prostitutes in France must be added five million who hover on the margin of existence and either have their haunts in the countryside itself or, with their rags and their children, continually desert the countryside for the towns and the towns for the countryside. The interests of the peasants, therefore, are no longer, as under Napoleon, in accord with, but in opposition to the interests of the bourgeoisie, to capital. Hence the peasants find their natural ally and leader in the *urban proletariat,* whose task is the overthrow of the bourgeois order. But *strong and unlimited government*—and this is the second *"idée napoléonienne,"* which the second Napoleon has to carry out—is called upon to defend this "material" order by force. This *"ordre matériel"* also serves as the catchword in all of Bonaparte's proclamations against the rebellious peasants.

Besides the mortgage which capital imposes on it, the smallholding is burdened by *taxes.* Taxes are the source of life for the bureaucracy, the army, the priests and the court, in short, for the whole apparatus of the executive power. Strong government and heavy taxes are identical. By its very nature, small-holding property forms a suitable basis for an all-powerful and innumerable bureaucracy. It creates a uniform level of relationships and persons over the whole surface of the land. Hence it also permits of uniform action from a supreme centre on all points of this uniform mass. It annihilates the aristocratic intermediate grades between the mass of the people and the state power. On all sides, therefore, it calls forth the direct interference of this state power and the interposition of its immediate organs. Finally, it produces an unemployed surplus population for which there is no place either on the land or in the towns, and which accordingly reaches out for state offices as a sort of respectable alms, and provokes the creation of state posts. By the new markets which he opened at the point of the bayonet, by the plundering of the Continent, Napoleon repaid the compulsory taxes with interest. These taxes were a spur to the industry of the peasant, whereas now they rob his industry of its last resources and complete his inability to resist pauperism. And an enormous bureaucracy, well-braided and well-fed, is the "*idée napoléonienne*" which is most congenial of all to the second Bonaparte. How could it be otherwise, seeing that alongside the actual classes of society he is forced to create an artificial caste, for which the maintenance of his regime becomes a bread-and-butter question? Accordingly, one of his first financial operations was the raising of officials' salaries to their old level and the creation of new sinecures.

Another "*idée napoléonienne*" is the domination of the *priests* as an instrument of government. But while in its accord with society, in its dependence on natural forces and its submission to the authority which protected it from above, the smallholding that had newly come into being was naturally religious, the smallholding that is ruined by debts, at odds with society and authority, and driven beyond its own limitations naturally becomes irreligious. Heaven was quite a pleasing accession to the narrow strip of land just won, especially as it makes the weather; it becomes an insult as soon as it is thrust forward as substitute for the smallholding. The priest then appears as only the anointed bloodhound of the earthly police—another "*idée napoléonienne.*" On the next occasion, the expedition against Rome will take place in France itself, but in a sense opposite to that of M. de Montalembert.

Lastly, the culminating point of the "*idées napoléoniennes*" is the preponderance of the *army*. The army was the *point d'honneur* of the smallholding peasants, it was they themselves transformed into heroes, defending their new possessions against the outer world, glorifying their recently won nationhood, plundering and revolutionising the world. The uniform was their own state dress; war was their poetry; the smallholding, extended and rounded off in imagination, was their fatherland, and patriotism the ideal form of their sense of property. But the enemies against whom the French peasant has now to defend his property are not the Cossacks; they are the *huissiers* and the tax collectors. The smallholding lies no longer in the so-called fatherland, but in the register of mortgages. The army itself is no longer the flower of the peasant youth; it is the swamp-flower of the peasant lumpenproletariat. It consists in large measure of *remplaçants*, of substitutes, just as the second Bonaparte is himself only a *remplaçant*, the substitute for Napoleon. It now performs its deeds of valour by hunting down the peasants like chamois, and in organised drives, by doing *gendarme* duty, and if the internal contradictions of his system chase the chief of the Society of December 10 over the French border, his army, after some acts of brigandage, will reap, not laurels, but thrashings.

One sees: *all "idées napoléoniennes" are ideas of the undeveloped smallholding in the freshness of its youth;* for the smallholding that has outlived its day they are an absurdity. They are only the hallucinations of its death struggle, words that are transformed into phrases, spirits transformed into ghosts. But the parody of the empire was necessary to free the mass of the French nation from the weight of tradition and to work out in pure form the opposition between the state power and society. With the progressive undermining of small-holding property, the state structure erected upon it collapses. The centralisation of the state that modern society requires arises only on the ruins of the military-bureaucratic government machinery which was forged in opposition to feudalism.

The condition of the French peasants provides us with the answer to the riddle of the *general elections of December 20 and 21,* which bore the second Bonaparte up Mount Sinai, not to receive laws, but to give them.

Manifestly, the bourgeoisie had now no choice but to elect Bonaparte. When the puritans at the Council of Constance complained of the dissolute lives of the popes and wailed about the necessity of moral reform, Cardinal Pierre d'Ailly thundered at them: "Only the devil in person can still save the Catholic Church, and you ask for angels." In like manner, after the coup d'état, the French bourgeoisie cried: Only the chief of the Society of December 10 can still save bourgeois society! Only theft can still save property; only perjury, religion; bastardy, the family; disorder, order!

As the executive authority which has made itself an independent power, Bonaparte feels it to be his mission to safeguard "bourgeois order." But the strength of this bourgeois order lies in the middle class. He looks on himself, therefore, as the representative of the middle class and issues decrees in this sense. Nevertheless, he is somebody solely due to the fact that he has broken the political power of this middle class and daily breaks it anew. Consequently, he looks on himself as the adversary of the political and literary power of the middle class. But by protecting its material power, he generates its political power anew. The cause must accordingly be kept alive; but the effect, where it manifests itself, must be done away with. But this cannot pass off without slight confusions of cause and effect, since in their interaction both lose their distinguishing features. New decrees that obliterate the border line. As against the bourgeoisie, Bonaparte looks on himself, at the same time, as the representative of the peasants and of the people in general, who wants to make the lower classes of the people happy within the framework of bourgeois society. New decrees that cheat the "true Socialists" of their statecraft in advance. But, above all, Bonaparte looks on himself as the chief of the Society of December 10, as the representative of the lumpenproletariat, to which he himself, his entourage, his government and his army belong, and whose prime consideration is to benefit itself and draw California lottery prizes from the state treasury. And he vindicates his position as chief of the Society of December 10 with decrees, without decrees and despite decrees.

This contradictory task of the man explains the contradictions of his government, the confused, blind to-ing and fro-ing which seeks now to win, now to humiliate first one class and then another and arrays all of them uniformly against him, whose practical uncertainty forms a highly comical contrast to the imperious, categorical style of the government decrees, a style which is faithfully copied from the uncle.

Industry and trade, hence the business affairs of the middle class, are to prosper in hothouse fashion under the strong government. The grant of innumerable railway concessions. But the Bonapartist lumpenproletariat is to enrich itself. The initiated play *tripotage* on the *bourse* with the railway concessions. But no capital is forthcoming for the railways. Obligation of the Bank to make advances on railways shares. But, at the same time, the Bank is to be exploited for personal ends and therefore must be cajoled. Release of the Bank from the obligation to publish its report weekly. Leonine agreement of the Bank with the government. The people are to be given employment. Initiation of public works. But the public works increase the obligations of the people in respect of taxes. Hence reduction of the taxes by an onslaught on the *rentiers*, by conversion of the five per cent bonds to four-and-a-half per cent. But, once more, the middle class must receive a *douceur.* Therefore doubling of the wine tax for the people, who buy it *en détail,* and halving of the wine tax for the middle class, who drink it *en gros.* Dissolution of the actual workers' associations, but promises of miracles of association in the future. The peasants are to be helped. Mortgage banks that expedite their getting into debt and accelerate the concentration of property. But these banks are to be used to make money out of the confiscated estates of the House of Orleans. No capitalist wants to agree to this condition, which is not in the decree, and the mortgage bank remains a mere decree, etc., etc.

Bonaparte would like to appear as the patriarchal benefactor of all classes. But he cannot give to one class without taking from another. Just as at the time of the Fronde it was said of the Duke of Guise that he was the most *obligeant* man in France because he had turned all his estates into his partisans' obligations to him, so Bonaparte would fain be the most *obligeant* man in France and turn all the property, all the labour of France into a personal obligation to himself. He would like to steal the whole of France in order to be able to make a present of her to France or, rather, in order to be able to buy France anew with French money, for as the chief of the Society of December 10 he must needs buy what ought to belong to him. And all the state institutions, the Senate, the

Council of State, the legislative body, the Legion of Honour, the soldiers' medals, the wash-houses, the public works, the railways, the *état-
major* of the National Guard excluding privates, and the confiscated
estates of the House of Orleans—all become parts of the institution of
purchase. Every place in the army and in the government machine becomes a means of purchase. But the most important feature of this
process, whereby France is taken in order to be given back, is the
percentages that find their way into the pockets of the head and the
members of the Society of December 10 during the transaction. The
witticism with which Countess L., the mistress of M. de Morny, characterised the confiscation of the Orleans estates: "*C'est le premier vol* de
l'aigle*" is applicable to every flight of this *eagle*, which is more like a
raven. He himself and his adherents call out to one another daily like
that Italian Carthusian admonishing the miser who, with boastful display,
counted up the goods on which he could yet live for years to come: "*Tu
fai conto sopra i beni, bisogna prima far il conto sopra gli anni.*"** Lest they
make a mistake in the years, they count the minutes. A gang of shady
characters push their way forward to the court, into the ministries, to the
head of the administration and the army, a crowd of the best of whom it
must be said that no one knows whence he comes, a noisy, disreputable,
rapacious bohème that crawls into braided coats with the same grotesque
dignity as the high dignitaries of Soulouque. One can visualise clearly
this upper stratum of the Society of December 10, if one reflects that
Véron-Crevel*** is its preacher of morals and *Granier de Cassagnac* its
thinker. When Guizot, at the time of his ministry, utilised this Granier
on a hole-and-corner newspaper against the dynastic opposition, he used
to boast of him with the quip: "*C'est le roi des drôles,*" "he is the king of
buffoons." One would do wrong to recall the Regency or Louis XV in
connection with Louis Bonaparte's court and clique. For "often already,
France has experienced a government of mistresses; but never before a
government of *hommes entretenus.*"†

Driven by the contradictory demands of his situation and being at the
same time, like a conjurer, under the necessity of keeping the public gaze
fixed on himself, as Napoleon's substitute, by springing constant sur-
prises, that is to say, under the necessity of executing a coup d'état *en*

---

* *Vol* means flight and theft.

** "Thou countest thy goods, thou shouldst first count thy years."

*** In his novel *Cousine Bette,* Balzac delineates the thoroughly dissolute Parisian
philistine in Crevel, a character based on Dr. Véron, owner of the *Constitu-
tionnel.*

† The words quoted are those of Madame Girardin.

miniature every day, Bonaparte throws the entire bourgeois economy into confusion, violates everything that seemed inviolable to the revolution of 1848, makes some tolerant of revolution, others desirous of revolution, and produces actual anarchy in the name of order, while at the same time stripping its halo from the entire state machine, profanes it and makes it at once loathsome and ridiculous. The cult of the Holy Coat of Trier he duplicates in Paris with the cult of the Napoleonic imperial mantle. But when the imperial mantle finally falls on the shoulders of Louis Bonaparte, the bronze statue of Napoleon will crash from the top of the Vendôme Column.

Preface to *A Contribution to the Critique of Political Economy*

Karl Marx

Marx spent the 1850's in London working on his critique of political economy and analysis of capitalism. He emerged from this period of intense theoretical work in 1859 with the publication of A Contribution to the Critique of Political Economy. *This work was an anticipation of the first part of volume one of* Capital, *which would appear eight years later, and is little read today except by scholars of Marx. What is read and widely controverted is the Preface to the 1859 essay. In the Preface, Marx first provides a thumbnail sketch of the development of his thinking on political economy, beginning with his early days with the* Rheinische Zeitung. *This can be taken as evidence that Marx saw a great deal of continuity in his work from his Young Hegelian days. He then presents a summary of "the guiding principle of my studies." This statement of the basic claims of historical materialism has become duly famous for pronouncements such as "It is not the consciousness of men that determines their existence, but their social existence that determines their consciousness" and "Mankind thus inevitably sets itself only such tasks as it is able to solve, since closer examination will always show that the problem itself arises only when the material conditions for its solution are already present or at least in the course of formation." The Preface seems to outline a fairly straightforward version of technological determinism. Controversy has concerned whether the Preface accurately represents Marx's actual theoretical views or is distorted by the attempt to be overly concise, and whether the view presented here is consistent with other of his theoretical and political writings.*

PREFACE

I examine the system of bourgeois economy in the following order: *capital, landed property, wage-labour; the State, foreign trade, world market.* The economic conditions of existence of the three great classes into which modern bourgeois society is divided are analyzed under the first three headings; the interconnection of the other three headings is self-

The translation is based on that of Salo Ryazanskaya and is taken from *Karl Marx/Friedrich Engels: Collected Works*, published by International Publishers.

evident. The first part of the first book, dealing with Capital, comprises the following chapters: 1. The commodity; 2. Money or simple circulation; 3. Capital in general. The present part consists of the first two chapters. The entire material lies before me in the form of monographs, which were written not for publication but for self-clarification at widely separated periods; their remoulding into an integrated whole according to the plan I have indicated will depend upon circumstances.

A general introduction, which I had drafted, is omitted, since on further consideration it seems to me confusing to anticipate results which still have to be substantiated, and the reader who really wishes to follow me will have to decide to advance from the particular to the general. A few brief remarks regarding the course of my study of political economy may, however, be appropriate here.

Although jurisprudence was my special study, I pursued it as a subject subordinated to philosophy and history. In the year 1842–43, as editor of the *Rheinische Zeitung*, I first found myself in the embarrassing position of having to discuss what is known as material interests. The deliberations of the Rhine Province Assembly in thefts of wood and the division of landed property; the official polemic started by Herr von Schaper, then Oberpräsident of the Rhine Province, against the *Rheinische Zeitung* about the condition of the Mosel peasantry, and finally the debates on free trade and protective tariffs caused me in the first instance to turn my attention to economic questions. On the other hand, at that time when good intentions "to push forward" often took the place of factual knowledge, an echo of French socialism and communism, slightly tinged by philosophy, was noticeable in the *Rheinische Zeitung*. I objected to this dilettantism, but at the same time frankly admitted in a controversy with the *Allgemeine Augsburger Zeitung* that my previous studies did not allow me to express any opinion on the content of the French theories. When the publishers of the *Rheinische Zeitung* conceived the illusion that by a more compliant policy on the part of the paper it might be possible to secure the abrogation of the death sentence passed upon it, I eagerly grasped the opportunity to withdraw from the public stage to my study.

The first work which I undertook to dispel the doubts assailing me was a critical re-examination of the Hegelian philosophy of law; the introduction to this work being published in the *Deutsch-Französische Jahrbücher* issued in Paris in 1844. My inquiry led me to the conclusion that neither legal relations nor political forms could be comprehended whether by themselves or on the basis of a so-called general development of the human mind, but that on the contrary they originate in the material conditions of life, the totality of which Hegel, following the example of English and French thinkers of the eighteenth century, embraces within the term "civil society"; that the anatomy of this civil society, however, has to be sought in political economy. The study of this, which I began in Paris, I continued in Brussels, where I moved owing to an expulsion order issued by M. Guizot. The general conclusion at which I arrived and which, once reached, became the guiding principle of my studies can be summarised as follows. In the social production of their existence, men inevitably enter into definite relations, which are independent of their will, namely relations of production appropriate to a given stage in the development of their material forces of production. The totality of these relations of production constitutes the economic structure of society, the real foundation, on which arises a legal and political superstructure and to which correspond definite forms of social consciousness. The mode of production of material life conditions the general process of social, political and intellectual life. It is not the consciousness of men that determines their existence, but their social existence that determines their consciousness. At a certain stage of development, the material productive forces of society come into conflict with the existing relations of production or—this merely expresses the same thing in legal terms—with the property relations within the framework of which they have operated hitherto. From forms of development of the productive forces these relations turn into their fetters. Then begins an era of social revolution. The changes in the economic foundation lead sooner or later to the transformation of the whole immense superstructure. In studying such transformations it is always necessary to distinguish between the material transformation of the economic conditions of production, which can be determined with the precision of natural science, and the legal, political, religious, artistic or philosophic—in short, ideological forms in which men become conscious of this conflict and fight it out. Just as one does not judge an individual by what he thinks about himself, so one cannot judge such a period of transformation by its consciousness, but, on the contrary, this consciousness must be explained from the contradictions of material life, from the conflict existing between the social forces of production and the relations of production. No social formation is ever destroyed before all the productive forces for which it is sufficient have been developed, and new superior relations of production never replace older ones before the material conditions for their existence have matured within the framework of the old society. Mankind thus inevitably sets itself only such tasks as it is able to solve, since closer examination will always show that the problem itself arises only when the material conditions for its solution are already present or at least in the course of formation. In broad outline, the Asiatic, ancient, feudal and modern bourgeois modes of production may be designated as epochs marking progress in the economic development of society. The bourgeois relations of production are the last antagonistic form of the social process of production— antagonistic not in the sense of individual antagonism but of an antagonism that emanates from the individuals' social conditions of existence— but the productive forces developing within bourgeois society create also the material conditions for a solution of this antagonism. The prehistory of human society accordingly closes with this social formation.

Friedrich Engels, with whom I maintained a constant exchange of ideas by correspondence since the publication of his brilliant essay on the critique of economic categories (printed in the *Deutsch-Französische Jahrbücher*), arrived by another road (compare his *Condition of the Working-Class in England*) at the same result as I, and when in the spring of 1845 he too came to live in Brussels, we decided to set forth together our conception as opposed to the ideological one of German philosophy, in fact to settle accounts with our former philosophical conscience. The intention was carried out in the form of a critique of post-Hegelian philosophy. The manuscript, two large octavo volumes, had long ago reached the publishers in Westphalia when we were informed that owing to changed circumstances it could not be printed. We abandoned the manuscript to the gnawing criticism of the mice all the more willingly since we have achieved our main purpose—self-clarification. Of the scattered works in which at that time we presented one or another aspect of our views to the public, I shall mention only the *Manifesto of the Communist Party*, jointly written by Engels and myself, and a *Speech on the Question of Free Trade*, which I myself published. The salient points of our conception were first outlined in an academic, although polemical, form in my *Poverty of Philosophy* . . . , this book which was aimed at Proudhon appeared in 1847. The publication of an essay on *Wage-Labour* written in German in which I combined the lectures I had held on this subject at the German Workers' Society in Brussels, was interrupted by the February Revolution and my forcible removal from Belgium in consequence.

The publication of the *Neue Rheinische Zeitung* in 1848 and 1849 and subsequent events cut short my economic studies, which I could only resume in London in 1850. The enormous amount of material relating to the history of political economy assembled in the British Museum, the fact that London is a convenient vantage point for the observation of bourgeois society, and finally the new stage of development which this society seemed to have entered with the discovery of gold in California and Australia, induced me to start again from the very beginning and to work carefully through the new material. These studies led partly of their own accord to apparently quite remote subjects on which I had to spend a certain amount of time. But it was in particular the imperative necessity of earning my living which reduced the time at my disposal. My collaboration, continued now for eight years, with the *New York Tribune,* the leading Anglo-American newspaper, necessitated an excessive fragmentation of my studies, for I wrote only exceptionally newspaper correspondence in the strict sense. Since a considerable part of my contributions consisted of articles dealing with important economic events in Britain and on the continent, I was compelled to become conversant with practical details which, strictly speaking, lie outside the sphere of political economy.

This sketch of the course of my studies in the domain of political economy is intended merely to show that my views—no matter how they may be judged and how little they conform to the interested prejudices of the ruling classes—are the outcome of conscientious research carried on over many years. At the entrance to science, as at the entrance to hell, the demand must be made:

> *Qui si convien lasciare ogni sospetto*
> *Ogni viltà convien che qui sia morta.*[1]

Karl Marx

London, January 1859

---

1. Here all mistrust must be abandoned, Here all cowardice must perish. (Dante, *The Divine Comedy,* 3:13)

III.
ECONOMIC
WRITINGS

Capital
Volume One
(selections)

Karl Marx

Capital (Das Kapital) *is without question Marx's major work. Although only the first part of what Marx sketched out in the* Grundrisse *(Notebooks from 1857–58) as his full research program,* Capital *itself was never completed. The first volume was published in 1867, but the second and third volumes were brought out under Engels's editorship only after Marx's death (Volume Two in 1885 and Volume Three in 1894). Marx's overall project was to comprehend and explain capitalism as a social formation and to analyze the nature and possibility of going beyond capitalism to a socialist society. This project, he realized, would require understanding, both historically and sociologically, all institutions of capitalist society, the state, law, culture, and religion, as well as the economy. But in accordance with his general theoretical approach, he began with the nature of the economy and especially the relations of production, for there were to be found the basic conditions out of which everything else grew. At the same time, as he strove to understand the nature of production and general economic relations in capitalism, Marx also engaged in an ongoing critique of other theorists, for he realized that an adequate understanding of the world could be had only by clearing out the distorted understandings that comprise a society's ideology. Hence the subtitle of* Capital, *"A Critique of Political Economy." Moreover, despite its initial appearance as a purely theoretical work in economic theory,* Capital *should be read as a philosophical investigation into the nature and possibility of human freedom. In this sense, it is continuous with the* Economic and Philosophic Manuscripts *of 1844. Capitalism oppresses, exploits, and alienates human beings. How did it come about? How does it operate to bring about these effects? How and why will it be overcome? These are the essential questions that inform the theoretical analysis of* Capital.

The selections given here are from Volume One. In the first part of that volume, Marx presents the basic categories of his economic theory: commodity, capital, money, use value, exchange value, and surplus value. These categories are put to work in the context of the specific form of the labor theory of value that Marx developed out of the writings of Smith, Ricardo, and other of the early political economists. The most striking fact about capitalist society is its accumulation of wealth on an unprecedented scale. And, as he notes in the beginning of Volume One, this wealth "appears as an 'immense collection of commodities.' " Commodities appear to carry their own value in themselves, and profit, which gives rise to accumulated wealth, appears to result from the exchange of commodities. This appearance, however, belies the real truth of capitalism, which is that profit, and hence accumulations of wealth, derives from the nature of the exchange between capitalist and proletarian. It is because of this exchange, the buying and selling of labor-power, that profit is possible. But profit is not produced in the marketplace, the sphere of exchange where the initial encounter takes place between capitalist and worker. Rather, it is the manner in which the capitalist uses the labor-power purchased to extract surplus value from the laborer in the factory that accounts for the possibility of profit. The secret of profit is to be found, then, not in the marketplace but in the sphere of production. Marx realized that, in order to understand this process, one had to explain both how labor is turned into the commodity, labor-power, and acquires a market price, and how the process of production is organized such that surplus value can be extracted. These are the fundamental tasks of Marx's theory of exploitation.

Section 4 of the first chapter, the famous "Fetishism of the Commodity" passage, concerns how the appearance that commodities assume as inherently valuable and having a life of their own is a distorted reflection of the reality of the underlying social relations. The movement of commodities around a capitalist economy appears to the producers as "a movement made by things, and these things, far from being under their control, in fact control them." The analogy Marx uses is with religion, which he analyzed as early as 1843 as a distorted reflection of the social relations of civil society. Just as the gods represent an alienated form of our own social relations, so do our commodities.

In the last part of Volume One, Marx turns to a discussion of the historical genesis of capitalism. How, Marx asks, did the initial accumulation of surplus value necessary to fuel the engine of capitalism first come into being? His answer: "In actual history, it is a notorious fact that conquest, enslavement, robbery, murder, in short, force, play the greatest part." The other important factor he notes was the creation of a pool of available labor by driving the agricultural peasantry off the land. In the penultimate chapter, originally meant to be the final chapter, Marx turns to the question of the future. In a sweeping statement, he outlines how the tendencies inherent in capitalism will lead to its demise. "The centralization of the means of production and the socialization of labor reach a point at which they become incompatible with their capitalist integument. This integument is burst asunder. The knell of capitalist private property sounds. The expropriators are expropriated."

Preface to the First Edition

This work, whose first volume I now submit to the public, forms the continuation of my book *Zur Kritik der Politischen Ökonomie*, published in 1859. The long pause between the first part and the continuation is due to an illness of many years' duration, which interrupted my work again and again.

The substance of that earlier work is summarized in the first chapter of this volume. This is done not merely for the sake of connectedness and completeness. The presentation is improved. As far as circumstances in any way permit, many points only hinted at in the earlier book are here worked out more fully, while, conversely, points worked out fully there are only touched upon in this volume. The sections on the history of the theories of value and of money are now, of course, left out altogether. However, the reader of the earlier work will find new sources relating to the history of those theories in the notes to the first chapter.

Beginnings are always difficult in all sciences. The understanding of the first chapter, especially the section that contains the analysis of commodities, will therefore present the greatest difficulty. I have popularized the passages concerning the substance of value and the magnitude of value as much as possible.[1] The value-form, whose fully

These selections include the Preface to the First Edition, sections 1, 2, and 4 of Chapter One, Chapter Two, an excerpt from Chapter Three, and Chapters Four, Six, Seven, Twenty-six, and Thirty-two, as translated from the German by Ben Fowkes.

---

1. This is the more necessary, in that even the section of Ferdinand Lassalle's work against Schulze-Delitzsch in which he professes to give 'the intellectual quintessence' of my explanations on these matters, contains important mistakes. If Ferdinand Lassalle has borrowed almost literally from my writings, and without any acknowledgement, all the general theoretical propositions in his economic works, for example those on the historical character of capital, on the connection between the relations of production and the mode of production, etc., etc., even down to the terminology created by me, this may perhaps be due to purposes of propaganda. I am of course not speaking here of his detailed

developed shape is the money-form, is very simple and slight in content. Nevertheless, the human mind has sought in vain for more than 2,000 years to get to the bottom of it, while on the other hand there has been at least an approximation to a successful analysis of forms which are much richer in content and more complex. Why? Because the complete body is easier to study than its cells. Moreover, in the analysis of economic forms neither microscopes nor chemical reagents are of assistance. The power of abstraction must replace both. But for bourgeois society, the commodity-form of the product of labour, or the value-form of the commodity, is the economic cell-form. To the superficial observer, the analysis of these forms seems to turn upon minutiae. It does in fact deal with minutiae, but so similarly does microscopic anatomy.

With the exception of the section on the form of value, therefore, this volume cannot stand accused on the score of difficulty. I assume, of course, a reader who is willing to learn something new and therefore to think for himself.

The physicist either observes natural processes where they occur in their most significant form, and are least affected by disturbing influences, or, wherever possible, he makes experiments under conditions which ensure that the process will occur in its pure state. What I have to examine in this work is the capitalist mode of production, and the relations of production and forms of intercourse [*Verkehrsverhältnisse*] that correspond to it. Until now, their *locus classicus* has been England. This is the reason why England is used as the main illustration of the theoretical developments I make. If, however, the German reader pharisaically shrugs his shoulders at the condition of the English industrial and agricultural workers, or optimistically comforts himself with the thought that in Germany things are not nearly so bad, I must plainly tell him: *De te fabula narratur!*

Intrinsically, it is not a question of the higher or lower degree of development of the social antagonisms that spring from the natural laws of capitalist production. It is a question of these laws themselves, of these tendencies winning their way through and working themselves out with iron necessity. The country that is more developed industrially only shows, to the less developed, the image of its own future.

But in any case, and apart from all this, where capitalist production

---

working-out and application of these propositions, which I have nothing to do with.*

*The footnotes are Marx's own and are numbered sequentially. (The numbering does not follow that of the translation from which the text was taken.)

has made itself fully at home amongst us, for instance in the factories properly so called, the situation is much worse than in England, because the counterpoise of the Factory Acts is absent. In all other spheres, and just like the rest of Continental Western Europe, we suffer not only from the development of capitalist production, but also from the incompleteness of that development. Alongside the modern evils, we are oppressed by a whole series of inherited evils, arising from the passive survival of archaic and outmoded modes of production, with their accompanying train of anachronistic social and political relations. We suffer not only from the living, but from the dead. *Le mort saisit le vif!*

The social statistics of Germany and the rest of Continental Western Europe are, in comparison with those of England, quite wretched. But they raise the veil just enough to let us catch a glimpse of the Medusa's head behind it. We should be appalled at our own circumstances if, as in England, our governments and parliaments periodically appointed commissions of inquiry into economic conditions; if these commissions were armed with the same plenary powers to get at the truth; if it were possible to find for this purpose men as competent, as free from partisanship and respect of persons as are England's factory inspectors, her medical reporters on public health, her commissioners of inquiry into the exploitation of women and children, into conditions of housing and nourishment, and so on. Perseus wore a magic cap so that the monsters he hunted down might not see him. We draw the magic cap down over our own eyes and ears so as to deny that there are any monsters.

Let us not deceive ourselves about this. Just as in the eighteenth century the American War of Independence sounded the tocsin for the European middle class, so in the nineteenth century the American Civil War did the same for the European working class. In England the process of transformation is palpably evident. When it has reached a certain point, it must react on the Continent. There it will take a form more brutal or more humane, according to the degree of development of the working class itself. Apart from any higher motives, then, the most basic interests of the present ruling classes dictate to them that they clear out of the way all the legally removable obstacles to the development of the working class. For this reason, among others, I have devoted a great deal of space in this volume to the history, the details, and the results of the English factory legislation. One nation can and should learn from others. Even when a society has begun to track down the natural laws of its movement—and it is the ultimate aim of this work to reveal the economic law of motion of modern society—it can neither leap over the natural phases of its development nor remove them by decree. But it can shorten and lessen the birth-pangs.

To prevent possible misunderstandings, let me say this. I do not by any means depict the capitalist and the landowner in rosy colours. But individuals are dealt with here only in so far as they are the personifications of economic categories, the bearers [*Träger*] of particular class-relations and interests. My standpoint, from which the development of the economic formation of society is viewed as a process of natural history, can less than any other make the individual responsible for relations whose creature he remains, socially speaking, however much he may subjectively raise himself above them.

In the domain of political economy, free scientific inquiry does not merely meet the same enemies as in all other domains. The peculiar nature of the material it deals with summons into the fray on the opposing side the most violent, sordid and malignant passions of the human breast, the Furies of private interest. The Established Church, for instance, will more readily pardon an attack on thirty-eight of its thirty-nine articles than on one thirty-ninth of its income. Nowadays atheism itself is a *culpa levis,* as compared with the criticism of existing property relations. Nevertheless, even here there is an unmistakable advance. I refer, as an example, to the Blue Book published within the last few weeks: 'Correspondence with Her Majesty's Missions Abroad, Regarding Industrial Questions and Trades' Unions.' There the representatives of the English Crown in foreign countries declare in plain language that in Germany, in France, in short in all the civilized states of the European Continent, a radical change in the existing relations between capital and labour is as evident and inevitable as in England. At the same time, on the other side of the Atlantic Ocean, Mr Wade, Vice-President of the United States, has declared in public meetings that, after the abolition of slavery, a radical transformation in the existing relations of capital and landed property is on the agenda. These are signs of the times, not to be hidden by purple mantles or black cassocks. They do not signify that tomorrow a miracle will occur. They do show that, within the ruling classes themselves, the foreboding is emerging that the present society is no solid crystal, but an organism capable of change, and constantly engaged in a process of change.

The second volume of this work will deal with the process of the circulation of capital (Book II) and the various forms of the process of capital in its totality (Book III), while the third and last volume (Book IV) will deal with the history of the theory.

I welcome every opinion based on scientific criticism. As to the prejudices of so-called public opinion, to which I have never made concessions, now, as ever, my maxim is that of the great Florentine:

'*Segui il tuo corso, e lascia dir le genti.*'

Karl Marx

London, 25 July 1867

Chapter 1: The Commodity
Sections 1, 2, and 4

1. The Two Factors of the Commodity: Use-Value and Value (Substance of Value, Magnitude of Value)

The wealth of societies in which the capitalist mode of production prevails appears as an 'immense collection of commodities';[2] the individual commodity appears as its elementary form. Our investigation therefore begins with the analysis of the commodity.

The commodity is, first of all, an external object, a thing which through its qualities satisfies human needs of whatever kind. The nature of these needs, whether they arise, for example, from the stomach, or the imagination, makes no difference.[3] Nor does it matter here how the thing satisfies man's need, whether directly as a means of subsistence, i.e. an object of consumption, or indirectly as a means of production.

Every useful thing, for example, iron, paper, etc., may be looked at from the two points of view of quality and quantity. Every useful thing is a whole composed of many properties; it can therefore be useful in various ways. The discovery of these ways and hence of the manifold uses of things is the work of history.[4] So also is the invention of socially recognized standards of measurement for the quantities of these useful objects. The diversity of the measures for commodities arises in part from the diverse nature of the objects to be measured, and in part from convention.

The usefulness of a thing makes it a use-value.[5] But this usefulness does not dangle in mid-air. It is conditioned by the physical properties of the commodity, and has no existence apart from the latter. It is therefore

---

2. Karl Marx, *Zur Kritik der Politischen Ökonomie*, Berlin, 1859, p. 3 [English translation, p. 27].

3. 'Desire implies want; it is the appetite of the mind, and as natural as hunger to the body . . . The greatest number (of things) have their value from supplying the wants of the mind' (Nicholas Barbon, *A Discourse on Coining the New Money Lighter. In Answer to Mr Locke's Considerations etc.*, London, 1696, pp. 2, 3).

4. 'Things have an intrinsick vertue' (this is Barbon's special term for use-value) 'which in all places have the same vertue; as the loadstone to attract iron' (op. cit., p. 6). The magnet's property of attracting iron only became useful once it had led to the discovery of magnetic polarity.

5. 'The natural worth of anything consists in its fitness to supply the necessities, or serve the conveniences of human life' (John Locke, 'Some Considerations on the Consequences of the Lowering of Interest' (1691), in *Works*, London, 1777, Vol. 2, p. 28). In English writers of the seventeenth century we still often find the word 'worth' used for use-value and 'value' for exchange-value. This is quite in accordance with the spirit of a language that likes to use a Teutonic word for the actual thing, and a Romance word for its reflection.

the physical body of the commodity itself, for instance iron, corn, a diamond, which is the use-value or useful thing. This property of a commodity is independent of the amount of labour required to appropriate its useful qualities. When examining use-values, we always assume we are dealing with definite quantities, such as dozens of watches, yards of linen, or tons of iron. The use-values of commodities provide the material for a special branch of knowledge, namely the commercial knowledge of commodities.[6] Use-values are only realized [*verwirklicht*] in use or in consumption. They constitute the material content of wealth, whatever its social form may be. In the form of society to be considered here they are also the material bearers [*Träger*] of . . . exchange-value.

Exchange-value appears first of all as the quantitative relation, the proportion, in which use-values of one kind exchange for use-values of another kind.[7] This relation changes constantly with time and place. Hence exchange-value appears to be something accidental and purely relative, and consequently an intrinsic value, i.e. an exchange-value that is inseparably connected with the commodity, inherent in it, seems a contradiction in terms.[8] Let us consider the matter more closely.

A given commodity, a quarter of wheat for example, is exchanged for *x* boot-polish, *y* silk, or *z* gold, etc. In short, it is exchanged for other commodities in the most diverse proportions. Therefore the wheat has many exchange values instead of one. But *x* boot-polish, *y* silk or *z* gold, etc., each represent the exchange-value of one quarter of wheat. Therefore *x* boot-polish, *y* silk, *z* gold, etc., must, as exchange-values, be mutually replaceable or of identical magnitude. It follows from this that, firstly, the valid exchange-values of a particular commodity express something equal, and secondly, exchange-value cannot be anything other than the mode of expression, the 'form of appearance,' of a content distinguishable from it.

Let us now take two commodities, for example corn and iron. Whatever their exchange relation may be, it can always be represented by an equation in which a given quantity of corn is equated to some quantity of iron, for instance 1 quarter of corn = *x* cwt of iron. What does

6. In bourgeois society the legal fiction prevails that each person, as a buyer, has an encyclopedic knowledge of commodities.

7. 'Value consists in the exchange relation between one thing and another, between a given amount of one product and a given amount of another' (Le Trosne, *De l'intérêt social,* in *Physiocrates,* ed. Daire, Paris, 1846, p. 889).

8. 'Nothing can have an intrinsick value' (N. Barbon, op. cit., p. 6); or as Butler says:

> 'The value of a thing
> Is just as much as it will bring.'

this equation signify? It signifies that a common element of identical magnitude exists in two different things, in 1 quarter of corn and similarly in x cwt of iron. Both are therefore equal to a third thing, which in itself is neither the one nor the other. Each of them, so far as it is exchange-value, must therefore be reducible to this third thing.

A simple geometrical example will illustrate this. In order to determine and compare the areas of all rectilinear figures we split them up into triangles. Then the triangle itself is reduced to an expression totally different from its visible shape: half the product of the base and the altitude. In the same way the exchange values of commodities must be reduced to a common element, of which they represent a greater or a lesser quantity.

This common element cannot be a geometrical, physical, chemical or other natural property of commodities. Such properties come into consideration only to the extent that they make the commodities useful, i.e. turn them into use-values. But clearly, the exchange relation of commodities is characterized precisely by its abstraction from their use-values. Within the exchange relation, one use-value is worth just as much as another, provided only that it is present in the appropriate quantity. Or, as old Barbon says: 'One sort of wares are as good as another, if the value be equal. There is no difference or distinction in things of equal value. . . . One hundred pounds worth of lead or iron, is of as great a value as one hundred pounds worth of silver and gold.'[9]

As use-values, commodities differ above all in quality, while as exchange-values they can only differ in quantity, and therefore do not contain an atom of use-value.

If then we disregard the use-value of commodities, only one property remains, that of being products of labour. But even the product of labour has already been transformed in our hands. If we make abstraction from its use-value, we abstract also from the material constituents and forms which make it a use-value. It is no longer a table, a house, a piece of yarn or any other useful thing. All its sensuous characteristics are extinguished. Nor is it any longer the product of the labour of the joiner, the mason or the spinner, or of any other particular kind of productive labour. With the disappearance of the useful character of the products of labour, the useful character of the kinds of labour embodied in them also disappears; this in turn entails the disappearance of the different concrete forms of labour. They can no longer be distinguished, but are all together reduced to the same kind of labour, human labour in the abstract.

9. N. Barbon, op. cit., pp. 53 and 7.

Let us now look at the residue of the products of labour. There is nothing left of them in each case but the same phantom-like objectivity; they are merely congealed quantities of homogeneous human labour, i.e. of human labour-power expended without regard to the form of its expenditure. All these things now tell us is that human labour-power has been expended to produce them, human labour is accumulated in them. As crystals of this social substance, which is common to them all, they are values—commodity values [*Warenwerte*].

We have seen that when commodities are in the relation of exchange, their exchange-value manifests itself as something totally independent of their use-value. But if we abstract from their use-value, there remains their value, as it has just been defined. The common factor in the exchange relation, or in the exchange-value of the commodity, is therefore its value. The progress of the investigation will lead us back to exchange-value as the necessary mode of expression, or form of appearance, of value. For the present, however, we must consider the nature of value independently of its form of appearance [*Erscheinungs form*].

A use-value, or useful article, therefore, has value only because abstract human labour is objectified [*vergegenständlicht*] or materialized in it. How, then, is the magnitude of this value to be measured? By means of the quantity of the 'value-forming substance,' the labour, contained in the article. This quantity is measured by its duration, and the labour-time is itself measured on the particular scale of hours, days etc.

It might seem that if the value of a commodity is determined by the quantity of labour expended to produce it, it would be the more valuable the more unskilful and lazy the worker who produced it, because he would need more time to complete the article. However, the labour that forms the substance of value is equal human labour, the expenditure of identical human labour-power. The total labour-power of society, which is manifested in the values of the world of commodities, counts here as one homogeneous mass of human labour-power, although composed of innumerable individual units of labour-power. Each of these units is the same as any other, to the extent that it has the character of a socially average unit of labour-power and acts as such, i.e. only needs, in order to produce a commodity, the labour time which is necessary on an average, or in other words is socially necessary. Socially necessary labour-time is the labour-time required to produce any use-value under the conditions of production normal for a given society and with the average degree of skill and intensity of labour prevalent in that society. The introduction of power-looms into England, for example, probably reduced by one half the labour required to convert a given quantity of yarn into woven fabric. In order to do this, the English hand-loom weaver in fact needed the same amount of labour-time as before; but the product of his individual hour of labour now only represented half an hour of social labour, and consequently fell to one half its former value.

What exclusively determines the magnitude of the value of any article is therefore the amount of labour socially necessary, or the labour-time socially necessary for its production.[10] The individual commodity counts here only as an average sample of its kind.[11] Commodities which contain equal quantities of labour, or which can be produced in the same time, have therefore the same value. The value of a commodity is related to the value of any other commodity as the labour-time necessary for the production of the one is related to the labour-time necessary for the production of the other. 'As exchange-values, all commodities are merely definite quantities of *congealed labour-time.*'[12]

The value of a commodity would therefore remain constant, if the labour-time required for its production also remained constant. But the latter changes with every variation in the productivity of labour. This is determined by a wide range of circumstances; it is determined amongst other things by the workers' average degree of skill, the level of development of science and its technological application, the social organization of the process of production, the extent and effectiveness of the means of production, and the conditions found in the natural environment. For example, the same quantity of labour is present in eight bushels of corn in favourable seasons and in only four bushels in unfavourable seasons. The same quantity of labour provides more metal in rich mines than in poor. Diamonds are of very rare occurrence on the earth's surface, and hence their discovery costs, on an average, a great deal of labour-time. Consequently much labour is represented in a small volume. Jacob questions whether gold has ever been paid for at its full value. This applies still more to diamonds. According to Eschwege, the total produce of the Brazilian diamond mines for the eighty years ending in 1823 still did not amount to the price of 1½ years' average produce of the sugar and coffee

10. 'The value of them' (the necessaries of life) 'when they are exchanged the one for another, is regulated by the quantity of labour necessarily required, and commonly taken in producing them' (*Some Thoughts on the Interest of Money in General, and Particularly in the Publick Funds,* London, pp. 36, 37). This remarkable anonymous work of the eighteenth century bears no date. However, it is clear from its contents that it appeared in the reign of George II, about 1739 or 1740.

11. 'Properly speaking, all products of the same kind form a single mass, and their price is determined in general and without regard to particular circumstances' (Le Trosne, op. cit., p. 893).

12. Karl Marx, op. cit., p. 6 [English translation, p. 30].

plantations of the same country, although the diamonds represented much more labour, therefore more value. With richer mines, the same quantity of labour would be embodied in more diamonds, and their value would fall. If man succeeded, without much labour, in transforming carbon into diamonds, their value might fall below that of bricks. In general, the greater the productivity of labour, the less the labour-time required to produce an article, the less the mass of labour crystallized in that article, and the less its value. Inversely, the less the productivity of labour, the greater the labour-time necessary to produce an article, and the greater its value. The value of a commodity, therefore, varies directly as the quantity, and inversely as the productivity, of the labour which finds its realization within the commodity. (Now we know the *substance* of value. It is *labour*. We know the *measure of its magnitude*. It is *labour-time*. The *form*, which stamps *value* as *exchange-value*, remains to be analysed. But before this we need to develop the characteristics we have already found somewhat more fully.)

A thing can be a use-value without being a value. This is the case whenever its utility to man is not mediated through labour. Air, virgin soil, natural meadows, unplanted forests, etc. fall into this category. A thing can be useful, and a product of human labour, without being a commodity. He who satisfies his own need with the product of his own labour admittedly creates use-values, but not commodities. In order to produce the latter, he must not only produce use-values, but use-values for others, social use-values. (And not merely for others. The medieval peasant produced a corn-rent for the feudal lord and a corn-tithe for the priest; but neither the corn-rent nor the corn-tithe became commodities simply by being produced for others. In order to become a commodity, the product must be transferred to the other person, for whom it serves as a use-value, through the medium of exchange.) Finally, nothing can be a value without being an object of utility. If the thing is useless, so is the labour contained in it; the labour does not count as labour, and therefore creates no value.

2. The Dual Character of the Labour Embodied In Commodities

Initially the commodity appeared to us as an object with a dual character, possessing both use-value and exchange-value. Later on it was seen that labour, too, has a dual character: in so far as it finds its expression in value, it no longer possesses the same characteristics as when it is the creator of use-values. I was the first to point out and examine critically this twofold nature of the labour contained in commodities.[13] As this

13. Karl Marx, op. cit., pp. 12, 13, and passim [English translation, pp. 41, 42].

point is crucial to an understanding of political economy, it requires further elucidation.

Let us take two commodities, such as a coat and 10 yards of linen, and let the value of the first be twice the value of the second, so that, if 10 yards of linen $= W$, the coat $= 2W$.

The coat is a use-value that satisfies a particular need. A specific kind of productive activity is required to bring it into existence. This activity is determined by its aim, mode of operation, object, means and result. We use the abbreviated expression 'useful labour' for labour whose utility is represented by the use-value of its product, or by the fact that its product is a use-value. In this connection we consider only its useful effect.

As the coat and the linen are qualitatively different use-values, so also are the forms of labour through which their existence is mediated— tailoring and weaving. If the use-values were not qualitatively different, hence not the products of qualitatively different forms of useful labour, they would be absolutely incapable of confronting each other as commodities. Coats cannot be exchanged for coats, one use-value cannot be exchanged for another of the same kind.

The totality of heterogeneous use-values or physical commodities reflects a totality of similarly heterogeneous forms of useful labour, which differ in order, genus, species and variety: in short, a social division of labour. This division of labour is a necessary condition for commodity production, although the converse does not hold; commodity production is not a necessary condition for the social division of labour. Labour is socially divided in the primitive Indian community, although the products do not thereby become commodities. Or, to take an example nearer home, labour is systematically divided in every factory, but the workers do not bring about this division by exchanging their individual products. Only the products of mutually independent acts of labour, performed in isolation, can confront each other as commodities.

To sum up, then: the use-value of every commodity contains useful labour, i.e. productive activity of a definite kind, carried on with a definite aim. Use-values cannot confront each other as commodities unless the useful labour contained in them is qualitatively different in each case. In a society whose products generally assume the form of commodities, i.e. in a society of commodity producers, this qualitative difference between the useful forms of labour which are carried on independently and privately by individual producers develops into a complex system, a social division of labour.

It is moreover a matter of indifference whether the coat is worn by the tailor or by his customer. In both cases it acts as a use-value. So, too, the relation between the coat and the labour that produced it is not in itself altered when tailoring becomes a special trade, an independent branch of the social division of labour. Men made clothes for thousands of years, under the compulsion of the need for clothing, without a single man ever becoming a tailor. But the existence of coats, of linen, of every element of material wealth not provided in advance by nature, had always to be mediated through a specific productive activity appropriate to its purpose, a productive activity that assimilated particular natural materials to particular human requirements. Labour, then, as the creator of use-values, as useful labour, is a condition of human existence which is independent of all forms of society; it is an eternal natural necessity which mediates the metabolism between man and nature, and therefore human life itself.

Use-values like coats, linen, etc., in short, the physical bodies of commodities, are combinations of two elements, the material provided by nature, and labour. If we subtract the total amount of useful labour of different kinds which is contained in the coat, the linen, etc., a material substratum is always left. This substratum is furnished by nature without human intervention. When man engages in production, he can only proceed as nature does herself, i.e. he can only change the form of the materials.[14] Furthermore, even in this work of modification he is constantly helped by natural forces. Labour is therefore not the only source of material wealth, i.e. of the use-values it produces. As William Petty says, labour is the father of material wealth, the earth is its mother.

Let us now pass from the commodity as an object of utility to the value of commodities.

We have assumed that the coat is worth twice as much as the linen. But this is merely a quantitative difference, and does not concern us at the moment. We shall therefore simply bear in mind that if the value of a coat is twice that of 10 yards of linen, 20 yards of linen will have the same value as a coat. As values, the coat and the linen have the same substance, they are the objective expressions of homogeneous labour. But tailoring and weaving are qualitatively different forms of labour.

14. 'All the phenomena of the universe, whether produced by the hand of man or indeed by the universal laws of physics, are not to be conceived of as acts of creation but solely as a reordering of matter. Composition and separation are the only elements found by the human mind whenever it analyses the notion of reproduction; and so it is with the reproduction of value' (use-value, although Verri himself, in this polemic against the Physiocrats, is not quite certain of the kind of value he is referring to) 'and wealth, whether earth, air and water are turned into corn in the fields, or the secretions of an insect are turned into silk by the hand of man, or some small pieces of metal are arranged together to form a repeating watch' (Pietro Verri, *Meditazioni sulla economia politica*—first printed in 1771—in Custodi's edition of the Italian economists, *Parte moderna*, Vol. 15, pp. 21, 22).

There are, however, states of society in which the same man alternately makes clothes and weaves. In this case, these two different modes of labour are only modifications of the labour of the same individual and not yet fixed functions peculiar to different individuals, just as the coat our tailor makes today, and the pair of trousers he makes tomorrow, require him only to vary his own individual labour. Moreover, we can see at a glance that in our capitalist society a given portion of labour is supplied alternately in the form of tailoring and in the form of weaving, in accordance with changes in the direction of the demand for labour. This change in the form of labour may well not take place without friction, but it must take place.

If we leave aside the determinate quality of productive activity, and therefore the useful character of the labour, what remains is its quality of being an expenditure of human labour-power. Tailoring and weaving, although they are qualitatively different productive activities, are both a productive expenditure of human brains, muscles, nerves, hands etc., and in this sense both human labour. They are merely two different forms of the expenditure of human labour-power. Of course, human labour-power must itself have attained a certain level of development before it can be expended in this or that form. But the value of a commodity represents human labour pure and simple, the expenditure of human labour in general. And just as, in civil society, a general or a banker plays a great part but man as such plays a very mean part,[15] so, here too, the same is true of human labour. It is the expenditure of simple labour-power, i.e. of the labour-power possessed in his bodily organism by every ordinary man, on the average, without being developed in any special way. *Simple average labour*, it is true, varies in character in different countries and at different cultural epochs, but in a particular society it is given. More complex labour counts only as *intensified*, or rather *multiplied* simple labour, so that a smaller quantity of complex labour is considered equal to a larger quantity of simple labour. Experience shows that this reduction is constantly being made. A commodity may be the outcome of the most complicated labour, but through its *value* it is posited as equal to the product of simple labour, hence it represents only a specific quantity of simple labour.[16] The various proportions in which different kinds of labour are reduced to simple labour as their unit of measurement are established by a social process that goes

15. Cf. Hegel, *Philosophie des Rechts*, Berlin, 1840, p. 250, para. 190.

16. The reader should note that we are not speaking here of the wages or value the worker receives for (e.g.) a day's labour, but of the value of the commodity in which his day of labour is objectified. At this stage of our presentation, the category of wages does not exist at all.

on behind the backs of the producers; these proportions therefore appear to the producers to have been handed down by tradition. In the interests of simplification, we shall henceforth view every form of labour-power directly as simple labour-power; by this we shall simply be saving ourselves the trouble of making the reduction.

Just as, in viewing the coat and the linen as values, we abstract from their different use-values, so, in the case of the labour represented by those values, do we disregard the difference between its useful forms, tailoring and weaving. The use-values coat and linen are combinations of, on the one hand, productive activity with a definite purpose, and, on the other, cloth and yarn; the values coat and linen, however, are merely congealed quantities of homogeneous labour. In the same way, the labour contained in these values does not count by virtue of its productive relation to cloth and yarn, but only as being an expenditure of human labour-power. Tailoring and weaving are the formative elements in the use-values coat and linen, precisely because these two kinds of labour are of different qualities; but only in so far as abstraction is made from their particular qualities, only in so far as both possess the same quality of being human labour, do tailoring and weaving form the substance of the values of the two articles mentioned.

Coats and linen, however, are not merely values in general, but values of definite magnitude, and, following our assumption, the coat is worth twice as much as the 10 yards of linen. Why is there this difference in value? Because the linen contains only half as much labour as the coat, so that labour-power had to be expended twice as long to produce the second as to produce the first.

While, therefore, with reference to use-value, the labour contained in a commodity counts only qualitatively, with reference to value it counts only quantitatively, once it has been reduced to human labour pure and simple. In the former case it was a matter of the 'how' and the 'what' of labour, in the latter of the 'how much,' of the temporal duration of labour. Since the magnitude of the value of a commodity represents nothing but the quantity of labour embodied in it, it follows that all commodities, when taken in certain proportions, must be equal in value.

If the productivity of all the different sorts of useful labour required, let us say, for the production of a coat remains unchanged, the total value of the coats produced will increase along with their quantity. If one coat represents x days' labour, two coats will represent $2x$ days' labour, and so on. But now assume that the duration of the labour necessary for the production of a coat is doubled or halved. In the first case, one coat is worth as much as two coats were before; in the second case two coats are only worth as much as one was before, although in both cases one coat performs the same service, and the useful labour contained in it remains of the same quality. One change has taken place, however: a change in the quantity of labour expended to produce the article.

In itself, an increase in the quantity of use-values constitutes an increase in material wealth. Two coats will clothe two men, one coat will only clothe one man, etc. Nevertheless, an increase in the amount of material wealth may correspond to a simultaneous fall in the magnitude of its value. This contradictory movement arises out of the twofold character of labour. By 'productivity' of course, we always mean the productivity of concrete useful labour; in reality this determines only the degree of effectiveness of productive activity directed towards a given purpose within a given period of time. Useful labour becomes, therefore, a more or less abundant source of products in direct proportion as its productivity rises or falls. As against this, however, variations in productivity have no impact whatever on the labour itself represented in value. As productivity is an attribute of labour in its concrete useful form, it naturally ceases to have any bearing on that labour as soon as we abstract from its concrete useful form. The same labour, therefore, performed for the same length of time, always yields the same amount of value, independently of any variations in productivity. But it provides different quantities of use-values during equal periods of time; more, if productivity rises; fewer, if it falls. For this reason, the same change in productivity which increases the fruitfulness of labour, and therefore the amount of use-values produced by it, also brings about a reduction in the value of this increased total amount, if it cuts down the total amount of labour-time necessary to produce the use-values. The converse also holds.

On the one hand, all labour is an expenditure of human labour-power, in the physiological sense, and it is in this quality of being equal, or abstract, human labour that it forms the value of commodities. On the other hand, all labour is an expenditure of human labour-power in a particular form and with a definite aim, and it is in this quality of being concrete useful labour that it produces use-values.[17]

4. The Fetishism of the Commodity and Its Secret

A commodity appears at first sight an extremely obvious, trivial thing. But its analysis brings out that it is a very strange thing, abounding in

17. In order to prove that 'labour alone is the ultimate and real standard by which the value of all commodities can at all times and places be estimated and compared,' Adam Smith says this: 'Equal quantities of labour, at all times and places, must have the same value for the labourer. In his ordinary state of health, strength and activity; in the ordinary degree of his skill and dexterity, he must

metaphysical subtleties and theological niceties. So far as it is a use-value, there is nothing mysterious about it, whether we consider it from the point of view that by its properties it satisfies human needs, or that it first takes on these properties as the product of human labour. It is absolutely clear that, by his activity, man changes the forms of the materials of nature in such a way as to make them useful to him. The form of wood, for instance, is altered if a table is made out of it. Nevertheless the table continues to be wood, an ordinary, sensuous thing. But as soon as it emerges as a commodity, it changes into a thing which transcends sensuousness. It not only stands with its feet on the ground, but, in relation to all other commodities, it stands on its head, and evolves out of its wooden brain grotesque ideas, far more wonderful than if it were to begin dancing of its own free will.[18]

The mystical character of the commodity does not therefore arise from its use-value. Just as little does it proceed from the nature of the determinants of value. For in the first place, however varied the useful kinds of labour, or productive activities, it is a physiological fact that they are functions of the human organism, and that each such function,

---

always lay down the same portion of his ease, his liberty, and his happiness' (*Wealth of Nations*, Bk I, Ch. 5 [pp. 104–5]). On the one hand, Adam Smith here (but not everywhere) confuses his determination of value by the quantity of labour expended in the production of commodities with the determination of the values of commodities by the value of labour, and therefore endeavours to prove that equal quantities of labour always have the same value. On the other hand, he has a suspicion that, insofar as labour manifests itself in the value of commodities, it only counts as an expenditure of labour-power; but then again he views this expenditure merely as the sacrifice of rest, freedom and happiness, not as also man's normal life-activity. Of course, he has the modern wage-labourer in mind. Adam Smith's anonymous predecessor, cited in note 9, is much nearer the mark when he says: 'One man has employed himself a week in providing this necessary of life . . . and he that gives him some other in exchange, cannot make a better estimate of what is a proper equivalent, than by comparing what cost him just as much labour and time: which in effect is no more than exchanging one man's labour in one thing for a time certain, for another man's labour in another thing for the same time' (*Some Thoughts on the Interest of Money in General etc.*, p. 39). [Note by Engels to the fourth German edition:] The English language has the advantage of possessing two separate words for these two different aspects of labour. Labour which creates use-values and is qualitatively determined is called 'work' as opposed to 'labour'; labour which creates value and is only measured quantitatively is called 'labour', as opposed to 'work'.

18. One may recall that China and the tables began to dance when the rest of the world appeared to be standing still—*pour encourager les autres*.

whatever may be its nature or its form, is essentially the expenditure of human brain, nerves, muscles and sense organs. Secondly, with regard to the foundation of the quantitative determination of value, namely the duration of that expenditure or the quantity of labour, this is quite palpably different from its quality. In all situations, the labour-time it costs to produce the means of subsistence must necessarily concern mankind, although not to the same degree at different stages of development.[19] And finally, as soon as men start to work for each other in any way, their labour also assumes a social form.

Whence, then, arises the enigmatic character of the product of labour, as soon as it assumes the form of a commodity? Clearly, it arises from this form itself. The equality of the kinds of human labour takes on a physical form in the equal objectivity of the products of labour as values; the measure of the expenditure of human labour-power by its duration takes on the form of the magnitude of the value of the products of labour; and finally the relationships between the producers, within which the social characteristics of their labours are manifested, take on the form of a social relation between the products of labour.

The mysterious character of the commodity-form consists therefore simply in the fact that the commodity reflects the social characteristics of men's own labour as objective characteristics of the products of labour themselves, as the socio-natural properties of these things. Hence it also reflects the social relation of the producers to the sum total of labour as a social relation between objects, a relation which exists apart from and outside the producers. Through this substitution, the products of labour become commodities, sensuous things which are at the same time supra-sensible or social. In the same way, the impression made by a thing on the optic nerve is perceived not as a subjective excitation of that nerve but as the objective form of a thing outside the eye. In the act of seeing, of course, light is really transmitted from one thing, the external object, to another thing, the eye. It is a physical relation between physical things. As against this, the commodity-form, and the value-relation of the products of labour within which it appears, have absolutely no connection with the physical nature of the commodity and the material [*dinglich*] relations arising out of this. It is nothing but the definite social relation between men themselves which assumes here, for them, the fantastic form of a

19. Among the ancient Germans the size of a piece of land was measured according to the labour of a day; hence the acre was called *Tagwerk*, *Tagwanne* (*jurnale*, or *terra jurnalis*, or *diornalis*), *Mannwerk*, *Mannskraft*, *Mannsmaad*, *Mannshauet*, etc. See Georg Ludwig von Maurer, *Einleitung zur Geschichte der Mark-, Hof-, usw. Verfassung*, Munich, 1854, p. 129 ff.

relation between things. In order, therefore, to find an analogy we must take flight into the misty realm of religion. There the products of the human brain appear as autonomous figures endowed with a life of their own, which enter into relations both with each other and with the human race. So it is in the world of commodities with the products of men's hands. I call this the fetishism which attaches itself to the products of labour as soon as they are produced as commodities, and is therefore inseparable from the production of commodities.

As the foregoing analysis has already demonstrated, this fetishism of the world of commodities arises from the peculiar social character of the labour which produces them.

Objects of utility become commodities only because they are the products of the labour of private individuals who work independently of each other. The sum total of the labour of all these private individuals forms the aggregate labour of society. Since the producers do not come into social contact until they exchange the products of their labour, the specific social characteristics of their private labours appear only within this exchange. In other words, the labour of the private individual manifests itself as an element of the total labour of society only through the relations which the act of exchange establishes between the products, and, through their mediation, between the producers. To the producers, therefore, the social relations between their private labours appear as what they are, i.e. they do not appear as direct social relations between persons in their work, but rather as material [*dinglich*] relations between persons and social relations between things.

It is only by being exchanged that the products of labour acquire a socially uniform objectivity as values, which is distinct from their sensuously varied objectivity as articles of utility. This division of the product of labour into a useful thing and a thing possessing value appears in practice only when exchange has already acquired a sufficient extension and importance to allow useful things to be produced for the purpose of being exchanged, so that their character as values has already to be taken into consideration during production. From this moment on, the labour of the individual producer acquires a twofold social character. On the one hand, it must, as a definite useful kind of labour, satisfy a definite social need, and thus maintain its position as an element of the total labour, as a branch of the social division of labour, which originally sprang up spontaneously. On the other hand, it can satisfy the manifold needs of the individual producer himself only in so far as every particular kind of useful private labour can be exchanged with, i.e. counts as the equal of, every other kind of useful private labour. Equality in the full sense between different kinds of labour can be arrived at only if we abstract from their real inequality, if we reduce them to the characteristic they have in common, that of being the expenditure of human labour-power, of human labour in the abstract. The private producer's brain reflects this twofold social character of his labour only in the forms which appear in practical intercourse, in the exchange of products. Hence the socially useful character of his private labour is reflected in the form that the product of labour has to be useful to others, and the social character of the equality of the various kinds of labour is reflected in the form of the common character, as values, possessed by these materially different things, the products of labour.

Men do not therefore bring the products of their labour into relation with each other as values because they see these objects merely as the material integuments of homogeneous human labour. The reverse is true: by equating their different products to each other in exchange as values, they equate their different kinds of labour as human labour. They do this without being aware of it.[20] Value, therefore, does not have its description branded on its forehead; it rather transforms every product of labour into a social hieroglyphic. Later on, men try to decipher the hieroglyphic, to get behind the secret of their own social product: for the characteristic which objects of utility have of being values is as much men's social product as is their language. The belated scientific discovery that the products of labour, in so far as they are values, are merely the material expressions of the human labour expended to produce them, marks an epoch in the history of mankind's development, but by no means banishes the semblance of objectivity possessed by the social characteristics of labour. Something which is only valid for this particular form of production, the production of commodities, namely the fact that the specific social character of private labours carried on independently of each other consists in their equality as human labour, and, in the product, assumes the form of the existence of value, appears to those caught up in the relations of commodity production (and this is true both before and after the above-mentioned scientific discovery) to be just as ultimately valid as the fact that the scientific dissection of the air into its component parts left the atmosphere itself unaltered in its physical configuration.

What initially concerns producers in practice when they make an exchange is how much of some other product they get for their own; in

20. Therefore, when Galiani said: Value is a relation between persons ('*La Ricchezza è una ragione tra due persone*') he ought to have added: a relation concealed beneath a material shell. (Galiani, *Della Moneta*, p. 222, Vol. 3 of Custodi's collection entitled *Scrittori classici italiani di economia politica, Parte moderna*, Milan, 1803.)

what proportions can the products be exchanged? As soon as these proportions have attained a certain customary stability, they appear to result
from the nature of the products, so that, for instance, one ton of iron
and two ounces of gold appear to be equal in value, in the same way as a
pound of gold and a pound of iron are equal in weight, despite their
different physical and chemical properties. The value character of the
products of labour becomes firmly established only when they act as
magnitudes of value. These magnitudes vary continually, independently
of the will, foreknowledge and actions of the exchangers. Their own
movement within society has for them the form of a movement made by
things, and these things, far from being under their control, in fact
control them. The production of commodities must be fully developed
before the scientific conviction emerges, from experience itself, that all
the different kinds of private labour (which are carried on independently
of each other, and yet, as spontaneously developed branches of the social
division of labour, are in a situation of all-round dependence on each
other) are continually being reduced to the quantitative proportions in
which society requires them. The reason for this reduction is that in the
midst of the accidental and ever-fluctuating exchange relations between
the products, the labour-time socially necessary to produce them asserts
itself as a regulative law of nature. In the same way, the law of gravity
asserts itself when a person's house collapses on top of him.[21] The
determination of the magnitude of value by labour-time is therefore a
secret hidden under the apparent movements in the relative values of
commodities. Its discovery destroys the semblance of the merely accidental determination of the magnitude of the value of the products of
labour, but by no means abolishes that determination's material form.

Reflection on the forms of human life, hence also scientific analysis of
those forms, takes a course directly opposite to their real development.
Reflection begins *post festum*, and therefore with the results of the process of development ready to hand. The forms which stamp products as
commodities and which are therefore the preliminary requirements for
the circulation of commodities, already possess the fixed quality of natural forms of social life before man seeks to give an account, not of their
historical character, for in his eyes they are immutable, but of their
content and meaning. Consequently, it was solely the analysis of the

---

21. 'What are we to think of a law which can only assert itself through periodic
crises? It is just a natural law which depends on the lack of awareness of the
people who undergo it' (Friedrich Engels, *Umrisse zu einer Kritik der Nationalökonomie*, in the *Deutsch-Französische Jahrbücher*, edited by Arnold Ruge
and Karl Marx, Paris, 1844) [English translation in Marx/Engels' *Collected Works*,
Vol. 3, London, 1975, p. 433].

prices of commodities which led to the determination of the magnitude of value, and solely the common expression of all commodities in money which led to the establishment of their character as values. It is however precisely this finished form of the world of commodities—the money form—which conceals the social character of private labour and the social relations between the individual workers, by making those relations appear as relations between material objects, instead of revealing them plainly. If I state that coats or boots stand in a relation to linen because the latter is the universal incarnation of abstract human labour, the absurdity of the statement is self-evident. Nevertheless, when the producers of coats and boots bring these commodities into a relation with linen, or with gold or silver (and this makes no difference here), as the universal equivalent, the relation between their own private labour and the collective labour of society appears to them in exactly this absurd form.

The categories of bourgeois economics consist precisely of forms of this kind. They are forms of thought which are socially valid, and therefore objective, for the relations of production belonging to this historically determined mode of social production, i.e. commodity production. The whole mystery of commodities, all the magic and necromancy that surrounds the products of labour on the basis of commodity production, vanishes therefore as soon as we come to other forms of production.

As political economists are fond of Robinson Crusoe stories,[22] let us first look at Robinson on his island. Undemanding though he is by nature, he still has needs to satisfy, and must therefore perform useful labours of various kinds: he must make tools, knock together furniture, tame llamas, fish, hunt and so on. Of his prayers and the like, we take no account here, since our friend takes pleasure in them and sees them as recreation. Despite the diversity of his productive functions, he knows that they are only different forms of activity of one and the same Robinson, hence only different modes of human labour. Necessity itself compels him to divide his time with precision between his different func-

---

22. Even Ricardo has his Robinson Crusoe stories. 'Ricardo makes his primitive fisherman and primitive hunter into owners of commodities who immediately exchange their fish and game in proportion to the labour-time which is materialized in these exchange-values. On this occasion he slips into the anachronism of allowing the primitive fisherman and hunter to calculate the value of their implements in accordance with the annuity tables used on the London Stock Exchange in 1817. Apart from bourgeois society, the "parallelograms of Mr Owen" seem to have been the only form of society Ricardo was acquainted with' (Karl Marx, *Zur Kritik etc.*, pp. 38–9) [English translation, p. 60].

tions. Whether one function occupies a greater space in his total activity than another depends on the magnitude of the difficulties to be overcome in attaining the useful effect aimed at. Our friend Robinson Crusoe learns this by experience, and having saved a watch, ledger, ink and pen from the shipwreck, he soon begins, like a good Englishman, to keep a set of books. His stock-book contains a catalogue of the useful objects he possesses, of the various operations necessary for their production, and finally of the labour-time that specific quantities of these products have on average cost him. All the relations between Robinson and these objects that form his self-created wealth are here so simple and transparent that even Mr Sedley Taylor could understand them. And yet those relations contain all the essential determinants of value.

Let us now transport ourselves from Robinson's island, bathed in light, to medieval Europe, shrouded in darkness. Here, instead of the independent man, we find everyone dependent—serfs and lords, vassals and suzerains, laymen and clerics. Personal dependence characterizes the social relations of material production as much as it does the other spheres of life based on that production. But precisely because relations of personal dependence form the given social foundation, there is no need for labour and its products to assume a fantastic form different from their reality. They take the shape, in the transactions of society, of services in kind and payments in kind. The natural form of labour, its particularity—and not, as in a society based on commodity production, its universality—is here its immediate social form. The *corvée* can be measured by time just as well as the labour which produces commodities, but every serf knows that what he expends in the service of his lord is a specific quantity of his own personal labour-power. The tithe owed to the priest is more clearly apparent than his blessing. Whatever we may think, then, of the different roles in which men confront each other in such a society, the social relations between individuals in the performance of their labour appear at all events as their own personal relations, and are not disguised as social relations between things, between the products of labour.

For an example of labour in common, i.e. directly associated labour, we do not need to go back to the spontaneously developed form which we find at the threshold of the history of all civilized peoples.[23] We have one

---

23. 'A ridiculous notion has spread abroad recently that communal property in its natural, spontaneous form is specifically Slav, indeed exclusively Russian. In fact, it is the primitive form that we can prove to have existed among Romans, Teutons and Celts, and which indeed still exists to this day in India, in a whole range of diverse patterns, albeit sometimes only as remnants. A more exact study of the Asiatic, and specifically of the Indian form of communal property would

nearer to hand in the patriarchal rural industry of a peasant family which produces corn, cattle, yarn, linen and clothing for its own use. These things confront the family as so many products of its collective labour, but they do not confront each other as commodities. The different kinds of labour which create these products—such as tilling the fields, tending the cattle, spinning, weaving and making clothes—are already in their natural form social functions; for they are functions of the family, which, just as much as a society based on commodity production, possesses its own spontaneously developed division of labour. The distribution of labour within the family and the labour-time expended by the individual members of the family, are regulated by differences of sex and age as well as by seasonal variations in the natural conditions of labour. The fact that the expenditure of the individual labour-powers is measured by duration appears here, by its very nature, as a social characteristic of labour itself, because the individual labour-powers, by their very nature, act only as instruments of the joint labour-power of the family.

Let us finally imagine, for a change, an association of free men, working with the means of production held in common, and expending their many different forms of labour-power in full self-awareness as one single social labour force. All the characteristics of Robinson's labour are repeated here, but with the difference that they are social instead of individual. All Robinson's products were exclusively the result of his own personal labour and they were therefore directly objects of utility for him personally. The total product of our imagined association is a social product. One part of this product serves as fresh means of production and remains social. But another part is consumed by the members of the association as means of subsistence. This part must therefore be divided amongst them. The way this division is made will vary with the particular kind of social organization of production and the corresponding level of social development attained by the producers. We shall assume, but only for the sake of a parallel with the production of commodities, that the share of each individual producer in the means of subsistence is determined by his labour-time. Labour-time would in that case play a double part. Its apportionment in accordance with a definite social plan maintains the correct proportion between the different functions of labour

---

indicate the way in which different forms of spontaneous, primitive communal property give rise to different forms of its dissolution. Thus the different original types of Roman and Germanic private property can be deduced from the different forms of Indian communal property' (Karl Marx, *Zur Kritik, etc.*, p. 10) [English translation, p. 33].

and the various needs of the associations. On the other hand, labour-time also serves as a measure of the part taken by each individual in the common labour, and of his share in the part of the total product destined for individual consumption. The social relations of the individual producers, both towards their labour and the products of their labour, are here transparent in their simplicity, in production as well as in distribution.

For a society of commodity producers, whose general social relation of production consists in the fact that they treat their products as commodities, hence as values, and in this material [*sachlich*] form bring their individual, private labours into relation with each other as homogeneous human labour, Christianity with its religious cult of man in the abstract, more particularly in its bourgeois development, i.e. in Protestantism, Deism, etc., is the most fitting form of religion. In the ancient Asiatic, Classical-antique, and other such modes of production, the transformation of the product into a commodity, and therefore men's existence as producers of commodities, plays a subordinate role, which however increases in importance as these communities approach nearer and nearer to the stage of their dissolution. Trading nations, properly so called, exist only in the interstices of the ancient world, like the gods of Epicurus in the *intermundia*, or Jews in the pores of Polish society. Those ancient social organisms of production are much more simple and transparent than those of bourgeois society. But they are founded either on the immaturity of man as an individual, when he has not yet torn himself loose from the umbilical cord of his natural species-connection with other men, or on direct relations of dominance and servitude. They are conditioned by a low stage of development of the productive powers of labour and correspondingly limited relations between men within the process of creating and reproducing their material life, hence also limited relations between man and nature. These real limitations are reflected in the ancient worship of nature, and in other elements of tribal religions. The religious reflections of the real world can, in any case, vanish only when the practical relations of everyday life between man and man, and man and nature, generally present themselves to him in a transparent and rational form. The veil is not removed from the countenance of the social life-process, i.e. the process of material production, until it becomes production by freely associated men, and stands under their conscious and planned control. This, however, requires that society possess a material foundation, or a series of material conditions of existence, which in their turn are the natural and spontaneous product of a long and tormented historical development.

Political economy has indeed analysed value and its magnitude, however incompletely,[24] and has uncovered the content concealed within these forms. But it has never once asked the question why this content has assumed that particular form, that is to say, why labour is expressed in value, and why the measurement of labour by its duration is expressed in the magnitude of the value of the product.[25] These formulas, which bear the unmistakable stamp of belonging to a social formation in which the

24. The insufficiency of Ricardo's analysis of the magnitude of value—and his analysis is by far the best—will appear from the third and fourth books of this work. As regards value in general, classical political economy in fact nowhere distinguishes explicitly and with a clear awareness between labour as it appears in the value of a product, and the same labour as it appears in the product's use-value. Of course the distinction is made in practice, since labour is treated sometimes from its quantitative aspect, and at other times qualitatively. But it does not occur to the economists that a purely quantitative distinction between the kinds of labour presupposes their qualitative unity or equality, and therefore their reduction to abstract human labour. For instance, Ricardo declares that he agrees with Destutt de Tracy when the latter says: 'As it is certain that our physical and moral faculties are alone our original riches, the employment of those faculties, labour of some kind, is our original treasure, and it is always from this employment that all those things are created which we call riches . . . It is certain too, that all those things only represent the labour which has created them, and if they have a value, or even two distinct values, they can only derive them from that' (the value) 'of the labour from which they emanate' (Ricardo, *The Principles of the Political Economy*, 3rd edn, London, 1821, p. 334). We would here only point out that Ricardo imposes his own more profound interpretation on the words of Destutt. Admittedly Destutt does say that all things which constitute wealth 'represent the labour which has created them,' but, on the other hand, he also says that they acquire their 'two different values' (use-value and exchange-value) from 'the value of labour.' He thus falls into the commonplace error of the vulgar economists, who assume the value of one commodity (here labour) in order in turn to use it to determine the values of other commodities. But Ricardo reads him as if he had said that labour (not the value of labour) is represented both in use-value and in exchange-value. Nevertheless, Ricardo himself makes so little of the dual character of the labour represented in this twofold way that he is forced to spend the whole of his chapter 'Value and Riches, their Distinctive Properties' on a laborious examination of the trivialities of a J. B. Say. And at the end he is therefore quite astonished to find that while Destutt agrees with him that labour is the source of value, he nevertheless also agrees with Say about the concept of value.

25. It is one of the chief failings of classical political economy that it has never succeeded, by means of its analysis of commodities, and in particular of their value, in discovering the form of value which in fact turns value into exchange-value. Even its best representatives, Adam Smith and Ricardo, treat the form of value as something of indifference, something external to the nature of the commodity itself. The explanation for this is not simply that their attention is

process of production has mastery over man, instead of the opposite, appear to the political economists' bourgeois consciousness to be as much a self-evident and nature-imposed necessity as productive labour itself. Hence the pre-bourgeois forms of the social organization of production are treated by political economy in much the same way as the Fathers of the Church treated pre-Christian religions.[26]

The degree to which some economists are misled by the fetishism

---

entirely absorbed by the analysis or the magnitude of value. It lies deeper. The value-form of the product of labour is the most abstract, but also the most universal form of the bourgeois mode of production; by that fact it stamps the bourgeois mode of production as a particular kind of social production of a historical and transitory character. If then we make the mistake of treating it as the eternal natural form of social production, we necessarily overlook the specificity of the value-form, and consequently of the commodity-form together with its further developments, the money form, the capital form, etc. We therefore find that economists who are entirely agreed that labour-time is the measure of the magnitude of value, have the strangest and most contradictory ideas about money, that is, about the universal equivalent in its finished form. This emerges sharply when they deal with banking, where the commonplace definitions of money will no longer hold water. Hence there has arisen in opposition to the classical economists a restored Mercantilist System (Ganilh etc.), which sees in value only the social form, or rather its insubstantial semblance. Let me point out once and for all that by classical, political economy I mean all the economists who, since the time of W. Petty, have investigated the real internal framework [*Zusammenhang*] of bourgeois relations of production, as opposed to the vulgar economists who only flounder around within the apparent framework of those relations, ceaselessly ruminate on the materials long since provided by scientific political economy, and seek there plausible explanations of the crudest phenomena for the domestic purposes of the bourgeoisie. Apart from this, the vulgar economists confine themselves to systematizing in a pedantic way, and proclaiming for everlasting truths, the banal and complacent notions held by the bourgeois agents of production about their own world, which is to them the best possible one.

26. 'The economists have a singular way of proceeding. For them, there are only two kinds of institutions, artificial and natural. The institutions of feudalism are artificial institutions, those of the bourgeoisie are natural institutions. In this they resemble the theologians, who likewise establish two kinds of religion. Every religion which is not theirs is an invention of men, while their own is an emanation of God . . . Thus there has been history, but there is no longer any' (Karl Marx, *Misère de la philosophie. Réponse à la philosophie de la misère de M. Proudhon*, 1847, p. 113). Truly comical is M. Bastiat, who imagines that the ancient Greeks and Romans lived by plunder alone. For if people live by plunder for centuries there must, after all, always be something there to plunder; in other

attached to the world of commodities, or by the objective appearance of the social characteristics of labour, is shown, among other things, by the dull and tedious dispute over the part played by nature in the formation of exchange-value. Since exchange-value is a definite social manner of expressing the labour bestowed on a thing, it can have no more natural content than has, for example, the rate of exchange.

As the commodity-form is the most general and the most undeveloped form of bourgeois production, it makes its appearance at an early date, though not in the same predominant and therefore characteristic manner as nowadays. Hence its fetish character is still relatively easy to penetrate. But when we come to more concrete forms, even this appearance of simplicity vanishes. Where did the illusions of the Monetary System come from? The adherents of the Monetary System did not see gold and silver as representing money as a social relation of production, but in the

---

words, the objects of plunder must be continually reproduced. It seems, there-fore, that even the Greeks and the Romans had a process of production, hence an economy, which constituted the material basis of their world as much as the bourgeois economy constitutes that of the present-day world. Or perhaps Bastiat means that a mode of production based on the labour of slaves is based on a system of plunder? In that case he is on dangerous ground. If a giant thinker like Aristotle could err in his evaluation of slave-labour, why should a dwarf economist like Bastiat be right in his evaluation of wage-labour? I seize this opportunity of briefly refuting an objection made by a German-American pub-lication to my work *Zur Kritik der Politischen Ökonomie*, 1859. My view is that each particular mode of production, and the relations of production correspond-ing to it at each given moment, in short 'the economic structure of society,' is 'the real foundation, on which arises a legal and political superstructure and to which correspond definite forms of social consciousness,' and that 'the mode of pro-duction of material life conditions the general process of social, political and intellectual life.' In the opinion of the German-American publication this is all very true for our own times, in which material interests are preponderant, but not for the Middle Ages, dominated by Catholicism, nor for Athens and Rome, dominated by politics. In the first place, it strikes us as odd that anyone should suppose that these well-worn phrases about the Middle Ages and the ancient world were unknown to anyone else. One thing is clear: the Middle Ages could not live on Catholicism, nor could the ancient world on politics. On the contrary, it is the manner in which they gained their livelihood which explains why in one case politics, in the other case Catholicism, played the chief part. For the rest, one needs no more than a slight acquaintance with, for example, the history of the Roman Republic, to be aware that its secret history is the history of landed property. And then there is Don Quixote, who long ago paid the penalty for wrongly imagining that knight errantry was compatible with all economic forms of society.

form of natural objects with peculiar social properties. And what of modern political economy, which looks down so disdainfully on the Monetary System? Does not its fetishism become quite palpable when it deals with capital? How long is it since the disappearance of the Physiocratic illusion that ground rent grows out of the soil, not out of society?

But, to avoid anticipating, we will content ourselves here with one more example relating to the commodity-form itself. If commodities could speak, they would say this: our use-value may interest men, but it does not belong to us as objects. What does belong to us as objects, however, is our value. Our own intercourse as commodities proves it. We relate to each other merely as exchange-values. Now listen how those commodities speak through the mouth of the economist:

'Value (i.e. exchange-value) is a property of things, riches (i.e. use-value) of man. Value, in this sense, necessarily implies exchanges, riches do not.'[27]

'Riches (use-value) are the attribute of man, value is the attribute of commodities. A man or a community is rich, a pearl or a diamond is valuable . . . A pearl or a diamond is valuable as a pearl or diamond.'[28]

So far no chemist has ever discovered exchange-value either in a pearl or a diamond. The economists who have discovered this chemical substance, and who lay special claim to critical acumen, nevertheless find that the use-value of material objects belongs to them independently of their material properties, while their value on the other hand, forms a part of them as objects. What confirms them in this view is the peculiar circumstance that the use-value of a thing is realized without exchange, i.e. in the direct relation between the thing and man, while, inversely, its value is realized only in exchange, i.e. in a social process. Who would not call to mind at this point the advice given by the good Dogberry to the night-watchman Seacoal?

'To be a well-favoured man is the gift of fortune; but reading and writing comes by nature.'[29]

27. *Observations on Some Verbal Disputes in Pol. Econ., Particularly Relating to Value, and to Supply and Demand*, London, 1821, p. 16.

28. S. Bailey, op. cit., p. 165.

29. Both the author of *Observations etc.*, and S. Bailey accuse Ricardo of converting exchange-value from something relative into something absolute. The reverse is true. He has reduced the apparent relativity which these things (diamonds, pearls, etc.) possess to the true relation hidden behind the appearance, namely their relativity as mere expressions of human labour. If the followers of Ricardo answer Bailey somewhat rudely, but by no means convincingly, this is because they are unable to find in Ricardo's own works any elucidation of the inner connection between value and the form of value, or exchange-value.

Chapter 2: The Process of Exchange

Commodities cannot themselves go to market and perform exchanges in
their own right. We must, therefore, have recourse to their guardians,
who are the possessors of commodities. Commodities are things, and
therefore lack the power to resist man. If they are unwilling, he can use
force; in other words, he can take possession of them.[30] In order that
these objects may enter into relation with each other as commodities,
their guardians must place themselves in relation to one another as
persons whose will resides in those objects, and must behave in such a
way that each does not appropriate the commodity of the other, and
alienate his own, except through an act to which both parties consent.
The guardians must therefore recognize each other as owners of private
property. This juridical relation, whose form is the contract, whether as
part of a developed legal system or not, is a relation between two wills
which mirrors the economic relation. The content of this juridical relation (or relation of two wills) is itself determined by the economic relation.[31] Here the persons exist for one another merely as representatives
and hence owners, of commodities. As we proceed to develop our investigation, we shall find, in general, that the characters who appear on the
economic stage are merely personifications of economic relations; it is as
the bearers of these economic relations that they come into contact with
each other.

What chiefly distinguishes a commodity from its owner is the fact that

30. In the twelfth century, so renowned for its piety, very delicate things often
appear among these commodities. Thus a French poet of the period enumerates
among the commodities to be found in the fair of Lendit, alongside clothing,
shoes, leather, implements of cultivation, skins, etc., also *'femmes folles de leur
corps.'*

31. Proudhon creates his ideal of justice, of *'justice éternelle,'* from the juridical
relations that correspond to the production of commodities: he thereby proves, to
the consolation of all good petty bourgeois, that the production of commodities
is a form as eternal as justice. Then he turns round and seeks to reform the
actual production of commodities, and the corresponding legal system, in accordance with this ideal. What would one think of a chemist who, instead of
studying the actual laws governing molecular interactions, and on that basis
solving definite problems, claimed to regulate those interactions by means of the
'eternal ideas' of *'naturalité'* and *'affinité'*? Do we really know any more about
'usury,' when we say it contradicts *'justice éternelle,'* *'équité éternelle,'* *'mutualité
éternelle,'* and other *'vérités éternelles'* than the fathers of the church did when
they said it was incompatible with *'grâce éternelle,'* *'foi éternelle,'* and *'la volunté
éternelle de Dieu'*?

every other commodity counts for it only as the form of appearance of its own value. A born leveller and cynic, it is always ready to exchange not only soul, but body, with each and every other commodity, be it more repulsive than Maritornes herself. The owner makes up for this lack in the commodity of a sense of the concrete, physical body of the other commodity, by his own five and more senses. For the owner, his commodity possesses no direct use-value. Otherwise, he would not bring it to market. It has use-value for others; but for himself its only direct use-value is as a bearer of exchange-value, and consequently, a means of exchange.[32] He therefore makes up his mind to sell it in return for commodities whose use-value is of service to him. All commodities are non-use-values for their owners, and use-values for their non-owners. Consequently, they must all change hands. But this changing of hands constitutes their exchange, and their exchange puts them in relation with each other as values and realizes them as values. Hence commodities must be realized as values before they can be realized as use-values.

On the other hand, they must stand the test as use-values before they can be realized as values. For the labour expended on them only counts in so far as it is expended in a form which is useful for others. However, only the act of exchange can prove whether that labour is useful for others, and its product consequently capable of satisfying the needs of others.

The owner of a commodity is prepared to part with it only in return for other commodities whose use-value satisfies his own need. So far, exchange is merely an individual process for him. On the other hand, he desires to realize his commodity, as a value, in any other suitable commodity of the same value. It does not matter to him whether his own commodity has any use-value for the owner of the other commodity or not. From this point of view, exchange is for him a general social process. But the same process cannot be simultaneously for all owners of commodities both exclusively individual and exclusively social and general.

Let us look at the matter a little more closely. To the owner of a commodity, every other commodity counts as the particular equivalent of his own commodity. Hence his own commodity is the universal equivalent for all the others. But since this applies to every owner, there is in

32. 'For twofold is the use of every object . . . The one is peculiar to the object as such, the other is not, as a sandal which may be worn and is also exchangeable. Both are uses of the sandal, for even he who exchanges the sandal for the money or food he is in need of, makes use of the sandal as a sandal. But not in its natural way. For it has been made for the sake of being exchanged' (Aristotle, *Republic*, I, i, c. 9).

fact no commodity acting as universal equivalent, and the commodities possess no general relative form of value under which they can be equated as values and have the magnitude of their values compared. Therefore they definitely do not confront each other as commodities, but as products or use-values only.

In their difficulties our commodity-owners think like Faust: 'In the beginning was the deed.' They have therefore already acted before thinking. The natural laws of the commodity have manifested themselves in the natural instinct of the owners of commodities. They can only bring their commodities into relation as values, and therefore as commodities, by bringing them into an opposing relation with some one other commodity, which serves as the universal equivalent. We have already reached that result by our analysis of the commodity. But only the action of society can turn a particular commodity into the universal equivalent. The social action of all other commodities, therefore, sets apart the particular commodity in which they all represent their values. The natural form of this commodity thereby becomes the socially recognized equivalent form. Through the agency of the social process it becomes the specific social function of the commodity which has been set apart to be the universal equivalent. It thus becomes—money.

'*Illi unum consilium habent et virtutem et potestatem suam bestiae tradunt . . . Et ne quis possit emere aut vendere, nisi qui habet characterem aut nomen bestiae, aut numerum nominis eius*' (Apocalypse).

Money necessarily crystallizes out of the process of exchange, in which different products of labour are in fact equated with each other, and thus converted into commodities. The historical broadening and deepening of the phenomenon of exchange develops the opposition between use-value and value which is latent in the nature of the commodity. The need to give an external expression to this opposition for the purposes of commercial intercourse produces the drive towards an independent form of value, which finds neither rest nor peace until an independent form has been achieved by the differentiation of commodities into commodities and money. At the same rate, then, as the transformation of the products of labour into commodities is accomplished, one particular commodity is transformed into money.[33]

33. From this we may form an estimate of the craftiness of petty-bourgeois socialism, which wants to perpetuate the production of commodities while simultaneously abolishing the 'antagonism between money and commodities,' i.e. abolishing money itself, since money only exists in and through this antagonism. One might just as well abolish the Pope while leaving Catholicism in existence. For more on this point see my work *Zur Kritik der Politischen Ökonomie*, p. 61 ff. [English translation, pp. 83–6].

The direct exchange of products has the form of the simple expression of value in one respect, but not as yet in another. That form was x commodity A $= y$ commodity B. The form of the direct exchange of products is x use-value A $= y$ use-value B.[34] The articles A and B in this case are not as yet commodities, but become so only through the act of exchange. The first way in which an object of utility attains the possibility of becoming an exchange-value is to exist as a non-use-value, as a quantum of use-value superfluous to the immediate needs of its owner. Things are in themselves external to man, and therefore alienable. In order that this alienation [*Veräusserung*] may be reciprocal, it is only necessary for men to agree tacitly to treat each other as the private owners of those alienable things, and, precisely for that reason, as persons who are independent of each other. But this relationship of reciprocal isolation and foreignness does not exist for the members of a primitive community of natural origin, whether it takes the form of a patriarchal family, an ancient Indian commune or an Inca state. The exchange of commodities begins where communities have their boundaries, at their points of contact with other communities, or with members of the latter. However, as soon as products have become commodities in the external relations of a community, they also, by reaction, become commodities in the internal life of the community. Their quantitative exchange-relation is at first determined purely by chance. They become exchangeable through the mutual desire of their owners to alienate them. In the meantime, the need for others' objects of utility gradually establishes itself. The constant repetition of exchange makes it a normal social process. In the course of time, therefore, at least some part of the products must be produced intentionally for the purpose of exchange. From that moment the distinction between the usefulness of things for direct consumption and their usefulness in exchange becomes firmly established. Their use-value becomes distinguished from their exchange-value. On the other hand, the quantitative proportion in which the things are exchangeable becomes dependent on their production itself. Custom fixes their values at definite magnitudes.

In the direct exchange of products, each commodity is a direct means of exchange to its owner, and an equivalent to those who do not possess

---

34. So long as a chaotic mass of articles is offered as the equivalent for a single article (as is often the case among savages), instead of two distinct objects of utility being exchanged, we are only at the threshold of even the direct exchange of products.

This is directed at the proposal of John Gray, in *The Social System* (1831), for the introduction of labour-money, later taken up by Proudhon.

it, although only in so far as it has use-value for them. At this stage, therefore, the articles exchanged do not acquire a value-form independent of their own use-value, or of the individual needs of the exchangers. The need for this form first develops with the increase in the number and variety of the commodities entering into the process of exchange. The problem and the means for its solution arise simultaneously. Commercial intercourse, in which the owners of commodities exchange and compare their own articles with various other articles, never takes place unless different kinds of commodities belonging to different owners are exchanged for, and equated as values with, one single further kind of commodity. This further commodity, by becoming the equivalent of various other commodities, directly acquires the form of a universal or social equivalent, if only within narrow limits. The universal equivalent form comes and goes with the momentary social contacts which call it into existence. It is transiently attached to this or that commodity in alternation. But with the development of exchange it fixes itself firmly and exclusively onto particular kinds of commodity, i.e. it crystallizes out into the money-form. The particular kind of commodity to which it sticks is at first a matter of accident. Nevertheless there are two circumstances which are by and large decisive. The money-form comes to be attached either to the most important articles of exchange from outside, which are in fact the primitive and spontaneous forms of manifestation of the exchange-value of local products, or to the object of utility which forms the chief element of indigenous alienable wealth, for example cattle. Nomadic peoples are the first to develop the money-form, because all their worldly possessions are in a movable and therefore directly alienable form, and because their mode of life, by continually bringing them into contact with foreign communities, encourages the exchange of products. Men have often made man himself into the primitive material of money, in the shape of the slave, but they have never done this with the land and soil. Such an idea could only arise in a bourgeois society, and one which was already well developed. It dates from the last third of the seventeenth century, and the first attempt to implement the idea on a national scale was made a century later, during the French bourgeois revolution.

In the same proportion as exchange bursts its local bonds, and the value of commodities accordingly expands more and more into the material embodiment of human labour as such, in that proportion does the money-form become transferred to commodities which are by nature fitted to perform the social function of a universal equivalent. Those commodities are the precious metals.

The truth of the statement that 'although gold and silver are not by nature money, money is by nature gold and silver,'[35] is shown by the appropriateness of their natural properties for the functions of money.[36] So far, however, we are acquainted with only one function of money, namely to serve as the form of appearance of the value of commodities, that is as the material in which the magnitudes of their values are socially expressed. Only a material whose every sample possesses the same uniform quality can be an adequate form of appearance of value, that is a material embodiment of abstract and therefore equal human labour. On the other hand, since the difference between the magnitudes of value is purely quantitative, the money commodity must be capable of purely quantitative differentiation, it must therefore be divisible at will, and it must also be possible to assemble it again from its component parts. Gold and silver possess these properties by nature.

The money commodity acquires a dual use-value. Alongside its special use-value as a commodity (gold, for instance, serves to fill hollow teeth, it forms the raw material for luxury articles, etc.) it acquires a formal use-value, arising out of its specific social function.

Since all other commodities are merely particular equivalents for money, the latter being their universal equivalent, they relate to money as particular commodities relate to the universal commodity.[37]

We have seen that the money-form is merely the reflection thrown upon a single commodity by the relations between all other commodities. That money is a commodity[38] is therefore only a discovery for those who proceed from its finished shape in order to analyse it afterwards. The

35. Karl Marx, op. cit., p. 135 [English translation, p. 155]. 'The metals . . . are by their nature money' (Galiani, *Della Moneta*, in Custodi's collection, *Parte moderna*, Vol. 3, p. 137).

36. For further details on this subject see the chapter on 'The Precious Metals' in my work cited above [English translation, pp. 153–7].

37. 'Money is the universal commodity' (Verri, op. cit., p. 16).

38. 'Silver and gold themselves, which we may call by the general name of Bullion, are . . . commodities . . . rising and falling in . . . value . . . Bullion then may be reckoned to be of higher value, where the smaller weight will purchase the greater quantity of the product or manufacture of the country etc.' (S. Clement, *A Discourse of the General Notions of Money, Trade, and Exchange, as They Stand in Relations to Each Other. By a Merchant*, London, 1695, p. 7). 'Silver and gold, coined or uncoined, tho' they are used for a measure of all other things, are no less a commodity than wine, oyl, tobacco, cloth or stuffs' (J. Child, *A Discourse Concerning Trade, and That in Particular of the East-Indies etc.*, London, 1689, p. 2). 'The stock and riches of the kingdom cannot properly be confined to money, nor ought gold and silver to be excluded from being merchandize' (T. Papillon, *The East-India Trade a Most Profitable Trade*, London, 1677, p. 4).

process of exchange gives to the commodity which it has converted into money not its value but its specific value-form. Confusion between these two attributes has misled some writers into maintaining that the value of gold and silver is imaginary.[39] The fact that money can, in certain functions, be replaced by mere symbols of itself, gave rise to another mistaken notion, that it is itself a mere symbol. Nevertheless, this error did contain the suspicion that the money-form of the thing is external to the thing itself, being simply the form of appearance of human relations hidden behind it. In this sense every commodity is a symbol, since, as value, it is only the material shell of the human labour expended on it.[40]

39. 'Gold and silver have value as metals before they are money' (Galiani, op. cit., p. 72). Locke says, 'The universal consent of mankind gave to silver, on account of its qualities which made it suitable for money, an imaginary value' (John Locke, *Some Considerations etc.*, 1691, in *Works*, ed. 1777, Vol. 2, p. 15). Law, on the other hand, says 'How could different nations give an imaginary value to any single thing . . . or how could this imaginary value have maintained itself?' But he himself understood very little of the matter, for example 'Silver was exchanged in proportion to the use-value it possessed, consequent in proportion to its real value. By its adoption as money it received an additional value (*une valeur additionnelle*)' (Jean Law, *Considérations sur le numéraire et le commerce*, in E. Daire's edition of *Économistes financiers du XVIII siècle*, pp. 469-70).

40. 'Money is their (the commodities') symbol' (V. de Forbonnais, *Élémens du commerce*, new edn, Leyden, 1776, Vol. 2, p. 143). 'As a symbol it is attracted by the commodities' (ibid. p. 155). 'Money is a symbol of a thing and represents it' (Montesquieu, *Esprit des lois*, *Œuvres*, London, 1767, Vol. 2, p. 3). 'Money is not a mere symbol, for it is itself wealth; it does not represent the values, it is their equivalent' (Le Trosne, op. cit., p. 910). 'If we consider the concept of value, we must look on the thing itself only as a symbol; it counts not as itself, but as what it is worth' (Hegel, op. cit., p. 100). Long before the economists, lawyers made fashionable the idea that money is a mere symbol, and that the value of the precious metals is purely imaginary. This they did in the sycophantic service of the royal power, supporting the right of the latter to debase the coinage, during the whole of the Middle Ages, by the traditions of the Roman Empire and the conceptions of money to be found in the Digest. 'Let no one call into question,' says their apt pupil, Philip of Valois, in a decree of 1346, 'that the trade, the composition, the supply, and the power of issuing ordinances on the currency . . . belongs exclusively to us and to our royal majesty, to fix such a rate and at such a price as it shall please us and seem good to us.' It was a maxim of Roman Law that the value of money was fixed by Imperial decree. It was expressly forbidden to treat money as a commodity. '*Pecunias vero nulli emere fas erit, nam in usu publico constitutas oportet non esse mercem.*' There is a good discussion of this by G. F. Pagnini, in *Saggio sopra il giusto pregio delle cose*, 1751, printed in Custodi's collection, *Parte moderna*, Vol. 2. In the second part of his work Pagnini directs his polemic especially against the legal gentlemen.

But if it is declared that the social characteristics assumed by material objects, or the material characteristics assumed by the social determinations of labour on the basis of a definite mode of production, are mere symbols, then it is also declared, at the same time, that these characteristics are the arbitrary product of human reflection. This was the kind of explanation favoured by the eighteenth century: in this way the Enlightenment endeavoured, at least temporarily, to remove the appearance of strangeness from the mysterious shapes assumed by human relations whose origins they were unable to decipher.

It has already been remarked above that the equivalent form of a commodity does not imply that the magnitude of its value can be determined. Therefore, even if we know that gold is money, and consequently directly exchangeable with all other commodities, this still does not tell us how much 10lb. of gold is worth, for instance. Money, like every other commodity, cannot express the magnitude of its value except relatively in other commodities. This value is determined by the labour-time required for its production, and is expressed in the quantity of any other commodity in which the same amount of labour-time is congealed.[41] This establishing of its relative value occurs at the source of its production by means of barter. As soon as it enters into circulation as money, its value is already given. In the last decades of the seventeenth century the first step in the analysis of money, the discovery that money is a commodity, had already been taken; but this was merely the first step, and nothing more. The difficulty lies not in comprehending that money is a commodity, but in discovering how, why and by what means a commodity becomes money.[42]

41. 'If a man can bring to London an ounce of silver out of the Earth of Peru, in the same time that he can produce a bushel of corn, then the one is the natural price of the other: now, if by reason of new or more easie mines a man can procure two ounces of silver as easily as he formerly did one, the corn will be as cheap at ten shillings the bushel as it was before at five shillings, *caeteris paribus*' (William Petty, *A Treatise of Texas and Contributions*, London, 1667, p. 32).

42. The learned Professor Roscher, after first informing us that 'the false definitions of money may be divided into two main groups: those which make it more, and those which make it less, than a commodity,' gives us a motley catalogue of works on the nature of money, which does not provide even the glimmer of an insight into the real history of the theory. He then draws this moral: 'For the rest, it is not to be denied that most of the later economists do not bear sufficiently in mind the peculiarities that distinguish money from other commodities' (it is then, after all, either more or less than a commodity!) . . . 'So far, the semi-mercantilist reaction of Ganilh is not altogether without foundation' (Wilhelm Roscher, *Die Grundlagen der Nationalökonomie*, 3rd edn, 1858, pp. 207–10).

We have already seen, from the simplest expression of value, *x* commodity A = *y* commodity B, that the thing in which the magnitude of the value of another thing is represented appears to have the equivalent form independently of this relation, as a social property inherent in its nature. We followed the process by which this false semblance became firmly established, a process which was completed when the universal equivalent form became identified with the natural form of a particular commodity, and thus crystallized into the money-form. What appears to happen is not that a particular commodity becomes money because all other commodities express their values in it, but, on the contrary, that all other commodities universally express their values in a particular commodity because it is money. The movement through which this process has been mediated vanishes in its own result, leaving no trace behind. Without any initiative on their part, the commodities find their own value-configuration ready to hand, in the form of a physical commodity existing outside but also alongside them. This physical object, gold or silver in its crude state, becomes, immediately on its emergence from the bowels of the earth, the direct incarnation of all human labour. Hence the magic of money. Men are henceforth related to each other in their social process of production in a purely atomistic way. Their own relations of production therefore assume a material shape which is independent of their control and their conscious individual action. This situation is manifested first by the fact that the products of men's labour universally take on the form of commodities. The riddle of the money fetish is therefore the riddle of the commodity fetish, now become visible and dazzling to our eyes.

From Chapter 3: Money, or the Circulation of Commodities

Money is the absolutely alienable commodity, because it is all other commodities divested of their shape, the product of their universal alienation. It reads all prices backwards, and thus as it were mirrors itself in the bodies of all other commodities, which provide the material through which it can come into being as a commodity. At the same time the prices, those wooing glances cast at money by commodities, define

More! Less! Not sufficiently! So far! Not altogether! What a way of determining one's concepts! And this eclectic professorial twaddle is modestly baptized by Herr Roscher 'the anatomico-physiological method' of political economy! However, he does deserve credit for one discovery, namely, that money is 'a pleasant commodity.'

the limit of its convertibility, namely its own quantity. Since every commodity disappears when it becomes money it is impossible to tell from the money itself how it got into the hands of its possessor, or what article has been changed into it. *Non olet*, from whatever source it may come. If it represents, on the one hand, a commodity which has been sold, it also represents, on the other hand, a commodity which can be bought.[43]

M—C, a purchase, is at the same time C—M, a sale; the concluding metamorphosis of one commodity is the first metamorphosis of another. For our weaver, the life of his commodity ends with the Bible into which he has reconverted his £2. But suppose the seller of the Bible turns the £2 set free by the weaver into brandy. M—C, the concluding phase of C—M—C (linen-money-Bible), is also C—M, the first phase of C—M—C (Bible-money-brandy). Since the producer of the commodity offers only a single product, he often sells it in large quantities, whereas the fact that he has many needs compels him to split up the price realized, the sum of money set free, into numerous purchases. Hence a sale leads to many purchases of different commodities. The concluding metamorphosis of a commodity thus constitutes an aggregate of the first metamorphoses of other commodities.

If we now consider the completed metamorphosis of a commodity as a whole, it appears in the first place that it is made up of two opposite and complementary movements, C—M and M—C. These two antithetical transmutations of the commodity are accomplished through two antithetical social processes in which the commodity-owner takes part, and are reflected in the antithetical economic characteristics of the two processes. By taking part in the act of sale, the commodity-owner becomes a seller; in the act of purchase, he becomes a buyer. But just as, in every transmutation of a commodity, its two forms, the commodity-form and the money-form, exist simultaneously but at opposite poles, so every seller is confronted with a buyer, every buyer with a seller. While the same commodity is successively passing through the two inverted transmutations, from a commodity into money and from money into another commodity, the owner of the commodity successively changes his role from seller to buyer. Being a seller and being a buyer are therefore not fixed roles, but constantly attach themselves to different persons in the course of the circulation of commodities.

The complete metamorphosis of a commodity, in its simplest form, implies four *dénouements* and three *dramatis personae*. First, a commodity

---

43. 'If money represents, in our hands, the things we can wish to buy, it also represents the things we have sold for this money' (Mercier de la Rivière, op. cit., p. 586).

comes face to face with money; the latter is the form taken by the value of the former, and exists over there in someone else's pocket in all its hard, material reality. A commodity-owner is thus confronted with a money-owner. Now as soon as the commodity has been changed into money, the money becomes its vanishing equivalent-form, whose use-value or content exists here on the spot, in the bodies of other commodities. Money, the final stage of the first transformation, is at the same time the starting-point for the second. The person who is a seller in the first transaction thus becomes a buyer in the second, in which a third commodity-owner comes to meet him as a seller.[44]

The two inverted phases of the movement which makes up the metamorphosis of a commodity constitute a circuit: commodity-form, stripping off of this form, and return to it. Of course, the commodity itself is here subject to contradictory determinations. At the starting-point it is a non-use-value to its owner; at the end it is a use-value. So too the money appears in the first phase as a solid crystal of value into which the commodity has been transformed, but afterwards it dissolves into the mere equivalent-form of the commodity.

The two metamorphoses which constitute the commodity's circular path are at the same time two inverse partial metamorphoses of two other commodities. One and the same commodity (the linen) opens the series of its own metamorphoses, and completes the metamorphosis of another (the wheat). In its first transformation, the sale, the linen plays these two parts in its own person. But then it goes the way of all flesh, enters the chrysalis state as gold, and thereby simultaneously completes the first metamorphosis of a third commodity. Hence the circuit made by one commodity in the course of its metamorphoses is inextricably entwined with the circuits of other commodities. This whole process constitutes the circulation of commodities.

The circulation of commodities differs from the direct exchange of products not only in form, but in its essence. We have only to consider the course of events. The weaver has undoubtedly exchanged his linen for a Bible, his own commodity for someone else's. But this phenomenon is only true for him. The Bible-pusher, who prefers a warming drink to cold sheets, had no intention of exchanging linen for his Bible; the weaver did not know that wheat had been exchanged for his linen. B's commodity replaces that of A, but A and B do not mutually exchange their commodities. It may in fact happen that A and B buy from each other, but a particular relationship of this kind is by no means the

44. 'There are accordingly . . . four final terms and three contracting parties, one of whom intervenes twice' (Le Trosne, op. cit., p. 909).

necessary result of the general conditions of the circulation of commodities. We see here, on the one hand, how the exchange of commodities breaks through all the individual and local limitations of the direct exchange of products, and develops the metabolic process of human labour. On the other hand, there develops a whole network of social connections of natural origin, entirely beyond the control of the human agents. Only because the farmer has sold his wheat is the weaver able to sell his linen, only because the weaver has sold his linen is our rash and intemperate friend able to sell his Bible, and only because the latter already has the water of everlasting life is the distiller able to sell his *eau-de-vie*. And so it goes on.

Chapter 4: The General Formula for Capital

The circulation of commodities is the starting-point of capital. The production of commodities and their circulation in its developed form, namely trade, form the historic presuppositions under which capital arises. World trade and the world market date from the sixteenth century, and from then on the modern history of capital starts to unfold.

If we disregard the material content of the circulation of commodities, i.e. the exchange of the various use-values, and consider only the economic forms brought into being by this process, we find that its ultimate product is money. This ultimate product of commodity circulation is the first form of appearance of capital.

Historically speaking, capital invariably first confronts landed property in the form of money; in the form of monetary wealth, merchants' capital and usurers' capital.[45] However, we do not need to look back at the history of capital's origins in order to recognize that money is its first form of appearance. Every day the same story is played out before our eyes. Even up to the present day, all new capital, in the first instance, steps onto the stage—i.e. the market, whether it is the commodity-market, the labour-market, or the money-market—in the shape of money, money which has to be transformed into capital by definite processes.

The first distinction between money as money and money as capital is nothing more than a difference in their form of circulation. The direct

45. The antagonism between the power of landed property, based on personal relations of domination and servitude, and the power of money, which is impersonal, is clearly expressed by the two French proverbs, '*Nulle terre sans seigneur,*' and '*L'argent n'a pas de maître.*'

form of the circulation of commodities is C—M—C, the transformation of commodities into money and the re-conversion of money into commodities: selling in order to buy. But alongside this form we find another form, which is quite distinct from the first: M—C—M, the transformation of money into commodities, and the re-conversion of commodities into money: buying in order to sell. Money which describes the latter course in its movement is transformed into capital, becomes capital, and, from the point of view of its function, already is capital.

Let us examine the circular movement M—C—M a little more closely. Just as in the case of simple circulation, it passes through two antithetical phases. In the first phase, M—C (the purchase), the money is changed into a commodity. In the second phase, C—M (the sale), the commodity is changed back again into money. These two phases, taken together in their unity, constitute the total movement which exchanges money for a commodity, and the same commodity for money, which buys a commodity in order to sell it, or, if one neglects the formal distinction between buying and selling, buys a commodity with money and then buys money with a commodity.[46] The result, in which the whole process vanishes, is the exchange for money for money, M—M. If I purchase 2,000 lb. of cotton for £100, and resell the 2,000 lb. of cotton for £110, I have in fact exchanged £100 for £110, money for money.

Now it is evident that the circulatory process M—C—M would be absurd and empty if the intention were, by using this roundabout route, to exchange two equal sums of money, £100 for £100. The miser's plan would be far simpler and surer: he holds on to his £100 instead of exposing it to the dangers of circulation. And yet, whether the merchant who has paid £100 for his cotton sells it for £110, or lets it go for £100, or even £50, his money has at all events described a characteristic and original path, quite different in kind from the path of simple circulation, as for instance in the case of the peasant who sells corn, and with the money thus set free buys clothes. First, then, we have to characterize the formal distinctions between the two circular paths M—C—M and C—M—C. This will simultaneously provide us with the difference in content which lies behind these formal distinctions.

Let us first see what the two forms have in common.

Both paths can be divided into the same two antithetical phases, C—M, sale, and M—C, purchase. In each phase the same material elements confront each other, namely a commodity and money, and same economic *dramatis personae*, a buyer and a seller. Each circular path is the unity of the same two antithetical phases, and in each case this unity

46. 'With money one buys commodities, and with commodities one buys money' (Mercier de la Rivière, *L'Ordre naturel et essentiel des sociétés politiques*, p. 543).

is mediated through the emergence of three participants in a contract, of whom one only sells, another only buys and the third both buys and sells.

What however first and foremost distinguishes the two paths C—M—C and M—C—M from each other is the inverted order of succession of the two opposed phases of circulation. The simple circulation of commodities begins with a sale and ends with a purchase, while the circulation of money as capital begins with a purchase and ends with a sale. In the one case both the starting-point and the terminating-point of the movement are commodities, in the other they are money. The whole process is mediated in the first form by money, and in the second, inversely, by a commodity.

In the circulation C—M—C, the money is in the end converted into a commodity which serves as a use-value; it has therefore been spent once and for all. In the inverted form M—C—M, on the contrary, the buyer lays out money in order that, as a seller, he may recover money. By the purchase of his commodity he throws money into circulation, in order to withdraw it again by the sale of the same commodity. He releases the money, but only with the cunning intention of getting it back again. The money therefore is not spent, it is merely advanced.[47]

In the form C—M—C, the same piece of money is displaced twice. The seller gets it from the buyer and pays it away to another seller. The whole process begins when money is received in return for commodities, and comes to an end when money is given up in return for commodities. In the form M—C—M this process is inverted. Here it is not the piece of money which is displaced twice, but the commodity. The buyer takes it from the hands of the seller and passes it into the hands of another buyer. Whilst in the simple circulation of commodities the twofold displacement of the same piece of money effects its definitive transfer from one hand into another, here the twofold displacement of the same commodity causes the money to flow back to its initial point of departure.

This reflux of money to its starting-point does not depend on the commodity's being sold for more than was paid for it. That only has a bearing on the amount of money which flows back. The phenomenon of reflux itself takes place as soon as the purchased commodity is resold, i.e. as soon as the cycle M—C—M has been completed. We have here, therefore, a palpable difference between the circulation of money as capital, and its circulation as mere money.

The cycle C—M—C reaches its conclusion when the money brought

47. 'When a thing is bought in order to be sold again, the sum employed is called money advanced; when it is bought not to be sold, it may be said to be expended' (James Steuart, *Works, etc.*, edited by General Sir James Steuart, his son, London, 1805, Vol. 1, p. 274).

in by the sale of one commodity is withdrawn again by the purchase of another. If there follows a reflux of money to its starting-point, this can happen only through a renewal or repetition of the whole course of the movement. If I sell a quarter of corn for £3, and with this £3 buy clothes, the money, so far as I am concerned, is irreversibly spent. I have nothing more to do with it. It belongs to the clothes merchant. If I now sell a second quarter of corn, money indeed flows back to me, not however as a result of the first transaction, but of its repetition. The money again leaves me as soon as I complete this second transaction by a fresh purchase. In the cycle C—M—C, therefore, the expenditure of money has nothing to do with its reflux. In M—C—M on the other hand the reflux of the money is conditioned by the very manner in which it is expended. Without this reflux, the operation fails, or the process is interrupted and incomplete, owing to the absence of its complementary and final phase, the sale.

The path C—M—C proceeds from the extreme constituted by one commodity, and ends with the extreme constituted by another, which falls out of circulation and into consumption. Consumption, the satisfaction of needs, in short use-value, is therefore its final goal. The path M—C—M, however, proceeds from the extreme of money and finally returns to that same extreme. Its driving and motivating force, its determining purpose, is therefore exchange-value.

In the simple circulation of commodities the two extremes have the same economic form. They are both commodities, and commodities of equal value. But they are also qualitatively different use-values, as for example corn and clothes. The exchange of products, the interchange carried out between the different materials in which social labour is embodied, forms here the content of the movement. It is otherwise in the cycle M—C—M. At first sight this appears to lack any content, because it is tautological. Both extremes have the same economic form. They are both money, and therefore are not qualitatively different use-values, for money is precisely the converted form of commodities, in which their particular use-values have been extinguished. To exchange £100 for cotton, and then to exchange this same cotton again for £100, is merely a roundabout way of exchanging money for money, the same for the same, and appears to be an operation as purposeless as it is absurd.[48]

48. 'One does not exchange money for money,' exclaims Mercier de la Rivière to the Mercantilists (op. cit., p. 486). In a work which professes to deal with 'trade' and 'speculation' there occurs the following: 'All trade consists in the exchange of things of different kinds; and the advantage' (to the merchant?) 'arises out of this difference. To exchange a pound of bread against a pound of bread . . . would be attended with no advantage; . . . Hence trade is advantageously contrasted with

One sum of money is distinguishable from another only by its amount. The process M—C—M does not therefore owe its content to any qualitative difference between its extremes, for they are both money, but solely to quantitative changes. More money is finally withdrawn from circulation than was thrown into it at the beginning. The cotton originally bought for £100 is for example re-sold at £100 + £10, i.e. £110. The complete form of this process is therefore M—C—M′, where M′ = M + Δ M, i.e. the original sum advanced plus an increment. This increment or excess over the original value I call 'surplus-value'. The value originally advanced, therefore, not only remains intact while in circulation, but increases its magnitude, adds to itself a surplus-value, or is valorized [*verwertet sich*]. And this movement converts it into capital.

Of course, it is also possible that in C—M—C the two extremes C and C, say corn and clothes, may represent quantitatively different magnitudes of value. The peasant may sell his corn above its value, or may buy the clothes at less than their value. He may, on the other hand, be cheated by the clothes merchant. Yet, for this particular form of circulation, such differences in value are purely accidental. The fact that the corn and the clothes are equivalents does not deprive the process of all sense and meaning, as it does in M—C—M. The equivalence of their values is rather a necessary condition of its normal course.

The repetition or renewal of the act of selling in order to buy finds its measure and its goal (as does the process itself) in a final purpose which lies outside it, namely consumption, the satisfaction of definite needs.

---

gambling, which consists in a mere exchange of money for money' (Th. Corbet, *An Inquiry into the Causes and Modes of the Wealth of Individuals; or the Principles of Trade and Speculation Explained*, London, 1841, p. 5). Although Corbet does not see that M—M, the exchange of money for money, is the characteristic form of circulation, not only of merchants' capital, but of all capital, yet at least he acknowledges that this form is common to gambling and to one species of trade, namely speculation. Then, however, MacCulloch comes on the scene, and asserts that to buy in order to sell is to speculate, and thus the distinction between speculation and trade vanishes. 'Every transaction in which an individual buys produce in order to sell it again is in fact a speculation' (MacCulloch, *A Dictionary, Practical etc., of Commerce*, London, 1847, p. 1009). With much more naïveté, Pinto, the Pindar of the Amsterdam Stock Exchange, remarks: 'Trade is a game' (this phrase is borrowed from Locke) 'and nothing can be won from beggars. If one won everything from everybody for long, it would be necessary to give back voluntarily the greater part of the profit in order to begin the game again' (Pinto, *Traité de la circulation et du crédit*, Amsterdam, 1771, p. 231).

Pindar (522–442 B.C.) composed odes in praise of Olympic victors; Pinto (A.D. 1715–87), rich Amsterdam speculator and merchant, wrote books in praise of his country's financial system.

But in buying in order to sell, on the contrary, the end and the beginning are the same, money or exchange-value and this very fact makes the movement an endless one. Certainly M becomes M + Δ M, £100 becomes £110. But, considered qualitatively, £100 is the same as £110, namely money; while, from the quantitative point of view, £110 is, like £100, a sum of definite and limited value. If the £110 is now spent as money, it ceases to play its part. It is no longer capital. Withdrawn from circulation, it is petrified into a hoard, and it could remain in that position until the Last Judgement without a single farthing accruing to it. If, then, we are concerned with the valorization [*Verwertung*] of value, the value of the £110 has the same need for valorization as the value of the £100, for they are both limited expressions of exchange-value, and therefore both have the same vocation, to approach, by quantitative increase, as near as possible to absolute wealth. Momentarily, indeed, the value originally advanced, the £100, is distinguishable from the surplus-value of £10, added to it during circulation; but the distinction vanishes immediately. At the end of the process, we do not receive on one hand the original £100, and on the other the surplus-value of £10. What emerges is rather a value of £110, which is in exactly the same form, appropriate for commencing the valorization process, as the original £100. At the end of the movement, money emerges once again as its starting-point.[49] Therefore the final result of each separate cycle, in which a purchase and consequent sale are completed, forms of itself the starting-point for a new cycle. The simple circulation of commodities— selling in order to buy—is a means to a final goal which lies outside circulation, namely the appropriation of use-values, the satisfaction of needs. As against this, the circulation of money as capital is an end in itself, for the valorization of value takes place only within this constantly renewed movement. The movement of capital is therefore limitless.[50]

49. 'Capital is divided . . . into the original capital and profit—the increment of capital . . . although in practice profit is immediately lumped together with capital and set into motion with it' (F. Engels, *Umrisse zu einer Kritik der Nationalökonomie*, in *Deutsch-Französische Jahrbücher*, edited by Arnold Ruge and Karl Marx, Paris, 1844, p. 99) [English translation, p. 430].

50. Aristotle contrasts economics with 'chrematistics.' He starts with economics. So far as it is the art of acquisition, it is limited to procuring the articles necessary to existence and useful either to a household or the state. 'True wealth (ὅ ἀληθινὸς πλοῦτος) consists of such use-values; for the amount of property which is needed for a good life is not unlimited . . . There is, however, a second mode of acquiring things, to which we may by preference and with correctness give the name of chrematistics, and in this case there appear to be no limits to riches and property. Trade (ἡ καπηλική is literally retail trade, and Aristotle chooses this form because use-values predominate in it) does not in its nature

As the conscious bearer [*Träger*] of this movement, the possessor of money becomes a capitalist. His person, or rather his pocket, is the point from which the money starts, and to which it returns. The objective content of the circulation we have been discussing—the valorization of value—is his subjective purpose, and it is only in so far as the appropriation of ever more wealth in the abstract is the sole driving force behind his operations that he functions as a capitalist, i.e. as capital personified and endowed with consciousness and a will. Use-values must therefore never be treated as the immediate aim of the capitalist;[51] nor must the profit on any single transaction. His aim is rather the unceasing movement of profit-making.[52] This boundless drive for enrichment, this passionate chase after value,[53] is common to the capitalist and the miser; but

belong to chrematistics, for here the exchange only has reference to what is necessary for (the buyer or the seller) themselves.' Therefore, as he goes on to show, the original form of trade was barter, but with the extension of the latter there arose the necessity for money. With the discovery of money, barter of necessity developed into καπηλική, into trading in commodities, and this again, in contradiction with its original tendency, grew into chrematistics, the art of making money. Now chrematistics can be distinguished from economics in that 'for chrematistics, circulation is the source of riches (ποιητικὴ χρημάτων . . . διὰ χρημάτων μεταβολῆς). And it appears to revolve around money, for money is the beginning and the end of this kind of exchange (το γὰρ νόμισμα στοιχεῖον καὶ πέρας τῆς ἀλλαγῆς ἐστιν). Therefore also riches, such as chrematistics strives for, are unlimited. Just as every art which is not a means to an end, but an end in itself, has no limit to its aims, because it seeks constantly to approach nearer and nearer to that end, while those arts which pursue means to an end are not boundless, since the goal itself imposes a limit on them, so with chrematistics there are no bounds to its aims, these aims being absolute wealth. Economics, unlike chrematistics, has a limit . . . for the object of the former is something different from money, of the latter the augmentation of money . . . By confusing these two forms, which overlap each other, some people have been led to look upon the preservation and increase of money *ad infinitum* as the final goal of economics' (Aristotle, *De Republica*, ed. Bekker, lib. I, c. 8, 9, passim).

51. 'Commodities' (here used in the sense of use-values) 'are not the terminating object of the trading capitalist, money is his terminating object' (T. Chalmers, *On Political Economy etc.*, 2nd edn, Glasgow, 1832, pp. 165–6).

52. 'Though the merchant does not count the profit he has just made as nothing, he nevertheless always has his eye on his future profit' (A. Genovesi, *Lezioni di economia civile* (1765), printed in Custodi's edition of the Italian economists, *Parte moderna*, Vol. 8, p. 139).

53. 'The inextinguishable passion for gain, the *auri sacra fames*, will always lead capitalists' (MacCulloch, *The Principles of Political Economy*, London, 1830, p. 179). This view, of course, does not prevent the same MacCulloch and his

while the miser is merely a capitalist gone mad, the capitalist is a rational miser. The ceaseless augmentation of value, which the miser seeks to attain by saving[54] his money from circulation, is achieved by the more acute capitalist by means of throwing his money again and again into circulation.[55]

The independent form, i.e. the monetary form, which the value of commodities assumes in simple circulation, does nothing but mediate the exchange of commodities, and it vanishes in the final result of the movement. On the other hand, in the circulation M—C—M both the money and the commodity function only as different modes of existence of value itself, the money as its general mode of existence, the commodity as its particular or, so to speak, disguised mode.[56] It is constantly changing from one form into the other, without becoming lost in this movement; it thus becomes transformed into an automatic subject. If we pin down the specific forms of appearance assumed in turn by self-valorizing value in the course of its life, we reach the following elucidation: capital is money, capital is commodities.[57] In truth, however, value is here the subject of a process in which, while constantly assuming the form in turn of money and commodities, it changes its own magnitude, throws off surplus-value from itself considered as original value, and thus valorizes itself independently. For the movement in the course of which it adds surplus-value is its own movement, its valorization is therefore self-valorization [_Selbstverwertung_]. By virtue of being value, it has acquired the occult ability to add value to itself. It brings forth living offspring, or at least lays golden eggs.

As the dominant subject [_übergreifendes Subjekt_] of this process, in which it alternately assumes and loses the form of money and the form

---

associates, when they are in theoretical difficulties, as for example in the treatment of over-production, from transforming the same capitalist into a good citizen, whose sole concern is for use-values, and who even develops an insatiable hunger for boots, hats, eggs, calico and other extremely common kinds of use-value.

54. Σώζειν [to save] is a characteristic Greek expression for hoarding. So in English the word 'to save' means both _retten_ [to rescue] and _sparen_ [to save].

55. 'Things possess an infinite quality when moving in a circle which they lack when advancing in a straight line' (Galiani, op. cit., p. 156).

56. 'It is not the material which forms capital, but the value of that material' (J. B. Say, _Traité d'économie politique_, 3rd edn, Paris, 1817, Vol. 2, p. 429).

57. 'Currency (!) employed in producing articles . . . is capital' (Macleod, _The Theory and Practice of Banking_, London, 1855, Vol. 1, Ch. 1, p. 55). 'Capital is commodities' (James Mill, _Elements of Political Economy_, London, 1821, p. 74).

of commodities, but preserves and expands itself through all these changes, value requires above all an independent form by means of which its identity with itself may be asserted. Only in the shape of money does it possess this form. Money therefore forms the starting-point and the conclusion of every valorization process. It was £100, and now it is £110, etc. But the money itself is only one of the two forms of value. Unless it takes the form of some commodity, it does not become capital. There is here no antagonism, as in the case of hoarding, between the money and commodities. The capitalist knows that all commodities, however tattered they may look, or however badly they may smell, are in faith and in truth money, are by nature circumcised Jews, and, what is more, a wonderful means for making still more money out of money.

In simple circulation, the value of commodities attained at the most a form independent of their use-values, i.e. the form of money. But now, in the circulation M—C—M, value suddenly presents itself as a self-moving substance which passes through a process of its own, and for which commodities and money are both mere forms. But there is more to come: instead of simply representing the relations of commodities, it now enters into a private relationship with itself, as it were. It differentiates itself as original value from itself as surplus-value, just as God the Father differentiates himself from himself as God the Son, although both are of the same age and form, in fact one single person; for only by the surplus-value of £10 does the £100 originally advanced become capital, and as soon as this has happened, as soon as the son has been created and, through the son, the father, their difference vanishes again, and both become one, £110.

Value therefore now becomes value in process, money in process, and, as such, capital. It comes out of circulation, enters into it again, preserves and multiplies itself within circulation, emerges from it with an increased size, and starts the same cycle again and again.[58] M—M, 'money which begets money,' such is the description of capital given by its first interpreters, the Mercantilists.

Buying in order to sell, or, more accurately, buying in order to sell dearer, M—C—M, seems admittedly to be a form peculiar to one kind of capital alone, merchants' capital. But industrial capital too is money which has been changed into commodities, and reconverted into more money by the sale of these commodities. Events which take place outside the sphere of circulation, in the interval between buying and selling, do

58. 'Capital . . . permanent self-multiplying value' (Sismondi, *Nouveaux Principes d'économie politique*, Vol. 1, p. 89) [cited in German in the original, and slightly altered].

not affect the form of this movement. Lastly, in the case of interest-bearing capital, the circulation M—C—M' presents itself in abridged form, in its final result and without any intermediate stage, in a concise style, so to speak, as M—M', i.e. money which is worth more money, value which is greater than itself.

M—C—M' is in fact therefore the general formula for capital, in the form in which it appears directly in the sphere of circulation.

Chapter 6: The Sale and Purchase of Labour-Power

The change in value of the money which has to be transformed into capital cannot take place in the money itself, since in its function as means of purchase and payment it does no more than realize [*realisieren*] the price of the commodity it buys or pays for, while, when it sticks to its own peculiar form, it petrifies into a mass of value of constant magnitude.[59] Just as little can this change originate in the second act of circulation, the resale of the commodity, for this act merely converts the commodity from its natural form back into its money-form. The change must therefore take place in the commodity which is bought in the first act of circulation, M—C, but not in its value, for it is equivalents which are being exchanged, and the commodity is paid for at its full value. The change can therefore originate only in the actual use-value of the commodity, i.e. in its consumption. In order to extract value out of the consumption of a commodity, our friend the money-owner must be lucky enough to find within the sphere of circulation, on the market, a commodity whose use-value possesses the peculiar property of being a source of value, whose actual consumption is therefore itself an objectification [*Vergegenständlichung*] of labour, hence a creation of value. The possessor of money does find such a special commodity on the market: the capacity for labour [*Arbeitsvermögen*], in other words labour-power [*Arbeitskraft*].

We mean by labour-power, or labour-capacity, the aggregate of those mental and physical capabilities existing in the physical form, the living personality, of a human being, capabilities which he sets in motion whenever he produces a use-value of any kind.

But in order that the owner of money may find labour-power on the market as a commodity, various conditions must first be fulfilled. In and for itself, the exchange of commodities implies no other relations of

---

59. 'In the form of money . . . capital is productive of no profit' (Ricardo, *Principles of Political Economy*, p. 267).

dependence than those which result from its own nature. On this assumption, labour-power can appear on the market as a commodity only if, and in so far as, its possessor, the individual whose labour-power it is, offers it for sale or sells it as a commodity. In order that its possessor may sell it as a commodity, he must have it at his disposal, he must be the free proprietor of his own labour-capacity, hence of his person.[60] He and the owner of money meet in the market, and enter into relations with each other on a footing of equality as owners of commodities, with the sole difference that one is a buyer, the other a seller; both are therefore equal in the eyes of the law. For this relation to continue, the proprietor of labour-power must always sell it for a limited period only, for if he were to sell it in a lump, once and for all, he would be selling himself, converting himself from a free man into a slave, from an owner of a commodity into a commodity. He must constantly treat his labour-power as his own property, his own commodity, and he can do this only by placing it at the disposal of the buyer, i.e. handing it over to the buyer for him to consume, for a definite period of time, temporarily. In this way he manages both to alienate [*veräussern*] his labour-power and to avoid renouncing his rights of ownership over it.[61]

60. In encyclopedias of classical antiquity one can reach such nonsense as this: In the ancient world capital was fully developed, 'except for the absence of the free worker and of a system of credit.' Mommsen too, in his *History of Rome*, commits one blunder after another in this respect.

61. Hence legislation in various countries fixes a maximum length for labour contracts. Wherever free labour is the rule, the law regulates the conditions for terminating this contract. In some states, particularly in Mexico (and before the American Civil War in the territories taken by the United States from Mexico, as also in practice in the Danubian Principalities until Cuza's *coup d'état*), slavery is hidden under the form of peonage. By means of advances repayable in labour, which are handed down from generation to generation, not only the individual worker, but also his family, become in fact the property of other persons and their families. Juarez abolished peonage, but the so-called Emperor Maximilian re-established it by a decree which was aptly denounced in the House of Representatives in Washington as a decree for the re-introduction of slavery into Mexico. 'Single products of my particular physical and mental skill and of my power to act I can alienate to someone else and I can give him the use of my abilities for a restricted period, because, on the strength of this restriction, my abilities acquire an external relation to the totality and universality of my being. By alienating the whole of my time, as crystallized in my work, and everything I produced, I would be making into another property the substance of my being, my universal activity and actuality, my personality' (Hegel, *Philosophie des Rechts*, Berlin, 1840, p. 104, para. 67) [English translation, p. 54].

The second essential condition which allows the owner of money to find labour-power in the market as a commodity is this, that the possessor of labour-power, instead of being able to sell commodities in which his labour has been objectified, must rather be compelled to offer for sale as a commodity that very labour-power which exists only in his living body.

In order that a man may be able to sell commodities other than his labour-power, he must of course possess means of production, such as raw materials, instruments of labour, etc. No boots can be made without leather. He requires also the means of subsistence. Nobody—not even a practitioner of *Zukunftsmusik*—can live on the products of the future, or on use-values whose production has not yet been completed; just as on the first day of his appearance on the world's stage, man must still consume every day, before and while he produces. If products are produced as commodities, they must be sold after they have been produced, and they can only satisfy the producer's needs after they have been sold. The time necessary for sale must be counted as well as the time of production.

For the transformation of money into capital, therefore, the owner of money must find the free worker available on the commodity-market; and this worker must be free in the double sense that as a free individual he can dispose of his labour-power as his own commodity, and that, on the other hand, he has no other commodity for sale, i.e. he is rid of them, he is free of all the objects needed for the realization [*Verwirklichung*] of his labour-power.

Why this free worker confronts him in the sphere of circulation is a question which does not interest the owner of money, for he finds the labour-market in existence as a particular branch of the commodity-market. And for the present it interests us just as little. We confine ourselves to the fact theoretically, as he does practically. One thing, however, is clear: nature does not produce on the one hand owners of money or commodities, and on the other hand men possessing nothing but their own labour-power. This relation has no basis in natural history, nor does it have a social basis common to all periods of human history. It is clearly the result of a past historical development, the product of many economic revolutions, of the extinction of a whole series of older formations of social production.

The economic categories already discussed similarly bear a historical imprint. Definite historical conditions are involved in the existence of the product as a commodity. In order to become a commodity, the product must cease to be produced as the immediate means of subsistence of the producer himself. Had we gone further, and inquired under what circumstances all, or even the majority of products take the form of commodities, we should have found that this only happens on the basis of one particular mode of production, the capitalist one. Such an investigation, however, would have been foreign to the analysis of commodities. The production and circulation of commodities can still take place even though the great mass of the objects produced are intended for the immediate requirements of their producers, and are not turned into commodities, so that the process of social production is as yet by no means dominated in its length and breadth by exchange-value. The appearance of products as commodities requires a level of development of the division of labour within society such that the separation of use-value from exchange-value, a separation which first begins with barter, has already been completed. But such a degree of development is common to many economic formations of society [*ökonomische Gesellschaftsformationen*], with the most diverse historical characteristics.

If we go on to consider money, its existence implies that a definite stage in the development of commodity exchange has been reached. The various forms of money (money as the mere equivalent of commodities, money as means of circulation, money as means of payment, money as hoard, or money as world currency) indicate very different levels of the process of social production, according to the extent and relative preponderance of one function or the other. Yet we know by experience that a relatively feeble development of commodity circulation suffices for the creation of all these forms. It is otherwise with capital. The historical conditions of its existence are by no means given with the mere circulation of money and commodities. It arises only when the owner of the means of production and subsistence finds the free worker available, on the market, as the seller of his own labour-power. And this one historical pre-condition comprises a world's history. Capital, therefore, announces from the outset a new epoch in the process of social production.[62]

This peculiar commodity, labour-power, must now be examined more closely. Like all other commodities it has a value.[63] How is that value determined?

---

62. The capitalist epoch is therefore characterized by the fact that labour-power, in the eyes of the worker himself, takes on the form of a commodity which is his property; his labour consequently takes on the form of wage-labour. On the other hand, it is only from this moment that the commodity-form of the products of labour becomes universal.

63. 'The value or worth of a man, is as of all other things his price—that is to say, so much as would be given for the use of his power' (T. Hobbes, *Leviathan*, in *Works*, ed. Molesworth, London, 1839–44, Vol. 3, p. 76).

The value of labour-power is determined, as in the case of every other commodity, by the labour-time necessary for the production, and consequently also the reproduction, of this specific article. In so far as it has value, it represents no more than a definite quantity of the average social labour objectified in it. Labour-power exists only as a capacity of the living individual. Its production consequently presupposes his existence. Given the existence of the individual, the production of labour-power consists in his reproduction of himself or his maintenance. For his maintenance he requires a certain quantity of the means of subsistence. Therefore the labour-time necessary for the production of labour-power is the same as that necessary for the production of those means of subsistence; in other words, the value of labour-power is the value of the means of subsistence necessary for the maintenance of its owner. However, labour-power becomes a reality only by being expressed; it is activated only through labour. But in the course of this activity, i.e. labour, a definite quantity of human muscle, nerve, brain, etc. is expended, and these things have to be replaced. Since more is expended, more must be received.[64] If the owner of labour-power works today, tomorrow he must again be able to repeat the same process in the same conditions as regards health and strength. His means of subsistence must therefore be sufficient to maintain him in his normal state as a working individual. His natural needs, such as food, clothing, fuel and housing vary according to the climatic and other physical peculiarities of his country. On the other hand, the number and extent of his so-called necessary requirements, as also the manner in which they are satisfied, are themselves products of history, and depend therefore to a great extent on the level of civilization attained by a country; in particular they depend on the conditions in which, and consequently on the habits and expectations with which, the class of free workers has been formed.[65] In contrast, therefore, with the case of other commodities, the determination of the value of labour-power contains a historical and moral element. Nevertheless, in a given country at a given period, the average amount of the means of subsistence necessary for the worker is a known *datum*.

The owner of labour-power is mortal. If then his appearance in the market is to be continuous, and the continuous transformation of money into capital assumes this, the seller of labour-power must perpetuate

---

64. In ancient Rome, therefore, the *villicus*, as the overseer of the agricultural slaves, received 'more meagre fare than working slaves, because his work was lighter' (T. Mommsen, *Römische Geschichte*, 1856, p. 810).

65. Cf. W. T. Thornton, *Over-Population and Its Remedy*, London, 1846.

himself 'in the way that every living individual perpetuates himself, by procreation.'[66] The labour-power withdrawn from the market by wear and tear, and by death, must be continually replaced by, at the very least, an equal amount of fresh labour-power. Hence the sum of means of subsistence necessary for the production of labour-power must include the means necessary for the worker's replacements, i.e. his children, in order that this race of peculiar commodity-owners may perpetuate its presence on the market.[67]

In order to modify the general nature of the human organism in such a way that it acquires skill and dexterity in a given branch of industry, and becomes labour-power of a developed and specific kind, a special education or training is needed, and this in turn costs an equivalent in commodities of a greater or lesser amount. The costs of education vary according to the degree of complexity of the labour-power required. These expenses (exceedingly small in the case of ordinary labour-power) form a part of the total value spent in producing it.

The value of labour-power can be resolved into the value of a definite quantity of the means of subsistence. It therefore varies with the value of the means of subsistence, i.e. with the quantity of labour-time required to produce them.

Some of the means of subsistence, such as food and fuel, are consumed every day, and must therefore be replaced every day. Others, such as clothes and furniture, last for longer periods and need to be replaced only at longer intervals. Articles of one kind must be bought or paid for every day, others every week, others every quarter and so on. But in whatever way the sum total of these outlays may be spread over the year, they must be covered by the average income, taking one day with another. If the total of the commodities required every day for the production of labour-power $= A$, and of those required every week $= B$, and of those required every quarter $= C$, and so on, the daily average of these commodities $= \frac{365A + 52B + 4C + \ldots}{365}$. Suppose that this mass of commodities required for the average day contains 6 hours of social labour, then every day half a day of average social labour is objectified in

66. Petty.

67. 'Its' (labour's) 'natural price . . . consists in such a quantity of necessaries and comforts of life, as, from the nature of the climate, and the habits of the country, are necessary to support the labourer, and to enable him to rear such a family as may preserve, in the market, an undiminished supply of labour' (R. Torrens, *An Essay on the External Corn Trade*, London, 1815, p. 62). The word labour is here wrongly used for labour-power.

labour-power, or in other words half a day of labour is required for the daily production of labour-power. This quantity of labour forms the value of a day's labour-power, or the value of the labour-power reproduced every day. If half a day of average social labour is present in 3 shillings, then 3 shillings is the price corresponding to the value of a day's labour-power. If its owner therefore offers it for sale at 3 shillings a day, its selling price is equal to its value, and according to our original assumption the owner of money, who is intent on transforming his 3 shillings into capital, pays this value.

The ultimate or minimum limit of the value of labour-power is formed by the value of the commodities which have to be supplied every day to the bearer of labour-power, the man, so that he can renew his life-process. That is to say, the limit is formed by the value of the physically indispensable means of subsistence. If the price of labour-power falls to this minimum, it falls below its value, since under such circumstances it can be maintained and developed only in a crippled state, and the value of every commodity is determined by the labour-time required to provide it in its normal quality.

It is an extraordinarily cheap kind of sentimentality which declares that this method of determining the value of labour-power, a method prescribed by the very nature of the case, is brutal, and which laments with Rossi in this matter: 'To conceive capacity for labour (*puissance de travail*) in abstraction from the workers' means of subsistence during the production process is to conceive a phantom (*être de raison*). When we speak of labour, or capacity for labour, we speak at the same time of the worker and his means of subsistence, of the worker and his wages.'[68] When we speak of capacity for labour, we do not speak of labour, any more than we speak of digestion when we speak of capacity for digestion. As is well known, the latter process requires something more than a good stomach. When we speak of capacity for labour, we do not abstract from the necessary means of subsistence. On the contrary, their value is expressed in its value. If his capacity for labour remains unsold, this is of no advantage to the worker. He will rather feel it to be a cruel nature-imposed necessity that his capacity for labour has required for its production a definite quantity of the means of subsistence, and will continue to require this for its reproduction. Then, like Sismondi, he will discover that 'the capacity for labour . . . is nothing unless it is sold.'[69]

One consequence of the peculiar nature of labour-power as a

68. Rossi, *Cours d'économie politique*, Brussels, 1842, pp. 370–71.
69. Sismondi, *Nouvelles Principes etc.*, Vol. 1, p. 113.

commodity is this, that it does not in reality pass straight away into the hands of the buyer on the conclusion of the contract between buyer and seller. Its value, like that of every other commodity, is already determined before it enters into circulation, for a definite quantity of social labour has been spent on the production of the labour-power. But its use-value consists in the subsequent exercise of that power. The alienation [*Veräusserung*] of labour-power and its real manifestation [*Äusserung*], i.e. the period of its existence as a use-value, do not coincide in time. But in those cases in which the formal alienation by sale of the use-value of a commodity is not simultaneous with its actual transfer to the buyer, the money of the buyer serves as means of payment.[70]

In every country where the capitalist mode of production prevails, it is the custom not to pay for labour-power until it has been exercised for the period fixed by the contract, for example, at the end of each week. In all cases, therefore, the worker advances the use-value of his labour-power to the capitalist. He lets the buyer consume it before he receives payment of the price. Everywhere the worker allows credit to the capitalist. That this credit is no mere fiction is shown not only by the occasional loss of the wages the worker has already advanced, when a capitalist goes bankrupt,[71] but also by a series of more long-lasting consequences.[72]

70. 'All labour is paid after it has ceased' (*An Inquiry into Those Principles, Respecting the Nature of Demand, etc.*, p. 104). 'The system of commercial credit had to start at the moment when the worker, the prime creator of products, could, thanks to his savings, wait for his wages until the end of the week, the fortnight, the month, the quarter, etc.' (C. Ganilh, *Des systèmes de l'économie politique*, 2nd edn, Paris, 1821, Vol. 1, p. 150).

71. 'The worker lends his industry,' says Storch. But he slyly adds to this the statement that the worker 'risks nothing,' except 'the loss of his wages . . . The worker does not hand over anything of a material nature' (Storch, *Cours d'économie politique*, St. Petersburg, 1815, Vol. 2, pp. 36–7).

72. One example. In London there are two sorts of bakers, the 'full priced,' who sell bread at its full value, and the 'undersellers,' who sell it at less than its value. The latter class comprises more than three-quarters of the total number of bakers (p. xxxii in the Report of H. S. Tremenheere, the commissioner appointed to examine 'the grievances complained of by the journeymen bakers,' etc., London, 1862). The undersellers, almost without exception, sell bread adulterated with alum, soap, pearl-ash, chalk, Derbyshire stone-dust and other similar agreeable, nourishing and wholesome ingredients. (See the above-cited Blue Book, as also the report of the select committee of 1855 on the adulteration of food, and Dr Hassall's *Adulterations Detected*, 2nd edn, London, 1861.) Sir John Gordon stated before the committee of 1855 that 'in consequence of these

Whether money serves as a means of purchase or a means of payment, this does not alter the nature of the exchange of commodities. The price of the labour-power is fixed by the contract, although it is not realized till later, like the rent of a house. The labour-power is sold, although it is paid for only at a later period. It will therefore be useful, if we want to conceive the relation in its purse form, to presuppose for the moment that the possessor of labour-power, on the occasion of each sale, immediately receives the price stipulated in the contract

We now know the manner of determining the value paid by the owner of money to the owner of this peculiar commodity, labour-power. The use-value which the former gets in exchange manifests itself only in the actual utilization, in the process of the consumption of the labour-power.

---

adulterations, the poor man, who lives on two pounds of bread a day, does not now get one-fourth part of nourishing matter, let alone the deleterious effects on his health.' Tremenheere states (op. cit., p. xlviii) as the reason why a 'very large part of the working class,' although well aware of this adulteration, nevertheless accept the alum, stone-dust, etc. as part of their purchase, that it is for them 'a matter of necessity to take from their baker or from the chandler's shop such bread as they choose to supply.' As they are not paid their wages before the end of the week, they in their turn are unable 'to pay for the bread consumed by their families during the week, before the end of the week,' and Tremenheere adds on the evidence of witnesses, 'it is notorious that bread composed of those mixtures is made expressly for sale in this manner.' 'In many English agricultural districts' (and still more in Scottish) 'wages are paid fortnightly and even monthly; with such long intervals between the payments, the agricultural labourer is obliged to buy on credit . . . He must pay higher prices, and is in fact tied to the shop which gives him credit. Thus at Horningham in Wilts., for example, where the wages are monthly, the same flour that he could buy elsewhere at 1s. 10d per stone, costs him 2s 4d. per stone' (*Public Health, Sixth Report* of the Medical Officer of the Privy Council, etc., 1864, p. 264). 'The block-printers of Paisley and Kilmarnock' (Western Scotland) 'enforced in 1833 by a strike the reduction of the period of payment from monthly to fortnightly' (*Reports of the Inspectors of Factories . . . 31 October 1853*, p. 34). As a further nice development from the credit given by the workers to the capitalist, we may refer to the method adopted by many English coal-owners whereby the worker is not paid till the end of the month, and in the meantime receives sums on account from the capitalist, often in goods for which the miner is obliged to pay more than the market price (truck system). 'It is a common practice with the coal masters to pay once a month, and advance cash to their workmen at the end of each intermediate week. The cash is given in the shop' (i.e. the tommy-shop which belongs to the master); 'the men take it on one side and lay it out on the other' (*Children's Employment Commission, Third Report*, London, 1864, p. 38, n. 192).

The money-owner buys everything necessary for this process, such as raw material, in the market, and pays the full price for it. The process of the consumption of labour-power is at the same time the production process of commodities and of surplus-value. The consumption of labour-power is completed, as in the case of every other commodity, outside the market or the sphere of circulation. Let us therefore, in company with the owner of money and the owner of labour-power, leave this noisy sphere, where everything takes place on the surface and in full view of everyone, and follow them into the hidden abode of production, on whose threshold there hangs the notice 'No admittance except on business.' Here we shall see, not only how capital produces, but how capital is itself produced. The secret of profit-making must at last be laid bare.

The sphere of circulation or commodity exchange, within whose boundaries the sale and purchase of labour-power goes on, is in fact a very Eden of the innate rights of man. It is the exclusive realm of Freedom, Equality, Property and Bentham. Freedom, because both buyer and seller of a commodity, let us say of labour-power, are determined only by their own free will. They contract as free persons, who are equal before the law. Their contract is the final result in which their joint will finds a common legal expression. Equality, because each enters into relation with the other, as with a simple owner of commodities, and they exchange equivalent for equivalent. Property, because each disposes only of what is his own. And Bentham, because each looks only to his own advantage. The only force bringing them together, and putting them into relation with each other, is the selfishness, the gain and the private interest of each. Each pays heed to himself only, and no one worries about the others. And precisely for that reason, either in accordance with the pre-established harmony of things, or under the auspices of an omniscient providence, they all work together to their mutual advantage, for the common weal, and in the common interest.

When we leave this sphere of simple circulation or the exchange of commodities, which provides the 'free-trader *vulgaris*' with his views, his concepts and the standard by which he judges the society of capital and wage-labour, a certain change takes place, or so it appears, in the physiognomy of our *dramatis personae*. He who was previously the money-owner now strides out in front as a capitalist; the possessor of labour-power follows as his worker. The one smirks self-importantly and is intent on business; the other is timid and holds back, like someone who has brought his own hide to market and now has nothing else to expect but—a tanning.

Chapter 7: The Labour Process and the Valorization Process

1. The Labour Process

The use of labour-power is labour itself. The purchaser of labour-power consumes it by setting the seller of it to work. By working, the latter becomes in actuality what previously he only was potentially, namely labour-power in action, a worker. In order to embody his labour in commodities, he must above all embody it in use-values, things which serve to satisfy needs of one kind or another. Hence what the capitalist sets the worker to produce is a particular use-value, a specific article. The fact that the production of use-values, or goods, is carried on under the control of a capitalist and on his behalf does not alter the general character of that production. We shall therefore, in the first place, have to consider the labour process independently of any specific social formation.

Labour is, first of all, a process between man and nature, a process by which man, through his own actions, mediates, regulates and controls the metabolism between himself and nature. He confronts the materials of nature as a force of nature. He sets in motion the natural forces which belong to his own body, his arms, legs, head and hands, in order to appropriate the materials of nature in a form adapted to his own needs. Through this movement he acts upon external nature and changes it, and in this way he simultaneously changes his own nature. He develops the potentialities slumbering within nature, and subjects the play of its forces to his own sovereign power. We are not dealing here with those first instinctive forms of labour which remain on the animal level. An immense interval of time separates the state of things in which a man brings his labour-power to market for sale as a commodity from the situation when human labour had not yet cast off its first instinctive form. We presuppose labour in a form in which it is an exclusively human characteristic. A spider conducts operations which resemble those of the weaver, and a bee would put many a human architect to shame by the construction of its honeycomb cells. But what distinguishes the worst architect from the best of bees is that the architect builds the cell in his mind before he constructs it in wax. At the end of every labour process, a result emerges which had already been conceived by the worker at the beginning, hence already existed ideally. Man not only effects a change of form in the materials of nature; he also realizes [*verwirklicht*] his own purpose in those materials. And this is a purpose he is conscious of, it determines the mode of his activity with the rigidity of a law, and he must subordinate his will to it. This subordination is no mere momentary act. Apart from the exertion of the working organs, a purposeful will is required for the entire duration of the work. This means close attention. The less he is attracted by the nature of the work and the way in which it has to be accomplished, and the less, therefore, he enjoys it as the free play of his own physical and mental powers, the closer his attention is forced to be.

The simple elements of the labour process are (1) purposeful activity, that is work itself, (2) the object on which that work is performed, and (3) the instruments of that work.

The land (and this, economically speaking, includes water) in its original state in which it supplies[73] man with necessaries or means of subsistence ready to hand is available without any effort on his part as the universal material for human labour. All those things which labour merely separates from immediate connection with their environment are objects of labour spontaneously provided by nature, such as fish caught and separated from their natural element, namely water, timber felled in virgin forests, and ores extracted from their veins. If, on the other hand, the object of labour has, so to speak, been filtered through previous labour, we call it raw material. For example, ore already extracted and ready for washing. All raw material is an object of labour [*Arbeitsgegenstand*], but not every object of labour is raw material; the object of labour counts as raw material only when it has already undergone some alteration by means of labour.

An instrument of labour is a thing, or a complex of things, which the worker interposes between himself and the object of his labour and which serves as a conductor, directing his activity onto that object. He makes use of the mechanical, physical and chemical properties of some substances in order to set them to work on other substances as instruments of his power, and in accordance with his purposes.[74] Leaving out

73. 'The earth's spontaneous productions being in small quantity, quite independent of man, appear, as it were, to be furnished by Nature, in the same way as a small sum is given to a young man, in order to put him in a way of industry, and of making his fortune' (James Steuart, *Principles of Political Economy*, Dublin, 1770, Vol. 1, p. 116).

74. 'Reason is as cunning as it is powerful. Cunning may be said to lie in the intermediative action which, while it permits the objects to follow their own bent and act upon one another till they waste away, and does not itself directly interfere in the process, is nevertheless only working out its own aims' (Hegel, *Enzyklopädie, Erster Theil, Die Logik*, Berlin, 1840, p. 382) [Para. 209, Addition. English translation: *Hegel's Logic*, tr. W. V. Wallace (revised by J. N. Findlay), Oxford, 1975, pp. 272–3].

of consideration such ready-made means of subsistence as fruits, in gathering which a man's bodily organs alone serve as the instruments of his labour, the object the worker directly takes possession of is not the object of labour but its instrument. Thus nature becomes one of the organs of his activity, which he annexes to his own bodily organs, adding stature to himself in spite of the Bible. As the earth is his original larder, so too it is his original tool house. It supplies him, for instance, with stones for throwing, grinding, pressing, cutting, etc. The earth itself is an instrument of labour, but its use in this way, in agriculture, presupposes a whole series of other instruments and a comparatively high stage of development of labour-power.[75] As soon as the labour process has undergone the slightest development, it requires specially prepared instruments. Thus we find stone implements and weapons in the oldest caves. In the earliest period of human history, domesticated animals, i.e. animals that have undergone modification by means of labour, that have been bred specially, play the chief part as instruments of labour along with stones, wood, bones and shells, which have also had work done on them.[76] The use and construction of instruments of labour, although present in germ among certain species of animals, is characteristic of the specifically human labour process, and Franklin therefore defines man as 'a tool-making animal.' Relics of bygone instruments of labour possess the same importance for the investigation of extinct economic formations of society as do fossil bones for the determination of extinct species of animals. It is not what is made but how, and by what instruments of labour, that distinguishes different economic epochs.[77] Instruments of labour not only supply a standard of the degree of development which human labour has attained, but they also indicate the social relations within which men work. Among the instruments of labour, those of a mechanical kind, which, taken as a whole, we may call the bones and

75. In his otherwise miserable work *Théorie de l'économie politique*, Paris, 1815, Ganilh enumerates in a striking manner in opposition to the Physiocrats the long series of labour processes which form the presupposition for agriculture properly so called.

'For the Physiocrats, the productivity of labour appeared as a *gift of nature, a productive power of nature* . . . Surplus-value therefore appeared as a *gift of nature*' (*Theories of Surplus-Value*, Part 1, pp. 49–51).

76. In his *Réflexions sur la formation et la distribution des richesses* (1766), Turgot gives a good account of the importance of domesticated animals for the beginnings of civilization.

77. The least important commodities of all for the technological comparison of different epochs of production are articles of real luxury.

muscles of production, offer much more decisive evidence of the character of a given social epoch of production than those which, like pipes, tubs, baskets, jars etc., serve only to hold the materials for labour, and may be given the general denotation of the vascular system of production. The latter first begins to play an important part in the chemical industries.[78]

In a wider sense we may include among the instruments of labour, in addition to things through which the impact of labour on its object is mediated, and which therefore, in one way or another, serve as conductors of activity, all the objective conditions necessary for carrying on the labour process. These do not enter directly into the process, but without them it is either impossible for it to take place, or possible only to a partial extent. Once again, the earth itself is a universal instrument of this kind, for it provides the worker with the ground beneath his feet and a 'field of employment' for his own particular process. Instruments of this kind, which have already been mediated through past labour, include workshops, canals, roads, etc.

In the labour process, therefore, man's activity, *via* the instruments of labour, effects an alteration in the object of labour which was intended from the outset. The process is extinguished in the product. The product of the process is a use-value, a piece of natural material adapted to human needs by means of a change in its form. Labour has become bound up in its object: labour has been objectified, the object has been worked on. What on the side of the worker appeared in the form of unrest [*Unruhe*] now appears, on the side of the product, in the form of being [*Sein*], as a fixed, immobile characteristic. The worker has spun, and the product is a spinning.[79]

If we look at the whole process from the point of view of its result, the product, it is plain that both the instruments and the object of labour are means of production and that the labour itself is productive labour.[80]

78. The writers of history have so far paid very little attention to the development of material production, which is the basis of all social life, and therefore of all real history. But prehistoric times at any rate have been classified on the basis of the investigations of natural science, rather than so-called historical research. Prehistory has been divided, according to the materials used to make tools and weapons, into the Stone Age, the Bronze Age and the Iron Age.

79. It appears paradoxical to assert that uncaught fish, for instance, are a means of production in the fishing industry. But hitherto no one has discovered the art of catching fish in waters that contain none.

80. This method of determining what is productive labour, from the standpoint of the simple labour process, is by no means sufficient to cover the capitalist process of production.

Although a use-value emerges from the labour process, in the form of a product, other use-values, products of previous labour, enter into it as means of production. The same use-value is both the product of a previous process, and a means of production in a later process. Products are therefore not only results of labour, but also its essential conditions.

With the exception of the extractive industries, such as mining, hunting, fishing (and agriculture, but only in so far as it starts by breaking up virgin soil), where the material for labour is provided directly by nature, all branches of industry deal with raw material, i.e. an object of labour which has already been filtered through labour, which is itself already a product of labour. An example is seed in agriculture. Animals and plants which we are accustomed to consider as products of nature, may be, in their present form, not only products of, say, last year's labour, but the result of a gradual transformation continued through many generations under human control, and through the agency of human labour. As regards the instruments of labour in particular, they show traces of the labour of past ages, even to the most superficial observer, in the great majority of cases.

Raw material may either form the principal substance of a product, or it may enter into its formation only as an accessory. An accessory may be consumed by the instruments of labour, such as coal by a steam-engine, oil by a wheel, hay by draft-horses, or it may be added to the raw material in order to produce some physical modification of it, as chlorine is added to unbleached linen, coal to iron, dye to wool, or again it may help to accomplish the work itself, as in the case of the materials used for heating and lighting workshops. The distinction between principal substance and accessory vanishes in the chemical industries proper, because there none of the raw material re-appears, in its original composition, in the substance of the product.[81]

Every object possesses various properties, and is thus capable of being applied to different uses. The same product may therefore form the raw material for very different labour processes. Corn, for example, is a raw material for millers, starch-manufacturers, distillers and cattle-breeders. It also enters as raw material into its own production in the shape of seed; coal both emerges from the mining industry as a product and enters into it as a means of production.

Again, a particular product may be used as both instrument of labour and raw material in the same process. Take, for instance, the fattening of cattle, where the animal is the raw material, and at the same time an instrument for the production of manure.

81. Storch distinguishes between raw material (*'matière'*) and accessory materials (*'matériaux'*). Cherbuliez describes accessories as *'matières instrumentales.'*

A product, though ready for immediate consumption, may nevertheless serve as raw material for a further product, as grapes do when they become the raw material for wine. On the other hand, labour may release its product in such a form that it can only be used as raw material. Raw material in this condition, such as cotton, thread and yarn, is called semi-manufactured, but should rather be described as having been manufactured up to a certain level. Although itself already a product, this raw material may have to go through a whole series of different processes, and in each of these it serves as raw material, changing its shape constantly, until it is precipitated from the last process of the series in finished form, either as means of subsistence or as instrument of labour. Hence we see that whether a use-value is to be regarded as raw material, as instrument of labour or as product is determined entirely by its specific function in the labour process, by the position it occupies there: as its position changes, so do its determining characteristics.

Therefore, whenever products enter as means of production into new labour processes, they lose their character of being products and function only as objective factors contributing to living labour. A spinner treats spindles only as a means for spinning, and flax as the material he spins. Of course it is impossible to spin without material and spindles; and therefore the availability of these products is presupposed at the beginning of the spinning operation. But in the process itself, the fact that they are the products of past labour is as irrelevant as, in the case of the digestive process, the fact that bread is the product of the previous labour of the farmer, the miller and the baker. On the contrary, it is by their imperfections that the means of production in any process bring to our attention their character of being the products of past labour. A knife which fails to cut, a piece of thread which keeps on snapping, forcibly remind us of Mr A, the cutler, or Mr B, the spinner. In a successful product, the role played by past labour in mediating its useful properties has been extinguished.

A machine which is not active in the labour process is useless. In addition, it falls prey to the destructive power of natural processes. Iron rusts; wood rots. Yarn with which we neither weave nor knit is cotton wasted. Living labour must seize on these things, awaken them from the dead, change them from merely possible into real and effective use-values. Bathed in the fire of labour, appropriated as part of its organism, and infused with vital energy for the performance of the functions appropriate to their concept and to their vocation in the process, they are indeed consumed, but to some purpose, as elements in the formation of new use-values, new products, which are capable of entering into individual consumption as means of subsistence or into a new labour process as means of production.

If then, on the one hand, finished products are not only results of the labour process, but also conditions of its existence, their induction into the process, their contact with living labour, is the sole means by which they can be made to retain their character of use-values, and be realized.

Labour uses up its material elements, its objects and its instruments. It consumes them, and is therefore a process of consumption. Such productive consumption is distinguished from individual consumption by this, that the latter uses up products as means of subsistence for the living individual; the former, as means of subsistence for labour, i.e. for the activity through which the living individual's labour-power manifests itself. Thus the product of individual consumption is the consumer himself; the result of productive consumption is a product distinct from the consumer.

In so far then as its instruments and its objects are themselves products, labour consumes products in order to create products, or in other words consumes one set of products by turning them into means of production for another set. But just as the labour process originally took place only between man and the earth (which was available independently of any human action), so even now we still employ in the process many means of production which are provided directly by nature and do not represent any combination of natural substances with human labour.

The labour process, as we have just presented it in its simple and abstract elements, is purposeful activity aimed at the production of use-values. It is an appropriation of what exists in nature for the requirements of man. It is the universal condition for the metabolic interaction [*Stoffwechsel*] between man and nature, the everlasting nature-imposed condition of human existence, and it is therefore independent of every form of that existence, or rather it is common to all forms of society in which human beings live. We did not, therefore, have to present the worker in his relationship with other workers; it was enough to present man and his labour on one side, nature and its materials on the other. The taste of porridge does not tell us who grew the oats, and the process we have presented does not reveal the conditions under which it takes place, whether it is happening under the slave-owner's brutal lash or the anxious eye of the capitalist, whether Cincinnatus undertakes it in tilling his couple of acres, or a savage, when he lays low a wild beast with a stone.[82]

82. By a wonderful feat of logical acumen, Colonel Torrens has discovered, in this stone of the savage, the origin of capital. 'In the first stone which the savage flings at the wild animal he pursues, in the first stick that he seizes to strike down the fruit which hangs above his reach, we see the appropriation of one article for the purpose of aiding in the acquisition of another, and thus discover the origin

Let us now return to our would-be capitalist. We left him just after he had purchased, in the open market, all the necessary factors of the labour process; its objective factors, the means of production, as well as its personal factor, labour-power. With the keen eye of an expert, he has selected the means of production and the kind of labour-power best adapted to his particular trade, be it spinning, bootmaking or any other kind. He then proceeds to consume the commodity, the labour-power he has just bought, i.e. he causes the worker, the bearer of that labour-power, to consume the means of production by his labour. The general character of the labour process is evidently not changed by the fact that the worker works for the capitalist instead of for himself; moreover, the particular methods and operations employed in bootmaking or spinning are not immediately altered by the intervention of the capitalist. He must begin by taking the labour-power as he finds it in the market, and consequently he must be satisfied with the kind of labour which arose in a period when there were as yet no capitalists. The transformation of the mode of production itself which results from the subordination of labour to capital can only occur later on, and we shall therefore deal with it in a later chapter.

The labour process, when it is the process by which the capitalist consumes labour-power, exhibits two characteristic phenomena.

First, the worker works under the control of the capitalist to whom his labour belongs; the capitalist takes good care that the work is done in a proper manner, and the means of production are applied directly to the purpose, so that the raw material is not wasted, and the instruments of labour are spared, i.e. only worn to the extent necessitated by their use in the work.

Secondly, the product is the property of the capitalist and not that of the worker, its immediate producer. Suppose that a capitalist pays for a day's worth of labour-power; then the right to use that power for a day belongs to him, just as much as the right to use any other commodity, such as a horse he had hired for the day. The use of a commodity belongs to its purchaser, and the seller of labour-power, by giving his labour, does no more, in reality, than part with the use-value he has sold. From the instant he steps into the workshop, the use-value of his labour-power and therefore also its use, which is labour, belongs to the capital-ist. By the purchase of labour-power, the capitalist incorporates labour, as a living agent of fermentation, into the lifeless constituents of the product, which also belong to him. From his point of view, the labour

of capital' (R. Torrens, *An Essay on the Production of Wealth, etc.*, pp. 70–71). No doubt this 'first stick' [*Stock*] would also explain why 'stock' in English is synon-ymous with capital.

process is nothing more than the consumption of the commodity pur-chased, i.e. of labour-power; but he can consume this labour-power only by adding the means of production to it. The labour process is a process between things the capitalist has purchased, things which belong to him. Thus the product of this process belongs to him just as much as the wine which is the product of the process of fermentation going on in his cellar.[83]

2. The Valorization Process

The product—the property of the capitalist—is a use-value, as yarn, for example, or boots. But although boots are, to some extent, the basis of social progress, and our capitalist is decidedly in favour of progress, he does not manufacture boots for their own sake. Use-value is certainly not *la chose qu'on aime pour lui-même* in the production of commodities. Use-values are produced by capitalists only because and in so far as they form the material substratum of exchange-value, are the bearers of exchange-value. Our capitalist has two objectives: in the first place, he wants to produce a use-value which has exchange-value, i.e. an article destined to be sold, a commodity; and secondly he wants to produce a commodity greater in value than the sum of the values of the com-modities used to produce it, namely the means of production and the labour-power he purchased with his good money on the open market. His aim is to produce not only a use-value, but a commodity; not only use-value, but value; and not just value, but also surplus-value.

It must be borne in mind that we are now dealing with the production

---

83. 'Products are appropriated before they are transformed into capital; this transformation does not withdraw them from that appropriation' (Cherbuliez, *Richesse ou pauvreté*, Paris, 1841, p. 54). 'The proletarian, by selling his labour for a definite quantity of the means of subsistence (*approvisionnement*), renounces all claim to a share in the product. The products continue to be appropriated as before; this is in no way altered by the bargain we have mentioned. The product belongs exclusively to the capitalist, who supplied the raw materials and the *approvisionnement*. This follows rigorously from the law of appropriation, a law whose fundamental principle was the exact opposite, namely that every worker has an exclusive right to the ownership of what he produces' (ibid., p. 58). 'When the labourers receive wages for their labour . . . the capitalist is then the owner not of the capital only' (i.e. the means of production) 'but of the labour also. If what is paid as wages is included, as it commonly is, in the term capital, it is absurd to talk of labour separately from capital. The word capital as thus em-ployed includes labour and capital both' (James Mill, *Elements of Political Econ-omy*, London, 1821, pp. 70–71).

of commodities, and that up to this point we have considered only one aspect of the process. Just as the commodity itself is a unity formed of use-value and value, so the process of production must be a unity, composed of the labour process and the process of creating value [*Wertbildungsprozess*].

Let us now examine production as a process of creating value.

We know that the value of each commodity is determined by the quantity of labour materialized in its use-value, by the labour-time socially necessary to produce it. This rule also holds good in the case of the product handed over to the capitalist as a result of the labour-process. Assuming this product to be yarn, our first step is to calculate the quantity of labour objectified in it.

For spinning the yarn, raw material is required; suppose in this case 10 lb. of cotton. We have no need at present to investigate the value of this cotton, for our capitalist has, we will assume, bought it at its full value, say 10 shillings. In this price the labour required for the production of the cotton is already expressed in terms of average social labour. We will further assume that the wear and tear of the spindle, which for our present purpose may represent all other instruments of labour employed, amounts to the value of 2 shillings. If then, twenty-four hours of labour, or two working days, are required to produce the quantity of gold represented by 12 shillings, it follows first of all that two days of labour are objectified in the yarn.

We should not let ourselves be misled by the circumstance that the cotton has changed its form and the worn-down portion of the spindle has entirely disappeared. According to the general law of value, if the value of 40 lb. of yarn = the value of 40 lb. of cotton + the value of a whole spindle, i.e. if the same amount of labour-time is required to produce the commodities on either side of this equation, then 10 lb. of yarn are an equivalent for 10 lb. of cotton, together with a quarter of spindle. In the case we are considering, the same amount of labour-time is represented in the 10 lb. of yarn on the one hand, and in the 10 lb. of cotton and the fraction of a spindle on the other. It is therefore a matter of indifference whether value appears in cotton, in a spindle or in yarn: its amount remains the same. The spindle and cotton, instead of resting quietly side by side, join together in the process, their forms are altered, and they are turned into yarn; but their value is no more affected by this fact than it would be if they had been simply exchanged for their equivalent in yarn.

The labour-time required for the production of the cotton, the raw material of the yarn, is part of the labour necessary to produce the yarn, and is therefore contained in the yarn. The same applies to the labour embodied in the spindle, without whose wear and tear the cotton could not be spun.[84]

Hence in determining the value of the yarn, or the labour-time required for its production, all the special processes carried on at various times and in different places which were necessary, first to produce the cotton and the wasted portion of the spindle, and then with the cotton and the spindle to spin the yarn, may together be looked on as different and successive phases of the same labour process. All the labour contained in the yarn is past labour; and it is a matter of no importance that the labour expended to produce its constituent elements lies further back in the past than the labour expended on the final process, the spinning. The former stands, as it were, in the pluperfect, the latter in the perfect tense, but this does not matter. If a definite quantity of labour, say thirty days, is needed to build a house, the total amount of labour incorporated in the house is not altered by the fact that the work of the last day was done twenty-nine days later than that of the first. Therefore the labour contained in the raw material and instruments of labour can be treated just as if it were labour expended in an earlier stage of the spinning process, before the labour finally added in the form of actual spinning.

The values of the means of production which are expressed in the price of 12 shillings (the cotton and the spindle) are therefore constituent parts of the value of the yarn, i.e. of the value of the product.

Two conditions must nevertheless be fulfilled. First, the cotton and the spindle must genuinely have served to produce a use-value; they must in the present case become yarn. Value is independent of the particular use-value by which it is borne, but a use-value of some kind has to act as its bearer. Second, the labour-time expended must not exceed what is necessary under the given social conditions of production. Therefore, if no more than 1 lb. of cotton is needed to spin 1 lb. of yarn, no more than this weight of cotton may be consumed in the production of 1 lb. of yarn. The same is true of the spindle. If the capitalist has a foible for using golden spindles instead of steel ones, the only labour that counts for anything in the value of the yarn remains that which would be required to produce a steel spindle, because no more is necessary under the given social conditions.

We now know what part of the value of the yarn is formed by the means of production, namely the cotton and the spindle. It is 12 shillings, i.e. the materialization of two days of labour. The next point to be

---

84. 'Not only the labour applied immediately to commodities affects their value, but the labour also which is bestowed on the implements, tools, and buildings with which such labour is assisted' (Ricardo, op. cit., p. 16).

considered is what part of the value of the yarn is added to the cotton by the labour of the spinner.

We have now to consider this labour from a standpoint quite different from that adopted for the labour process. There we viewed it solely as the activity which has the purpose of changing cotton into yarn; there, the more appropriate the work was to its purpose, the better the yarn, other circumstances remaining the same. In that case the labour of the spinner was specifically different from other kinds of productive labour, and this difference revealed itself both subjectively in the particular purpose of spinning, and objectively in the special character of its operations, the special nature of its means of production, and the special use-value of its product. For the operation of spinning, cotton and spindles are a necessity, but for making rifled cannon they would be of no use whatever. Here, on the contrary, where we consider the labour of the spinner only in so far as it creates value, i.e. is a source of value, that labour differs in no respect from the labour of the man who bores cannon, or (what concerns us more closely here) from the labour of the cotton-planter and the spindle-maker which is realized in the means of production of the yarn. It is solely by reason of this identity that cotton planting, spindle-making and spinning are capable of forming the component parts of one whole, namely the value of the yarn, differing only quantitatively from each other. Here we are no longer concerned with the quality, the character and the content of the labour, but merely with its quantity. And this simply requires to be calculated. We assume that spinning is simple labour, the average labour of a given society. Later it will be seen that the contrary assumption would make no difference.

During the labour process, the worker's labour constantly undergoes a transformation, from the form of unrest [*Unruhe*] into that of being [*Sein*], from the form of motion [*Bewegung*] into that of objectivity [*Gegenständlichkeit*]. At the end of one hour, the spinning motion is represented in a certain quantity of yarn; in other words, a definite quantity of labour, namely that of one hour, has been objectified in the cotton. We say labour, i.e. the expenditure of his vital force by the spinner, and not spinning labour, because the special work of spinning counts here only in so far as it is the expenditure of labour-power in general, and not the specific labour of the spinner.

In the process we are now considering it is of extreme importance that no more time be consumed in the work of transforming the cotton into yarn than is necessary under the given social conditions. If under normal, i.e. average social conditions of production, x pounds of cotton are made into y pounds of yarn by one hour's labour, then a day's labour does not count as 12 hours' labour unless $12x$ lb. of cotton have been made into

12y lb. of yarn; for only socially necessary labour-time counts towards the creation of value.

Not only the labour, but also the raw material and the product now appear in quite a new light, very different from that in which we viewed them in the labour process pure and simple. Now the raw material merely serves to absorb a definite quantity of labour. By being soaked in labour, the raw material is in fact changed into yarn, because labour-power is expended in the form of spinning and added to it; but the product, the yarn, is now nothing more than a measure of the labour absorbed by the cotton. If in one hour 1⅔ lb. of cotton can be spun into 1⅔ lb. of yarn, then 10 lb. of yarn indicate the absorption of 6 hours of labour. Definite quantities of product, quantities which are determined by experience, now represent nothing but definite quantities of labour, definite masses of crystallized labour-time. They are now simply the material shape taken by a given number of hours or days of social labour.

The fact that the labour is precisely the labour of spinning, that its material is cotton, its product yarn, is as irrelevant here as it is that the object of labour is itself already a product, hence already raw material. If the worker, instead of spinning, were to be employed in a coal-mine, the object on which he worked would be coal, which is present in nature; nevertheless, a definite quantity of coal, when extracted from its seam, would represent a definite quantity of absorbed labour.

We assumed, on the occasion of its sale, that the value of a day's labour-power was 3 shillings, and that 6 hours of labour was incorporated in that sum; and consequently that this amount of labour was needed to produce the worker's average daily means of subsistence. If now our spinner, by working for one hour, can convert 1⅔ lb. of cotton into 1⅔ lb. of yarn,[85] it follows that in 6 hours he will convert 10 lb. of cotton into 10 lb. of yarn. Hence, during the spinning process, the cotton absorbs 6 hours of labour. The same quantity of labour is also embodied in a piece of gold of the value of 3 shillings. A value of 3 shillings, therefore, is added to the cotton by the labour of spinning.

Let us now consider the total value of the product, the 10 lb. of yarn. Two and a half days of labour have been objectified in it. Out of this, two days were contained in the cotton and the worn-down portion of the spindle, and half a day was absorbed during the process of spinning. This two and a half days of labour is represented by a piece of gold of the value of 15 shillings. Hence 15 shillings is an adequate price for the 10 lb. of yarn, and the price of 1 lb is 1s. 6d.

Our capitalist stares in astonishment. The value of the product is

85. These figures are entirely arbitrary.

equal to the value of the capital advanced. The value advanced has not been valorized, no surplus-value has been created, and consequently money has not been transformed into capital. The price of the yarn is 15 shillings, and 15 shillings were spent in the open market on the constituent elements of the product or, what amounts to the same thing, on the factors of the labour process; 10 shillings were paid for the cotton, 2 shillings for the wear of the spindle and 3 shillings for the labour-power. The swollen value of the yarn is of no avail, for it is merely the sum of the values formerly existing in the cotton, the spindle and the labour-power: out of such a simple addition of existing values, no surplus-value can possibly arise.[86] These values are now all concentrated in one thing; but so they were in the sum of 15 shillings, before it was split up into three parts by the purchase of the commodities.

In itself this result is not particularly strange. The value of one pound of yarn is 1s. 6d., and our capitalist would therefore have to pay 15 shillings for 10 lb. of yarn on the open market. It is clear that whether a man buys his house ready built, or has it built for him, neither of these operations will increase the amount of money laid out on the house.

Our capitalist, who is at home in vulgar economics, may perhaps say that he advanced his money with the intention of making more money out of it. The road to hell is paved with good intentions, and he might just as well have intended to make money without producing at all.[87] He makes threats. He will not be caught napping again. In future he will buy the commodities in the market, instead of manufacturing them himself. But if all his brother capitalists were to do the same, where would he find his commodities on the market? And he cannot eat his money. He recites the catechism: 'Consider my abstinence. I might have squandered the 15 shillings, but instead I consumed it productively and made yarn

86. This is the fundamental proposition which forms the basis of the doctrine of the Physiocrats that all non-agricultural labour is unproductive. For the professional economist it is irrefutable. 'This method of adding to one particular object the value of numerous others' (for example adding the living costs of the weaver to the flax) 'of as it were heaping up various values in layers on top of one single value, has the result that this value grows to the same extent . . . The expression "addition" gives a very clear picture of the way in which the price of a manufactured product is formed; this price is only the sum of a number of values which have been consumed, and it is arrived at by adding them together; however, addition is not the same as multiplication' (Mercier de la Rivière, op. cit., p. 599).

87. Thus from 1844 to 1847 he withdrew part of his capital from productive employment in order to throw it away in railway speculations; and so also, during the American Civil War, he closed his factory and turned the workers onto the street in order to gamble on the Liverpool cotton exchange.

with it.' Very true; and as a reward he is now in possession of good yarn instead of a bad conscience. As for playing the part of a miser, it would never do for him to relapse into such bad ways; we have already seen what such asceticism leads to. Besides, where there is nothing, the king has lost his rights; whatever the merits of his abstinence there is no money there to recompense him, because the value of the product is merely the sum of the values thrown into the process of production. Let him therefore console himself with the reflection that virtue is its own reward. But no, on the contrary, he becomes insistent. The yarn is of no use to him, he says. He produced it in order to sell it. In that case let him sell it, or, easier still, let him in future produce only things he needs himself, a remedy already prescribed by his personal physician Mac-Culloch as being of proven efficacy against an epidemic of over-production. Now our capitalist grows defiant. 'Can the worker produce commodities out of nothing, merely by using his arms and legs? Did I not provide him with the materials through which, and in which alone, his labour could be embodied? And as the greater part of society consists of such impecunious creatures, have I not rendered society an incalculable service by providing my instruments of production, my cotton and my spindle, and the worker too, for have I not provided him with the means of subsistence? Am I to be allowed nothing in return for all this service?' But has the worker not performed an equivalent service in return, by changing his cotton and his spindle into yarn? In any case, here the question of service does not arise.[88] A service is nothing other than the useful effect of a use-value, be it that of a commodity, or that of the labour.[89] But here we are dealing with exchange-value. The capitalist

88. 'Let whoever wants to do so extol himself, put on finery and adorn himself [but pay no heed and keep firmly to the scriptures] . . . Whoever takes more or better than he gives, that is usury and does not signify a service but a wrong done to his neighbour, as when one steals and robs. Not everything described as a service and a benefit to one's neighbour is in fact a service and a benefit. An adulteress and an adulterer do each other a great service and pleasure. A horseman does great service to a robber by helping him to rob on the highway, and attack the people and the land. The papists do our people a great service in that they do not drown, burn, or murder them all, or let them rot in prison, but let some live and drive them out or take from them what they have. The devil himself does his servants a great, inestimable service . . . To sum up: the world is full of great, excellent daily services and good deeds' (Martin Luther, *An die Pfarrherrn, wider den Wucher zu predigen. Vermanung*, Wittenberg, 1540).

89. In *Zur Kritik der politischen Ökonomie*, p. 14 [English edition, p. 37], I make the following remark on this point: 'It is easy to understand what "service" the category "service" must render to economists like J. B. Say and F. Bastiat.'

paid to the worker a value of 3 shillings, and the worker gave him back an exact equivalent in the value of 3 shillings he added to the cotton: he gave him value for value. Our friend, who has up till now displayed all the arrogance of capital, suddenly takes on the unassuming demeanour of one of his own workers, and exclaims: 'Have I myself not worked? Have I not performed the labour of superintendence, of overseeing the spinner? And does not this labour, too, create value?' The capitalist's own overseer and manager shrug their shoulders. In the meantime, with a hearty laugh, he recovers his composure. The whole litany he has just recited was simply meant to pull the wool over our eyes. He himself does not care twopence for it. He leaves this and all similar subterfuges and conjuring tricks to the professors of political economy, who are paid for it. He himself is a practical man, and although he does not always consider what he says outside his business, within his business he knows what he is doing.

Let us examine the matter more closely. The value of a day's labour-power amounts to 3 shillings, because on our assumption half a day's labour is objectified in that quantity of labour-power, i.e. because the means of subsistence required every day for the production of labour-power cost half a day's labour. But the past labour embodied in the labour-power and the living labour it can perform, and the daily cost of maintaining labour-power and its daily expenditure in work, are two totally different things. The former determines the exchange-value of the labour-power, the latter is its use-value. The fact that half a day's labour is necessary to keep the worker alive during 24 hours does not in any way prevent him from working a whole day. Therefore the value of labour-power, and the value which that labour-power valorizes [*verwertet*] in the labour-process, are two entirely different magnitudes; and this difference was what the capitalist had in mind when he was purchasing the labour-power. The useful quality of labour-power, by virtue of which it makes yarn or boots, was to the capitalist merely the necessary condition for his activity; for in order to create value labour must be expended in a useful manner. What was really decisive for him was the specific use-value which this commodity possesses of being a source not only of value, but of more value than it has itself. This is the specific service the capitalist expects from labour-power, and in this transaction he acts in accordance with the eternal laws of commodity-exchange. In fact, the seller of labour-power, like the seller of any other commodity, realizes [*realisiert*] its exchange-value, and alienates [*veräussert*] its use-value. He cannot take the one without giving the other. The use-value of labour-power, in other words labour, belongs just as little to its seller as the use-value of oil after it has been sold belongs to the dealer who sold it. The

owner of the money has paid the value of a day's labour-power; he
therefore has the use of it for a day, a day's labour belongs to him. On the
one hand the daily sustenance of labour-power costs only half a day's
labour, while on the other hand the very same labour-power can remain
effective, can work, during a whole day, and consequently the value
which its use during one day creates is double what the capitalist pays for
that use; this circumstance is a piece of good luck for the buyer, but by
no means an injustice towards the seller.

Our capitalist foresaw this situation, and that was the cause of his
laughter. The worker therefore finds, in the workshop, the means of
production necessary for working not just 6 but 12 hours. If 10 lb. of
cotton could absorb 6 hours' labour, and become 10 lb. of yarn, now
20 lb. of cotton will absorb 12 hours' labour and be changed into 20 lb.
of yarn. Let us examine the product of this extended labour-process.
Now five days of labour are objectified in this 20 lb. of yarn; four days
are due to the cotton and the lost steel of the spindle, the remaining day
has been absorbed by the cotton during the spinning process. Expressed
in gold, the labour of five days is 30 shillings. This is therefore the price
of the 20 lb. of yarn, giving, as before, 1s. 6d. as the price of 1 lb. But the
sum of the values of the commodities thrown into the process amounts
to 27 shillings. The value of the yarn is 30 shillings. Therefore the value
of the product is one-ninth greater than the value advanced to produce
it; 27 shillings have turned into 30 shillings; a surplus-value of 3 shillings has been precipitated. The trick has at last worked: money has been
transformed into capital.

Every condition of the problem is satisfied, while the laws governing
the exchange of commodities have not been violated in any way. Equivalent has been exchanged for equivalent. For the capitalist as buyer paid
the full value for each commodity, for the cotton, for the spindle and for
the labour-power. He then did what is done by every purchaser of
commodities: he consumed their use-value. The process of consuming
labour-power, which was also the process of producing commodities,
resulted in 20 lb. of yarn, with a value of 30 shillings. The capitalist,
formerly a buyer, now returns to the market as a seller. He sells his yarn
at 1s. 6d. a pound, which is its exact value. Yet for all that he withdraws
3 shillings more from circulation than he originally threw into it. This
whole course of events, the transformation of money into capital, both
takes place and does not take place in the sphere of circulation. It takes
place through the mediation of circulation because it is conditioned by
the purchase of the labour-power in the market; it does not take place in
circulation because what happens there is only an introduction to the
valorization process, which is entirely confined to the sphere of production. And so 'everything is for the best in the best of all possible worlds.'

By turning his money into commodities which serve as the building materials for a new product, and as factors in the labour process, by incorporating living labour into their lifeless objectivity, the capitalist simultaneously transforms value, i.e. past labour in its objectified and lifeless form, into capital, value which can perform its own valorization process, an animated monster which begins to 'work,' 'as if its body were by love possessed.'

If we now compare the process of creating value with the process of valorization, we see that the latter is nothing but the continuation of the former beyond a definite point. If the process is not carried beyond the point where the value paid by the capitalist for the labour-power is replaced by an exact equivalent, it is simply a process of creating value; but if is continued beyond that point, it becomes a process of valorization.

If we proceed further, and compare the process of creating value with the labour process, we find that the latter consists in the useful labour which produces use-values. Here the movement of production is viewed qualitatively, with regard to the particular kind of article produced, and in accordance with the purpose and content of the movement. But if it is viewed as a value-creating process the same labour process appears only quantitatively. Here it is a question merely of the time needed to do the work, of the period, that is, during which the labour-power is usefully expended. Here the commodities which enter into the labour process no longer count as functionally determined and material elements on which labour-power acts with a given purpose. They count merely as definite quantities of objectified labour. Whether it was already contained in the means of production, or has just been added by the action of labour-power, that labour counts only according to its duration. It amounts to so many hours, or days, etc.

Moreover, the time spent in production counts only in so far as it is socially necessary for the production of a use-value. This has various consequences. First, the labour-power must be functioning under normal conditions. If a self-acting mule is the socially predominant instrument of labour for spinning, it would be impermissible to supply the spinner with a spinning-wheel. The cotton too must not be such rubbish as to tear at every other moment, but must be of suitable quality. Otherwise the spinner would spend more time than socially necessary in producing his pound of yarn, and in this case the excess of time would create neither value nor money. But whether the objective factors of labour are normal or not does not depend on the worker, but rather on the capitalist. A further condition is that the labour-power itself must be of normal effectiveness. In the trade in which it is being employed, it must possess the average skill, dexterity and speed prevalent in that trade, and our capitalist took good care to buy labour-power of such normal quality. It must be expended with the average amount of exertion and the usual degree of intensity; and the capitalist is as careful to see that this is done, as he is to ensure that his workmen are not idle for a single moment. He has bought the use of the labour-power for a definite period, and he insists on his rights. He has no intention of being robbed. Lastly—and for this purpose our friend has a penal code of his own—all wasteful consumption of raw material or instruments of labour is strictly forbidden, because what is wasted in this way represents a superfluous expenditure of quantities of objectified labour, labour that does not count in the product or enter into its value.[90]

We now see that the difference between labour, considered on the one

90. This is one of the circumstances which make production based on slavery more expensive. Under slavery, according to the striking expression employed in antiquity, the worker is distinguishable only as *instrumentum vocale* from an animal, which is *instrumentum semi-vocale,* and from a lifeless implement, which is *instrumentum mutum.* But he himself takes care to let both beast and implement feel that he is none of them, but rather a human being. He gives himself the satisfaction of knowing that he is different by treating the one with brutality and damaging the other *con amore.* Hence the economic principle, universally applied in this mode of production, of employing only the rudest and heaviest implements, which are difficult to damage owing to their very clumsiness. In the slave states bordering on the Gulf of Mexico, down to the date of the Civil War, the only ploughs to be found were those constructed on the old Chinese model, which turned up the earth like a pig or a mole, instead of making furrows. Cf. J. E. Cairnes, *The Slave Power,* London, 1862, pp. 46 ff. In his *Seaboard Slave States,* Olmsted says, among other things, 'I am here shown tools that no man in his senses, with us, would allow a labourer, for whom he was paying wages, to be encumbered with; and the excessive weight and clumsiness of which, I would judge, would make work at least ten per cent greater than with those ordinarily used with us. And I am assured that, with the careless and clumsy treatment they always must get from the slaves, anything lighter or less rude could not be furnished them with good economy, and that such tools as we constantly give our labourers and find our profit in giving them, would not last a day in a Virginia cornfield—much lighter and more free from stones though it be than ours. So, too, when I ask why mules are so universally substituted for horses on the farm, the first reason given, and confessedly the most conclusive one, is that horses are always soon foundered or crippled by them, while mules will bear cudgelling, or lose a meal or two now and then, and not be materially injured, and they do not take cold or get sick, if neglected or overworked. But I do not need to go further than to the window of the room in which I am writing, to see at almost any time, treatment of cattle that would ensure the immediate discharge of the driver by almost any farmer owning them in the North.'

hand as producing utilities, and on the other hand as creating value, a difference which we discovered by our analysis of a commodity, resolves itself into a distinction between two aspects of the production process.

The production process, considered as the unity of the labour process and the process of creating value, is the process of production of commodities; considered as the unity of labour process and the process of valorization, it is the capitalist process of production, or the capitalist form of the production of commodities.

We stated on a previous page that in the valorization process it does not in the least matter whether the labour appropriated by the capitalist is simple labour of average social quality, or more complex labour, labour with a higher specific gravity as it were. All labour of a higher, or more complicated, character than average labour is expenditure of labour-power of a more costly kind, labour-power whose production has cost more time and labour than unskilled or simple labour-power, and which therefore has a higher value. This power being of higher value, it expresses itself in labour of a higher sort, and therefore becomes objectified, during an equal amount of time, in proportionally higher values. Whatever difference in skill there may be between the labour of a spinner and that of a jeweller, the portion of his labour by which the jeweller merely replaces the value of his own labour-power does not in any way differ in quality from the additional portion by which he creates surplus-value. In both cases, the surplus-value results only from a quantitative excess of labour, from a lengthening of one and the same labour-process: in the one case, the process of making jewels, in the other, the process of making yarn.[91]

91. The distinction between higher and simple labour, 'skilled labour' and 'unskilled labour,' rests in part on pure illusion or, to say the least, on distinctions that have long since ceased to be real, and survive only by virtue of a traditional convention; and in part on the helpless condition of some section of the working class, a condition that prevents them from exacting equally with the rest the value of their labour-power. Accidental circumstances here play so great a part that these two forms of labour sometimes change places. Where, for instance, the physique of the working class has deteriorated and is, relatively speaking, exhausted, which is the case in all countries when capitalist production is highly developed, the lower forms of labour, which demand great expenditure of muscle, are in general considered as higher forms compared with much more delicate forms of labour; the latter sink down to the level of simple labour. Take as an example the labour of a bricklayer which in England occupies a much higher level than that of a damask weaver. Again, although the labour of a fustian-cutter demands greater bodily exertion, and is at the same time unhealthy, it counts only as simple labour. Moreover, we must not imagine that so-called 'skilled' labour

But, on the other hand, in every process of creating value the reduction of the higher type of labour to average social labour, for instance one day of the former to x days of the latter, is unavoidable.[92] We therefore save ourselves a superfluous operation, and simplify our analysis, by the assumption that the labour of the worker employed by the capitalist is average simple labour.

Chapter 26: The Secret of Primitive Accumulation

We have seen how money is transformed into capital; how surplus-value is made through capital, and how more capital is made from surplus-value. But the accumulation of capital presupposes surplus-value; surplus-value presupposes capitalist production; capitalist production presupposes the availability of considerable masses of capital and labour-power in the hands of commodity producers. The whole movement, therefore, seems to turn around in a never-ending circle, which we can only get out of by assuming a primitive accumulation (the 'previous accumulation' of Adam Smith) which precedes capitalist accumulation; an accumulation which is not the result of the capitalist mode of production but its point of departure.

This primitive accumulation plays approximately the same role in political economy as original sin does in theology. Adam bit the apple, and thereupon sin fell on the human race. Its origin is supposed to be explained when it is told as an anecdote about the past. Long, long ago

---

forms a large part of the whole of the nation's labour. Laing estimates that in England (and Wales) the livelihood of 11,300,000 people depends on unskilled labour. If from the total population of 18,000,000 living at the time when he wrote, deduct 1,000,000 for the 'genteel population,' 1,500,000 for paupers, vagrants, criminals and prostitutes, and 4,650,000 who compose the middle class, there remain the above-mentioned 11,000,000. But in his middle class he includes people who live on the interest of small investments, officials, men of letters, artists, schoolmasters and the like, and in order to swell the number he also includes in these 4,650,000 the better paid portion of the 'factory workers'! The bricklayers, too, figure amongst these 'high-class workers' (S. Laing, *National Distress etc.*, London, 1844). 'The great class who have nothing to give for food but ordinary labour, are the great bulk of the people' (James Mill, in the article 'Colony,' *Supplement to the Encyclopaedia Britannica*, 1831).

92. 'Where reference is made to labour as a measure of value, it necessarily implies labour of one particular kind . . . the proportion which the other kinds bear to it being easily ascertained' ([J. Cazenove], *Outlines of Political Economy*, London, 1832, pp. 22–3).

there were two sorts of people; one, the diligent, intelligent and above all frugal élite; the other, lazy rascals, spending their substance, and more, in riotous living. The legend of theological original sin tells us certainly how man came to be condemned to eat his bread in the sweat of his brow; but the history of economic original sin reveals to us that there are people to whom this is by no means essential. Never mind! Thus it came to pass that the former sort accumulated wealth, and the latter sort finally had nothing to sell except their own skins. And from this original sin dates the poverty of the great majority who, despite all their labour, have up to now nothing to sell but themselves, and the wealth of the few that increases constantly, although they have long ceased to work. Such insipid childishness is every day preached to us in the defence of property. M. Thiers, for example, still repeats it with all the solemnity of a statesman to the French people, who were once so full of wit and ingenuity. But as soon as the question of property is at stake, it becomes a sacred duty to proclaim the standpoint of the nursery tale as the one thing fit for all age-groups and all stages of development. In actual history, it is a notorious fact that conquest, enslavement, robbery, murder, in short, force, play the greatest part. In the tender annals of political economy, the idyllic reigns from time immemorial. Right and 'labour' were from the beginning of time the sole means of enrichment, 'this year' of course always excepted. As a matter of fact, the methods of primitive accumulation are anything but idyllic.

In themselves, money and commodities are no more capital than the means of production and subsistence are. They need to be transformed into capital. But this transformation can itself only take place under particular circumstances, which meet together at this point: the confrontation of, and the contact between, two very different kinds of commodity owners; on the one hand, the owners of money, means of production, means of subsistence, who are eager to valorize the sum of values they have appropriated by buying the labour-power of others; on the other hand, free workers, the sellers of their own labour-power, and therefore the sellers of labour. Free workers, in the double sense that they neither form part of the means of production themselves, as would be the case with slaves, serfs, etc., nor do they own the means of production, as would be the case with self-employed peasant proprietors. The free workers are therefore free from, unencumbered by, any means of production of their own. With the polarization of the commodity-market into these two classes, the fundamental conditions of capitalist production are present. The capital-relation presupposes a complete separation between the workers and the ownership of the conditions for the realization of their labour. As soon as capitalist production stands on its own feet, it not only maintains this separation, but reproduces it on a constantly extending scale. The process, therefore, which creates the capital-relation can be nothing other than the process which divorces the worker from the ownership of the conditions of his own labour; it is a process which operates two transformations, whereby the social means of subsistence and production are turned into capital, and the immediate producers are turned into wage-labourers. So-called primitive accumulation, therefore, is nothing else than the historical process of divorcing the producer from the means of production. It appears as 'primitive' because it forms the pre-history of capital, and of the mode of production corresponding to capital.

The economic structure of capitalist society has grown out of the economic structure of feudal society. The dissolution of the latter set free the elements of the former.

The immediate producer, the worker, could dispose of his own person only after he had ceased to be bound to the soil, and ceased to be the slave or serf of another person. To become a free seller of labour-power, who carries his commodity wherever he can find a market for it, he must further have escaped from the regime of the guilds, their rules for apprentices and journeymen, and their restrictive labour regulations. Hence the historical movement which changes the producers into wage-labourers appears, on the one hand, as their emancipation from serfdom and from the fetters of the guilds, and it is this aspect of the movement which alone exists for our bourgeois historians. But, on the other hand, these newly freed men became sellers of themselves only after they had been robbed of all their own means of production, and all the guarantees of existence afforded by the old feudal arrangements. And this history, the history of their expropriation, is written in the annals of mankind in letters of blood and fire.

The industrial capitalists, these new potentates, had on their part not only to displace the guild masters of handicrafts, but also the feudal lords, who were in possession of the sources of wealth. In this respect, the rise of the industrial capitalists appears as the fruit of a victorious struggle both against feudal power and its disgusting prerogatives, and against the guilds, and the fetters by which the latter restricted the free development of production and the free exploitation of man by man. The knights of industry, however, only succeeded in supplanting the knights of the sword by making use of events in which they had played no part whatsoever. They rose by means as base as those once used by the Roman freedman to make himself the master of his *patronus.*

The starting-point of the development that gave rise both to the wage-labourer and to the capitalist was the enslavement of the worker. The advance made consisted in a change in the form of this servitude, in the transformation of feudal exploitation into capitalist exploitation. To understand the course taken by this change, we do not need to go back very far at all. Although we come across the first sporadic traces of capitalist production as early as the fourteenth or fifteenth centuries in certain towns of the Mediterranean, the capitalist era dates from the sixteenth century. Wherever it appears, the abolition of serfdom has long since been completed, and the most brilliant achievement of the Middle Ages, the existence of independent city-states, has already been on the wane for a considerable length of time.

In the history of primitive accumulation, all revolutions are epoch-making that act as levers for the capitalist class in the course of its formation; but this is true above all for those moments when great masses of men are suddenly and forcibly torn from their means of subsistence, and hurled onto the labour-market as free, unprotected and rightless proletarians. The expropriation of the agricultural producer, of the peasant, from the soil is the basis of the whole process. The history of this expropriation assumes different aspects in different countries, and runs through its various phases in different orders of succession, and at different historical epochs. Only in England, which we therefore take as our example, has it the classic form.[93]

Chapter 32: The Historical Tendency of Capitalist Accumulation

What does the primitive accumulation of capital, i.e. its historical genesis, resolve itself into? In so far as it is not the direct transformation of slaves and serfs into wage-labourers, and therefore a mere change of form, it only means the expropriation of the immediate producers, i.e. the dissolution of private property based on the labour of its owner. Private property, as the antithesis to social, collective property, exists only

---

93. In Italy, where capitalist production developed earliest, the dissolution of serfdom also took place earlier than elsewhere. There the serf was emancipated before he had acquired any prescriptive right to the soil. His emancipation at once transformed him into a 'free' proletarian, without any legal rights, and he found a master ready and waiting for him in the towns, which had been for the most part handed down from Roman times. When the revolution which took place in the world market at about the end of the fifteenth century had annihilated northern Italy's commercial supremacy, a movement in the reverse direction set in. The urban workers were driven *en masse* into the countryside, and gave a previously unheard-of impulse to small-scale cultivation, carried on in the form of market gardening.

where the means of labour and the external conditions of labour belong to private individuals. But according to whether these private individuals are workers or non-workers, private property has a different character. The innumerable different shades of private property which appear at first sight are only reflections of the intermediate situations which lie between the two extremes.

The private property of the worker in his means of production is the foundation of small-scale industry, and small-scale industry is a necessary condition for the development of social production and of the free individuality of the worker himself. Of course, this mode of production also exists under slavery, serfdom and other situations of dependence. But it flourishes, unleashes the whole of its energy, attains its adequate classical form, only where the worker is the free proprietor of the conditions of his labour, and sets them in motion himself: where the peasant owns the land he cultivates, or the artisan owns the tool with which he is an accomplished performer.

This mode of production presupposes the fragmentation of holdings, and the dispersal of the other means of production. As it excludes the concentration of these means of production, so it also excludes co-operation, division of labour within each separate process of production, the social control and regulation of the forces of nature, and the free development of the productive forces of society. It is compatible only with a system of production and a society moving within narrow limits which are of natural origin. To perpetuate it would be, as Pecqueur rightly says, 'to decree universal mediocrity.' At a certain stage of development, it brings into the world the material means of its own destruction. From that moment, new forces and new passions spring up in the bosom of society, forces and passions which feel themselves to be fettered by that society. It has to be annihilated; it is annihilated. Its annihilation, the transformation of the individualized and scattered means of production into socially concentrated means of production, the transformation, therefore, of the dwarf-like property of the many into the giant property of the few and the expropriation of the great mass of the people from the soil, from the means of subsistence and from the instruments of labour, this terrible and arduously accomplished expropriation of the mass of the people forms the pre-history of capital. It comprises a whole series of forcible methods, and we have only passed in review those that have been epoch-making as methods of the primitive accumulation of capital. The expropriation of the direct producers was accomplished by means of the most merciless barbarism, and under the stimulus of the most infamous, the most sordid, the most petty and the most odious of passions. Private property which is personally earned, i.e. which is based, as it were, on the fusing together of the isolated, independent working individual with the conditions of his labour, is supplanted by capitalist private property, which rests on the exploitation of alien, but formally free labour.[94]

As soon as this metamorphosis has sufficiently decomposed the old society throughout its depth and breadth, as soon as the workers have been turned into proletarians, and their means of labour into capital, as soon as the capitalist mode of production stands on its own feet, the further socialization of labour and the further transformation of the soil and other means of production into socially exploited and therefore communal means of production takes on a new form. What is now to be expropriated is not the self-employed worker, but the capitalist who exploits a large number of workers.

This expropriation is accomplished through the action of the immanent laws of capitalist production itself, through the centralization of capitals. One capitalist always strikes down many others. Hand in hand with this centralization, or this expropriation of many capitalists by a few, other developments take place on an ever-increasing scale, such as the growth of the cooperative form of the labour process, the conscious technical application of science, the planned exploitation of the soil, the transformation of the means of labour into forms in which they can only be used in common, the economizing of all means of production by their use as the means of production of combined, socialized labour, the entanglement of all peoples in the net of the world market, and, with this, the growth of the international character of the capitalist regime. Along with the constant decrease in the number of capitalist magnates, who usurp and monopolize all the advantages of this process of transformation, the mass of misery, oppression, slavery, degradation and exploitation grows; but with this there also grows the revolt of the working class, a class constantly increasing in numbers, and trained, united and organized by the very mechanism of the capitalist process of production. The monopoly of capital becomes a fetter upon the mode of production which has flourished alongside and under it. The centralization of the means of production and the socialization of labour reach a point at which they become incompatible with their capitalist integument. This integument is burst asunder. The knell of capitalist private property sounds. The expropriators are expropriated.

94. 'We are in a situation which is entirely new for society . . . we are striving to separate every kind of property from every kind of labour' (Sismondi, *Nouveaux Principes d'économie politique*, Vol. 2, p. 434).

The capitalist mode of appropriation, which springs from the capitalist mode of production, produces capitalist private property. This is the first negation of individual private property, as founded on the labour of its proprietor. But capitalist production begets, with the inexorability of a natural process, its own negation. This is the negation of the negation. It does not re-establish private property, but it does indeed establish individual property on the basis of the achievements of the capitalist era: namely cooperation and the possession in common of the land and the means of production produced by labour itself.

The transformation of scattered private property resting on the personal labour of the individuals themselves into capitalist private property is naturally an incomparably more protracted, violent and difficult process than the transformation of capitalist private property, which in fact already rests on the carrying on of production by society, into social property. In the former case, it was a matter of the expropriation of the mass of the people by a few usurpers; but in this case, we have the expropriation of a few usurpers by the mass of the people.[95]

95. 'The advance of industry, whose involuntary but willing promoter is the bourgeoisie, replaces the isolation of the workers, due to competition, with their revolutionary combination, due to association. The development of large-scale industry, therefore, cuts from under its feet the very foundation on which the bourgeoisie produces and appropriates products for itself. What the bourgeoisie, therefore, produces, above all, are its own grave-diggers. Its fall and the victory of the proletariat are equally inevitable . . . Of all the classes which confront the bourgeoisie today, the proletariat alone is a really revolutionary class. The other classes decay and disappear in the face of large-scale industry, the proletariat is its most characteristic product. The lower middle classes, the small manufacturers, the shopkeepers, the artisans, the peasants, all these fight against the bourgeoisie in order to save from extinction their existence as parts of the middle class . . . they are reactionary, for they try to roll back the wheel of history' (Karl Marx and F. Engels, *Manifest der Kommunistischen Partei*, London, 1848, pp. 11, 9) [English translation: Karl Marx, *The Revolutions of 1848*, Pelican Marx Library, pp. 79,77].

*The Civil
War in France
(excerpt)*

Karl Marx

*The empire that Louis Bonaparte had established in France in 1851 came to
a dismal end at the hands of the Prussians in the Franco-Prussion War of
1870–71. With the emperor dethroned and the Prussian armies at the gates
of the capital, the workers of Paris declared the creation of a Commune in
March of 1871; they ruled Paris until May of that year. Meanwhile, a
Provisional Government, which became the Third Republic, had been in-
stalled at Versailles under Adolphe Thiers and had opened negotiations with
the Prussians. The Commune met a bloody end in late May when it was
finally overcome by the Thiers government.*

*Marx, watching these events from London, had a decidedly mixed opinion
about the Commune and was pessimistic about its chances for success. Nonetheless, he proposed writing an Address to the People of Paris that would be
endorsed by the General Council of the First International in London. The
Address went through three drafts that survive, the final one being presented
to the General Council on May 30, 1871, only two days after the final collapse of the Commune.*

*The Address has four sections. The first two discuss the nature of the Pro-
visional Government of the new republic and the events leading up to the
establishment of the Commune. In the third and most famous section, Marx
discusses the nature and structure of the Commune itself. "The working
class," Marx declares, "cannot simply lay hold of the ready-made State
machinery, and wield it for its own purposes." It must set up its own form of
government. He goes on to describe the intentions of the Communards in
somewhat fanciful terms since there had been a lack of agreement among them
concerning what to do and little time in which to do it. The Commune, he
claims, "aimed at the expropriation of the expropriators. It wanted to make
individual property a truth by transforming the means of production, land
and capital, now chiefly the means of enslaving and exploiting labour, into
mere instruments of free and associated labour." The Commune, however, is
not to be confused with a final form of revolutionary society, Marx cautions.
The working class "know that in order to work out their own emancipation, . . . they will have to pass through long struggles, through a series of
historic processes, transforming circumstances and men." The fourth section*

*goes on to describe the demise of the Commune, and Marx ends the Address
by paying tribute to the victims of the repression. "Working men's Paris, with
its Commune, will be for ever celebrated as the glorious harbinger of a new
society. Its martyrs are enshrined in the great heart of the working class."*

The Civil War in France *is considered important both as a historical pam-
phlet and as one of Marx's longest discussions of what the post-revolutionary
"dictatorship of the proletariat" might look like. In this latter vein, it was
used to support Leninist interpretations of Marx's theory of revolution.*

What follows is the third section of the Address from the English original.

On the dawn of the 18th of March, Paris arose to the thunderburst of
"Vive la Commune!" What is the Commune, that sphinx so tantalizing to
the bourgeois mind?

> "The proletarians of Paris," said the Central Committee in its manifesto of
> the 18th March, "amidst the failures and treasons of the ruling classes, have
> understood that the hour has struck for them to save the situation by taking
> into their own hands the direction of public affairs. . . . They have understood
> that it is their imperious duty and their absolute right to render themselves
> master of their own destinies, by seizing upon the governmental power."

But the working class cannot simply lay hold of the ready-made State
machinery, and wield it for its own purposes.

The centralized State power, with its ubiquitous organs of standing
army, police, bureaucracy, clergy, and judicature—organs wrought after
the plan of a systematic and hierarchic division of labour—originates
from the days of absolute monarchy, serving nascent middle-class society
as a mighty weapon in its struggles against feudalism. Still, its development remained clogged by all manner of mediaeval rubbish, seignorial
rights, local privileges, municipal and guild monopolies and provincial
constitutions. The gigantic broom of the French Revolution of the eighteenth century swept away all these relics of bygone times, thus clearing
simultaneously the social soil of its last hindrances to the superstructure
of the modern State edifice raised under the First Empire, itself the
offspring of the coalition wars of old semi-feudal Europe against modern France. During the subsequent *régimes* the Government, placed under parliamentary control—that is, under the direct control of the prop-

ertied classes—became not only a hotbed of huge national debts and crushing taxes; with its irresistible allurements of place, pelf, and patronage, it became not only the bone of contention between the rival factions and adventurers of the ruling classes; but its political character changed simultaneously with the economic changes of society. At the same pace at which the progress of modern industry developed, widened, intensified the class antagonism between capital and labour, the State power assumed more and more the character of the national power of capital over labour, of a public force organized for social enslavement, of an engine of class despotism. After every revolution marking a progressive phase in the class struggle, the purely repressive character of the State power stands out in bolder and bolder relief. The Revolution of 1830, resulting in the transfer of Government from the landlords to the capitalists, transferred it from the more remote to the more direct antagonists of the working men. The bourgeois Republicans, who, in the name of the Revolution of February, took the State power, used it for the June massacres, in order to convince the working class that "social" republic meant the republic ensuring their social subjection, and in order to convince the royalist bulk of the bourgeois and landlord class that they might safely leave the cares and emoluments of government to the bourgeois "Republicans." However, after their one heroic exploit of June, the bourgeois Republicans had, from the front, to fall back to the rear of the "Party of Order"—a combination formed by all the rival fractions and factions of the appropriating class in their now openly declared antagonism to the producing classes. The proper form of their joint-stock Government was the *Parliamentary Republic*, with Louis Bonaparte for its President. Theirs was a *régime* of avowed class terrorism and deliberate insult towards the "vile multitude." If the Parliamentary Republic, as M. Thiers said, "divided them (the different fractions of the ruling class) least," it opened an abyss between that class and the whole body of society outside their spare ranks. The restraints by which their own divisions had under former *régimes* still checked the State power, were removed by their union; and in view of the threatening upheaval of the proletariate, they now used that State power mercilessly and ostentatiously as the national war-engine of capital against labour. In their uninterrupted crusade against the producing masses they were, however, bound not only to invest the executive with continually increased powers of repression, but at the same time to divest their own parliamentary stronghold—the National Assembly—one by one, of all its own means of defence against the Executive. The Executive, in the person of Louis Bonaparte, turned them out. The natural offspring of the "Party-of-Order" Republic was the Second Empire.

The Empire, with the *coup d'état* for its certificate of birth, universal suffrage for its sanction, and the sword for its sceptre, professed to rest upon the peasantry, the large mass of producers not directly involved in the struggle of capital and labour. It professed to save the working class by breaking down Parliamentarism, and, with it, the undisguised subserviency of Government to the propertied classes. It professed to save the propertied classes by upholding their economic supremacy over the working class; and, finally, it professed to unite all classes by reviving for all the chimera of national glory. In reality, it was the only form of government possible at a time when the bourgeoisie had already lost, and the working class had not yet acquired, the faculty of ruling the nation. It was acclaimed throughout the world as the saviour of society. Under its sway, bourgeois society, freed from political cares, attained a development unexpected even by itself. Its industry and commerce expanded to colossal dimensions; financial swindling celebrated cosmopolitan orgies; the misery of the masses was set off by a shameless display of gorgeous, meretricious, and debased luxury. The State power, apparently soaring high above society, was at the same time itself the greatest scandal of that society and the very hotbed of all its corruptions. Its own rottenness, and the rottenness of the society it had saved, were laid bare by the bayonet of Prussia, herself eagerly bent upon transferring the supreme seat of the *régime* from Paris to Berlin. Imperialism is, at the same time, the most prostitute and the ultimate form of the State power which nascent middle-class society had commenced to elaborate as a means of its own emancipation from feudalism, and which full-grown bourgeois society had finally transformed into a means for the enslavement of labour by capital.

The direct antithesis to the Empire was the Commune. The cry of "Social Republic," with which the revolution of February was ushered in by the Paris proletariate, did but express a vague aspiration after a Republic that was not only to supersede the monarchical form of class-rule, but class-rule itself. The Commune was the positive form of that Republic.

Paris, the central seat of the old governmental power, and, at the same time, the social stronghold of the French working class, had risen in arms against the attempt of Thiers and the Rurals to restore and perpetuate that old governmental power bequeathed to them by the Empire. Paris could resist only because, in consequence of the siege, it had got rid of the army, and replaced it by a National Guard, the bulk of which consisted of working men. This fact was now to be transformed into an institution. The first decree of the Commune, therefore, was the suppression of the standing army, and the substitution for it of the armed people.

The Commune was formed of the municipal councillors, chosen by universal suffrage in the various wards of the town, responsible and revocable at short terms. The majority of its members were naturally working men, of acknowledged representatives of the working class. The Commune was to be a working, not a parliamentary, body, executive and legislative at the same time. Instead of continuing to be the agent of the Central Government, the police was at once stripped of its political attributes, and turned into the responsible and at all times revocable agent of the Commune. So were the officials of all other branches of the Administration. From the members of the Commune downwards, the public service had to be done at *workmen's wages.* The vested interests and the representation allowances of the high dignitaries of State disappeared along with the high dignitaries themselves. Public functions ceased to be the private property of the tools of the Central Government. Not only municipal administration, but the whole initiative hitherto exercised by the State was laid into the hands of the Commune.

Having once got rid of the standing army and the police, the physical force elements of the old Government, the Commune was anxious to break the spiritual force of repression, the "parson-power," by the disestablishment and disendowment of all churches as proprietary bodies. The priests were sent back to the recesses of private life, there to feed upon the alms of the faithful in imitation of their predecessors, the Apostles. The whole of the educational institutions were opened to the people gratuitously, and at the same time cleared of all interference of Church and State. Thus, not only was education made accessible to all, but science itself freed from the fetters which class prejudice and governmental force had imposed upon it.

The judicial functionaries were to be divested of that sham independence which had but served to mask their abject subserviency to all succeeding governments to which, in turn, they had taken, and broken, the oaths of allegiance. Like the rest of public servants, magistrates and judges were to be elective, responsible, and revocable.

The Paris Commune was, of course, to serve as a model to all the great industrial centres of France. The communal *régime* once established in Paris and the secondary centres, the old centralized Government would in the provinces, too, have to give way to the self-government of the producers. In a rough sketch of national organization which the Commune had no time to develop, it states clearly that the Commune was to be the political form of even the smallest country hamlet, and that in the rural districts the standing army was to be replaced by a national militia, with an extremely short term of service. The rural communes of every district were to administer their common affairs by an assembly of delegates in the central town, and these district assemblies were again to send deputies to the National Delegation in Paris, each delegate to be at any time revocable and bound by the *mandat impératif* (formal instructions) of his constituents. The few but important functions which still would remain for a central government were not to be suppressed, as has been intentionally misstated, but were to be discharged by Communal, and therefore strictly responsible agents. The unity of the nation was not to be broken, but, on the contrary, to be organized by the Communal constitution, and to become a reality by the destruction of the State power which claimed to be the embodiment of that unity independent of, and superior to, the nation itself, from which it was but a parasitic excrescence. While the merely repressive organs of the old governmental power were to be amputated, its legitimate functions were to be wrested from an authority usurping pre-eminence over society itself, and restored to the responsible agents of society. Instead of deciding once in three or six years which member of the ruling class was to misrepresent the people in Parliament, universal suffrage was to serve the people, constituted in Communes, as individual suffrage serves every other employer in the search for the workmen and managers in his business. And it is well known that companies, like individuals, in matters of real business generally know how to put the right man in the right place, and, if they for once make a mistake, to redress it promptly. On the other hand, nothing could be more foreign to the spirit of the Commune than to supersede universal suffrage by hierarchic investiture.

It is generally the fate of completely new historical creations to be mistaken for the counterpart of older and even defunct forms of social life, to which they may bear a certain likeness. Thus, this new Commune, which breaks the modern State power, has been mistaken for a reproduction of the mediaeval Communes, which first preceded, and afterwards became the substratum of, that very State power.—The communal constitution has been mistaken for an attempt to break up into a federation of small States, as dreamt of by Montesquieu and the Girondins, that unity of great nations, which, if originally brought about by political force, has now become a powerful coefficient of social production.—The antagonism of the Commune against the State power has been mistaken for an exaggerated form of the ancient struggle against over-centralization. Peculiar historical circumstances may have prevented the classical development, as in France, of the bourgeois form of government, and may have allowed, as in England, to complete the great central State organs by corrupt vestries, jobbing councillors, and ferocious poor-law guardians in the towns, and virtually hereditary magistrates in the counties. The Communal Constitution would have restored to the social body all the forces hitherto absorbed by the State parasite feeding upon, and clogging the free movement of, society. By this one act it would have initiated the regeneration of France.—The provincial French middle-class saw in the Commune an attempt to restore the sway their order had held over the country under Louis Philippe, and which, under Louis Napoleon, was supplanted by the pretended rule of the country over the towns. In reality, the Communal Constitution brought the rural pro-ducers under the intellectual lead of the central towns of their districts, and there secured to them, in the working men, the natural trustees of their interests.—The very existence of the Commune involved, as a matter of course, local municipal liberty, but no longer as a check upon the, now superseded, State power. It could only enter into the head of a Bismarck, who, when not engaged on his intrigues of blood and iron, always likes to resume his old trade, so befitting his mental calibre, of contributor to *Kladderadatsch* (the Berlin *Punch*), it could only enter into such a head, to ascribe to the Paris Commune aspirations after that caricature of the old French municipal organization of 1791, the Prus-sian municipal constitution which degrades the town governments to mere secondary wheels in the police-machinery of the Prussian State. The Commune made that catch-word of bourgeois revolutions, cheap government, a reality, by destroying the two greatest sources of expendi-ture—the standing army and State functionarism. Its very existence pre-supposed the non-existence of monarchy, which, in Europe at least, is the normal incumbrance and indispensable cloak of class-rule. It sup-plied the Republic with the basis of really democratic institutions. But neither cheap government nor the "true Republic" was its ultimate aim; they were its mere concomitants.

The multiplicity of interpretations to which the Commune has been subjected, and the multiplicity of interests which construed it in their favour, show that it was a thoroughly expansive political form, while all previous forms of government had been emphatically repressive. Its true secret was this. It was essentially a working-class government, the pro-duce of the struggle of the producing against the appropriating class, the political form at last discovered under which to work out the economical emancipation of Labour.

Except on this last condition, the Communal Constitution would have been an impossibility and a delusion. The political rule of the producer cannot coexist with the perpetuation of his social slavery. The Commune was therefore to serve as a lever for uprooting the economical founda-tions upon which rests the existence of classes, and therefore of class rule. With labour emancipated, every man becomes a working man, and productive labour ceases to be a class attribute.

It is a strange fact. In spite of all the tall talk and all the immense literature, for the last sixty years, about Emancipation of Labour, no sooner do the working men anywhere take the subject into their own hands with a will, than uprises at once all the apologetic phraseology of the mouthpieces of present society with its two poles of Capital and Wage-slavery (the landlord now is but the sleeping partner of the capitalist), as if capitalist society was still in its purest state of virgin innocence, with its antagonisms still undeveloped, with its delusions still unexploded, with its prostitute realities not yet laid bare. The Commune, they exclaim, intends to abolish property, the basis of all civilization! Yes, gentlemen, the Commune intended to abolish that class-property which makes the labour of the many the wealth of the few. It aimed at the expropriation of the expropriators. It wanted to make individual property a truth by transforming the means of production, land and capital, now chiefly the means of enslaving and exploiting labour, into mere instruments of free and associated labour.—But this is Communism, "impossible" Communism! Why, those members of the ruling classes who are intelligent enough to perceive the impossibility of continuing the present system—and they are many—have become the obtrusive and full-mouthed apostles of cooperative production. If cooperative production is not to remain a sham and a snare; if it is to supersede the Capitalist system; if united cooperative societies are to regulate national production upon a common plan, thus taking it under their own control, and putting an end to the constant anarchy and periodical convulsions which are the fatality of Capitalist production—what else, gentlemen, would it be but Communism, "possible" Communism?

The working class did not expect miracles from the Commune. They have no ready-made utopias to introduce *par décret du peuple.* They know that in order to work out their own emancipation, and along with it that higher form to which present society is irresistibly tending by its own economical agencies, they will have to pass through long struggles, through a series of historic processes, transforming circumstances and men. They have no ideals to realize, but to set free elements of the new society with which old collapsing bourgeois society itself is pregnant. In the full consciousness of their historic mission, and with the heroic resolve to act up to it, the working class can afford to smile at the coarse invective of the gentlemen's gentlemen with the pen and inkhorn, and at the didactic patronage of well-wishing bourgeois-doctrinaires, pouring forth their ignorant platitudes and sectarian crotchets in the oracular tone of scientific infallibility.

When the Paris Commune took the management of the revolution in its own hands; when plain working men for the first time dared to fringe upon the Governmental privilege of their "natural superiors," and, under circumstances of unexampled difficulty, performed their work modestly, conscientiously, and efficiently—performed it at salaries the highest of which barely amounted to one-fifth of what, according to high scientific authority, is the minimum required for a secretary to a certain metropolitan school-board,—the old world writhed in convulsions of rage at the sight of the Red Flag, the symbol of the Republic of Labour, floating over the Hôtel de Ville.

And yet, this was the first revolution in which the working class was openly acknowledged as the only class capable of social initiative, even by the great bulk of the Paris middle class—shopkeepers, tradesmen, merchants—the wealthy capitalists alone excepted. The Commune had saved them by a sagacious settlement of that ever-recurring cause of dispute among the middle classes themselves—the debtor and creditor accounts. The same portion of the middle class, after they had assisted in putting down the working men's insurrection of June, 1848, had been at once unceremoniously sacrificed to their creditors by the then Constituent Assembly. But this was not their motive for now rallying round the working class. They felt that there was but one alternative—the Commune, or the Empire—under whatever name it might reappear. The Empire had ruined them economically by the havoc it made of public wealth, by the wholesale financial swindling it fostered, by the props it lent to the artificially accelerated centralization of capital, and the concomitant expropriation of their own ranks. It had suppressed them politically, it had shocked them morally by its orgies, it had insulted their Voltairianism by handing over the education of their children to the *frères Ignorantins*, it had revolted their national feeling as Frenchmen by precipitating them headlong into a war which left only one equivalent for the ruins it made—the disappearance of the Empire. In fact, after the exodus from Paris of the high Bonapartist and capitalist *Bohême*, the true middle-class Party of Order came out in the shape of the "Union Républicaine," enrolling themselves under the colours of the Commune and defending it against the wilful misconstruction of Thiers. Whether the gratitude of this great body of the middle class will stand the present severe trial, time must show.

The Commune was perfectly right in telling the peasants that "its victory was their only hope." Of all the lies hatched at Versailles and re-echoed by the glorious European penny-a-liner, one of the most tremendous was that the Rurals represented the French peasantry. Think only of the love of the French peasant for the men to whom, after 1815, he had to pay the milliard of indemnity! In the eyes of the French peasant, the very existence of a great landed proprietor is in itself an encroachment on his conquests of 1789. The bourgeois, in 1848, had burthened his plot of land with the additional tax of forty-five cents in the franc; but then he did so in the name of the revolution; while now he had fomented a civil war against the revolution, to shift on to the peasant's shoulders the chief load of the five milliards of indemnity to be paid to the Prussians. The Commune, on the other hand, in one of its first proclamations, declared that the true originators of the war would be made to pay its cost. The Commune would have delivered the peasant of the blood tax,—would have given him a cheap government,—transformed his present blood-suckers, the notary, advocate, executor, and other judicial vampires, into salaried communal agents, elected by, and responsible to, himself. It would have freed him of the tyranny of the *garde champêtre*, the gendarme, and the prefect, would have put enlightenment by the schoolmaster in the place of stuntification by the priest. And the French peasant is, above all, a man of reckoning. He would find it extremely reasonable that the pay of the priest, instead of being extorted by the tax-gatherer, should only depend upon the spontaneous action of the parishioners' religious instincts. Such were the great immediate boons which the rule of the Commune—and that rule alone—held out to the French peasantry. It is, therefore, quite superfluous here to expatiate upon the more complicated but vital problems which the Commune alone was able, and at the same time compelled, to solve in favour of the peasant, viz., the hypothecary debt, lying like an incubus upon his parcel of soil, the *prolétariat foncier* (the rural proletariate), daily growing upon it, and his expropriation from it enforced, at a more and more rapid rate, by the very development of modern agriculture and the competition of capitalist farming.

The French peasant had elected Louis Bonaparte president of the Republic; but the Party of Order created the Empire. What the French peasant really wants he commenced to show in 1849 and 1850, by opposing his maire to the Government's prefect, his schoolmaster to the Government's priest, and himself to the Government's gendarme. All the laws made by the Party of Order in January and February, 1850, were avowed measures of repression against the peasant. The peasant was a Bonapartist, because the great Revolution, with all its benefits to him, was, in his eyes, personified in Napoleon. This delusion, rapidly breaking down under the Second Empire (and in its very nature hostile to the Rurals), this prejudice of the past, how could it have withstood the appeal of the Commune to the living interests and urgent wants of the peasantry?

The Rurals—this was, in fact, their chief apprehension—knew that three months' free communication of Communal Paris with the provinces would bring about a general rising of the peasants, and hence their anxiety to establish a police blockade around Paris, so as to stop the spread of the rinderpest.

If the Commune was thus the true representative of all the healthy elements of French society, and therefore the truly national Government, it was, at the same time, as a working men's Government, as the bold champion of the emancipation of labour, emphatically international. Within sight of the Prussian army, that had annexed to Germany two French provinces, the Commune annexed to France the working people all over the world.

The Second Empire had been the jubilee of cosmopolitan black-leggism, the rakes of all countries rushing in at its call for a share in its orgies and in the plunder of the French people. Even at this moment the right hand of Thiers is Ganesco, the foul Wallachian, and his left hand is Markowski, the Russian spy. The Commune admitted all foreigners to the honour of dying for an immortal cause. Between the foreign war lost by their treason, and the civil war fomented by their conspiracy with the foreign invader, the bourgeoisie had found the time to display their patriotism by organizing police-hunts upon the Germans in France. The Commune made a German working-man its Minister of Labour. Thiers, the bourgeoisie, the Second Empire, had continually deluded Poland by loud professions of sympathy, while in reality betraying her to, and doing the dirty work of, Russia. The Commune honoured the heroic sons of Poland by placing them at the head of the defenders of Paris. And, to broadly mark the new era of history it was conscious of initiating, under the eyes of the conquering Prussians on the one side, and of the Bonapartist army, led by Bonapartist generals, on the other, the Commune pulled down that colossal symbol of martial glory, the Vendôme column.

The great social measure of the Commune was its own working existence. Its special measures could but betoken the tendency of a government of the people by the people. Such were the abolition of the night-work of journeymen bakers; the prohibition, under penalty, of the employers' practice to reduce wages by levying upon their workpeople fines under manifold pretexts,—a process in which the employer combines in his own person the parts of legislator, judge, and executor, and filches the money to boot. Another measure of this class was the surrender, to associations of workmen, under reserve of compensation, of all closed workshops and factories, no matter whether the respective capitalists had absconded or preferred to strike work.

The financial measures of the Commune, remarkable for their sagacity and moderation, could only be such as were compatible with the state of a besieged town. Considering the colossal robberies committed upon the city of Paris by the great financial companies and contractors, under the protection of Haussmann, the Commune would have had an incomparably better title to confiscate their property than Louis Napoleon had against the Orléans family. The Hohenzollern and the English oligarchs who both have derived a good deal of their estates from Church plunder, were, of course, greatly shocked at the Commune clearing but 8,000f. out of secularisation.

While the Versailles Government, as soon as it had recovered some spirit and strength, used the most violent means against the Commune; while it put down the free expression of opinion all over France, even to the forbidding of meetings of delegates from the large towns; while it subjected Versailles and the rest of France to an espionage far surpassing that of the Second Empire; while it burned by its gendarme inquisitors all papers printed at Paris, and sifted all correspondence from and to Paris; while in the National Assembly the most timid attempts to put in a word for Paris were howled down in a manner unknown even to the *Chambre introuvable* of 1816; with the savage warfare of Versailles outside, and its attempts at corruption and conspiracy inside Paris—would the Commune not have shamefully betrayed its trust by affecting to keep up all the decencies and appearances of liberalism as in a time of profound peace? Had the Government of the Commune been akin to that of M. Thiers, there would have been no more occasion to suppress Party-of-Order papers at Paris than there was to suppress Communal papers at Versailles.

It was irritating indeed to the Rurals that at the very same time they declared the return to the Church to be the only means of salvation for France, the infidel Commune unearthed the peculiar mysteries of the Picpus nunnery, and of the Church of Saint Laurent. It was a satire upon M. Thiers that, while he showered grand crosses upon the Bonapartist generals in acknowledgment of their mastery in losing battles, signing capitulations, and turning cigarettes at Wilhelmshöhe, the Commune dismissed and arrested its generals whenever they were suspected of neglecting their duties. The expulsion from, and arrest by, the Commune of one of its members who had slipped in under a false name, and had undergone at Lyons six days' imprisonment for simple bankruptcy, was it not a deliberate insult hurled at the forger, Jules Favre, then still the foreign minister of France, still selling France to Bismarck, and still dictating his orders to that paragon Government of Belgium? But indeed the Commune did not pretend to infallibility, the invariable attribute of all governments of the old stamp. It published its doings and sayings, it initiated the public into all its shortcomings.

In every revolution there intrude, at the side of its true agents, men of a different stamp; some of them survivors of and devotees to past revolutions, without insight into the present movement, but preserving popular influence by their known honesty and courage, or by the sheer force of tradition; others mere bawlers, who, by dint of repeating year after year the same set of stereotyped declamations against the Government of the day, have sneaked into the reputation of revolutionists of the first water. After the 18th of March, some such men did also turn up, and in some cases contrived to play preeminent parts. As far as their power went, they hampered the real action of the working class, exactly as men of that sort have hampered the full development of every previous revolution. They are an unavoidable evil; with time they are shaken off; but time was not allowed to the Commune.

Wonderful, indeed, was the change the Commune had wrought in Paris! No longer any trace of the meretricious Paris of the Second Empire. No longer was Paris the rendezvous of British landlords, Irish absentees, American ex-slaveholders and shoddy men, Russian ex-serfowners, and Wallachian boyards. No more corpses at the Morgue, no nocturnal burglaries, scarcely any robberies; in fact, for the first time since the days of February, 1848, the streets of Paris were safe, and that without any police of any kind.

> "We," said a member of the Commune, "hear no longer of assassination, theft, and personal assault; it seems indeed as if the police had dragged along with it to Versailles all its Conservative friends."

The *cocottes* had refound the scent of their protectors—the absconding men of family, religion, and, above all, of property. In their stead, the real women of Paris showed again at the surface—heroic, noble, and devoted, like the women of antiquity. Working, thinking, fighting, bleeding Paris—almost forgetful, in its incubation of a new society, of the cannibals at its gates—radiant in the enthusiasm of its historic initiative!

Opposed to this new world at Paris, behold the old world at Versailles—that assembly of the ghouls of all defunct *régimes*, Legitimists and Orleanists, eager to feed upon the carcass of the nation,—with a tail of antediluvian Republicans, sanctioning, by their presence in the Assembly, the slaveholders' rebellion, relying for the maintenance of their Parliamentary Republic upon the vanity of the senile mountebank at its head, and caricaturing 1789 by holding their ghastly meetings in the *Jeu de Paume*.* There it was, this Assembly, the representative of everything dead in France, propped up to the semblance of life by nothing but the

---

*"The tennis court where the National Assembly of 1789 adopted its famous decisions." *(Engels' Note to the 1871 German edition.)*

swords of the generals of Louis Bonaparte. Paris all truth, Versailles all lie; and that lie vented through the mouth of Thiers.

Thiers tells a deputation of the mayors of the Seine-et-Oise,—

"You may rely upon my word, which I have *never* broken!"

He tells the Assembly itself that "it was the most freely elected and most Liberal Assembly France ever possessed"; he tells his motley sol- diery that it was "the admiration of the world, and the finest army France every possessed"; he tells the provinces that the bombardment of Paris by him was a myth:

"If some cannon-shots have been fired, it is not the deed of the army of Versailles, but of some insurgents trying to make believe that they are fighting, while they dare not show their faces."

He again tells the provinces that

"the artillery of Versailles does not bombard Paris, but only cannonades it."

He tells the Archbishop of Paris that the pretended executions and reprisals (!) attributed to the Versailles troops were all moonshine. He tells Paris that he was only anxious "to free it from the hideous tyrants who oppress it," and that, in fact, the Paris of the Commune was "but a handful of criminals."

The Paris of M. Thiers was not the real Paris of the "vile multitude," but a phantom Paris, the Paris of the *francs-fileurs*, the Paris of the Boulevards, male and female—the rich, the capitalist, the gilded, the idle Paris, now thronging with its lackeys, its blacklegs, its literary *bohême*, and its *cocottes* at Versailles, Saint-Denis, Rueil, and Saint-Germain; considering the civil war but an agreeable diversion, eyeing the battle going on through telescopes, counting the rounds of cannon, and swear- ing by their own honour and that of their prostitutes, that the perfor- mance was far better got up than it used to be at the Porte St. Martin. The men who fell were really dead; the cries of the wounded were cries in good earnest; and, besides the whole thing was so intensely historical.

This is the Paris of M. Thiers, as the Emigration of Coblenz was the France of M. de Calonne.

Critique of the Gotha Program

Karl Marx

The First International did not officially dissolve until 1876, but it lost much of its influence in the early 1870s, and Marx had ceased to be active in it at that point. With the unification of Germany following the Franco-Prussian War, Marx's political attention had returned to Germany, which had one of the more active working-class movements. The German movement was organized chiefly around two major parties: the Social Democratic Workers' Party (SDAP), towards which Marx was sympathetic, and the General Union of German Workers (ADAV), which was comprised mostly of the followers of Ferdinand Lassalle. The two parties entered into discussions aimed at unifying their efforts, and in May of 1875, in the town of Gotha, they adopted a common program. When Marx saw the draft of the program he was furious and wrote a critique of it to be circulated prior to the unification vote among the leaders of the SDAP. This document, officially known as "Marginal Notes on the Program of the German Workers' Party," was first published in 1891 by Engels under the title "Critique of the Gotha Program."

In the "Critique," Marx attacked what he saw as the Lassallean elements in the program that gave it too much of a bourgeois and nationalist cast. What the document has become famous for, however, are the remarks Marx makes, in the process of criticizing these elements, about questions of distributive justice and the nature of the state in post-revolutionary society. He notes that immediately after the revolution, a new form of society will emerge "from capitalist society, which is thus in every respect, economically, morally, and intellectually, still stamped with the birthmarks of the old society from whose womb it emerges." In this society, the worker will receive for his or her labor an amount exactly equal to his or her contribution, less a deduction to finance social necessities. But Marx comments, this sense of equal right is still a bourgeois concept and in effect means that all workers have the right to be unequal. Bourgeois distributive justice, even in this advanced form, ignores the particularities of the worker's situation and needs. These defects cannot be avoided, however, for "Right can never be higher than the economic structure of society and its cultural development which this determines."

But a higher stage of communist society will evolve in which labor becomes "not only a means of life but life's prime want." In this stage, the product will no longer be distributed according to bourgeois standards of justice but according to a truly communist standard: "From each according to his abilities, to each according to his needs." With regard to the state, Marx notes

315

*again that an initial stage of postrevolutionary society must be differentiated
from fully developed communism. This first stage "is also a political transition period in which the state can be nothing but the revolutionary dictatorship of the proletariat."*

The translation used here is taken from Karl Marx/Friedrich Engels:
Collected Works, *published by International Publishers.*

I

1. "Labour is the source of all wealth and all culture, and *since* useful labour
is possible only in society and through society, the proceeds of labour belong
undiminished with equal right to all members of society."

First part of the paragraph: "Labour is the source of all wealth and all
culture."

Labour is *not the source* of all wealth. *Nature* is just as much the source
of use values (and it is surely of such that material wealth consists!) as
labour, which itself is only the manifestation of a force of nature, human
labour power. The above phrase is to be found in all children's primers
and is correct insofar as it is *implied* that labour is performed with the
pertinent objects and instruments. But a socialist programme cannot
allow such bourgeois phrases to pass over in silence the *conditions* that
alone give them meaning. And insofar as man from the outset behaves
towards nature, the primary source of all instruments and objects of
labour, as an owner, treats her as belonging to him, his labour becomes
the source of use values, therefore also of wealth. The bourgeois have
very good grounds for ascribing *supernatural creative power* to labour;
since precisely from the fact that labour is determined by nature, it
follows that the man who possesses no other property than his labour
power must, in all conditions of society and culture, be the slave of other
men who have made themselves the owners of the material conditions of
labour. He can work only with their permission, hence live only with
their permission.

Let us now leave the sentence as it stands, or rather limps. What would
one have expected in conclusion? Obviously this:

"Since labour is the source of all wealth, no one in society can appropriate wealth except as the product of labour. Therefore, if he himself
does not work, he lives by the labour of others and also acquires his
culture at the expense of the labour of others."

Instead of this, by means of the verbal rivet "*and since*" a second
proposition is added in order to draw a conclusion from this and not
from the first one.

Second part of the paragraph: "Useful labour is possible only in society and through society."

According to the first proposition, labour was the source of all wealth and all culture; therefore no society is possible without labour. Now we learn, conversely, that no "useful" labour is possible without society.

One could just as well have said that only in society can useless and even socially harmful labour become a gainful occupation, that only in society can one live by being idle, etc., etc.—in short, one could just as well have copied the whole of Rousseau.

And what is "useful" labour? Surely only labour which produces the intended useful result. A savage—and man was a savage after he had ceased to be an ape—who kills an animal with a stone, who collects fruits, etc., performs "useful" labour.

Thirdly. The conclusion: "And since useful labour is possible only in society and through society, the proceeds of labour belong undiminished with equal right to all members of society."

A fine conclusion! If useful labour is possible only in society and through society, the proceeds of labour belong to society—and only so much therefrom accrues to the individual worker as is not required to maintain the "condition" of labour, society.

In fact, this proposition has at all times been made use of *by the champions of the state of society prevailing at any given time.* First come the claims of the government and everything that sticks to it, since it is the social organ for the maintenance of the social order; then come the claims of the various kinds of private owners for the various kinds of private property are the foundations of society, etc. One sees that such hollow phrases can be twisted and turned as desired.

The first and second parts of the paragraph have some intelligible connection only in the following wording:

"Labour becomes the source of wealth and culture only as social labour," or, what is the same thing, "in and through society."

This proposition is incontestably correct, for although isolated labour (its material conditions presupposed) can create use values, it can create neither wealth nor culture.

But equally incontestable is the other proposition:

"In proportion as labour develops socially, and becomes thereby a source of wealth and culture, poverty and destitution develop among the workers, and wealth and culture among the non-workers."

This is the law of all history hitherto. What, therefore, had to be done here, instead of setting down general phrases about "*labour*" and "*society*," was to prove concretely how in present capitalist society the material, etc., conditions have at last been created which enable and compel the workers to lift this historical curse.

In fact, however, the whole paragraph, bungled in style and content, is only there in order to inscribe the Lassallean catchword of the "undiminished proceeds of labour" as a slogan at the top of the party banner. I shall return later to the "proceeds of labour," "equal right," etc., since the same thing recurs in a somewhat different form further on.

> 2. "In present-day society, the means of labour are the monopoly of the capitalist class; the resulting dependence of the working class is the cause of misery and servitude in all their forms."

This sentence, borrowed from the Rules of the International, is incorrect in this "improved" edition.

In present-day society the means of labour are the monopoly of the landowners (the monopoly of land ownership is even the basis of the monopoly of capital) *and* the capitalists. In the passage in question, the Rules of the International mention neither the one nor the other class of monopolists. They speak of the "*monopoly of the means of labour, that is, the sources of life.*" The addition, "sources of life," makes it sufficiently clear that land is included in the means of labour.

The correction was introduced because Lassalle, for reasons now generally known, attacked *only* the capitalist class and not the landowners. In England, the capitalist is mostly not even the owner of the land on which his factory stands.

> 3. "The emancipation of labour demands the raising of the means of labour to the common property of society and the collective regulation of the total labour with a fair distribution of the proceeds of labour."

"The raising of the means of labour to common property"! Ought obviously to read their "conversion into common property." But this only in passing.

What are "*proceeds of labour*"? The product of labour or its value? And in the latter case, is it the total value of the product or only that part of the value which labour has newly added to the value of the means of production consumed?

"Proceeds of labour" is a loose notion which Lassalle has put in the place of definite economic concepts.

What is "fair" distribution?

Do not the bourgeois assert that present-day distribution is "fair"? And is it not, in fact, the only "fair" distribution on the basis of the present-day mode of production? Are economic relations regulated by legal concepts or do not, on the contrary, legal relations arise from economic ones? Have not also the socialist sectarians the most varied notions about "fair" distribution?

To understand what is implied in this connection by the phrase "fair distribution," we must take the first paragraph and this one together. The latter presupposes a society wherein "the means of labour are common property and the total labour is collectively regulated," and from the first paragraph we learn that "the proceeds of labour belong undiminished with equal right to all members of society."

"To all members of society"? To those who do not work as well? What remains then of "the undiminished proceeds of labour"? Only to those members of society who work? What remains then of "the equal right" of all members of society?

But "all members of society" and "equal right" are obviously mere phrases. The crucial point is this, that in this communist society every worker must receive his "undiminished" Lassallean "proceeds of labour."

Let us take first of all the words "proceeds of labour" in the sense of the product of labour; then the collective proceeds of labour are the *total social product*.

From this must now be deducted:

First, cover for replacement of the means of production used up.

Secondly, additional portion for expansion of production.

Thirdly, reserve or insurance funds to provide against accidents, disturbances caused by natural factors, etc.

These deductions from the "undiminished proceeds of labour" are an economic necessity and their magnitude is to be determined according to available means and forces, and party by computation of probabilities, but they are in no way calculable by equity.

There remains the other part of the total product, intended to serve as means of consumption.

Before this is divided among the individuals, there has to be again deducted from it:

First, the general costs of administration not directly appertaining to production.

This part will, from the outset, be very considerably restricted in comparison with present-day society and it diminishes in proportion as the new society develops.

Secondly, that which is intended for the common satisfaction of needs, such as schools, health services, etc.

From the outset this part grows considerably in comparison with present-day society and it grows in proportion as the new society develops.

Thirdly, funds for those unable to work, etc., in short, for what is included under so-called official poor relief today.

Only now do we come to the "distribution" which the programme, under Lassallean influence, has alone in view in its narrow fashion, namely, to that part of the means of consumption which is divided among the individual producers of the collective.

The "undiminished proceeds of labour" have already unnoticeably become converted into the "diminished" proceeds, although what the producer is deprived of in his capacity as a private individual benefits him directly or indirectly in his capacity as a member of society.

Just as the phrase of the "undiminished proceeds of labour" has disappeared, so now does the phrase of the "proceeds of labour" disappear altogether.

Within the collective society based on common ownership of the means of production, the producers do not exchange their products; just as little does the labour employed on the products appear here *as the value* of these products, as a material quality possessed by them, since now, in contrast to capitalist society, individual labour no longer exists in an indirect fashion but directly as a component part of the total labour. The phrase "proceeds of labour," objectionable even today on account of its ambiguity, thus loses all meaning.

What we are dealing with here is a communist society, not as it has *developed* on its own foundations, but on the contrary, just as it *emerges* from capitalist society, which is thus in every respect, economically, morally and intellectually, still stamped with the birth-marks of the old society from whose womb it emerges. Accordingly, the individual producer receives back from society—after the deductions have been made—exactly what he gives to it. What he has given to it is his individual quantum of labour. For example, the social working day consists of the sum of the individual hours of work; the individual labour time of the individual producer is the part of the social working day contributed by him, his share in it. He receives a certificate from society that he has furnished such and such an amount of labour (after deducting his labour for the common funds), and with this certificate he draws from the social stock of means of consumption as much as the same amount of labour costs. The same amount of labour which he has given to society in one form he receives back in another.

Here obviously the same principle prevails as that which regulates the exchange of commodities, as far as this is the exchange of equal values. Content and form are changed, because under the altered circumstances no one can give anything except his labour, and because, on the other hand, nothing can pass to the ownership of individuals except individual means of consumption. But, as far as the distribution of the latter among the individual producers is concerned, the same principle prevails as in the exchange of commodity-equivalents: a given amount of labour in one form is exchanged for an equal amount of labour in another form.

Hence, *equal right* here is still in principle—*bourgeois right,* although principle and practice are no longer at loggerheads, while the exchange of equivalents in commodity exchange only exists *on the average* and not in the individual case.

In spite of this advance, this *equal right* is still constantly encumbered by a bourgeois limitation. The right of the producers is *proportional* to the labour they supply; the equality consists in the fact that measurement is made with an *equal standard,* labour. But one man is superior to another physically or mentally and so supplies more labour in the same time, or can work for a longer time; and labour, to serve as a measure, must be defined by its duration or intensity, otherwise it ceases to be a standard of measurement. This *equal* right is an unequal right for unequal labour. It recognises no class distinctions, because everyone is only a worker like everyone else; but it tacitly recognises the unequal individual endowment and thus productive capacity of the workers as natural privileges. *It is, therefore, a right of inequality, in its content, like every right.* Right by its nature can exist only as the application of an equal standard; but unequal individuals (and they would not be different individuals if they were not unequal) are measurable by an equal standard only insofar as they are made subject to an equal criterion, are taken from a *certain* side only, for instance, in the present case, are regarded *only as workers* and nothing more is seen in them, everything else being ignored. Besides, one worker is married, another not; one has more children than another, etc., etc. Thus, given an equal amount of work done, and hence an equal share in the social consumption fund, one will in fact receive more than another, one will be richer than another, etc. To avoid all these defects, right would have to be unequal rather than equal.

But these defects are inevitable in the first phase of communist society as it is when it has just emerged after prolonged birth-pangs from capitalist society. Right can never be higher than the economic structure of society and its cultural development which this determines.

In a higher phase of communist society, after the enslaving subordination of the individual to the division of labour, and thereby also the antithesis between mental and physical labour, has vanished; after labour has become not only a means of life but life's prime want; after the productive forces have also increased with the all-round development of the individual, and all the springs of common wealth flow more abundantly—only then can the narrow horizon of bourgeois right be crossed in its entirety and society inscribe on its banners: From each according to his abilities, to each according to his needs!

I have dealt at greater length with the "undiminished proceeds of labour," on the one hand, and with "equal right" and "fair distribution," on the other, in order to show what a crime it is to attempt, on the one hand, to force on our Party again, as dogmas, ideas which in a certain period had some meaning but have now become obsolete verbal rubbish, while again perverting, on the other, the realistic outlook, which it cost so much effort to instil into the Party but which has now taken root in it, by means of ideological, legal and other trash so common among the Democrats and French Socialists.

Quite apart from the analysis so far given, it was in general a mistake to make a fuss about so-called *distribution* and put the principal stress on it.

Any distribution whatever of the means of consumption is only a consequence of the distribution of the conditions of production themselves. The latter distribution, however, is a feature of the mode of production itself. The capitalist mode of production, for example, rests on the fact that the material conditions of production are in the hands of non-workers in the form of capital and land ownership, while the masses are only owners of the personal condition of production, of labour power. If the elements of production are so distributed, then the present-day distribution of the means of consumption results automatically. If the material conditions of production are the collective property of the workers themselves, then there likewise results a distribution of the means of consumption different from the present one. The vulgar socialists (and from them in turn a section of the Democrats) have taken over from the bourgeois economists the consideration and treatment of distribution as independent of the mode of production and hence the presentation of socialism as turning principally on distribution. After the real relation has long been made clear, why retrogress again?

4. "The emancipation of labour must be the work of the working class, in relation to which all other classes are *only one reactionary mass*."

The main clause is taken from the introductory words of the Rules of the International, but "improved." There it is said: "The emancipation of the working classes must be conquered by the working classes themselves"; here, on the contrary, the "working class" has to emancipate— what? "Labour." Let him understand who can.

In compensation, the subordinate clause, on the other hand, is a Lassallean quotation of the first water: "in relation to which (the working class) all other classes are *only one reactionary mass.*"

In the *Communist Manifesto* it is said: "Of all the classes that stand face to face with the bourgeoisie today, the proletariat alone is a *really revolutionary class.* The other classes decay and finally disappear in the face of Modern Industry; the proletariat is its special and essential product."

The bourgeoisie is here conceived as a revolutionary class—as the bearer of large-scale industry—in relation to the feudal lords and the middle estates, who desire to maintain all social positions that are the creation of obsolete modes of production. Thus they do not form *together with the bourgeoisie* only one reactionary mass.

On the other hand, the proletariat is revolutionary in relation to the bourgeoisie because, having itself grown up on the basis of large-scale industry, it strives to strip off from production the capitalist character that the bourgeoisie seeks to perpetuate. But the *Manifesto* adds that the "middle estates" are becoming revolutionary "in view of their impending transfer into the proletariat."

From this point of view, therefore, it is again nonsense to say that they, "together with the bourgeoisie," and with the feudal lords into the bargain, "form only one reactionary mass" in relation to the working class.

Did anyone proclaim to the artisans, small manufacturers, etc., and *peasants* during the last elections: In relation to us you, together with the bourgeoisie and feudal lords, form only one reactionary mass?

Lassalle knew the *Communist Manifesto* by heart, as his faithful followers know the gospels written by him. If, therefore, he has falsified it so grossly, this has occurred only to put a good colour on his alliance with absolutist and feudal opponents against the bourgeoisie.

In the above paragraph, moreover, his oracular saying is dragged in by the hair, without any connection with the botched quotation from the Rules of the International. Thus it is here simply an impertinence, and indeed not at all displeasing to Mr. Bismarck, one of those cheap pieces of insolence in which the Marat of Berlin deals.

5. "The working class strives for its emancipation first of all *within the framework of the present-day national state,* conscious that the necessary result of its efforts, which are common to the workers of all civilised countries, will be the international brotherhood of peoples."

Lassalle, in opposition to the *Communist Manifesto* and to all earlier socialism, conceived the workers' movement from the narrowest national standpoint. He is being followed in this—and that after the work of the International!

It is altogether self-evident that, to be able to fight at all, the working class must organise itself at home *as a class* and that its own country is the immediate arena of its struggle. To this extent its class struggle is national, not in substance, but, as the *Communist Manifesto* says, "in form." But the "framework of the present-day national state," for instance, the German Empire, is itself in its turn economically "within the framework of the world market," politically "within the framework of the system of states." Every businessman knows that German trade is at the same time foreign trade, and the greatness of Mr. Bismarck consists, to be sure, precisely in his pursuing his kind of *international* policy.

And to what does the German workers' party reduce its internationalism? To the consciousness that the result of its efforts "will be the *international brotherhood of peoples*"—a phrase borrowed from the bourgeois League of Peace and Freedom, which is intended to pass as equivalent to the international brotherhood of the working classes in the joint struggle against the ruling classes and their governments. So not a word *about the international functions* of the German working class! And it is thus that it is to defy its own bourgeoisie—which is already linked up in brotherhood against it with the bourgeois of all other countries—and Mr. Bismarck's international policy of conspiracy!

In fact, the internationalism of the programme stands *even infinitely below* that of the Free Trade Party. The latter also asserts that the result of its efforts will be "the international brotherhood of peoples." But it also *does* something to make trade international and by no means contents itself with the consciousness—that all peoples are carrying on trade at home.

The international activity of the working classes does not in any way depend on the existence of the "*International Working Men's Association.*" This was only the first attempt to create a central organ for that activity; an attempt which was a lasting success on account of the impulse which it gave, but which was no longer realisable in *its first historical form* after the fall of the Paris Commune.

Bismarck's *Norddeutsche* was absolutely right when it announced, to the satisfaction of its master, that the German workers' party had forsworn internationalism in the new programme.

II

"Starting from these basic principles, the German workers' party strives by all legal means for the *free state—and—*socialist society; the abolition of the wage system *together with* the *iron law of wages—*and—exploitation in every form; the elimination of all social and political inequality."

I shall return to the "free" state later.

So, in future, the German workers' party has got to believe in

Lassalle's "iron law of wages"! That this may not be lost, the nonsense is perpetrated of speaking of the "abolition of the wage system" (it should read: system of wage labour) "*together with* the iron law of wages." If I abolish wage labour, then naturally I abolish its laws too, whether they are of "iron" or sponge. But Lassalle's attack on wage labour turns almost solely on this so-called law. In order, therefore, to prove that the Lassallean sect has won, the "wage system" must be abolished "*together with* the iron law of wages" and not without it.

It is well known that nothing of the "iron law of wages" is Lassalle's except the word "iron" borrowed from Goethe's "eternal, iron, great laws." The word *iron* is a label by which the true believers recognise one another. But if I take the law with Lassalle's stamp on it and, consequently, in his sense, then I must also take it with his substantiation. And what is that? As Lange already showed, shortly after Lassalle's death, it is the Malthusian theory of population (preached by Lange himself). But if this theory is correct, then again I can*not* abolish the law even if I abolish wage labour a hundred time over, because the law then governs not only the system of wage labour but *every* social system. Basing themselves directly on this, the economists have been proving for fifty years and more that socialism cannot abolish destitution, *which has its basis in nature*, but can only make it *general*, distribute it simultaneously over the whole surface of society!

But all this is not the main thing. *Quite apart* from the *false* Lassallean formulation of the law, the truly outrageous retrogression consists in the following:

Since Lassalle's death there has asserted itself in *our* Party the scientific understanding that *wages* are not what they *appear* to be, namely the *value*, or *price, of labour*, but only a masked form for the *value*, or *price, of labour power*. Thereby the whole bourgeois conception of wages hitherto, as well as all the criticism hitherto directed against this conception, was thrown overboard once for all and it was made clear that the wage-worker has permission to work for his own subsistence, that is, *to live* only insofar as he works for a certain time gratis for the capitalist (and hence also for the latter's co-consumers of surplus value); that the whole capitalist system of production turns on increasing this gratis labour by extending the working day or by developing productivity, that is, increasing the intensity of labour power, etc.; that, consequently, the system of wage labour is a system of slavery, and indeed of a slavery which becomes more severe in proportion as the social productive forces of labour develop, whether the worker receives better or worse payment. And after this understanding has gained more and more ground in our Party, one returns to Lassalle's dogmas although one must have known that Lassalle *did not know* what wages were, but following in the wake of the bourgeois economists took the appearance for the essence of the matter.

It is as if, among slaves who have at last got behind the secret of slavery and broken out in rebellion, a slave still in thrall to obsolete notions were to inscribe on the programme of the rebellion: Slavery must be abolished because the feeding of slaves in the system of slavery cannot exceed a certain low maximum!

Does not the mere fact that the representatives of our Party were capable of perpetrating such a monstrous attack on the understanding that has spread among the mass of our Party prove by itself with what criminal levity and with what lack of conscience they set to work in drawing up this compromise programme!

Instead of the indefinite concluding phrase of the paragraph, "the elimination of all social and political inequality," is ought to have been said that with the abolition of class distinctions all social and political inequality arising from them would disappear of itself.

III

"The German workers' party, in order *to pave the way for the solution of the social question,* demands the establishment of producers' cooperative societies with *state aid under the democratic control of the working people.* The producers' cooperative societies *are to be called into being* for industry and agriculture on such a scale *that the socialist organisation of the total labour will arise from them.*"

After the Lassallean "iron law of wages," the panacea of the prophet. The way for it is "paved" in worthy fashion. In place of the existing class struggle appears a newspaper scribbler's phrase: "*the* social *question,*" for the "*solution*" of which one "paves the way." Instead of arising from the revolutionary process of the transformation of society, the "socialist organisation of the total labour" "arises" from the "state aid" that the state gives to the producers' cooperative societies which the *state,* not the worker, "*calls into being.*" It is worthy of Lassalle's imagination that with state loans one can build a new society just as well as a new railway!

From the remnants of a sense of shame, "state aid" has been put— "under the democratic control of the working people."

In the first place, the "working people" in Germany consist in their majority of peasants, and not of proletarians.

Secondly, "democratic" means in German "*volksherrschaftlich*" ["by the rule of the people"]. But what does "control of the working people by the rule of the people" mean? And particularly in the case of working people who, through these demands that they put to the state, express their full consciousness that they neither rule nor are ripe for rule!

It would be superfluous to deal here with the criticism of the recipe prescribed by Buchez in the reign of Louis Philippe in *opposition* to the French Socialists and accepted by the reactionary workers of the *Atelier.* The chief offence does not lie in having inscribed this specific nostrum in the programme, but in taking a retrograde step at all from the standpoint of a class movement to that of a sectarian movement.

That the workers desire to establish the conditions for cooperative production on a social scale, and first of all on a national scale, in their own country, only means that they are working to transform the present conditions of production, and it has nothing in common with the foundation of cooperative societies with state aid. But as far as the present cooperative societies are concerned, they are of value *only* insofar as they are the independent creations of the workers and not protégés either of the governments or of the bourgeois.

IV

I come now to the democratic section.

A. *"The free basis of the state."*

First of all, according to II, the German workers' party strives for "the free state."

Free state—what is it?

It is by no means the purpose of the workers, who have got rid of the narrow mentality of humble subjects, to set the state "free." In the German Empire the "state" is almost as "free" as in Russia. Freedom consists in converting the state from an organ superimposed upon society into one completely subordinate to it, and even today forms of state are more free or less free to the extent that they restrict the "freedom of the state."

The German workers' party—at least if it adopts the programme—shows that its socialist ideas are not even skin-deep, in that, instead of treating existing society (and this holds good for any future one) as the *basis* of the existing *state* (or of the future state in the case of future society), it treats the state rather as an independent entity that possesses its own *"intellectual, ethical and libertarian bases."*

And what of the wild abuse which the programme makes of the words *"present-day state," "present-day society,"* and of the still more riotous misconception it creates in regard to the state to which it addresses its demands?

"Present-day society" is capitalist society, which exists in all civilised countries, more or less free from medieval admixture, more or less modified by the particular historical development of each country, more or less developed. On the other hand, the "present-day state" changes with a country's frontier. It is different in the Prusso-German Empire from that in Switzerland, and different in England from that in the United States. "The *present-day* state" is, therefore, a fiction.

Nevertheless, the different states of the different civilised countries, in spite of their motley diversity of form, all have this in common that they are based on modern bourgeois society, more or less capitalistically developed. They have, therefore, also certain essential characteristics in common. In this sense it is possible to speak of the "present-day state," in contrast with the future, in which its present root, bourgeois society, will have died off.

The question then arises: what transformation will the state undergo in communist society? In other words, what social functions will remain in existence there that are analogous to present state functions? This question can only be answered scientifically, and one does not get a flea-hop nearer to the problem by a thousandfold combination of the word people with the word state.

Between capitalist and communist society lies the period of the revolutionary transformation of the one into the other. Corresponding to this is also a political transition period in which the state can be nothing but *the revolutionary dictatorship of the proletariat.*

Now the programme deals neither with this nor with the future state of communist society.

Its political demands contain nothing beyond the old democratic litany familiar to all: universal suffrage, direct legislation, popular rights, a people's militia, etc. They are a mere echo of the bourgeois People's Party, of the League of Peace and Freedom. They are all demands which, insofar as they are not exaggerated in fantastic presentation, have already been *implemented.* Only the state to which they belong does not lie within the borders of the German Empire, but in Switzerland, the United States, etc. This sort of "state of the future" is a *present-day state,* although existing outside the "framework" of the German Empire.

But one thing has been forgotten. Since the German worker's party expressly declares that it acts within "the present-day national state," hence within its own state, the Prusso-German Empire—its demands would indeed otherwise be largely meaningless, since one only demands what one has not yet got—it should not have forgotten the chief thing, namely that all those pretty little gewgaws rest on the recognition of what is called sovereignty of the people and hence are appropriate only in a *democratic republic.*

Since one has not the courage—and wisely so, for the circumstances demand caution—to demand the democratic republic, as the French workers' programmes under Louis Philippe and under Louis Napoleon did, one should not have resorted to the subterfuge, neither "honest" nor decent, of demanding things which have meaning only in a democratic republic from a state which is nothing but a police-guarded military despotism, embellished with parliamentary forms, alloyed with a feudal admixture and at the same time already influenced by the bourgeoisie, and bureaucratically carpentered, and then assuring this state into the bargain that one imagines one will be able to force such things upon it "by legal means."

Even vulgar democracy, which sees the millennium in the democratic republic and has no suspicion that it is precisely in this last form of state of bourgeois society that the class struggle has to be fought out to a conclusion—even it towers mountains above this kind of democratism which keeps within the limits of what is permitted by the police and not permitted by logic.

That, in fact, by the word "state" is meant the government machine or the state insofar as it forms a special organism separated from society through division of labour, is shown alone by the words

"the German workers' party demands *as the economic basis of the state:* a single progressive income tax," etc.

Taxes are the economic basis of the government machinery and of nothing else. In the state of the future existing in Switzerland, this demand has been pretty well fulfilled. Income tax presupposes various sources of income of the various social classes, and hence capitalist society. It is, therefore, nothing remarkable that the Liverpool FINANCIAL REFORMERS, bourgeois headed by Gladstone's brother, are putting forward the same demand as the programme.

B. "The German workers' party demands as the intellectual and ethical basis of the state:

1. "Universal and *equal education of the people* by the state. Universal compulsory school attendance. Free instruction."

Equal education of the people? What idea lies behind these words? Is it believed that in present-day society (and it is only with this that one is dealing) education can be *equal* for all classes? Or is it demanded that the upper classes also shall be compulsorily reduced to the modicum of education—the elementary school—that alone is compatible with the economic conditions not only of the wage labourers but of the peasants as well?

"Universal compulsory school attendance. Free instruction." The former exists even in Germany, the latter in Switzerland and in the United States in the case of elementary schools. If in some states of the latter country "upper" educational institutions are also "free," that only means in fact defraying the cost of the education of the upper classes from the general tax receipts. Incidentally, the same holds good for "free administration of justice" demanded under A, 5. The administration of criminal justice is to be had free everywhere; that of civil justice is concerned almost exclusively with conflicts over property and hence affects almost exclusively the propertied classes. Are they to carry on their litigation at the expense of the national coffers?

The paragraph on the schools should at least have demanded technical schools (theoretical and practical) in combination with the elementary school.

"*Education of the people by the state*" is altogether objectionable. Defining by a general law the expenditures on the elementary schools, the qualifications of the teaching staff, the subjects of instruction, etc., and, as is done in the United States, supervising the fulfilment of these legal specifications by state inspectors, is a very different thing from appointing the state as the educator of the people! Government and Church should rather be equally excluded from any influence on the school. Particularly, indeed, in the Prusso-German Empire (and one should not take refuge in the rotten subterfuge that one is speaking of a "state of the future;" we have seen how matters stand in this respect) the state has need, on the contrary, of a very stern education by the people.

But the whole programme, for all its democratic clang, is tainted through and through by the Lassallean sect's servile belief in the state, or, what is no better, by a democratic belief in miracles, or rather it is a compromise between these two kinds of belief in miracles, both equally remote from socialism.

"Freedom of science" says a paragraph of the Prussian Constitution. Why, then, here?

"*Freedom of conscience*"! If one desired at this time of the *Kulturkampf* to remind liberalism of its old catchwords, it surely could have been done only in the following form: Everyone should be able to attend to his religious as well as his bodily needs without the police sticking their noses in. But the workers' party ought at any rate in this connection to have expressed its awareness of the fact that bourgeois "freedom of conscience" is nothing but the toleration of all possible kinds of *religious unfreedom of conscience*, and that for its part it endeavours rather to liberate the conscience from the witchery of religion. But one chooses not to transgress the "bourgeois" level.

I have now come to the end, for the appendix that now follows in the programme does not constitute a *characteristic* component part of it. Hence I can be very brief here.

2. *"Normal working day."*

In no other country has the workers' party limited itself to such a vague demand, but has always fixed the length of the working day that it considers normal under the given circumstances.

3. "Restriction of female labour and prohibition of child labour."

The standardisation of the working day must include the restriction of female labour, insofar as it relates to the duration, breaks, etc., of the working day; otherwise it could only mean the exclusion of female labour from branches of industry that are especially unhealthy for the female body or are morally objectionable to the female sex. If that is what was meant, it should have been said.

"Prohibition of child labour"! Here it is absolutely essential to state the *age limit.*

A *general prohibition* of child labour is incompatible with the existence of large-scale industry and hence an empty, pious wish.

Its implementation—if it were possible—would be reactionary, since, with a strict regulation of the working time according to the different age groups and other precautionary stipulations for the protection of children, an early combination of productive labour with education is one of the most potent means for the transformation of present-day society.

4. "State supervision of factory, workshop and domestic industry."

In consideration of the Prusso-German state it should definitely have been demanded that the inspectors are to be removable only by a court of law; that any worker can have them prosecuted for neglect of duty; that they must belong to the medical profession.

5. "Regulation of prison labour."

A petty demand in a general workers' programme. In any case, it should have been clearly stated that there is no intention from fear of competition to allow ordinary criminals to be treated like beasts, and especially that there is no desire to deprive them of their sole means of betterment, productive labour. This was surely the least one might have expected from Socialists.

6. "An effective liability law."

It should have been stated what is meant by an "effective" liability law.

Let it be noted, incidentally, that in speaking of the normal working day the part of factory legislation that deals with health regulations and safety measures, etc., has been overlooked. The liability law only comes into operation when these regulations are infringed.

In short, this appendix too is distinguished by slovenly editing.

Dixi et salvavi animam meam.[1]

1. I have spoken and saved my soul. (Ezekiel 3:18–19)

Marginal Notes On Bakunin's
Statism and Anarchy
(excerpt)

Karl Marx

Mikhail Bakunin (1814–76), a Russian revolutionary and one of the founders of modern anarchism, was perhaps Marx's chief antagonist within the ranks of the First International. Bakunin published Statism and Anarchy *in Geneva in 1873. Marx, in late 1874, took notes on the book in his usual fashion by copying out excerpts and adding critical commentary. The notes, which often display Marx at his most polemical and sarcastic, are fairly extensive, taking up thirty-eight pages in the* Collected Works, *although much of it takes the form of long passages quoted from Bakunin. The thrust of Marx's comments are aimed at refuting anarchism in general and Bakunin's views in particular.*

The notes are of interest today largely for remarks about the nature of the state after the revolution. Bakunin, the anarchist, is skeptical of state power in any form and sees the danger of the revolutionary state that replaces the bourgeois state oppressing the workers with no real gain in freedom. "Schoolboyish rot," Marx replies. Bakunin understands "absolutely nothing of social revolution, only its political rhetoric; its economic conditions simply do not exist for him." He misunderstands, that is, how political relations are determined by economic relations. While Bakunin is afraid of a new despotism in the form of a ruling minority "that is all the more dangerous as it appears as the expression of the so-called will of the people," Marx sees no danger here for "the class rule *of the workers over the strata of the old world who are struggling against them can only last as long as the economic basis of class society has not been destroyed." A question lurking for us behind this exchange is who, in light of the experience of the twentieth century, has the more correct insight.*

The translation used here is taken from Karl Marx/Friedrich Engels: Collected Works, *published by International Publishers. The passages from Bakunin are in small type, with interjections by Marx in parentheses. Marx's commentary is in the larger type.*

. . . The question is, if the proletariat is to be the ruling class, over whom will it rule? This means that another proletariat will remain which will be subject to this new domination, this new state.

It implies that as long as the other classes, above all the capitalist class, still exist, and as long as the proletariat is still fighting against it (for when the proletariat obtains control of the government its enemies and the old organisation of society will not yet have disappeared), it must use *forcible* means, that is to say, governmental means; as long as it remains a class itself, and the economic conditions which give rise to the class struggle and the existence of classes have not vanished they must be removed or transformed by force, and the process of transforming them must be accelerated by force.

For example, . . . the vulgar peasants, the peasant rabble, who, as is well known, do not enjoy the goodwill of the Marxists and who, standing on the lowest rung of civilisation, will probably be governed by the urban and factory proletariat.

That is to say, where peasants en masse exist as owners of private property, where they even form a more or less considerable majority, as in all the states of the West European continent, where they have not yet disappeared and have not been replaced by agricultural day labourers, as in England, there the following may happen: either the peasants prevent or bring about the downfall of every workers' revolution, as they have done hitherto in France; or else the proletariat (for the peasant proprietor does not belong to the proletariat, and even if he does belong to it in terms of his actual position, he does not think of himself as belonging to it) must, as the government, take measures needed to enable the peasant to directly improve his condition, i.e. to win him over to the revolution; these measures, however, contain the seeds which will facilitate the transition from the private ownership of the land to collective ownership, so that the peasant arrives at this economically of his own accord; but it is important not to antagonise the peasant, e.g. by proclaiming the abolition of the right of inheritance or the abolition of his property; the latter is possible only where the capitalist tenant farmer has ousted the peasants, so that the actual farmer is as much a proletarian, a wage-labourer, as the urban worker, so that he has the same interests as the latter *directly* and not indirectly. Still less should smallholdings be strengthened by increasing the size of allotments simply by dividing up the large estates among the peasantry, as in Bakunin's revolutionary campaign.

Or, if this question is considered from the national point of view, then it must be assumed that for the Germans the Slavs will, for the same reason, be placed in the same relationship of slavish dependency on the victorious German proletariat as that in which the latter finds itself vis-à-vis its own bourgeoisie

Schoolboyish rot! A radical social revolution is bound up with definite historical conditions of economic development; these are its premisses. It is only possible, therefore, where alongside capitalist production the industrial proletariat accounts for at least a significant portion of the mass of the people. And for it to have any chance of victory, it must be able *mutatis mutandis* at the very least to do as much directly for the peasants as the French bourgeoisie did in its revolution for the French peasantry at that time. A fine idea to imagine that the rule of the workers implies the oppression of rural labour! But this is where we glimpse Mr. Bakunin's innermost thought. He understands absolutely nothing of social revolution, only its political rhetoric; its economic conditions simply do not exist for him. Now since all previous economic formations, whether developed or undeveloped, have entailed the enslavement of the worker (whether as wage labourer, peasant, etc.), he imagines that *radical revolution* is equally possible in all these formations. What is more, he wants the European social revolution, whose economic basis is capitalist production, to be carried out on the level of the Russian or Slav agricultural and pastoral peoples, and that it should not surpass this level, even though he can see that *navigation* creates distinctions among brethren; but of course he only thinks of *navigation* because this distinction is familiar to all politicians! *Willpower*, not economic conditions, is the basis of his social revolution.

Where there is a state there is inevitably domination and consequently there is also slavery; domination without slavery, hidden or masked, is unthinkable— that is why we are enemies of the state.

What does it mean to talk of the proletariat raised to the level of the ruling estate?

It means that the proletariat, instead of fighting in individual instances against the economically privileged classes, has gained sufficient strength and organisation to use general means of coercion in its struggle against them; but it can only make use of such economic means as abolish its own character as wage labourer and hence as a class; when its victory is complete, its rule too is therefore at an end, since its class character will have disappeared.

Will perhaps the entire proletariat stand at the head of the government?

In a TRADES UNION, for example, does the entire union form its executive committee? Will all division of labour in the factory come to an end as well as the various functions arising from it? And with Bakunin's constitution from below, will everyone be at the top? If so, there will be no one at the bottom. Will all the members of the community at the same time administer the common interests of the region? If so, there will be no distinction between community and region.

There are about 40 million Germans. Does this mean that all 40 million will be members of the government?

CERTAINLY! For the system starts with the self-government of the communities.

The entire people will rule, and no one will be ruled.

When a person rules himself, he does not do so according to this principle; for he is only himself and not another.

Then there will be no government, no state, but if there is a state, there will be both rulers and slaves.

That just means when class rule has disappeared there [will] be no state in the present political sense.

The dilemma in the theory of the Marxists is easily resolved. By people's government they (i.e. Bakunin) understand the government of the people by means of a small number of representatives chosen (elected) by the people.

Asine! This is democratic twaddle, political claptrap! Elections—a political form found in the tiniest Russian commune and in the artel. The character of an election does not depend on this name but on the economic foundation, the economic interrelations of the voters, and as soon as the functions have ceased to be political, 1) government functions no longer exist; 2) the distribution of general functions has become a routine matter which entails no domination; 3) elections lose their present political character.

The universal suffrage of the whole people—

such a thing as the whole people, in the present meaning of the word, is an illusion—

to elect its representatives and rulers of state—that is the last word of the Marxists and also of the democratic school—is a lie which conceals the despotism of the *ruling minority*, a lie that is all the more dangerous as it appears as the expression of the so-called will of the people.

With collective ownership the so-called will of the people disappears and makes way for the genuine will of the cooperative.

So the result is the control of the vast majority of the people by a privileged minority. But this minority, the Marxists say,

Where?

will consist of workers. Yes, quite possibly of former workers, but, as soon as they have become the representatives or rulers of the people, *they cease to be workers—*

no more than a factory owner today ceases to be a capitalist when he becomes a municipal councillor—

and will gaze down upon the whole world of the common workers from the eminence of statehood; they will no longer represent the people, but only themselves and their claims to govern the people. Anyone who can doubt this knows nothing of human nature.

If Mr. Bakunin were familiar even with the position of a manager in a workers' cooperative factory, all his fantasies about domination would go to the devil. He should have asked himself: what forms could management functions assume within such a workers' state, if he wants to call it that?

But these chosen people will become passionately convinced as well as learned socialists. The words '*learned socialism*'"—

never used—

'scientific socialism'—

used only in contrast to utopian socialism which wishes to foist new illusions onto the people instead of confining its scientific investigations to the social movement created by the people itself; see my book against Proudhon—

which recur repeatedly in the writings and speeches of the Lassalleans and Marxists, prove themselves that the so-called people's state will be nothing more than the highly despotic direction of the masses of the people by a new and very small aristocracy of genuinely or supposedly learned men. The people is not scientific; that means it will be wholly liberated from the cares of government, it will be completely incorporated into the herd that is to be governed. A fine liberation!

The Marxists perceive this (!) contradiction and, recognising that a government of scholars (*quelle rêverie!*) will be the most oppressive, most hated and most despicable in the world, and that for all its democratic forms it will actually be a dictatorship, they console themselves with the thought that this dictatorship will be provisional and brief.

Non, mon cher!—The *class rule* of the workers over the strata of the old world who are struggling against them can only last as long as the economic basis of class society has not been destroyed.

They say that their sole concern and objective will be *to educate and uplift the people* (ale-house politician!) both economically and politically to such a level that all government will soon become unnecessary and the state will completely lose its political, i.e. its dominating character, and will change of its own accord into the free organisation of economic interests and communities. This is an evident contradiction. If their state is truly a people's state, why destroy it, and if its abolition is necessary for the real liberation of the people, then how dare they call it a people's state?

Apart from his harping on Liebknecht's *people's state*, which is nonsense directed against the *Communist Manifesto*, etc., it only means that, as the proletariat in the period of struggle leading to the overthrow of the old society still acts on the basis of the old society and hence still moves within political forms which more or less correspond to it, it has at that stage not yet arrived at its final organisation, and hence to achieve its liberation has recourse to methods which will be discarded once that liberation has been attained. Hence Mr. Bakunin deduces that the proletariat should rather do nothing at all . . . and just wait for the *day of universal liquidation*—the Last Judgement. . . .

Index of Topics

feudal
  mode of production, xx
  ownership, 109–10
  socialism, 176–78
  society, 19, 161–64
  system, 150
First International, 315
freedom (*see* emancipation)
free state, 327
  attitude toward religion, 7
French civil war, 301, 303–14
  bourgeois society, 304
  centralized state power, 302–3
  Commune, 302–5
  imperialism, 304
  parliamentary republic, 303
French revolution (*also see* Revolution of 1848)
  bourgeois society, 189
General Union of German Workers (ADAV), 315
German (true) socialism, 179–81
German governments, 35
German ideology, 105–53
German middle class, 37
German philosophy, 29, 32, 107–21
  critical struggle against German world, 33
  law and state, 32–33
Germany
  comparison with England, 218
  emancipation of, 38–39
  social statistics of, 218
Gotha program, critique of, 315–32
Hegel, critique of, 79–81
  phenomenology, 81–97
Hegelian dialectic, relationship to, 79–80
historical materialism, x, xvii–xxiii, 102, 211
history, 88, 115–16, 122
  collisions in, 142
  consciousness and, 115–21
  economic developments, xxxiii
  German, 126–27
  German philosophy as extension of, 32
  hegemony of spirit in, 131
  industry, 76
  men making their own, 188–89
  ordering rule of ideas, 132
  rule of idea or illusions, 132
  sharing illusion of epochs, 125–26
  spheres interacting, 122
  theory of, 102
history of class struggle, xxi–xxii
human activity, exchange of, 45
human beings, objectifying themselves, 83
human emancipation, 5
human existence, 115
human nature, 85
human science, 76
human senses, 73–74
humanism, 71, 87, 92
ideology, 105–53
imperfect state, 11
imperialism, 304

income taxes, 175
individual
  as person, 73, 147–48
  deprived of life content, 151
industrial capitalists, 165
industry, history, 76
inheritance, abolishing, 176
intellectual power, xxiii
internationalism, 324
iron law of wages, 325–26
irreligious criticism, 28
Jewish question, 1–26
Jewish religion
  foundation of, 24
  interpretation of, 21–22
  relationship to Christian religion, 21–26
Jews
  contradiction between practical power and political rights, 23
  emancipation of, 2–23
  social emancipation, 26
knowing, 89
labor, xix, 55, 59, 84, 150–51, 274
  accumulated, 171
  act of production, 62
  alienated, 48, 58–68
  combined, socialized, 299
  complex, 228
  contained in commodity, 229
  continuous transformation of, 285
  definite quantities of objectified, 291
  direct relationship to products, 61
  directly associated, 237–238
  division of, 49, 108, 117–20, 130, 132–36
  dual character of, 225–30
  emancipating, 322
  equal right, 321
  equal standard, 321
  equality of kinds, 232
  expressed as value, 240
  externalization, 61–62
  fair distribution of proceeds of, 318–19
  forced, 62
  instrument of, 275–77
  iron law of, 325–26
  liability of all, 176
  life activity, 63
  living, 171
  means of, 318
  means of life, 60
  measurement, 240
  not source of all wealth, 316
  objectification, 59–60
  objects of, 275
  political economy proceeding from, 66
  proceeds, 317–20
  process of consumption, 280
  productive life, 63
  products as values, 233–35
  products becoming commodities, 232–33
  products of, 222–23
  products of past, 279

Index of Names